WITHDRAWN

CULTURE INCARNATE

CULTURE INCARNATE

Native Anthropology from Russia

Edited by
Marjorie Mandelstam Balzer

M.E. Sharpe
Armonk, New York
London, England

Copyright © 1995 by M. E. Sharpe, Inc.

Translations copyright © 1992, 1993, 1994, and 1995 by M. E. Sharpe, Inc.

All rights reserved. No part of this book may be reproduced in any form
without written permission from the publisher, M. E. Sharpe, Inc.,
80 Business Park Drive, Armonk, New York 10504.

Library of Congress Cataloging-in-Publication Data

Culture incarnate : native anthropology from Russia /
edited by Marjorie Mandelstam Balzer.
p. cm.
Includes bibliographical references and index.
ISBN 1-56324-534-5 (alk. paper) — ISBN 1-56324-535-3 (pbk. : alk paper)
1. Ethnology—Russia (Federation)
2. Political anthropology—Russia (Federation)
3. Symbolic anthropology—Russia (Federation)
4. Russia (Federation)—Social life and customs.
I. Balzer, Marjorie Mandelstam.
DK510.33.C85 1995
305.8′00974—dc20   94-33956
CIP

Cover Art: Amur River appliqué art using a paper cut-out technique
based on older cloth and fur cutting. The artist is Nanai (Goldy)
master Anna A. Samar, sister of the ethnographer and political
activist Evdokiya A. Gaer. The art (made between courses at a
dinner table) was a gift to Marjorie M. Balzer in 1991.

Printed in the United States of America

The paper used in this publication meets the minimum requirements of
American National Standard for Information Sciences—
Permanence of Paper for Printed Library Materials,
ANSI Z 39.48-1984.

BM (c) 10 9 8 7 6 5 4 3 2 1
BM (p) 10 9 8 7 6 5 4 3 2 1

In memory of Isabella Vasil´evna Mimykg Avtonova,
Naukan Iupik (Eskimo) schoolteacher and ethnographer,
who lived "betwixt and between"
multiple medical systems and cultures.

Contents

About the Editor and Contributors   ix

Map: The Russian Federation and Its Internal Divisions   xiii

Introduction: What's "Native" About Non-Russian Anthropology?
Marjorie Mandelstam Balzer   3

I. **Ethnohistory: Seeking Roots and Self-Identity**

    The Mordva: Ethnonym or Ethnopholism?
    Nikolai F. Mokshin   31

    Ethnogenesis and Ethnocultural Relationships of the Turkic
    Peoples of the Volga and Urals: Problems and Tasks
    Raul G. Kuzeev and Shamil F. Mukhamediarov   46

    Several Features of the Yakut (Sakha) Ethnoculture
    Anatolii I. Gogolev   63

    The Question of the Khakas Ethnonym
    Viktor Ia. Butanaev   70

II. **Political Anthropology: Interpreting Ethnicity,**
    Ethnic Conflict, and Sociocultural Norms

    The Former Checheno-Ingushetia: Interethnic Relations and
    Ethnic Conflicts
    Galina U. Soldatova   83

    Ethnic Relations in Tuva
    Zoia V. Anaibin   102

    The Problems of Sovereignty and Interethnic Relations in the
    Republic of Tatarstan
    Roza N. Musina   113

    Cultural Norms in the Baikal Region
    Zoia P. Morokhoeva   123

III. Symbolic Anthropology: Seeking Riches of Folk Wisdom and Values in Ritual and Tradition

Birth Rituals of the Nanai
Evdokiya A. Gaer   143

Marriage Customs of the Yakuts (Sakha)
Platon A. Sleptsov   173

Traditions, Rituals, and Beliefs of the Asiatic Eskimos
Tassan S. Tein   209

Tuvan Shamanic Folklore
Mongush B. Kenin-Lopsan   215

IV. Native Ethnographers Unite: A Folklore Manifesto

The Study of Northern Languages, Folklore, and Cultures
Aleksandr B. Soktoev   257

Index   265

About the Editor and Contributors

Marjorie Mandelstam Balzer (Ph.D. 1979) teaches in the Sociology and Russian Area Studies departments of Georgetown University. She is editor of the journal *Anthropology and Archeology of Eurasia*, where versions of some of the studies translated here previously appeared, and of the volumes *Shamanism: Soviet Studies of Traditional Religion in Siberia and Central Asia* (1990) and *Russian Traditional Culture: Religion, Gender, and Customary Law* (1992). She has taught at Grinnell College and the universities of Illinois and Pennsylvania and has held postdoctoral research appointments at Harvard, Columbia, and the Wilson Center's Kennan Institute for Advanced Russian Studies. Since 1975, she has written on nationalism, religion, and gender for the *American Anthropologist, Slavic Review, Journal of Soviet Nationalities, Arctic Anthropology, Social Science and Medicine*, and various edited volumes, using data from several years of fieldwork in the former Soviet Union and Russia (especially Siberia). Forthcoming books include *The Tenacity of Ethnicity* and *Siberian Women's Lives: Autobiographies from the Sakha Republic (Yakutia)*.

Zoia Vasil'evna Anaibin is a researcher in the Russian Academy of Sciences Institute of Languages, Literature, and History in Kyzyl, Republic of Tuva. She is the author of ethnosociological articles and a participant in a multiethnic project examining ethnic relations in the Russian Federation. Readers are referred to her articles in the institute's *Uchenye zapiski* (Scientific notes).

Viktor Iakovlevich Butanaev is a foremost ethnographer of the Khakas people, a Kandidat of Historical Sciences, and a senior researcher in the Khakas Scientific Research Institute of Languages, Literature, and History in Abakhan, Khakasia. Author of numerous ethnohistorical articles and monographs, he has also compiled a dictionary of personal names of the Khakas.

Evdokiya Alexandrovna Gaer, a graduate of the Institute of Ethnography in Moscow, is a Kandidat of Historical Sciences and a member of the ethnography division of the Institute of History in Vladivostok. She chairs the division of the Minorities of the North of the Academy of Natural

Sciences in Moscow. She was an elected deputy to the Soviet parliament representing the entire Far East and served as a member of the Supreme Soviet of the Soviet Union. In the Supreme Soviet, she was head of the Committee for Minority Peoples, and later became advisor to the Committee for Minority Peoples in the Russian parliament. She is also a vice-director of Goskomsevera in Moscow; an executive of the International Fund for the Development of Ethnic Groups in the Russian Federation; and a founding executive committee member of the Association for the Nationalities of the North, Siberia, and the Far East (formerly Association of the Small Populations of the North). Gaer now serves as head of the International League of the Minority Peoples of the North.

Anatolii Ignatevich Gogolev is Professor of History at Yakut State University and a Doctor of Historical Sciences. His Kandidat and Doktorat degrees are both from the Russian Academy of Sciences (St. Petersburg) and he is a member of the Sakha Republic Academy of Sciences. He is the author of numerous articles and five major monographs, including three in his own series *Istoricheskaia etnografiia iakutov* (Historical ethnography of the Yakut). He has led numerous archeological and ethnographic expeditions throughout Yakutia, was the scientific organizer for the International Conference on Shamanism held in the Sakha Republic August 1992, and is revered by many in the republic as the foremost authority on Yakut cultural history. Readers are referred to his *Yakutia* (Yakutsk: Ministry of Culture, 1993).

Mongush Borakhovich Kenin-Lopsan is a senior researcher of the Institute of Languages, Literature, and History (IaLI) of the Russian Academy of Sciences, Siberian Division, Kyzyl branch, Republic of Tuva. He is the author of numerous articles and books, including two volumes of collected works and the book excerpted here, *Obriadovaia praktika i fol'klor tuvinskogo shamanstva. Konets XIX–nachalo XXv* (Ritual Practice and Folklore of Tuvinian Shamanism: Late Nineteenth to Early Twentieth Century) (Novosibirsk: Nauka, 1987).

Raul Gumerovich Kuzeev is a Doctor of Historical Sciences and the director of the Museum of Archeology and Ethnography of the Scientific Center of the Ural Division of the Russian Academy of Sciences, in Ufa, Bashkortostan. He is the author of numerous works and is also a member of the Committee of Turkologists.

Nikolai Feodorovich Mokshin is a Doctor of Historical Sciences and senior researcher in the Institute of Languages, Literature, History, and Economics of the Saransk, Mordova, branch of the Russian Academy of Sciences. He is author of many articles and books on the Mordva culture and has occupied the post of ethnography division head.

Zoia Petrovna Morokhoeva is a Kandidat of Philosophy and a researcher in the Buryat Institute of Social Sciences, Russian Academy of Sciences, in Ulan-Ude, the capital of the Buryat Republic. In 1994 she founded a "laboratory of cultural anthropology" within the Teacher's Training Institute of the Ministry of Education. Readers are referred to her *Lichnost' v kul'turakh vostoka i zapada: k postanovke problemy* (Personality in the Cultures of the East and West: Toward a Formulation of the Problem) (Novosibirsk: Nauka, 1994).

Shamil Fatikhovich Mukhamediarov is a senior scientific researcher at the Institute of History of the Russian Academy of Sciences in Moscow. Extensively published in Russian and in Tatar, he is a Kandidat of Historical Sciences and a member of the Committee of Turkologists.

Roza Nurievna Musina is a senior researcher in the Academy of Sciences Institute of Languages, Literature, and History in Kazan, Tatarstan. She is an ethnosociologist with extensive survey research experience and is the author of numerous articles and book chapters. Readers are referred to her edited volume, *Sovremennye natsional'nye protsessy v respublike Tatarstana* (Contemporary National Processes in the Republic of Tatarstan) (Kazan: Kazan Scientific Center, 1992).

Platon Alekseevich Sleptsov teaches ethnography at Yakutsk State University in the Sakha Republic. Until 1993 he was a scientific researcher in the ethnosociology sector of the Institute of Languages, Literature, and History (IaLI) of the Russian Academy of Sciences, Siberian Division, Yakutsk branch, Republic of Sakha. He was active in the organization of a 1992 conference on shamanism, sponsored by the Museum of Music and Folklore under the republic's Ministry of Culture, and has become a consultant to the minister of education. He is the author of numerous articles and the book excerpted here, *Traditsionnaia sem'ia i obriadnost' u iakutov (XIX–nachalo XXv)* (Traditional Family and Ritual of the Yakut: Nineteenth to Early Twentieth Century) (Yakutsk: "Yakutsk" Book Publishers, 1989).

Aleksandr Badmaevich Soktoev is the director of the Institute of Philology of the Russian Academy of Sciences, in Novosibirsk. He is a Doctor of Philology and a corresponding member of the Russian Academy of Sciences and author of many articles and monographs. Readers are referred to his *Khotsa Namsaraev* (Ulan-Ude, 1971) and *Istoriia sovetskoi literatury Buriatov* (The History of Soviet Buryat Literature) (Ulan-Ude, 1967). He has recently devoted most of his time to organizing the forthcoming sixty-volume series, *Pamiatniki fol'klora narodov Sibirii Dal'nogo Vostoka* (advertised in English as "Folklore of Siberia and the Far East").

Galina Urtanbekovna Soldatova is a researcher at the Institute of Ethnology and Anthropology of the Russian Academy of Sciences in Moscow and holds a Kandidat of Historical Sciences degree. She is author of numerous ethnographic articles on the North Caucasus and was an established scholar in Ossetia before moving to Moscow. Readers are referred to her article "Interethnic Communication: The Cognitive Structure of Ethnic Self-Awareness," *Soviet Psychology*, vol. 29, no. 3 (May–June 1991), pp. 111–26.

Tassan S. Tein is a senior researcher of the Combined Scientific Research Institute of North-Eastern Studies (SVKNII) of the Russian Academy of Sciences, Siberian Division, Magadan branch, Chukotka. He is the author of works on Iupik (Eskimo) folk tradition published both in regional collections and more mainstream Russian ones, for example, "Shamans of the Siberian Eskimo," (Shamany Sibirskikh Eskimosov) in *Problemy istorii obshchestvennogo soznaniia aborigenov sibiri* (Problems in the History of Social Consciousness of the Aboriginal Siberians) (Leningrad: Nauka, 1981).

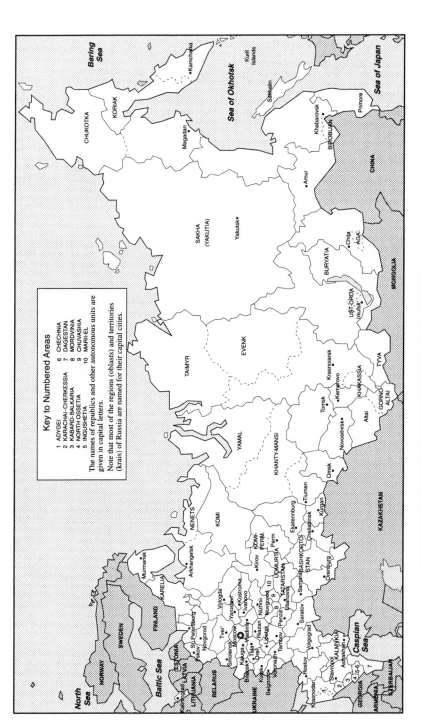

THE RUSSIAN FEDERATION AND ITS INTERNAL DIVISIONS

Key to Numbered Areas

1	ADYGEI	6	CHECHNIA
2	KARACHAI-CHERKESSIA	7	DAGESTAN
3	KABARD-BALKARIA	8	MORDVINIA
4	NORTH OSSETIA	9	CHUVASHIA
5	INGUSHETIA	10	MARII-EL

The names of republics and other autonomous units are given in capital letters.

Note that most of the regions (oblasts) and territories (krais) of Russia are named for their capital cities.

CULTURE
INCARNATE

Rooted. Anatolii I. Gogolev, ethnographer and archeologist of the Sakha (Yakut), of Eastern Siberia. Photo by M.M. Balzer, taken in a sacred grove near Kachikats village, Kangalassk Region, Yakutia, spring 1986.

Introduction

What's "Native" About Non-Russian Anthropology?

Marjorie Mandelstam Balzer

Who has the right to claim authoritative interpretations of the ethnohistory and cultural anthropology of a given people? Do "insiders" do it better, or is it more appropriate for carefully trained professionals from another culture to attempt to attain knowledge of a particular society without "going Native"? These classic anthropology questions have special relevance in the current *fin-de-siècle* and *fin-de-Soviet* period of political uncertainty, cultural multiplicity, and ethnic assertion. The answers are by no means obvious, for standards of anthropology are shifting both in the "West" and in the "East." It is not even clear who is "Native" and who is not, for many truly multicultural people of mixed ethnic and educational backgrounds have become our most talented and sensitive anthropologists worldwide.

The phrase "Native anthropologist" is used here interchangeably with "indigenous anthropologist." The word "native" has itself been subject to some political critique, given dangers of ghettoizing anthropologists who write about their own cultures, and given anthropologists' memories of the notorious colonial stereotype phrase "the natives [read primitive other] are restless." I feel relatively comfortable with "native," however, since I am willing to describe myself as a "native anthropologist" (without capitalization) when I write about my own indigenous suburbs of Washington, D.C.

As old national boundaries erode and new ones emerge, new voices of anthropologists, ethnographers, and ethnosociologists studying their own cultures have begun to be heard more clearly. Indigenous anthropologists, as representatives of their own cultures, are often the incarnation of traditions that they themselves choose to describe and interpret. With anthropological training, they are both of their cultures—culture incarnate—and in positions to critique those cultures in times of turmoil. While this is an international phenomenon, it is nowhere more blatant than on the territory of the former Soviet Union, including inside the Russian Federation. The thesis of this book is that non-Russian anthropologists of Russia have much to contribute and have not yet been heard well enough.

The history of Native ethnography in Russia began before the 1917 Revolution with a few token but striking examples representing the development of indigenous intelligentsias. In Buryatia, the Orientalist Dorzhi Banzarov in the first half of the nineteenth century set a standard for Buddhist cultural and medical scholarship, followed later by Mikhail N. Khangalov. The famed turn-of-the-century Tatar Islamic reformist Ismail Bei Gasprali (Gasprinskii) was a collector of Turkic ethnography as well as the founder of the Jadid movement. The Khakas scholar Nikolai F. Khatanov studied his own people and the related Urankhai Tuvans. From the Russian empire border, the Kyrgyz ethnographer Chikan Ch. Valikhanov and the Kazakh Gomozhap Sibikov became well known and well respected in Russian intellectual circles. Early-twentieth-century Sakha (Yakut) ethnography and folklore was furthered by the meticulous scholarship of Gavril V. Ksenofontov, Aleksei E. Kulakovskii, and Platon A. Oiunskii (Sleptsov), all of whom were later persecuted for political activism.[1]

Despite the initial Stalinist repression of Native intelligentsias, one of the more benevolent legacies of Soviet rule in its Russian mini-empire is that numerous non-Russian peoples have had opportunities for education, in their home districts, in regional centers, and in Moscow. Within each ethnic group in Russia, a few ethnographers, both amateur and professional, developed their own skills, and contributed greatly to their peoples' knowledge of their history and culture. The degree to which this process was smooth or restricted, influenced by world anthropological trends or ideologically constrained, varied with individual situations and with the time period. By the demise of the Soviet Union, a number of talented anthropologist-ethnographers had emerged, with varying degrees of awareness of Western scholarship and varying tendencies to think for themselves. Some encountered considerable prejudices along the way of their quota-oriented education and others received special accelerated career treatment. Most lived with a mixture of both.

A father of Soviet anthropology, Lev Shternberg, whose ten commandments of ethnography were perhaps more often breached than followed, said in the 1920s that a good anthropologist should know more than one culture well.[2] A few Native ethnographers trained in Leningrad and Moscow took this seriously, doing fieldwork in various parts of the Soviet Union, far from their homes, but most kept their focus fixed on their own cultures. Self-knowledge and understanding of their own cultural roots was what had brought them into anthropology in the first place. Besides, they were bicultural and bilingual in the Russian/Soviet context. They thus had built-in exposure, socialized at an early age, to issues of negotiating dual (if not multiple) sets of values and traditions.

Such Native scholars make fascinating and creative anthropologists. Their writings and life histories enable us to explore insider/outsider reflexivity issues that can transcend our own disciplinary parochialism.[3] The anthropology featured in this volume is selected from a wide range of scholarship. The materials chosen, from articles, book chapters, and unpublished manuscripts, present a sampling of Native anthropology produced in recent years in Russia. The authors represent a range of professional training and experience. Some are older members of Academy of Sciences elites and others are younger mavericks. They define themselves variously as ethnographers, philosophers, ethnopsychologists, ethnosociologists, and ethnohistorians—thus falling within a broad Western conception of sociocultural anthropology.[4]

The authors showcased here are Bashkir, Buryat, Iupik (Eskimo), Khakhas, Mordva, Nanai (Goldy), Ossetian, Tatar, Tyvan (Tuvan), and Sakha (Yakut) scholars. The geographical territory covered is thus enormous, ranging from the European parts of Russia (e.g., Mordvinia, Tatarstan, Bashkortostan) to the North Caucasus (Ossetia, Ingushetia, Chechnia), to Siberia (Tuva, Buryatia, Sakha) and the Far East (Amur River, Chukotka). This includes a representative but by no means inclusive sample, for over 100 different nationalities live within the Russian Federation, depending on how they are counted. Officially, 33 ethnically based republics, regions, or districts exist within Russia (although the Chechen unilaterally consider themselves to have already seceded).[5]

Several consistent themes dominate the anthropological literature of Russia, and particularly, the literature written by Native anthropologists. These themes, in Western parlance, come under the seemingly simple headings of ethnohistory and political and symbolic anthropology. As with any "scientific" terminology, the conceptions embraced are more subtle and complex than these glosses imply.

Within the category of ethnohistory is included debates about ethnic origins (deepest cultural and genetic roots of an ethnic group), ethnogenesis (evolution of an ethnic group from various others), ethnonyms (ethnic group self-names), and ethnic identity in a more modern or postmodern sense. The debates about such issues have enormous political implications for current claims, literally on the ground in boundary disputes, and in people's heads, in the changing ways people think of themselves.[6]

A separate category of "political anthropology" has been slowly evolving out of the relatively new disciplines of "ethnosociology" and "ethnopsychology." Younger anthropologists have been probing not only their ethnic roots but also the sources of their peoples' conflicts with their neighbors and their diverse political relations within the "*matrioshka* nationalism" framework of the former Soviet Union and of Russia. Non-Russian anthropologists carefully emphasize the word *Rossiia* for Russia (rather than *Rus*), or use "the Russian Federation," to focus on the multiethnic character of Russia. Concerned with questions of culturally shaped values, ecology, "character," and behavior, some of these anthropologists think of nationalism in its modern, potentially nation-building context.[7]

The third thematic category, symbolic anthropology, has been rapidly growing since official proclamations of "glasnost" relegitimized religion and made acceptable the possibility of diverse worldviews and interpretations of those views. In certain constrained forms, research akin to symbolic anthropology was a staple in the Soviet Union well before the 1980s. Ethnographers writing about their own cultures have long been fascinated by both their spiritual and their esthetic roots, and yet removed from those roots through formal Soviet education and informal socialization. They used study of traditional (labeled prerevolutionary) ritual and folk wisdom as ways to uncover the rich symbolic meanings embedded in their cultures. In this way, both consciously and unconsciously (depending on the individuals), they helped bolster their own and their peoples' sagging pride in their cultures. As part of their personal searches for deeper cultural understanding, Native ethnographers delved into the harsh religious histories of their peoples through interviews with elders and systematic archival research. In the 1990s, they have also been active participants, even leaders, in rituals they once proclaimed dead.[8] In them, culture incarnate comes to life.

Ethnohistory

The first chapter in the ethnohistory section, by the well-established Mordva ethnographer Nikolai Feodorovich Mokshin, plunges directly into a debate about the name "Mordva," and who the Mordva people are historically. It raises critical issues about how we describe ethnic processes, how we understand inchoate ethnic splits and consolidations, and how Soviet-Marxist thinking has influenced Native scholars. Most significant, the article provides a poignant example of the theoretical problems that can arise from reliance on "ethnonyms" (self-names)—when even these obvious ethnic markers and their meanings are not agreed upon by the people themselves. At root, the problem becomes "when is a group an ethnic group?"

and how can we, in the intensely politicized late twentieth century, determine this for peoples who lived centuries earlier and who had their own, different politics. Mokshin has a definite view, supporting the current and historical validity of the term Mordva in defiance of some recent local attacks, and despite his own family name, which is nearly congruent with one of the two main subgroups of the Mordva—Moksha (as opposed to Erzia).[9]

Authors of the second chapter grapple with similar issues, describing historical patterns using the highly charged example of Turkic peoples inside Russia. The authors, Raul Gumerovich Kuzeev and Shamil Fatikhovich Mukhamediarov, are, respectively, Bashkir and Tatar ethnohistorians. The main strength of this chapter is that together the authors argue for the methodological benefits of studying interrelated groups in a large historically defined region. In what becomes nearly a manifesto, they plead: "When the history of a group of peoples is closely interconnected, it is helpful to study ethnic history as the simultaneous consolidation of a number of related and nonrelated ethnoses, after considerable time in economic, cultural, and other kinds of contact" (p. 47). These may not seem like fighting words, but the position they take runs against currents of specific-group ethnogenesis in traditional Soviet ethnography and also against more recent tendencies of Native scholars to be exclusive, even chauvinist (especially anti-Russian), in their orientation to one ethnic group. The authors also rail against and even sarcastically mock recent proclamations of deep Turkic roots for a given people, for example diverse unproven claims of Turkic links to Scythians and Sumerians. Their ethnic foci range from Bulgars to the peoples of the Ural mountains, and their eclectic approach incorporates the concept of Turkicization, including of Slavic peoples. Addressing more modern trends, they argue for better urban anthropology and for recognition of the ways in which the Soviet state itself influenced development of national consciousness through its republic structures. Ironically, these data-oriented ethnohistorians are attracted to some of the over-systematizing ethnic-group typologies that became fashionable under former Institute of Ethnography director Iulian Bromlei. This may be a function of when the article was written (1990). But their coverage of the interrelation of ethnicity and religion is especially valuable. Their work reminds us there are many histories of Islam and many kinds of Islam.

Anatolii Ignatevich Gogolev has been quietly and diligently working for years on topics that have recently become fashionable because of a renewed search for an understanding of Sakha (Yakut) roots, for a sense of the relationship between Sakha and Turkic cultures, and for new concepts of historical processes that have shaped the Sakha into a nation. For many historical questions that the Sakha intelligentsia of East Siberia has been asking with increasing intensity, Anatolii Gogolev has suggested detailed and nuanced answers, which he occasionally publishes in popular as well as academic venues. His work is in the tradition of a classical "four fields" anthropology that integrates data from multiple sources: biological, linguistic, archeological, and sociocultural. Within Soviet scholarship, this was, at its best, the methodology of numerous "ethnogenetic" studies. Yet much of the theory of "ethnogenesis" was marred by a standardized Eurocentric framework of "Progress," which diluted the power of specific case studies. Gogolev's work for the most part transcends this by a wide search for historical interconnections without prejudging their content or meaning. In this sense, while certainly an evolutionary theorist, he comes closer to a cross between Franz Boas and Julian Steward than Marx and Engels in the goals he sets for himself.[10]

The respected Khakas ethnographer Viktor Iakovlevich Butanaev is also concerned with the Turkic roots of his people, and became embroiled in a vicious debate about Khakas history that burst into the pages of the preeminent journal *Sovetskaia etnografiia* in 1992. The work published here is his contribution to that debate. He argues that the Khakas ethnonym is a figment of the Soviet period, as indeed is the development of the Khakas people's sense of themselves as a separate nationality. Nonetheless, the Khakas use the term "Tadar" in their spoken language for themselves, and this in turn refers to a group of people described in most relevant Soviet ethnographic literature as aboriginal to the Middle Yenisei valley. Butanaev's assertion that the present-day Khakas are very different from their Yenisei predecessors, from the Khakas mentioned in Chinese chronicles, or from possible Khakas kin of the Kyrgyz (of the Kyrgyz state) makes his views correlate well with those of Western anthropologists who insist ethnic identity is a modern, fluid, and highly political phenomenon.[11]

Political Anthropology

Anthropologists concerned more explicitly with politics include those who are puzzling over the roots and meanings of ethnic conflicts throughout the former Soviet Union. The very survival of the Russian Federation has been questioned, with one of its republics, Chechnia, having already unilaterally declared independence. How the federation will evolve very much depends on a center–periphery dynamic that is still being played out. The insights of local anthropologists into this process are critical for our understanding of whether Russia will go the way of the former Soviet Union or will transform itself from a mini-empire into a truly federal state.

One of the most serious hotspots is in the North Caucasus mountains, on

Harmonious Circassian presentation of self to outsiders at a mountain lake in the now turbulent North Caucasus. Photo by M.M. Balzer, October 1983.

the border with Georgia and very much including Chechnia. The magnificent mountains and valleys of the North Caucasus (see photo) were the site of some of the most violent and protracted fighting in Russian history, during the nineteenth-century Caucasus War for consolidation of the Russian empire periphery. At that time, this region of myriad peoples and languages was shaped and marked politically and ethnically by the fighting, for groups that had earlier had little sense of cohesion came together both as allies and as self-identifying, evolving clan-based ethnic groups. That process of testing and cohesion, fighting and reconciling is still going on today, in a time of transition exacerbated by memory of the brutal treatment against many of these same Caucasus peoples when they were deported *en masse* to Central Asia as traitors, under Stalin during and just after World War II, especially in 1943 and 1944. While geography is hardly destiny, it provides constraints and possibilities of which local peoples are acutely aware as they debate land ownership and cultural-political unity.[12]

Crystallizing incidents of violence create cycles of revenge and retaliation. The chapter by the Ossetian ethnopsychologist Galina U. Soldatova on Chechen, Ingush, Ossetian, and Russian relations is particularly significant for its depiction of an intertwined anatomy of ethnic polarization. The very horror of war in Ingushetia and Chechnia, however, gave literal pause to hostilities between nearby Kabardei and Balkar groups—thus serving as an object lesson for peoples on the brink of the insanity of bloodshed.[13] Galina Soldatova's article covers political, demographic, and "sociopsychological" aspects of ethnic polarization. In her psychological generalizations about whole ethnic groups she borders on older anthropological discussions of national character, and thus may be controversial for some readers. She herself is well aware of the pitfalls of ethnic stereotyping, and thus tries to rely on interview data in which people themselves discuss their own "ethnic self-perceptions."

Another Russian border area scarred by recent ethnic violence is the tiny mountainous republic of Tuva, where Tuvan youths attacked Russian newcomers in 1989 and 1990. Similar to the Baltic states, Tuva was not incorporated into the Soviet Union until 1944. Modern Tuvans thus have retained a very strong memory of their culture and past status as an independent, albeit client state, at the Soviet-Mongolian border.[14] The Tuvan ethnosociologist Zoia V. Anaibin outlines current Tuvan demographic and political contexts for both tensions and rapprochement between the majority Tuvans and minority Slavic population of Tuva. Although many skilled Russian workers have been leaving Tuva, Zoia Anaibin characterizes Tuvan nationalism as under control and for the most part not secessionist. Her own ties to the more conservative Tuvan former communist political elite may make this assessment premature, but nonetheless her analysis provides rare data about a critically strategic (culturally and politically) people within the potentially unstable Russian Federation.

A third sharply contested political space within Russia is the republic of Tatarstan. Ethnosociologist Roza N. Musina briefly yet effectively outlines historical, demographic, and social backgrounds of Russian-Tatar relations before discussing the emergence of various political groups in Tatarstan. She places these groups in three blocks: nationalist, democratic, and socialist. Politics in Tatarstan is fluctuating every day, as is the center–periphery dynamic that led Tatar leaders not to sign the 1992 Federal Treaty. The bilateral treaty signed in spring 1994 between Moscow (President Yeltsin) and Kazan (President Shamiev) represents an important step in federal relations, which may serve as a model for others. Roza Musina's work grounds the reader with basic information that can help in interpretation of future flux. She is one of several ethnosociologists in Tatarstan known for excellent standards of survey research and has recently become a team member of a Moscow-based project to compare various secessionist and ethnic conflict tendencies within the Russian Federation.[15] Musina contends that Tatarstan is not only a politically pivotal republic for the survival of the Russian Federation, but even the most legally and symbolically diagnostic.

An important and complex aspect of interethnic politics in Russia involves the ecology movement, born as early as the 1960s in the Lake Baikal region. Baikal is the center of the Buryat homeland, with its ecosystem extending south into Mongolia, as well as north into Siberia. But it is also claimed by patriotic Russians as a jewel worth saving for Russia. The region around Lake Baikal, like so many others in Russia, has become multiethnic without being fully integrated. At Baikal, as elsewhere, Soviet socioeconomic lifestyles and values permeated the cultures of both indigenous and newcomer populations, although to varying degrees. The Buryats, a Mongolic people, have become a distinct minority in their own lands, divided (gerrymandered) officially into three regions. However, Buryats and Russians have worked together to try to save Lake Baikal from industrial pollution, especially that caused by a notorious cellulose plant.[16]

The author of the chapter featured here on Lake Baikal is a Buryat cultural anthropologist, Zoia I. Morokhoeva, who has written a broad philosophical essay on the cultural implications of various approaches to Baikal's survival. She is justifiably worried about the ad-hocracy and political in-fighting that has characterized much of Baikal's recent development history. She also gently criticizes some Russian and Western legal management land zoning strategies as potentially clashing with the harmony of Buryat Eastern traditions that have always been more fully at one with nature and not outside or above it. Straining back to the values that nourished Buryat Buddhist and animist traditions is, as Morokhoeva recognizes, not easy in the current context. But it is, she argues, crucial for the survival of her people.

Symbolic anthropology

The study of symbols can theoretically embrace material culture, the political use or development of key cultural icons, and the understanding of rituals with multiple functions and meanings. Selections here focus on some of the most blatant and basic aspects of symbolic anthropology, concentrating on the nexus of ritual, religion, esthetics, and ideology.

The reasoning behind religious thought is revealed in Evdokiya Alexandrovna Gaer's detailed ethnography of the birth rituals of the Amur River peoples. Gaer does not limit her focus to her own people, the Nanai (formerly Goldy), but also compares other Amur peoples, the Nivkh (formerly Gilyak) and the Ulchi (sometimes Olchi). She is a Moscow Institute of Ethnography–trained anthropologist, whose rich and productive fieldwork in the 1970s and 1980s provides a fine complement to classic earlier ethnographies of the region by Lev Shternberg, L.I. Shrenk, and B.O. Pilsudski (among others). Particularly noteworthy is her attention to, and

Evdokiya A. Gaer in the study of Marjorie M. Balzer, November 1991.
Photo by Harley D. Balzer.

reporting of, the precise language of her interviews. In keeping with standards of Soviet ethnography, Evdokiya Gaer focused her interviews with elderly informants on their prerevolutionary period memories. Her interest was in the "traditional," rather than "modern" adaptations or maladaptations to disintegrating conditions, cultural and ecological. Nonetheless, from her texts and from conversations with her, it is clear that more than "memory culture" or "salvage anthropology" is being described. A syncretic mixture of traditional and modern ideologies is evident in current ritual practices related to shamanism, bear ceremonialism, and life-crisis rituals.[17] And small indications of "postmodern" cultural revival movements in the Amur region are manifest in folklore groups (e.g., Mangbo), the prominence of Native writers like Vladimir Sangi, the rise of ecological activists like Iurii Samar (also educated as an ethnographer), and in Evdokiya Gaer's own political career (see photo above).

The Sakha (Yakut) ethnographer Platon A. Sleptsov has become firmly established as one of the bright younger scholars in the Sakha intelligentsia (see photo, facing page). Trained in both Yakutsk and Leningrad in the early to mid-1980s, he was influenced by rigorous standards of holistic and comparative anthropology, paired with specific knowledge of Turkic cultures. Thus the fieldwork-focused traditions of Lev Ia. Shternberg and Rudolf F. Its, plus his mentors Dmitrii G. Savinov and Anatolii I. Gogolev are easily recogniz-

Platon A. Sleptsov with his baby daughter. Photo by M.M. Balzer, Yakutsk, Sakha Republic, August 1994.

able in his meticulous work. Platon Sleptsov's professional career in the Yakutsk branch of the Academy of Science began during the death throes of Soviet activist demands that ethnographers aid propagandists in concocting new secular rituals of birth, marriage, and death. Thus on the eve of Gorbachev's perestroika, Platon Sleptsov served on a committee to recreate Yakut marriage rituals, mixing a small dose of Sakha tradition with large doses of socialist messages. He easily survived this sterile exercise of imposing culture "from above" and has recently been active in far more productive, locally generated projects. These include Sakha republic reformist education and language programs, as well as projects to help revive respect for selected aspects of shamanism and pre-Soviet life-crisis rituals.[18]

Platon Sleptsov's research on marriage ritual and belief typically, and safely, focuses on the late-nineteenth, early-twentieth-century time period just prior to the revolution. This allows him, and every other ethnographer who has adhered to this standard strategy, to mask problems inherent in defining the word "traditional" when used in the Soviet context. Also typical is a Marxist-influenced striving for identification of developmental stages within marriage customs, positing transitions from matriarchy into patriarchy through analysis of "survivals." Nonetheless, Sleptsov's analysis cannot be fully stereotyped, for he stresses pragmatic, material, exchange aspects of marriage together with the significance of spiritual and social symbolism, using the work of Elena Novik, Claude Lévi-Strauss, and Victor Turner. His interpretation of Turkic and "proto-Turkic" ethnogenetic commonalities rests on a thorough search of the ethnographic and archeological literature and is made particularly cogent through description of parallel rituals in Turkic and Buryat cultures using linguistic terms and colorful glosses for those rituals.

Tassan S. Tein is a Iupik Eskimo writing ethnography since the 1970s, based in Magadan, with roots among the Chaplino and Naukan peoples of Chukotka.[19] The data presented here, which touch on shamanism and much else, are presented with far less ideological baggage than those of many researchers in today's Russia. His conclusions are direct and less self-conscious than those of many of us contorted by competing anthropological theories while interpreting the vast marketplace of cross-cultural experience. Thus Tein simply stresses the importance of seeing a range of "traditions, rituals, omens, and beliefs" as part of religion. Religion *per se* is neither elevated nor condemned, at least not in this chapter.

At moments in the text, written recently and passed to me in manuscript form, Tassan Tein generalizes back to all "ancient Eskimo," as if they had a belief system that could be projected through time, capturing some essential Eskimo-ness, or at least Asian Eskimo tradition. But other descriptions are more refined, noting, for example, that one bad omen means the reverse in a nearby village. Most significant, Tein gives a flavor for the kinds of reasoning and beliefs that permeated Eskimo everyday life through the Soviet period, despite Soviet propaganda. His work defies standard Western or Soviet ethnographic categorization, as does any anthropology that attempts to interpret the spirit of Native thinking. Thus he highlights women's appeasement of mice (after stealing from their burrows), men's hunting etiquette, and the use of urine to discourage the return of the dead as spirits. Some of the customs mentioned have correlations among other northern Siberian peoples, but no effort is made to fit Eskimo practices into others' linguistic or ethnogenetic frameworks. Tense changes in the original manuscript have been preserved in the translation provided here, for they show a wavering between discussion of outmoded concepts and current ones. Even with this sensitivity, however, any "objective" assessment of current worldview is clearly elusive. Rather, readers should sit back and enjoy a poetically potent description of (some) Chaplino, Naukan, and Providenia concepts related to sea-mammal and bear hunting, to death, to dreaming, and to initiation into a world not as fully bygone as some anthropologists have claimed.

Mongush B. Kenin-Lopsan also pays assiduous attention to the importance of language, analyzing shamanic folklore as not only a reflection of a Tuvan worldview, but also as poetry.[20] Mongush Kenin-Lopsan is of an older generation of Native ethnographers, one of the most prominent of his people to take advantage of Soviet education programs allowing for careers in ethnography. While predominantly Kyzyl-based, he too was influenced by the Leningrad University tradition of ethnography, through Rudolf F. Its and Dmitrii G. Savinov, as well as by his colleague in Tuvan studies, Moscow Institute of Ethnography (now Institute of Ethnology and Anthropology) scholar Sevyan Vainshtein. The thoroughness of his methodology is indicated by his list of informants, mostly elders whose special interests and talents he notes, along with more conventional information. He spent many years building rapport and mutual respect with villagers and recent urban residents, including former shamans and their helpers. This is not surprising, given that his father was the folklorist Borakh K. Mongush, who was able to relate family shamanic traditions to his son.

Mongush Kenin-Lopsan wrote the work excerpted here before the strong recent post-Soviet cultural and political revival movement had taken hold in the sovereign republic of Tuva. He mentioned in his "afterword" that "professional shamanism . . . remains only in the memory of the people," little dreaming that a revival of interest in shamanism and Buddhism would bring traditional spiritual and medical practitioners back into repute. However, as an ethnographer interested in the full context of the belief systems of his people, he also noted that, despite Soviet rule, "elements of the cult of the shamanic tree, the mineral spring *arzhaan*, and certain beliefs indirectly related to shamanism are preserved." Thus he described a foundation from which the current revival movement has grown and adapted (see photo). Kenin-Lopsan in print showed no nostalgia for the pre-Soviet past, noting there is much yet to do to "overcome the religious superstitions." However, like many of his Siberian ethnographer colleagues, he has dramatically modified his definitions of these "superstitions" in recent years. And by early and consistently stressing the

A Tuvan (or Soyot) shaman of the Altai Region, c. 1900. Photo in archives of the Hamburgisches Museum für Völkerkunde.

richness of Tuvan folklore esthetics, he usually side-stepped most political implications of his work during his career.

"Natives" on ethnography and change

The anthropologists featured here have in common a thirst for detail combined with a cultural insider's understanding of the reasoning behind many of the traditions studied. Most of all, they are joined in a conception of themselves, representatives of diverse cultures, as struggling through unavoidable processes of change without total acculturation of Russian, Soviet, industrial, and "postmodern" ways. When they talk or write of themselves, a strong sense of mission often emerges—that it is their destiny to contribute to their own peoples' understanding of their cultures. Helping one's people to shake cycles of ecological and spiritual neglect and to respect their own cultural values, lore, and traditional wisdom is an explicit goal of many Native anthropologists. Along the way, if they also help variously defined "others" understand that culture, so much the better.

As individuals, Native scholars in Russia have taken various paths toward realizing goals that brought them into anthropology. Many have highly respected academic research and teaching careers. Some have become cultural activists, educating their people through popular articles. Others have plunged headlong into politics, becoming parliament deputies. Still others have become spiritual leaders or ecological activists.

An interesting example is the Naukan (Eskimo) schoolteacher, Isabella Avtonova, to whom this book is dedicated, who spent years collecting a catalogue of the edible plants that are known to the local Chukchi and Eskimo of Chukotka. Her work represents not only recovery of traditional lore for posterity, but also a faith in the living wisdom and usefulness of that lore. She integrated her folk knowledge with a reverence that included making small food offerings in four directions when collecting plants. In the introduction to her catalogue, she anticipated objections that, since European foods are well known and used in Chukotka, Native dishes should be superseded. She argued for a full range of knowledge of multiple, enriching ways of food and medicinal preparation. She thus created an apt metaphor, using food, for the coexistence of cultures in general, and the Russian, Chukchi, and Eskimo cultures in specific. She wrote:

> I would like to say a word about ecology, which is a very important issue in our civilization. I am not against the building of roads, houses, and so forth. Yet how heedlessly and badly the workers treat the tundra, hauling sand and gravel and totally ignoring the plant world. Surely, before taking natural material from the tundra, the project supervisors should consult with the local population; they should at least pay a little respect to us, the native inhabitants of the tundra, who gather edible plants during the brief summer.... Interacting with the world of nature not only provides material benefits and invigorates health, but also replenishes our spiritual riches and makes life more meaningful. One who experiences the joy of communing with nature becomes a better person.[21]

A more famous ecological and political activist is the Nanai ethnographer Evdokiya Gaer, discussed above, who won a seat in the all-Union parliament in 1989, became a member of the Supreme Soviet, and later was elected to the Russian Federation duma. To win her first election, she defeated the Russian head of the entire Far East Military District. While clearly an opposition candidate, she was elected on the basis of effective appeal to both Russians and Native peoples for reform. She came to my attention when an especially striking story was printed in *Literaturnaia gazeta* (12 July 1989, p. 3), which she later confirmed. One day, after her energy appeared to flag as she stood beside Yeltsin in a television interview, an elderly female shaman from her region decided to fly to Moscow to help her. With the delight of an ethnographer, a compatriot, and a patient, Evdokiya Gaer agreed to a late-night seance, which she said did help revive her health, spirits, and energy.

Gaer and I had several significant conversations about the virtues of being an "insider" anthropologist, well-versed not only in the language but the euphemisms of one's own people. On a field visit in the 1980s, she overheard metaphorical talk among her own female relatives about a shamanic curing seance that they were planning to hold in secret. If she had not understood their extremely vague allusion, she would never have been allowed to participate. On the other hand, there were times when even she felt like an outsider, as, for example, when she tried innocently to help in an elderly woman's home by sweeping in the evening, and the alarmed hostess told her she was disturbing spirits. Being "Native" clearly is itself a matter of degree and variation; by her academic degrees and her status in the outside world, Gaer has removed herself from the world of her childhood and from complete rapport with her own people. Instead, she has become an important interpreter of their culture and their grief at its loss.

One early morning, in the midst of the 1991 Anthropology Association convention, Evdokiya Gaer told me a frightening dream which she had just had, and which she gave permission to relate. In the dream, she and family and friends were all crammed together in a traditional large canoe, rowing down the Amur River in a sunny, lush environment. Suddenly, up ahead they saw a huge wall of dark-green slime coming toward them, killing everything in its wake. She awoke before it arrived, interpreting the dream as a metaphor for her own, and her people's, fear of nuclear destruction and ecological devastation.[22]

Sensitivity to dreams, art, and poetry is characteristic of many non-Russian ethnographers of Russia, as is fascination with shamanism. Sometimes that fascination crosses over, especially in the 1990s, into active participation in shamanic ritual. The esteemed Tuvan ethnographer Mongush Kenin-Lopsan has taken on not only roles of elder statesman of Tuvan ethnography, but also spiritual guide for young Tuvans and foreign visitors, who shared shamanic curing techniques in Tuva in summer 1993.[23] The Buryat ethnographer Taras Mikhailov, long known as a Soviet-style propagandist against shamanism (even while he studied its details), emerged at a conference in Yakutsk in 1990 as a defender of the creation of shamanic schools in Buryatia, and has gained a reputation as a shaman.[24]

The issue of how deeply a Native ethnographer believes in aspects of the spiritual traditions she or he is studying goes directly to the core of the "authoritativeness" of Native ethnography. Pseudo-objectivity, in some successful cases, can be traded for a subtle, informed, and self-conscious subjectivity. This is neither guaranteed in, nor exclusive to, Native ethnography. Some excellent "outsider" anthropologists, who spend years emersed in a focal culture, gain the kind of insider, experiential knowledge that turns them into spiritual practitioners. Some initially foreign ethnographers become fellow-travelers along a philosophical road of linguistic nuance, and a mystical road of belief in "nonordinary reality." But this is more likely to occur among Native ethnographers, whose own cultural knowledge and participation is itself a matter of degree.[25]

The two Sakha ethnographers featured here illustrate contrasting styles and approaches to insider knowledge. I choose the Sakha case because I am attempting to fellow-travel in it most intensively. But other cases could easily serve as well (for example the two Tuvan specialists in this volume). Anatolii Gogolev and Platon Sleptsov are teacher and student, both with ethnographic training in Leningrad (now St. Petersburg), and very close friends. One is far more inclined than the other toward believing in traditional Sakha religion. This became apparent early in our interactions, in my first few months of fieldwork, when many of my Sakha friends tended to hide the degree to which they observed non-Soviet rituals. (Some also had reawakenings when this became possible, later revealing they had become believers between 1986 and 1990.) In 1986, I was thrilled to be driven by Anatolii Gogolev to a sacred grove, the first in Yakutia that I ever saw. But he waited in the car while I went with Platon to put a ribbon on a sacred tree and revel in a magnificent mountain valley view. When we returned, we discovered Anatolii reading a detective novel.[26]

Does it matter? Readers probably could not tell from the entries here which author is spiritually closer to his traditions, because both scholars have used techniques of objectifying removal of themselves from their texts and have written about the distant or recent past. Anatolii Gogolev, the more senior and synthetic author, has an encyclopedic wealth of folklore, ethnographic, and archeological data in his memory. Platon Sleptsov is on the way to developing ethnographic depth. The contrast in their approach to data may well become more apparent in the post-Soviet future, as they choose different topics and interrelated theories for focus. Gogolev, leery of "superstition," remains the descriptive digger, deciphering the special Sakha mix of Turkic, Mongolic, Ugrian, Samoedic, and Yukagiric traditions over huge swaths of historical time. And Sleptsov is becoming one of the young ethnographers interested in writing about the painful reinvention of Sakha tradition and belief in the present. In a territory as vast as the Sakha Republic (four times the size of Texas), and as diverse in its population history and fluctuating networks of commercial and political influence, it would be surprising if multiple styles and mixed feelings were not present in current-day Sakha and other ethnic minority conceptions of themselves (see photos that follow).

Yakut National Theater actor Afanasii Fedorov playing the shaman at an art opening for an exhibition of shamanic images, summer 1992. The actor has also been helping patients by practicing some shamanic curing techniques.

The Artist as Ethnographer. Yukagir artist Nikolai N. Kurilov is known for his depictions of Yukagir life in the Far North of the Sakha Republic where the Yukagir number just over 1,000. Photo by Viktor Iakovlev in the artist's studio in the village of Chersk, 1993.

Yet another approach to the urgent need to recover locally defined tradition and meaning in the chaotic post-Soviet world is represented by a quite literally monumental project to publish the major epics and lore of Siberian and Far Eastern peoples in a multivolume series. This project is led by the Buryat folklorist Aleksandr Badmaevich Soktoev, who is based in Novosibirsk, and who has made his life's mission the recovery and dissemination of the cultural riches of all Siberian peoples. As with many Siberian activist academics, Soktoev's own sense of identity extends in multiple rings beyond his native Buryatia to embrace solidarity with Siberian and Far Eastern indigenous peoples. This was especially evident in an opening address he gave to a 1993 conference, "Languages, Culture, and the Future of Arctic Peoples," held in Yakutsk. That address, graciously naming many Native ethnographers and folklorists with whom he works, concludes this volume in order to give readers a fuller understanding of the scholarship that developed in the Soviet period as non-Russian peoples increasingly took on responsibility for the descriptions and interpretations of their own cultures.

It is ironic that at a time of shrinking support for anthropology and increased fears for the cultural survival of some of the smaller indigenous populations, there have never been more Native ethnographers in Russia. It is crucial that we incorporate their diverse worldviews and theories into the intellectual cacophony of international anthropology.

Slaughtering: A reindeer round-up from Nikolai N. Kurilov's series "the artist in the tundra," using an applique techniqué, 1990. Photo by Albert Stepanov.

The Dance: A reindeer round-up by Nikolai N. Kurilov using an appliqué technique, 1985. Photo by Albert Stepanov.

Notes

1. This brief historical review owes much to Dmitrii Glebovich Savinov, whose lively lectures at Leningrad University were bright spots while I was waiting for permission to go to Yakutia in fall 1985. See also A.N. Pypin, *Istoriia russkoi etnografii* (St. Petersburg, 1890–92, 4 vols.); S.A. Tokarev, *Istoriia russkoi etnografii (Dooktiabr'ski period)* (Moscow: Academy of Sciences, 1966). A modern synthetic history of pre-revolutionary anthropology in Russia, outlining contributions of both Russians and non-Russians, remains to be written, although the historian Catherine Clay's current research touches on aspects of this. For samples of native ethnography from the 1800s to the 1920s, see Dorzhi Banzarov, *Sobranie sochinenii* (Moscow: Academy of Sciences, 1955, original Kazan 1846); Mikhail N. Khangalov, *Sobranie sochinenii* (Ulan-Ude: Buriat knizh. izdat, 1958–60, 3 vols.); Ismail Bei Gasprinskii (Gasprali), *Russkoe musul'manstvo* (Oxford: Obshchestvo issledovanie Srednei Azii, 1985, reprint no. 6); Nikolai F. Khatanov, *Obraztsy narodnoi literatury tiurkskikh plemen* (St. Petersburg, 1907); Chikan Ch. Valikhov, *Sobranie sochinenii* (Alma-Alta: GRKSE, 1985, 5 vols.); Gavriil V. Ksenofontov, *Shamanizm: izbrannye trudy* (Yakutsk: Sever-Iug, 1992); Aleksei E. Kulakovskii, *Nauchnye trudy* (Yakutsk: Iakutsk. knizhnoe izdatel'stvo, 1979).

2. For Shternberg's progress-oriented, humanistic Ten Commandments, see N.I. Gagen-Torn, "The Leningrad Ethnographic School in the 1920s," *Soviet Anthropology and Archeology*, 1971, vol. 10, pp. 161–62. The anthropologist Igor Krupnik (Smithsonian lecture, December 1991) has raised the important issue that Native anthropologists with shrinking access to or desire for Moscow intellectual circles and education may become increasingly parochial in their outlooks and foci in the post-Soviet environment. This does not necessarily follow, however, and may vary as individuals seek diverse international contacts.

3. See the excellent articles outlining the complexities of defining "Native" by Kirin Narayan, "How Native Is a 'Native' Anthropologist?" *American Anthropologist*, 1993, vol. 95, no. 3, pp. 671–86; and José Limón, "Representation, Ethnicity and the Precursory Ethnography: Notes of a Native Anthropologist," *Recapturing Anthropology*, ed. Richard Fox, (Santa Fe, NM: School of American Research Press, 1991), pp. 115–36. The Japanese-American anthropologist Emiko Ohnuki-Tierney, who has grappled extensively with such concerns in her illustrious career, concludes in " 'Native' Anthropologists," *American Ethnologist*, 1984, vol. 11, pp. 584–86: "If native anthropologists can gain enough distance between their personal selves and their collective selves—their cultures—they can make an important contribution to anthropology because of their access to intimate knowledge of their own culture. The task is not an automatic or even easy one, however, and there are definite advantages for nonnative anthropologists. The two can indeed perform complementary roles in studying a culture." Other examples of outstanding and internationally known Native ethnographers include: Alfonso Ortiz, *The Tewa World: Space, Time Being and Becoming in a Pueblo Society* (Chicago: University of Chicago Press, 1969); Mysore Naras Srinivas, *On Living in a Revolution and Other Essays* (Delhi, New York: Oxford, 1992); Stanley Jeyar Tambiah, *Buddhism Betrayed? Religion, Politics and Violence in Sri Lanka* (Chicago: University of Chicago Press, 1992); and Gananath Obeyesekere, *Medusa's Hair: An Essay on Personal Symbols and Religious Experience* (Chicago: University of Chicago Press, 1981). See also Hussein Fahim, *Indigenous Anthropology in Non-Western Countries* (Durham, NC: Carolina Academic Press, 1982); H. Russell Bernard, *Native Ethnography: A Mexican Indian Describes His Culture* (Newberry Park, CA: Sage, 1989); and Margaret Mead, *The School in American Culture* (Cambridge: Harvard University Press, 1951).

4. In choosing this sample, I was not driven by a need to represent any particular ethnic group, and there are obviously many gaps. Some of the material came to me through personal connections. Thus both accident and my own knowledge of those who study Turkic cultures has played some role in which authors were chosen. Excluded here are related genres of life histories, and material-culture studies. Given the history of the discipline, it is probably no accident that the articles under "political anthropology" are written by younger female scholars and those under "ethnohistory" are by older, more established male ethnographers. For profiles of many of the peoples of the Russian Federation, see Paul Friedrich, ed., *Handbook of the Peoples of Post-Soviet Eurasia* (New York: G.K. Hall for Human Relations Area Files, 1994); Nikolai Vaktin, *Native Peoples of the Russian Far North* (London: Minority Group Rights International, 1992).

5. Leokadiia M. Drobizheva, "Kazhdomu—svoi," *Rodina*, 1991, pp. 19–22; Marjorie Mandelstam Balzer, "From Ethnicity to Nationalism: Turmoil in the Russian Mini-Empire," in *Social Legacies of Communism*, eds. James Millar and Sharon Wolchik (Cambridge: Cambridge University Press, 1994), pp. 56–88. Depending on how they are counted, 126 non-Russian groups were represented within Russia in the 1989 census, and some researchers have recently revised this to about 160. Their population, based on the 1989 census, is approximately 30 million, or about 20 percent of the population of Russia (150 million).

6. Ethnohistorians besides those featured here include the Itelmen N.K. Starkova, the Nanai N.B. Kile, the Nivkhs G.A. Otaina and Ch.M. Taksami, the Evens V.D. Lebedev and A.E. Alekseev, the Tuvan K.A. Bicheldei, the Sakha V.F. Ivanov, the Kumyk S.Sh. Gadzhieva; and the Kalmyks M.L. Kichikov (Ochirov) and V.P. Sanchirov. For perspective on Soviet ethnohistory, see Iulian V. Bromlei, "Osnovnye napravleniia etnograficheskikh issledovanii v SSSR," *Voprosy istorii*, 1968, no. 1, pp. 37–56 (translated as "Major Trends in Ethnographic Research in the USSR," *Soviet Anthropology and Archeology*, 1969, no. 1, pp. 3–42); B.P. Polevoi and Ch.M. Taksami, *Etnograficheskie issledovaniia na Sovetskom dal'nem vostoke v XVII–XX vv.* (Moscow: Nauka, 1979); K.V. Chistov, "Iz istorii sovetskoi etnografii 30–80 godov XX veka," *Sovetskaia etnografiia*, 1983, no. 3, pp. 3–18; M.V. Kriukov, I. Zel'nov, eds., *Etnografiia i smezhnye distsipliny* (Moscow: Nauka, 1988); S.A. Arutiunov, *Narody i kul'tury: razvitie i vzaimodeistvie* (Moscow: Nauka, 1989); V.A. Shnirel'man, "Zlokliucheniia odnoi nauki: etnogeneticheskie issledovaniia i Stalinskaia natsional'naia politika," *Etnograficheskoe obozrenie*, 1993, no. 3, pp. 52–68. See also D.B. Shimkin, "Recent Trends in Soviet Anthropology," *American Anthropologist*, 1949, vol. 51, no. 4, pp. 621–25; Stephen P. Dunn and Ethel Dunn, eds., *Introduction to Soviet Ethnography* (Berkeley: Highgate Road Social Science Research Station, 1973, 2 vols.); David Zil'berman, "Ethnography in Soviet Russia," *Dialectical Anthropology*, 1976, no. 1; Ernest Gellner, "The Soviet and the Savage," *Current Anthropology*, 1975, vol. 16, no. 4, pp. 595–617; Ernest Gellner, ed., *Soviet and Western Anthropology* (New York: Columbia University Press, 1980; M. Goncharuk, ed., *Soviet Studies in Ethnography* (Moscow: Social Sciences Today, 1978); Yuri Slezkine, "The Fall of Soviet Ethnography, 1928–1938," *Current Anthropology*, 1991, vol. 32, no. 4, pp. 476–84.

7. Others whose diverse work nonetheless resembles political anthropology include the Sakha ethnopsychologist Uliana A. Vinokurova and the Gagauz social linguist Mikhail N. Guboglo. The evolution of political anthropology analogous to that practiced in the West is a very new phenomenon, although in another sense the (neo-)Marxist ideologizing of scholarship in the Soviet Union meant all anthropology was political. Self-reflection on this includes: V.A. Tishkov, "Sovetskaia etnografiia: preodeolenie krizisa," *Etnicheskoe obozrenie*, 1992, no. 1, pp. 5–20; B.N. Basilov, "Etnografiia: est' li u nee budyshchee?" *Etnicheskoe obozrenie*, 1992, no. 4, pp. 3–17. Compare "Crisis in

Anthropology," *Anthropology and Archeology of Eurasia*, vol. 33, no. 3 (Winter 1994–95); and "The Soviet Multiethnic State," *Soviet Anthropology and Archeology*, vol. 28, no. 3 (Winter 1989–90). See also George E. Marcus, ed., *Perilous States: Conversations on Culture, Politics and Nation* (Chicago: University of Chicago Press, 1993); Ian Bremmer and Ray Taras, eds., *Nations and Politics in the Soviet Successor States* (Cambridge: Cambridge University Press, 1993); Gail Lapidus and Victor Zaslavsky, eds., *From Union to Commonwealth* (Cambridge: Cambridge University Press, 1992); Graham Smith, ed., *The Nationalities Question in the Soviet Union* (London: Longman, 1990); Michel Aucouturier, ed., "L'Anthropologie soviétique," *Cahier du monde russe et soviétique*, 1990, vol. 31, no. 2–3; Victor Zaslavsky, *The Neo-Stalinist State: Class Ethnicity and Consensus in Soviet Society*, rev. ed. (Armonk, NY: M.E. Sharpe, 1994).

8. Examples include Taras Mikhailov of Buryatia, Mongush Kenin-Lopsan of Tuva, Chuner Taksami of the Amur Nivkh, and Tat'iana Moldanova of the Khanty-Mansi region. Recent Soviet and post-Soviet scholarship touching on issues related to symbolic anthropology includes studies of religion, gender, and semiotics. See B.N. Basilov, *Shamanstvo u narodov Srednei Azii i Kazakhstana* (Moscow: Nauka, 1992); A.K. Baiburin and I.S. Kon, eds., *Etnicheskie stereotypy muzhskogo i zhenskogo povedeniia* (St. Petersburg: Nauka, 1991); L.M. Drobizheva and M.S. Kashuba, eds., *Traditsii v sovremennom obshchestve* (Moscow: Nauka, 1990); A.S. Myl'nikov, *Etnograficheskoe izuchenie znakovykh sredstv kul'tury* (Leningrad: Nauka, 1989). See also "Semiotics and Politics," *Anthropology and Archeology of Eurasia*, vol. 32, no. 3 (Winter 1993–94).

9. I have tried not to take sides in the debate because I do not know enough about it, although just using the term "subgroup" for Moksha and Erzia could already be construed as biased against seeing them as wholly separate ethnic groups. See Ronald Wixman, "Mordvinian," in *The Peoples of the USSR: An Ethnographic Handbook* (Armonk, NY: M.E. Sharpe, 1984), p. 137.

10. The difference between the ethnonym "Sakha" and the word "Yakut" requires explanation. According to the Sakha ethnographer A.E. Kulakovskii, *Nauchnyi trudy* (Yakutsk: Iakutskoe knizhnoe izdatel'stvo, 1979), p. 414, Yakut is a corruption of a name that the Tungusic neighbors of the Sakha used, which was then picked up by Russians. When I confronted Anatolii Gogolev about whether to change his use of "Yakut" to the ethnonym "Sakha," he sighed, "No, leave it with Yakut. That is what my other writings use and what most readers know us as." For references to A.I. Gogolev's most significant works, see *Anthropology and Archeology of Eurasia*, vol. 31, no. 2 (Fall 1992), plus articles in *Poliarnaia zvezda*, e.g., "Srednevekovoe nasledie Iakutov," 1992, no. 3, pp. 155–57; "Istoriia dukhovnoi kul'tury Iakutov-Sakha," 1992, no. 1, pp. 136–40. Compare: Franz Boas, *Race, Language and Culture* (New York: Free Press, 1966, original 1940); Julian Steward, *Theory of Culture Change: The Methodology of Multilinear Evolution* (Urbana: University of Illinois Press, 1972, original 1955); David B. Givens and Susan N. Skomal, "The Four Fields: Myth or Reality?" *Anthropology Newsletter*, 1992, vol. 33, no. 7, pp. 1, 17.

11. For more on the Khakas origins debate, see "Ethnonyms and Origins," *Anthropology and Archeology of Eurasia*, vol. 32, no. 4 (Spring 1994). The reverence Khakas intellectuals have for Viktor Ia. Butanaev was recently emphasized to me by Valerii Ivanovich Ivanzaev, the head of the Khakas popular movement called Chon Chobi.

12. For more on the tragic North Caucasus history, see "Punished Peoples: An Update on the Situation in the North Caucasus and Kalmykia," *Anthropology and Archeology of Eurasia*, vol. 31, no. 4 (Spring 1993). See also Aleksandr M. Nekrich, *The Punished Peoples: The Deportation and Fate of Soviet Minorities at the End of the Second World War*, trans. George Saunders (New York: Norton, 1978); Robert Conquest, *The Nation Killers (the Soviet Deportation of Nationalities)* (New York: Macmillan, 1970).

13. I am grateful to Sergei Arutiunov, the head of the Caucasus division of the Institute of Ethnology and Anthropology of the Russian Academy of Sciences for this information, explained in March 1993. The peoples of the Caucasus have been divided into three main language groups: Altaic, Indo-European, and Ibero-Caucasian. For background, see Ronald Wixman, *Language Aspects of Ethnic Patterns and Processes in the North Caucasus* (Chicago: University of Chicago Press, 1980); Natalia Sadomskaya, ed., "Studies of the North Caucasus," *Soviet Anthropology and Archeology*, vol. 25, no. 2 (Fall 1986); Jane Ormrod, "The North Caucasus: Fragmentation or Federation?" in *Nations and Politics in the Soviet Successor States*, eds. Ian Bremmer and Ray Taras (Cambridge: Cambridge University Press, 1993), pp. 448–76; Shirin Akiner, *Islamic Peoples of the Soviet Union* (London: Kegan, Paul, 1983); Alexandre Bennigsen and S. Enders Wimbush, *Muslims of the Soviet Empire* (Bloomington: Indiana University Press, 1986). See also N.G. Volkova, *Etnonima i plemennye nazvaniia Severnogo Kavkaza* (Moscow: Nauka, 1973), N.G. Volkova, "Etnicheskaia istoriia, soderzhanie, poniatiia," *Sovetskaia etnografiia*, 1985 no. 5; and articles by Iuri Anchabadze in *Sovetskaia etnografiia*, for example "Ostrakism na Kavkaze," 1979 no. 5; "Strannye pominki," 1982 no. 1; and "Prikrasnyi obychai gostepriimstva," 1985 no. 4. For a strong dose of indigenous Soviet condemnation of outmoded but lingering Caucasian traditions, see O. Soia-Serko, "You Do Not Get Rid of Prejudices by Miracles," *Soviet Anthropology and Archeology*, vol. 10, no. 2, 1971, pp. 125–34.

14. See Toomas Alatalu, "Tuva—A State Reawakens," *Soviet Studies*, 1991, vol. 44, no. 5, pp. 881–95; Robert A. Rupen, "The Absorption of Tuva," in *The Anatomy of Communist Takeovers*, ed., Thomas T. Hammond. (New Haven: Yale University Press, 1975), pp. 148–50; Balzer, "From Ethnicity to Nationalism: Turmoil in the Russian Mini-Empire," pp. 56–88. See also Sevyan Vainshtein, *Nomads of South Siberia* (Cambridge: Cambridge University Press, 1980), and Caroline Humphrey's introduction in the same volume. Tuvans numbered 207,000 in the 1989 census.

15. The first three of the authors featured in the political anthropology section are members of the project "Post-Communist Nationalism, Ethnic Identity and Conflict Resolution in the Russian Federation," directed by Leokadiia Mikhailovna Drobizheva, head of the ethnosociology division of the Russian Academy of Sciences Institute of Anthropology and Ethnology, in Moscow, funded by the MacArthur Foundation. I am grateful to the authors and to Leokadiia M. Drobizheva for enabling publication here.

16. See O.K. Gusev, *Sviashchenyi Baikal: zapovednye zemli Baikala* (Moscow: Agropromizdat, 1986); "Spotlight on Lake Baikal," *Surviving Together*, Winter 1993, no. 33, pp. 35–43, especially statements by G. Gordon Davis (an American legal activist) and Sergei Shapkhaev (a Buryat ecology leader); Ze'ev Wolfson, *The Geography of Survival: Ecology in the Post-Soviet Era* (Armonk, NY: M.E. Sharpe, 1994). For more on Buryat culture and politics, see Caroline Humphrey, *The Karl Marx Collective: Ecomony, Society and Religion in a Siberian Collective Farm* (Cambridge: Cambridge University Press, 1983); Caroline Humphrey, "The Buryats," in *The Nationalities Question in the Soviet Union*, ed., Graham Smith (London: Longman, 1990), pp. 290–303; Irina Urbanaeva, "The Fate of Baikal Within Russia," *Anthropology and Archeology of Eurasia*, vol. 32, no. 4 (Spring 1994); Balzer, "From Ethnicity to Nationalism: Turmoil in the Russian Mini-Empire," pp. 56–88. The Buryats numbered 353,000 in the 1979 census, and were about 25 percent of the population of the Buryat Republic.

17. See also Evdokiya Gaer, "The Way of the Soul to the Otherworld and the Nanai Shaman," in *Shamanism: Past and Present*, eds., M. Hoppál and O.J. von Sadovsky (Budapest: Akademii Kiado, 1989), pp. 233–39; Chuner M. Taksami, *Osnovnye problemy etnografii i istorii Nivkhov* (Leningrad: Nauka, 1975).

18. Platon Alekseevich Sleptsov was named for one of the Sakha revolutionary

heroes, Platon Oiunskii, who was also one of the first Sakha ethnographers and collectors of epic folklore, and founder of the Institute of Languages, Literature, and History. He comes from a village in the Namsk region, where his father was known for his traditional knowledge and for special telepathic skills. I am grateful to Platon Sleptsov for many insights into Sakha cultural complexity, change, and resistance to change. For background, see "Cultural History of the Yakut (Sakha) People: The Work of Anatolii I. Gogolev," *Anthropology and Archeology of Eurasia*, vol. 31, no. 2 (Fall 1992); Piers Vitebsky, "Yakut," in *The Nationalities Question in the Soviet Union*, ed., Graham Smith (London: Longman, 1990), pp. 304–21; and Marjorie Mandelstam Balzer, "Dilemmas of the Spirit: Religion and Atheism in the Yakut-Sakha Republic," in *Religious Policy in the Soviet Union*, ed., Sabrina Ramet (Cambridge: Cambridge University Press, 1993), pp. 231–51. The Sakha numbered 382,000 in the 1989 census.

19. I am following Asiatic Eskimo practice of referring to themselves as "Eskimo," rather than "Inuit," the term Canadian Eskimo prefer. However, the Chukotka Eskimo also refer to themselves as "Iupik," and are Iupik speakers, with kinship and linguistic links to the nearby Iupik of Alaska and St. Lawrence Island. Siberian Iupik numbered only 1,718 in the 1989 census. I am grateful to Richard Condon, editor of *Arctic Anthropology*, for transferring this manuscript to me. See also Tassan S. Tein's "Shamans of the Siberian Eskimos," *Arctic Anthropology*, 1993, vol. 30, no. 1, translated and with an introduction by Dmitrii B. Shimkin. For ethnographic background, see Waldemar Bogoras (Bogaraz-tan), *The Eskimo of Siberia* (New York: Brill, Leiden and Stechert, Memoir of the American Museum of Natural History, vol. 12, 1913, original Jesup North Pacific Expedition, vol. 8, pt. 3); G.A. Menovshchikov, *Eskimosy* (Magadan: Magadan Knizhnoe Izdatel'stvo, 1959); Igor I. Krupnik, *Arkticheskiia etnoekologiia* (Moscow: Nauka, 1989); idem., *Arctic Adaptations: Native Whalers and Reindeer Herders of Northern Eurasia*, trans. and ed., Marcia Levenson (Hanover: Dartmouth, 1993).

20. Recognition of shamanic seance texts as poetry is exemplified in John Leavitt, ed., *Poetry and Prophecy* (Chicago: University of Chicago, forthcoming). The esthetics of shamanism was the main theme of the 1993 International Conference on Shamanism held in Budapest, Hungary, organized by Mihaly Hoppal. See also Ivan Brady, ed., *Anthropological Poetics* (Savage, MD: Rowman and Littlefield, 1991). I am grateful to Boris Chichlo for first mentioning the significance of Mongush Kenin-Lopsan's work. Transliterations used here represent sounds as closely as possible for the altered Cyrillic of the Turkic Tuvan and Sakha languages, adapting the Library of Congress system.

21. See I.V. Mimykg Avtonova, "Edible Wild Plants in Our Foods (Chukchi, Eskimo)," *Anthropology and Archeology of Eurasia*, vol. 31, no. 1 (Summer 1992), p. 89–90. I am grateful to Deborah Schindler for providing the catalogue for publication and for insights into its author. See also Deborah L. Schindler, "Indigenous Rights and Powers in Chukotka," *Inuit Studies*, 1992, vol. 15, no. 1–2.

22. I am grateful to Evdokiya Gaer for sharing this dream, and for allowing me to return her Moscow hospitality in Washington.

23. For a published account see Larry Peters, "In the Land of the Eagles: Experiences on the Shamanic Path in Tuva," *Shaman's Drum*, 1993, no. 33, pp. 42–49. I am grateful to trip leader Bill Brunton (personal communication, July 1993) for describing the rapport and successful cures of Western and Tuvan healers during their summer 1993 trip, sponsored by the Foundation for Shamanic Studies and the Tuvan Republic president. See also their film "The Foundation for Shamanic Studies Expedition to Tuva."

24. See Taras M. Mikhailov, *Buriatskii shamanism: istoriia, struktura i sotsial'nye funktsii* (Novosibirsk: Nauka, 1987). For a short excerpt, see "Buriat Shamanism: History, Function and Social Structure," in *Shamanism: Soviet Studies of Traditional Religion in*

Siberia and Central Asia, ed., M.M. Balzer (Armonk, NY: M.E. Sharpe, 1990), pp. 110–20.

25. Native anthropologists with particular depth and relevance include: Kayano Shigeru, *The Ainu Speak: The Land Was a Forest*, trans. Kyoko Selden and Lili Selden (Boulder: Westview, 1994); Nita Kumar, *Friends, Brothers and Informants: Fieldwork Memoirs of Banaras* (Berkeley: University of California Press, 1992); Kirin Narayan, *Storytellers, Saints and Scoundrels: Folk Narrative in Hindu Religious Teaching* (Philadelphia: University of Pennsylvania Press, 1989). Some "outsider" anthropologists, such as Ann Chowning in Melanesia, Frank Steward in North America, and Eva Schmidt in Siberia, gain reputations for deep cultural knowledge and reticence to publish sacred secrets for moral reasons. See also Barbara Tedlock, *The Beautiful and the Dangerous: Encounters with the Zuni Indians* (New York: Viking, 1992); Paul Stollar and Cheryl Olkes, *In Sorcery's Shadow* (Chicago: University of Chicago Press, 1987). For fruitful recent collaborations, see Ruth Behar, *Translated Woman: Crossing the Border with Esperanza's Story* (Boston: Beacon Press, 1993); Michael M.J. Fischer and Mehdi Abedi, *Debating Muslims: Cultural Dialogues in Postmodernity and Tradition* (Madison: University of Wisconsin Press, 1990).

26. Some tension has evolved in the republic between those who consider themselves practitioners of traditional beliefs and those who, at some remove, study rituals as ethnographers and folklorists. During an argument in June 1992 over how to organize the elaborate rituals of the annual *yhyakh* festival celebrating national solidarity, *kumys* (fermented mare's milk), fertility, and the advent of summer, a leader of the cultural revival group *Kut-Siur* (Soul-Mind) told Ministry of Culture consultants that they should yield expertise to those Sakha who were true believers of traditional Sakha religion (personal communication Lazar Afanaseev, *Kut-Siur* leader, August 1992).

I

**Ethnohistory:
Seeking Roots and Self-Identity**

The Mordva
Ethnonym or Ethnopholism?

Nikolai F. Mokshin

Recently in Mordova, there is renewed talk of the ethnonym "Mordva," its origin and usage—not only in spoken word, but also in radio and television broadcasts in the local and even in the central press, owing to the revived interest in national processes and relations between nationalities. Certain authors have even emphasized its allegedly negative, ethnophol (derogatory) nature. The authors of a letter sent to *Literaturnaia gazeta* from the Mordva village of Al'kino, Kovylkinsk region, Mordva ASSR, call this ethnonym "a very nonsensical parasite-word," "a slur," "an awkward nickname" that can be blamed for the fact that "people have come to renounce their true origin, and have rushed in droves (especially the young people) to become 'Russians.' And perhaps history may soon witness that sorry time when the world's civilization, in an instant, will lose forever two remarkable nationalities, and Mordova will be nothing more than the term for an administrative territory...."[1]

Again, as in the time when Mordva autonomy was created, there are proposals to use the terms Moksha-Erzia or Erzia-Moksha, instead of Mordva.

How well-founded is this argument? Should one not listen to its proponents and satisfy their demands? In order to give a full answer to these difficult questions, one must not only analyze the contemporary trends in the ethnonational development of the Mordva, but also consult the deep roots of their ethnic history.

The Mordva ethnos is one of the ancient aboriginal peoples of Eastern

Russian text © 1991 by "Nauka" Publishers and "Sovetskaia etnografiia." "Mordva: etnonim ili etnofolizm?" *Sovetskaia etnografiia*, 1991, no. 4, pp. 84–93. A publication of the former Institute of Ethnography, USSR Academy of Sciences. Translated by Ronald Radzai.

Europe, arising between the end of the first millennium B.C. and the beginning of the first millennium A.D. Its ethnic territory was located between the Volga and the Oka rivers. Naturally, this territory changed somewhat during the various historical periods, alternately expanding and contracting. In the period of early feudalism (before the thirteenth century), the western boundary of the Mordva settlements can be considered the Oka River, as testified by chronicle sources as well as by hydronymics that can be located in the Oka basin: the Mordves, Mordovka, and several other rivers. The northern boundary marched with the Oka and the Volga (*Rav* in Mordvin), the eastern with the Sura, and the southern with the natural dividing line between forest and steppe. The Erzia occupied the northern portion of the "Mordova land" (as it was called in the Russian annals), and the Moksha the southern.

In the west and northwest, the neighbors of the Mordva were the Muroma, the Eastern Slavs (primarily the Viatichi), the Russians (*ruzt* in Mordvin). In the south, the Khazars, then the Pechenegs, from the eleventh century on the Polovtsy and Kumans or Oguz (*guzt* in Mordvin), and then the Tatar (*pechkast* in Mordvin); in the east, the Volga Bulgars, and afterwards the Chuvash (*vet'ket'* in Mordvin).

The ethnonym *mordva* appears quite early in written sources. Of these, we should mention, first, the book of the Byzantine Bishop Jordanus (a Goth by origin), "Getica" ("On the Origin and History of the Goths"), completed in 551. Speaking of the campaigns of the king of the Goths, Hermanarich (died 375 or 376), whom many ancient writers compared to Alexander the Great, Jordanus states that the king defeated many war-like tribes and forced them to obey his laws. Among these he mentions the *Mordens*,[2] meaning the Mordva. According to the Byzantine Emperor Constantine Porphyrogenetus (905–959), Mordia was located ten days' march from the Pechenegs.[3]

In Western European medieval sources, the Mordva are also called *Merdas, Merdinis, Merdium, Mordani, Mordua, Morduinos*. In the old Russian chronicles, the ethnonym *mordva* is found from the eleventh to thirteenth centuries. Along with *mordva*, they also contain the term *mordvichi*. A false patronym formation for ethnonyms using *-ichi* was used quite commonly in old Russian sources (Vogulichi, Dregovichi, Krivichi, Nemchichi, Rusichi, Toimichi, etc.).

As we know, the ethnonym Mordva goes back to Iranian-Scythian languages (cf. Persian *mard*—man, Tajik *mard*—man). In the Mordvin languages, this word has survived to denote husband/spouse (*mirde*). In the Russian word "Mordva," the suffix *va* carries a nuance of collectivity. It may be compared with the ethnonyms Litva, Tatarva. In Russian sources down to the seventeenth century, the Mordva appear only under the ethnonym *mordva*.

One of the earliest written notices of the ethnonym *erzia* (*arisu*) has come down to us in an epistle of the Kagan of Khazaria, Iosif (tenth century). However, some think this is not the first written evidence of the Erzia. Earlier mentions are found in the works of the ancient Greeks Strabo (*aorsy*) and Ptolemy (*arsiity*).[4]

The earliest written information on the ethnonym *moksha* (Moxel) is contained in the notes of the thirteenth-century Flemish traveler Guillaume Rubruquis, and also in the "Jami-al-tavarikh" ("Compendium of Chronicles," in Persian) of the Iranian historian and statesman Rashid-al-Din (1247–1318), which is considered one of the fundamental sources on the political and socioeconomic history of the Mongols. As the latter mentions, in the year of the hen, corresponding to 634 (from September 4, 1236 to August 23, 1237), the sons of Juchi Batu, Orda and Berke, the son of the Ugetai Kagan, Kadan, the grandson of Chagatai Buri and the son of Chingiz Khan, Kulkan, "took up war with the Moksha, the Burtasy, and the Ardzhans (Erzia) and in a short while conquered them."[5]

It is generally assumed that, while the etymology of the ethnonym "Mordva" is of Indo-European origin, the etymology of the ethnonyms "Erzia" and "Moksha" has local, Mordvin roots. But recent investigations do not confirm this, and indicate an Indo-European origin for these ethnonyms.[6] *Erzia* most likely goes back to the Iranian lexicon (Persian *arshan*—male, man, hero), and *Moksha* to an Indo-European hydronymic (cf. Sanskrit *moksha*—spilling, flowing away, liberation).

"The Mordva himself,[a]" wrote A.A. Shakhmatov in the early twentieth century, "to this day does not call himself by this name; the Mordva speaks of himself as an Erzia or a Moksha (these are two different tribes of Mordvas); the Erzia and Moksha call the Russians the Mordva. Evidently, the Russians coming from the south encountered the Mordva and called them by the old south Russian term Mordva, in origin a Scythian word."[7]

However, Shakhmatov's belief that "the Mordva himself to this day does not call himself by this name" is not entirely true. The ethnonyms "Erzia" and "Moksha" are used more often within the ethnic group. But the ethnonym "Mordva," originally employed by other ethnic groups, chiefly Indo-European, to distinguish them, has long since been used by the Mordva themselves as an endoethnonym [internal self-defining term]. This, in turn, has played no small role in making the tribes that constituted the ancient Mordva conscious of their common origin. As scholars have observed, certain protoethnic groups, having definite traits of an ethnos, lack a word for themselves (an endoethnonym). On the other hand, their neighbors, based on the presence of these objective traits, gave them special names, seeing in them more or less discrete groups. As V.A. Shnirel'man justly notes: "That is why it is characteristic among early peoples for an ethnos to adopt, as the word for themselves, an ethnonym derived from their neighbors. Only in the event that such an ethnonym had an openly humiliating or derogatory nuance was it not used."[8]

Already in the first half of the first millennium A.D., the lines of evolution of the Moksha and Erzia groups began to emerge in the ancient Mordva family of tribes, thereafter becoming increasingly prominent. One of the major reasons for this split was the expansive territory inhabited by them, which made contact difficult between tribal groups. Territorial segregation meant that these tribes were in contact with other ethnic groups, giving rise to peculiarities in language, anthropological appearance, culture, and the daily life of the Moksha and the Erzia. Another not unimportant reason for the dualization of the ancient Mordva was the migration processes taking place on their ethnic territory. An especially significant role in the alteration of the ethnic situation, in the awakening of divergent processes within the ancient Mordva tribes, in the breakup of their ethnolinguistic continuity, was probably played by the incursion of Turkic tribes from the southern steppe in the second half of the first millennium A.D. Later on, a number of other political (e.g., the Mongol-Tatar invasion and yoke, the conquests of the Khanate of Kazan), socioeconomic, and ethnocultural factors helped to strengthen the binary nature of the Mordva ethnos, which has survived till the present.

At the start of the second millennium A.D., the formation of the Mordva nationality on the basis of the ancient Mordva tribes can be discerned. This was caused by a change in the socioeconomic structure of the ancient Mordva and formation of early class relations. The international situation, which was very eventful at the time, played no small part in the consolidation of the Mordva nationality. The campaigns of the Khazars and the Kievan princes against the Mordva resulted in their being forced to pay tribute, at first to the Khazar khanate, and after the decline of this, to Kievan Rus'. But the Russian princes sometimes also suffered defeats in conflicts with the Mordva. The "Primary Chronicle of Kiev" reports, under the year 1103: "This same year, Iaroslav fought the Mordva in the month of March, the 4th day, and Iaroslav was beaten."[9] This passage reveals the existence of a military organization among the Mordva, which also doubtlessly hastened the consolidation of the Mordva ethnos.

From the end of the twelfth to the first third of the thirteenth centuries, the Mordva were led by Purgas, under whom a sizable segment of the Mordva were concentrated in the bounds of the "Purgas *volost'*" of the

Russian chronicles. To this day we have not established the boundaries, or even the center of this *volost'*, although it has been conjectured that this might have been the Purgas stronghold, remains of which have been excavated 60 km to the east of the town of Kadom. The "Purgas *volost'*," created by the unification of at least some of the Mordva tribes, was the political and governing formation that brought about the territorial cohesion of these tribes. It strengthened the commonalty of their socioeconomic and ethnic interests and hastened their transformation into a feudal Mordva nationality.

The beginning consolidation of Mordva tribes into a single nationality, which provisionally may be called a nationality of a higher taxonomic level, was accompanied by the consolidation of the Erzia and Moksha groups of tribes, which in turn formed two closely related nationalities—the Erzia and the Moksha. These can be called nationalities of a lower taxonomic level. The above processes can be termed, respectively, macroconsolidation and microconsolidation. The existence of nationalities of different levels and the hierarchical ordering of their ethnic awareness is one of the characteristic features of ethnic development during the time of the feudal socioeconomic formation.[b]

The unification of the Mordva with Russia was a lengthy process, stretching over whole centuries. It began at a time when Rus' was not yet an integrated whole, i.e., the period of its feudal fragmentation, when there were independent and sometimes warring Russian princedoms, and it ended with the formation of the unified Russian state. The joint struggle of the Russians and Mordva against the yoke of the Golden Horde, and then the Khanate of Kazan, had considerable influence in bringing them together.

The yoke of the Golden Horde, followed by the oppression of the Khanate of Kazan, had a negative effect on the consolidation of the Mordva nationality, disturbing its normal development as an ethnosocial whole. This cost much effort, resources, and human lives, and aggravated the Erzia-Moksha ethnic differences. The annexation of the Mordva to the Russian state and its inclusion in the Russian social body had much positive impact, not only on the socioeconomic and political, but also the ethnic development of the Mordva nationality. It put an end to its fragmentation between two constantly warring nations—the Great Principality of Moscow and the Khanate of Kazan—and stimulated the consolidation of the Mordva. The annexation to Russia made it possible for many Mordva driven off into captivity to return from Kazan to their homeland, to the Moksha and the Sura, and for the Mordva to return to a peaceful, less troubled and dangerous mode of life.

The incorporation of the Mordva into Russia had great progressive significance, not only for the Mordva, but also for the Russian people. The

Mordva were the first populous and well-known nation to be annexed to Russia. Their example had considerable impact on the ethnic orientation of other Volga peoples (and not only in that region), who were incorporated into Russia in the immediate wake of the Mordva. Thus, the annexation of the Mordva to Russia was an important factor in the history of the creation of the multinational Russian state.

To be sure, we are far from idealizing the processes of ethnic development of the Mordva people under the conditions of tsarist Russia, yet we should not move to the opposite extreme, portraying the prerevolutionary past of the Mordva people only in dark tones. Thus, we cannot agree with the opinion of several authors that the prerevolutionary Mordva were in a condition of dying out and vanishing.[10] Our analysis of the full census materials for the 1897 population of Russia and certain other sources indicates that, despite a number of negative factors that reduced the Mordva birthrate, on the whole their numbers increased. The predictions of a number of prerevolutionary scholars as to the imminent and total russification of the Mordva people proved wrong, and the very raising of the issue of the absorption of the Mordva as a whole ethnos by the Russian ethnos was unfounded. Naturally one cannot entirely deny certain assimilative processes as a result of the multifaceted objective nature of Mordva-Russian society, stemming from the full range of socioeconomic development of the country. These did indeed occur, and were actually mutual, although the issue of the assimilation of the Russians by the Mordva, their Mordvinization, has not yet been properly researched.[c]

Lenin's characterization is applicable to the historical fate of the pre-October Mordva, stressing that "the national movement is not yet complete here, and is *still* taking place, the awakening of the masses to master their native tongue and its literature (a necessary condition and concomitant with the full development of capitalism, the full penetration of exchange down to the last peasant family)."[11] Therefore, in our view, it is something of an exaggeration to say that the Mordva in the prerevolutionary period were a capitalistic (bourgeois) nation.[12] It is probably more accurate to call them a capitalistic nationality, developing in association with the Russian capitalistic nation.

October 1917 put an end to the economic and social oppression and ethnic discrimination against the Mordva, as well as all other peoples of Russia, and created a possibility for their self-determination. In 1921, at Samara, on the initiative of the Central Committee of the Russian Communist Party (Bolsheviks) [CC RCP(B)], the First All-Russian Congress of Mordva Communists was convened. This decided that it was necessary to "separate the Mordva into an autonomous entity with an administration corresponding to the constitution of the RSFSR."[13] In 1925, the resolution of the All-Russian Central Executive Committee (ARCEC) was adopted, "On the making of the territory inhabited by the Mordva population into an independent administrative entity"; in 1928, the Mordva Okrug with center at Saransk was created within the Middle Volga Oblast; in 1930, the Presidium of the ARCEC changed the Mordva Okrug into the Mordva Autonomous Oblast, and in 1934 by resolution of the Presidium of the ARCEC this oblast with the identical boundaries, in keeping with the will of its working population, was proclaimed the Mordva Autonomous Soviet Socialist Republic. The formation of a Mordva soviet socialist state not only had great significance for the development of the national economy and culture of the Mordva, but also created more propitious conditions for its transformation into a nation.[d]

In the first years after the October Revolution, in addition to a tendency toward further integration of the Erzia and Moksha, the ethnostructure of the fledgling Mordva nation also revealed a tendency toward differentiation not only on the intraethnic (subethnic) level, but also on the level of major ethnic groups: the ethnoses (peoples), as also found expression in a series of official documents. Thus, a report by the head of a Mordva division of the Narkomnats (People's Commissariat on Affairs of the Nationalities of the RSFSR), sent to the CC RCP(B), stated: "By resolution of the governing board at the meeting of March 7, 1921, it was decided to convene a congress of responsible party members among our backward [*otstaloi*] Mordva nation, and also to make the *Mordva peoples* (emphasis mine) into an independent autonomous entity. . . . With the convening of the congress and the handling of the matter of forming an autonomous entity we hope to weld together the *Mordva peoples* and foster closer relations between them and other nationalities in the way of cultural development and enlightenment."[14]

In 1921, the First All-Russian Congress of Communists of the Mordva adopted an "Appeal to the Mordva Peoples." A telegram addressed to the CC RCP(B), Lenin, Stalin, Zinoviev, and Trotsky, in the name of this congress, stated: "The First All-Russian Congress of Mordva Communists, assembled in Samara under the wing of the Third Congress of the Comintern, for the quickest implementation of the policy of the Soviet State in the area of the backward national minorities, including the *Mordva peoples*, sends its warmest greetings to the leaders of the world revolution and expresses its deep trust in the handling of these problems under their guidance"[15] (emphasis mine). In later party and soviet documents, the term "Mordva peoples" is no longer used, and the usual term is "Mordva people," "Mordva nationality," "Mordva nation," which are used as synonyms.

An ethnodifferentiating tendency also appeared in the discussion of the draft of the first Constitution of the Mordva ASSR, adopted in 1937. An amendment was proposed for the first article, "to adopt the name of the republic as the Moksha-Erzia ASSR." However, the constitutional commission, headed by N.G. Surdin, chairman of the Central Executive Committee of the Mordva ASSR, came to the conclusion that the republic "is more properly termed the Mordva ASSR" because "historically, all peoples know the Mordva nationality, but not its individual elements—the Moksha and the Erzia. Furthermore, even the Mordva people—both Moksha and Erzia—call themselves the Mordva. Thus, there is little need to create another name artificially."[16]

Perhaps because of the example of a number of other peoples (the Mari, the Udmurt, etc.), who changed their former official ethnonyms after the Revolution, the Mordva intelligentsia in the 1920s also began to express the view that the ethnonym "Mordva" should be replaced by another, more self-derived name. Common views that the word *mordva* is not an ethnonym at all, but a nickname derived from the Russian word *morda* ("mug, snout"), received some currency. This also encouraged an undesirable anti-Russian stance among some of the Mordva population.

The holding of such views was also related to lack of information, at that time, on the history of the Mordva people, and ethnography in general. As for the science of onomastics, it was only just in its infancy. Even in scholarly circles, interpretations very far from the mark were proposed for the ethnonym "Mordva." P.D. Stepanov, for example, asserted that this ethnonym consists of two words: *mor* or *mort*—person, people, humans, husband, and *tuwa* (*tuwo*)—pig.[17] On this basis, he constructed a complete hypothesis about the Mordva as a "swine-eating people." True, he later admitted that his "hypothesis as to the origin of the term 'Mordva' in the midst of alien tribes according to the characteristic attribute in the diet of the ancient Mordva tribes should be abandoned as having little foundation from the standpoint of linguistics."[18e]

In the 1920s, variants were proposed instead of the ethnonym "Mordva": *moksherziat* (from Moksha + Erzia) and *erziamokshot* (from Erzia + Moksha), which came to be used with reference to the Mordva in the Mordvin-language literature. This desire to combine both ethnonyms into one itself reflected centripetal, consolidation processes. In the Moksha press, there was a tendency to employ the form Moksherziat, and in the Erzia press the form Erziamokshot. This tendency is also discerned in sphragistic materials. For example, the seal of the Mordva Oblast Executive Committee read: "R.S.F.S.R. Erzian'-mokshon' Avtonomnoi oblasten' ispolnitel'noi komitetos'," while the seal of the Mordva delegation to the Presidium of the ARCEC had: "*R.S.F.S.R. TsIKon Prezidiumon' Moksherzian'*

Avtonomiian' mastoron' (oblasten') Predstavitel'stvaz'."[19]

Today, the use of this ethnonym has become more unified, more often in the form *moksherziat,* less often *erziamokshot.* Yet these are ethnonyms of artificial, bookish origin, never used by the Mordva in this combination, and it is unlikely that they will be instilled in the people. Along with them, the national press is now making broad use of the ethnonym *mordvat* to designate all of the Mordva, but the terms *"erziat* and *mokshot"* or *"mokshat* and *erziat"* continue to be the usual way of designating the entire Mordva.

As shown by our field research,[20] the peculiar rivalry between the Moksha and the Erzia for priority claim on the designation Mordva survives in part to this day. Among the Erzia, for example, it is commonly held that they are the Mordva. "We of Ivantsev are Mordva, while the Moksha live in Pechi and Sanki."[21] On the other hand, certain Moksha declare that it is they who are the Mordva: "We are the Mordva, and the Erzia are not Mordva."[22] "We Moksha are pure Mordva, and the Erzia are a different nation."[23]

At the same time, the majority of the Mordva are conscious that the Erzia and the Moksha together form a single people, the Mordva. Thus, when the Moksha are asked whether or not the Erzia are Mordva, they usually reply: "Why certainly they are Mordva, but we do not understand their language. We say *traks* (cow), they say *skal,* we say *shumbas* (rabbit), they say *numolo....*"[24] "The Erzia also have their own kind. If you are an Erzia you can get closer to them, feel more comfortable with them in the market, or anywhere else."[25] "Our son-in-law is an Erzia. They talk differently from us, but they are the same people, the Mordva."[26] "The Moksha and the Erzia are both Mordva. I worked with the Erzia, they are good people. True, their language has words that we cannot understand. We say *iliat* (evening), they *chokshne*; the Moksha word is *ucha* (sheep), their word is *reve....*"[27]

The Erzia also give similar answers to this question. "The Moksha are also Mordva, like us, but they don't talk like us, you will understand one word and not another. I was in the army and served with a Moksha. He was my friend. We usually talked in Russian. We tried in Mordva, but it didn't work. It was hard for me to understand him, and he me. Still, you can understand 50 percent, if you listen well. Now, with Chuvash, for example, you can't understand anything, unless you know it."[28] "Both the Erzia and the Moksha are Mordva, but we Erzia have a different language from the Moksha. I was at Magadan, staying with my son, who works there. His neighbor was a Moksha. She was glad that I was a Mordva. We began to talk, I in Erzia, she in Moksha, and it was hard to understand each other. Then we started to talk in Russian."[29]

The tendency for awareness of the unity of the Mordva people is especially notable among city dwellers. It can also be seen in the countryside, but it does not appear as strongly there as in the city. Even so, the examples above, as well as other data obtained from massive ethnographic surveys,[30] indicate that ethnic consolidation of the Mordva is taking place, although this process is not complete. Indeed, conclusions of this type [stressing consolidation] have been drawn.[31] These reflect the desire, revealed by certain Mordva authors, and not only by them, to outrun the processes that are actually taking place, to represent their nation as being more monolithic than it is in fact. These conclusions are not altogether harmless, if only because they have long hindered the study of contemporary ethnonational processes among the Mordva, and have also disoriented the governing bodies, distracting their attention from one of the major problems in the development of the Mordva nation.

Regulation of national processes, as well as the relations between nationalities, demands a profound knowledge of the ethnic structure of the people involved. The ethnic structure of a people has usually meant, in Soviet historical and ethnographical literature, its constituent subethnic components (subethnoses) and ethnographic groups, as well as their interactions. The most characteristic trait of a subethnos is the presence of self-awareness and a name to designate themselves, whereas ethnographic groups, lacking these traits, are primarily distinguished by their linguistic, traditional culture, and religious-ethnographic features.

The best-known ethnic structure subdivisions of the Mordva are the Erzia and the Moksha, although their contemporary ethnic status is far from clear. In the ethnographic literature they are usually termed "appendages," "branches," "parts," "subgroups," "groups," "large groups," "major groups," "sizable groups," or "main groups" of the Mordva. However, all of these terms, which provide an approximate idea as to the binary ethnic structure of the Mordva at the present day, are extremely loose and indefinite in meaning. They do not allow a sufficiently clear understanding of the nature of these subdivisions of the Mordva ethnos.

Neither is the term "ethnic group," also used to refer to the Erzia and the Moksha, altogether exact, for in certain cases it is used to refer to an internal subdivision of an ethnos possessing self-awareness, and in others to "fragments" of an ethnos. Since the term "ethnic group" is better suited to distinguishing "fragments" of an ethnos, it seems better to call the Erzia and the Moksha, not ethnic groups, but subethnoses, to which are assigned collections of people within self-aware ethnoses that are marked by specific traits. Such self-awareness is characteristic of the Erzia and the Moksha. It is reflected in the ethnonyms *erzia* and *moksha* (actually, subethnonyms), which have endured till the present.[32] The recent attempts of certain authors to consider the Erzia and Moksha at the present stage of historical development as independent ethnoses or peoples do not have sufficient foundation.[33] Not only are they unscientific, but also politically harmful, for they disorient the social organism, especially the Erzia and the Moksha, and deform their ethnic guideposts.

Iu.V. Bromlei has pointed out similar attempts to consider certain other subethnoses as peoples or ethnoses. In one of his last publications before his death, he wrote: "It should also be noted that another extreme has recently emerged in the question of the ethnonational structure of the country, namely, the desire to treat certain subethnoses as peoples or ethnoses. Let us say that such Tatar subethnoses as the Teptiari and Mishari try to represent themselves as individual peoples or ethnoses; or another example—the attempt to consider the Latgaltsy as an independent ethnos, instead of a subethnos of the Latvians. Moreover, the issue is being raised as to whether every group name of ethnic character should be taken as evidence of the existence of an independent ethnos. With such an approach, the number of independent peoples of the country could reach several hundred. It seems rather obvious that this clearly ignores the ethnic consolidation processes, not only those occurring at present, but also those that took place in the years before the Revolution."[34]

In the scholarly literature on the Mordva it is commonly held that the Mordva, besides the Erzia and the Moksha, include another three subdivisions of equal ethnotaxonomic order, namely, the *shoksha*, the *karatai*, and the *teriukhan*. In many publications (as though it were self-evident), these terms are used as ethnonyms, although in fact they were never such. A vicious circle is created, for which we can blame the (as it were) glamor of the ethnonym: for it is believed that, once there are ethnonyms, there will also be different ethnic collectivities to be designated by them.[35]

The word *shoksha*, as an ethnonym, came to be used rather recently, in the past two or three decades, to designate the Erzia of the Tengushevsk and Torbeevsk regions of the Mordva republic. This group of Mordva calls itself "Mordva," "Mordva-Erzia," "Erzia," the neighboring Moksha usually call them "Erzia," and the Russians "Mordva." Shoksha is the name of a tributary of the Moksha River and a village on its banks. The name of the village is derived from the hydronym Shoksha. In historical documents there is also mention of a village, Russkaia Shoksha (now the village of Riazanovka, Ermishinsk region, Riazan' Oblast), where Russians live. It was located next to the Mordva village of Shoksha. Today, this group of Erzia lives in fifteen populated points of Tengushevsk region and five of Torbeevsk region, amounting to around 10,000 people. Having long lived in close proximity to the Moksha, this group of Erzia has borrowed several household and cultural articles from them. Even so, this influence has not been deep enough to cause them to lose their Erzia self-awareness.

The so-called Karatai live in three small villages (Mordovsk Karatai, Zaovrazhnye Karatai, Shershalan) of the Kamsko-Ust'insk region of the Tatar SSR. They consider themselves Mordva, but no longer recall whether their ancestors were Moksha or Erzia. The Tatar of neighboring villages call them *mukshiliar*, i.e., Moksha, and the Russians, Mordva. They have a good command of the Tatar language, and practice the Orthodox religion.

Today, the Karatai Mordva are drawing ever closer to the Russians, as encouraged by working together at one state farm, "Kamsko-Ust'insk," schooling, and mixed marriages. According to a house-by-house survey that we conducted in the village of Mordovskie Karatai in 1976, 6.7 percent of all households are Mordva-Russian, and 2.2 percent are Mordva-Tatar. In 1958, the population of Mordva in these villages amounted to a thousand people, in 1976 it had dropped to three hundred, due to a number of factors, the most significant of which may be migration to the city.[36]

The Karatai Mordva draw a clear distinction between the name of their village and their own ethnic name. "Karatai is our village. We call ourselves Mordva. . . . We do not call ourselves Karatai, nor does anyone else. They say, there are the Karatai, that is, those from the village of Karatai. But in terms of nationality, we are Mordva."[37]

Teriukhan in the special literature is used for an ethnographic group of Mordva, probably Erzia, living in the past on the territory of Teriushevsk *volost'*, Nizhegorodsk *uezd*, Nizhegorodsk *guberniia* (today, the Dal'ne konstantinovsk region of Nizhegorodsk oblast), wholly russified at the start of the twentieth century. The word *teriukhan* was not the ethnic name of the Teriushevsk Mordva for themselves, nor was it used by their Russian neighbors as an ethnonym. In origin, it is connected with the name of Teriushevsk *volost'*, which in turn goes back to the toponym Bol'shoe Teriushevo, the name of a village that used to be the center of the *volost'*. The inhabitants of these villages remained non-Christian right down till the middle of the eighteenth century, though this did not prevent them from having close contact with the surrounding Russian population. They adopted the Russian language long before becoming Christians, while keeping their Mordva ethnic name, pre-Christian beliefs, and traditional rituals.

The Russian language of the non-Christian Teriushevians led Bishop Dmitrii of Nizhegorodsk and Alatyrsk to declare "they wrongly call themselves Mordva, as they were never Mordva and do not or did not ever know the Mordva language, but speak like Suzdal or Iaroslav peasants."[38] In a meeting with them, the governor of Nizhnii Novgorog, Prince Dutskii, wondered why they did not speak Mordvin, if they were indeed Mordva.

They replied: "our fathers and forefathers did not know the Mordvin tongue, nor do we know it, we have spoken Russian from olden times. . . ."[39] In the second half of the latter century, the Teriushevsk Mordva population was in the final stage of russification, and in the first decades of the twentieth century they entirely lost their Mordva self-awareness, fully merging with the Russian ethnos. It is hardly legitimate to now call this Russian group an ethnographic division of Mordva.

Thus, the ethnic structure of the Mordva people at present reveals two subethnoses—Erzia and Moksha—and two ethnographic groups—so-called Shoksha and Karatai.

Editor's notes

a. The original text has a combination of gender-neutral and male terms. Since the quote is from the early twentieth century, it has been necessary to keep the linguistic bias intact.

b. This paragraph is an indicator of the kind of pressures put on Soviet researchers to be "scientific," to order and create hierarchies, or to squeeze the unsqueezable, ethnic consciousness, into a ranking within Marxist terminology. The author posits both consolidation and splitting of protoethnic groups in the Mordva past, and both may indeed have occurred at different times.

c. This assimilation of Russians was true in many areas of the Russian Empire, for example throughout the North, and has become a recent, local, theme for many native scholars.

d. This ironic situation, the pushing of a given people into formal political-national identity beyond their previous ethnic consciousness through Soviet organization, has been stressed by many Western scholars. See Ronald Grigor Suny, *The Making of the Georgian Nation* (Bloomington: Indiana University Press, 1988). The argument is made particularly with regard to the Caucasus and Soviet Central Asia, with various degrees of validity, depending on the cases and the borders discussed.

e. The linguistic confusion indicated here says much about the politicization of linguistics in the Stalin era, particularly through the theories of N.Ia. Marr. See Loren R. Graham, *The Soviet Academy of Sciences and the Communist Party 1927–1932* (Princeton: Princeton University Press, 1967), pp. 216–17.

Notes

1. *Literaturnaia gazeta*, 6 December 1989, p. 4.

2. Jordanus, *O proiskhozhdenii i deianiikh getov* (Moscow, 1960), pp. 89, 150.

3. Konstantin Bagrianorodnyi, "Ob upravlenii gosudarstvom," *Izv. Gosudarstvennoi akademii istorii material'noi kul'tury*, no. 91 (Moscow-Leningrad, 1934), p. 16.

4. Cited in: F.I. Gordeev, "Baltiiskie i iranskie zaimstvovaniia v Lariiskom iazyke," *Proiskhozhdenie mariiskogo naroda* (Ioshkar-Ola, 1967), pp. 194–95.

5. *Sbornik materialov, otnosiashchikhsia k Zolotoi Orde*, vol. 2 (Moscow-Leningrad, 1941), p. 96.

6. N.F. Mokshin, "Proiskhozhdenie etnonima erzia," *Voprosy geografii mordovskoi ASSR* (Moscow, 1974), pp. 34–36; ibid., "O teonime Mokosh', gidronime i etnonime Moksha," *Onomastika Povolzh'ia*, vol. 4 (Saransk, 1976), p. 331.

7. A.A. Shakhmatov, *Vvedenie v kurs istorii russkogo iazyka*, pt. 1 (Petrograd, 1916), p. 38.

8. V.A. Shnirel'man, "Protoetnos okhotnikov i sobiratelei po avstraliiskim dannym," *Etnos v doklassovom i ranneklassovom obshchestve* (Moscow, 1982), p. 99.

9. *Polnoe sobranie russkikh letopisei*, vol. 1 (Leningrad, 1926), p. 11.

10. A. Martynov, "Mordva v Nizhegorodskom uezde," *Nizhegorodskii gubernskie vedomosti, chast'* neofitsial'naia, 1865, no. 24, p. 194; L. Grebnev, "Mordva Samarskoi gubernii," *Samara eparkhial'nye vedomosti, chast'* neofitsial'naia, 1886, no. 23, no. 462; A.L. Kiselev, *Sotsialisticheskaia kul'tura mordovii* (Saransk, 1959), p. 7; N.Ia. Nazarkin, *Narodonaselenie i okhrana zdorov'ia v mordovii* (Saransk, 1973), pp. 83–84, 89–90.

11. V.I. Lenin, "O karikature na marksizm i ob 'imperialisticheskom' ekonomisme," *Polnoe sobranie sochinenii*, vol. 30, p. 89.

12. L.G. Filatov, "K voprosu formirovaniia i razvitiia mordovskoi sotsialisticheskoi natsii," *Tr. mordov. NII iazyka, literatury, istorii i ekonomiki*, no. 24 (Saransk, 1963), p. 26; A.I. Sukharev, *Sotsial'nyi oblik Sovetskoi mordovii* (Saransk, 1980), p. 14.

13. Tsentral'nyi gosudarstvennyi arkhiv Oktiabr'skoi revoliutsii (hereafter, TsGAOR), f. 1318 (Narkomnats), op. 1, d. 1010, l. 59.

14. Ibid., d. 1011, l. 33–33 ob.

15. Ibid., l. 57.

16. Tsentral'nyi gosudarstvennyi arkhiv Mordovskoi ASSR, f. R–175 (Sovety), op. 5, d. 192, l. 37.

17. P.D. Stepanov, "K voprosu o proiskhozhdenii mordvy," *Zapiski mordov. NII sotsialisticheskoi kul'tury*, no. 3 (Saransk, 1941), p. 26.

18. Idem, "Drevneishii period istorii mordovskogo naroda," *Zapiski mordov. NII iazyka, literatury, istorii i ekonomiki*, no. 15 (Saransk, 1952), p. 173.

19. TsGAOR, f. 1235 (VTsIK), op. 125, d. 182, l. 395, 405.

20. N.F. Moksha, *Etnicheskaia istoriia mordvy* (Saransk, 1977), pp. 211–12.

21. Author's field materials, 1961. Recorded from a Mordva (Erzia) woman, E.F. Biiushkina, born 1893 (Ivantsevo village, Lukoianovsk region, Nizhegorodsk oblast).

22. Ibid., recorded in 1973 from a Mordva (Moksha) woman, A.A. Nadina, born 1900 (Novoe Drakino village, Kovylkinsk region, Mordva ASSR).

23. Ibid., recorded in 1984 from a Mordva (Moksha) woman, E.A. Ermashova, born 1930 (Mordovsk Pimbur village, Zubovo-Poliansk region, Mordva ASSR).

24. Ibid., recorded in 1973 from a Mordva (Moksha) woman, A.K. Chizhaeva, born 1930 (Zhuravkino village, Zubovo-Poliansk region, Mordva ASSR).

25. Ibid., recorded in 1973 from a Mordva (Moksha) woman, V.P. Semkina, born 1910 (Zhuravkino).

26. Ibid., recorded in 1973 from a Mordva (Moksha) man, D.V. Ageev, born 1928 (Glushkovo village, Insarsk region, Mordva ASSR).

27. Ibid., recorded in 1973 from a Mordva (Moksha) woman, E.I. Iakushkina, born 1892 (Novoe Drakino village, Kovylkinsk region, Mordva ASSR).

28. Ibid., recorded in 1975 from a Mordva (Erzia) man, A.L. Chuzhaikin, born 1924 (Voroshilovo settlement, Alatyrsk region, Chuvash SSR).

29. Ibid., recorded in 1975 from a Mordva (Erzia) woman, L.I. Dolgova, born 1912 (Atrat' village, Alatyrsk region, Chuvash ASSR).

30. Moksha, *Etnicheskaia istoriia mordvy*, p. 212.

31. V.V. Gorbunov, "K voprosu o formirovanii mordovskoi sotsialisticheskoi natsii," *Materialy nauchnoi sessii po voprosam mordovskogo iazykoznaniia* (Saransk, 1955), p. 58; L.V. Dorozhkin and I.A. Iashkin, "Mordovskaia gosudarstvennost'— detishche leninskoi natsional'noi politiki," *Po zavetam Lenina* (Saransk, 1970), p. 94;

Sukharev, *Sotsial'nyi oblik Sovetskoi mordovii*, pp. 16–18; L.V. Dorozhkin and V.I. Kozlov, "Etnicheskie protsessy," *Mordva (istoriko-etnograficheskie ocherki)* (Saransk, 1981), p. 314.

32. N.F. Moksha, "Etnonimy mordva, erzia, moksha i ikh upotreblenie," *Onomastika Povolzh'ia*, vol. 2 (Gor'kii, 1971), pp. 285–91.

33. D. Nad'kin, "Doroga k khramu," *Sovetskaia mordoviia*, 31 October 1989, p. 3; R. Kemaikina, "Kiian mon?" *Siatko*, 1990, no. 4, pp. 79–84; S. K. Gur'ianov, "Osobennosti mordovskogo natsional'nostogo samosoznaniia," *Sovetskaia etnografiia*, 1990, no. 4, pp. 126–28.

34. Iu.V. Bromlei, "K razrabotke poniatiino-terminologicheskikh aspektov natsional'noi problematiki," *Sovetskaia etnografiia*, 1989, no. 6, p. 10.

35. O.S. Tomanovskaia, "Etnos i etnonim v predklassovom obshchestve: chastnye aspekty ikh sootnosheniia," *Etnos v doklassovom i ranneklassovom obshchestve* (Moscow, 1982), p. 204.

36. N.F. Moksha, *Mordovskii etnos* (Saransk, 1989), p. 64.

37. Author's field materials. Recorded from I.Z. Demin, a resident of Mordovskie Karatai, born 1924.

38. Tsentral'nyi gosudarstvennyi arkhiv drevnikh aktov (TsGADA), f. 248, Pravitel'stvuiushchii Senat, op. 14, ed. khr. 805, l. 7.

39. Ibid., l. 12.

Ethnogenesis and Ethnocultural Relationships of the Turkic Peoples of the Volga and Urals

Problems and Tasks

Raul G. Kuzeev and Shamil F. Mukhamediarov

The present stage of development of Soviet Turkic studies is characterized by a broadening and deepening range of vital issues under examination and growth in the general theoretical level of the research. In general works on the history of the republics and oblasts with a Turkic-speaking population, the most important aspect is now ethnogenesis, the ethnic history and the historical-cultural contacts among Turkic peoples. However, it is becoming increasingly clear that only a further elaboration of the interdisciplinary approach to the questions of ethnogenesis, in close connection with the organization of work on the study of the group of historically interacting ethnoses, long in contact with each other on the same common territory, can identify with sufficient objectivity the processes of a people's formation. Such an interdisciplinary approach to the study of ethnogenesis has already been utilized in a number of scholarly meetings devoted to the origin of the Turkic peoples, and in the corresponding monograph publications [1–12].

A lively interest in the origin, history, and culture of one's own people is a characteristic of the modern age, due to the unprecedented growth of national self-awareness among the peoples of the USSR. This has led to the elaboration, on the initiative of the History Division of the USSR Academy of Sciences, of two comprehensive programs—"Ethnogenesis and ethnic processes of the modern age" (under Iu.V. Bromlei) and "A comprehensive

Russian text © 1990 by "Sovetskaia tiurkologiia." "Etnoiazykovye sviazi. Etnogenez i etnokul'turnye sviazi tiurkskikh narodov povolzh'ia i priural'ia: problemy i zadachi," *Sovetskaia tiurkologiia*, 1990, no. 2, pp. 48–60. A publication of the USSR Academy of Sciences. Translated by Ronald Radzai.

program on the cultural history of the peoples of the USSR" (under B.A. Rybakov) [13, 14]. An All-Union School/Seminar featured "Methodology and techniques of studying ethnic history" (Zvenigorod, November 1987). Convened in November 1988, an all-union scientific conference discussed the question of the ethnogenesis and ethnic history of the peoples of Central Asia and Kazakhstan [15]. Soviet scholars under Iu.V. Bromlei took part in an International Conference, Questions of National Self-Awareness in Russia (USSR) and Eastern Europe in Modern and Recent Times, organized in March 1989 by the University of London. The most intense work on questions of the ethnogenesis of the Turkic peoples (as well as other peoples of the USSR) was carried out in the postwar years, when the Institute of Ethnography of the USSR Academy of Sciences headed up the preparation and publication of a fundamental multivolume series, "Peoples of the World," and social scientists of the Union and autonomous republics issued their own general works on the history of the republics.

Experience from the study of ethnic questions shows that a monoethnic approach is not always productive in an understanding of ethnogenesis. Often it prevents comparison and analysis of findings from the study of ethnogenetic processes among neighboring, even ethnically related peoples, due to a subjective difference in the views of the authors as to the time periods involved in the ethnic history and a different assessment of the influence of economic, political, and other factors on the process of ethnogenesis. There is a tendency to ethnocentric interpretation of the origin of one's own people.

When the history of a group of peoples is closely interconnected, it is helpful to study ethnic history as the simultaneous consolidation of a number of related and nonrelated ethnoses, after considerable time in economic, cultural, and other kinds of contact. Such a relatively higher methodological approach to the investigation of the issue encourages publications on the ethnic history of populations of vast historico-ethnographical regions [16–19, and elsewhere]. Particularly interesting was the discussion, by the IIIaL BNTs UrO AN SSSR [Institute of History, Language, and Literature of the Bashkir Scientific Center of the Urals Division of the Academy of Sciences] in late 1987, of the ethnic history of the Turkic and Finno-Ugrian peoples of the Volga/Ural historico-ethnographical province [20]. Among many other issues at this seminar, aspects of the ethnic development of regional peoples during feudalism and capitalism were debated, using the concepts of stadial (formative) types of an ethnos. A constructive theory was advanced that the level of consolidation of an ethnos in terms of the stage of socioeconomic development that it has attained has only a relative correlation with a people's level of cultural accomplishments. Despite a difference of views, the idea is finding increasing acceptance that a nation, as a historical community, is formed not only by ethnic relationships, even highly developed ones, but by class-social, ideological, economic, and other relationships characteristic of capitalism. Under this perspective, the formative approach to the typology of ethnoses is indeed the most objective indicator of their progress in history. Each specific ethnos on its historical path may experience both ascending and descending stages of consolidation. But in a period of progressive development, ethnoses periodically experience impulses of consolidation that are directly or indirectly related to the basic trends of socioeconomic and political development.

Recently, general works have appeared on the history and ethnogenesis of the ancient and medieval Turkic ethnic formations of Eurasia, which are of value in working out ethnogenetic problems of the Volga/Ural region as well [21–32]. These include works on the history of the Huns [33], Khazars [34, 35], Oguz [36], Kimaks and Kypchaks [37–39], and others. These works, as well as the recent extensive bibliography that has appeared on the peoples of the Middle Volga and the Southern Urals [40–52], make it possible to move on to a new phase of investigation, and to the writing of general surveys.

The urgency of ethnogenetic research has notably grown in recent time. The historical investigation of the ethnocultural interactions of peoples long settled in our country from earliest times, differing significantly from each other in numbers, level of socioeconomic development, language and culture, anthropological makeup, and certain other parameters, does much to help in the understanding of the present ethnic situation. However, these ethnic and cultural processes have been understudied. The task of investigating interethnic contacts in an overall context of human past and recent history remains urgent. First and foremost, it is necessary to overcome the limited approaches to the study of the history of the Turkic peoples. It is hard to agree with desires to assign the ancient Scythians, Sarmatians, Saks, Massagetes, and Alans predominantly to ethnoses of Turkic origin [53–56], as there are no grounds for a renewed theory of the genesis and evolution of the Altaic community or its Turkic branch. Also dubious is the tendency to push back in time the ethnogenesis of a number of Turkic peoples, and to analyze their ethnic and ethnopolitical history in a vacuum from other peoples and from development of the major historico-cultural regions that have emerged in the past. A.P. Novosel'tsev, I. Aliev, R.G. Kuzeev, and others have recently come out with well-founded criticism of such constructs [57–59]. The treatment of a number of issues, including ethnocultural ones concerning the history of Volga and Ural peoples, was subjected to just criticism at a coordination conference of USSR union and autonomous republic directors of historical institutions [60]. Literature of the past two decades indeed developed concepts concerning the repeated massive turkicization of the Volga/Ural region before the Bulgars, indicating that many of the cultures of the Middle Volga and Urals from the first millennium B.C. onward were Turkic, that the Chuvash ethnos was formed on the basis of Turkic-speaking builders of the Piseral'sko-Andreevsk mounds of the second and third centuries A.D., and stressing the critical role of pre-Bulgar turkicization in forming an ethnic base for all regional Turkic peoples. The idea that the Polomskaia (third to ninth centuries) and the Lomovatskaia (fifth to ninth centuries) cultures in the basin of the Middle Kama were Ugrian-Turkic or Turkic speakers is being postulated with increasing frequency [61, p. 4]. Provided new materials and proofs are amassed, it may be quite possible to push back the time (perhaps by several centuries) for the ethnogenesis of a particular people. Processes of turkicization of the Iranian-speaking tribes and complicated ethnogenesis of known Turkic groupings from a Europoid base in the Middle Ages (e.g., some of the Pechenegs) are also well known from the literature.

However, the interpretation of archeological cultures of Eastern Europe in the second and first millennia B.C. as belonging wholly or partly to Turkic-speaking tribes, and their identification with the ancient Turks on the sole basis of etymological analysis of the tribal names of the ancient period, does not seem convincing. These tendencies are basically an attempt to revise the Central Asian concept of the genesis of the Altaic linguistic community with no Eurasian archeological foundation, relying simply on a "revamped" interpretation of the known archeological sources, along with ethnonym data in the confines of certain regions.

Recently, given significant pushing back of the advent of the Turks on the Middle Volga, in the Urals, on the Kama, in Kazakhstan, Azerbaijan, and the North Caucasus, a rupture has formed between the renewed "Turkic" interpretation of archeological and ethnonym material and the well-known hypothesis concerning the Altaic community evolution, although it is still too early to consider this theory shaken. This rupture also involves many ideas and hypotheses as to the early (second to first millennia B.C.) turkicization of the Middle Volga, the Kama and Urals, Transcaucasia: that the Iirk and Argipe, mentioned by Herodotus, were Turkic speakers; that the Scythians, Sauromatians, Sarmatians, Saks, and even the tribes of the Ananian culture were entirely or partly Turkic speakers, and so on. An extreme manifestation of such views are ideas—which are being advanced more and more frequently—of Turkic-Sumerian, Kypchak-Sumerian, Chuvash-Sumerian, and Bashkir-Sumerian ethnic and linguistic relationships. As a result, concepts of extreme autochthonism are being revived by those investigating the ethnogenesis of Volga/Ural Turkic peoples. In view of this tendency, it becomes necessary to point out, once again, the correlation between the date for the start of massive penetration of Turks into the Volga/Ural province and the proven fact of the migration to the Middle Volga from the Sea of Aral and the North Caucasus of the ancient Bulgar tribes, given the fundamental importance of the Volga Bulgar ethnopolitical world in the historical and cultural processes in the region [62, 63, etc.].

In connection with the chronology of the migrations of the ancient Turkic peoples, interesting works include those of S.G. Kliashtornyi on ancient Turkic paleography and archeologist V.A. Ivanov analyzing statistical materials on ancient Turkic burial customs of the seventh to ninth centuries using 163 burial sites of the Altai, Tuva, Kazakhstan, and Central Asia. No persistent combinations of ancient Turkic burial attributes from the seventh to ninth centuries are found west of the boundary "defined by burial at Samarkand and mounds at Zhaksy-Arganaty, Iegiz-Koitas, Boshchekul, Bobrovka in Central and Eastern Kazakhstan" [64, p. 148]. Equally interesting is the fact that this coincides with the western limits established according to the texts of runic inscriptions by Kliashtornyi at "the Buzgal pass in the Baisun-tau mountains, on the road from Samarkand to Balkh, 90 km south of Shakhrisiabz" [66, p. 156].

Thus, at present it is not possible to include the southern Urals and adjoining areas, or the Middle Volga, in the active sphere of ethnocultural influence of ancient Turkic tribes. Hence, the study of the course and chronological framework of the process of turkicization in the vast panorama of Eurasia still remains a task for interdisciplinary research. With the examples given above we should like to point out, once more, that the questions of the chronology and extent of processes of turkicization in Eurasia, the relations and interactions between the Turkic and the Indo-Iranian worlds, and especially the hypotheses of a Turkic attribution of the language and mythology of the Sumerians or the presence of Turkic parallels in the languages of the ancient tribes of Mesoamerica must all be studied not in the context of the history and ethnic development of a single people, exclusively or predominantly, but on the scale of broad ethnolinguistic groupings and territories. The new conclusions should obviously be accompanied by well-substantiated revisions or corrections of the existing concepts as to the genesis and historical development of the Turkic languages and, perhaps, of the Altaic system as a whole. Lacking such an approach, the plausibility of many hypotheses and chronologies of Turkic ethnogenesis is greatly reduced.

A recent concept is that the Volga Bulgars provided an ethnic and ethnocultural basis for the formation of all the Turkic peoples of the Middle

Volga and the Urals, and also exerted influence on the formation of the Finno-Ugrian peoples of the region. Of course, this does not involve a simplified idea of the "equal rights" of all peoples of the region to claim a Bulgar ethnic and cultural heritage. The historical process was certainly much more complicated. Yet this concept moves the framework in which questions of ethnogenesis and ethnic history are addressed from the bounds of single nations to the substantially larger domain of the Volga/Ural historico-ethnographical province. And we believe that this is a fruitful and promising concept to develop further. Incidentally, the concept has already received some coverage in recent works [67–70].

We are firmly convinced that this means the Bulgar period, which is in many ways crucial in ethnic and ethnocultural respects, simply underscores the need to gather new sources and further investigate the periods both before and after the Bulgars in the history of the Volga/Ural region.

In terms of the pre-Bulgar period, the research of specialists should be targeted and shifted to the Caspian/North Caucasus, Aral/Central Asia, and Southern/Western Siberia regions, where cultural remains of the multiclass ethnocultural world of the Volga Bulgars might be found. At the same time, research in the Volga/Ural region itself is not yet complete, where (for example) the issue of a Burtas-Bulgar-Mishar line of development has now been raised in a new and interesting way [71]. Also worthy of serious analysis is the role of the Bulgar ethnic and cultural population over a large span of time in the ethnocultural processes of all Turkic ethnoses of the Volga-Oka-Ural-Tobol region.

No less difficult in terms of ethnogenetic and cultural-political issues is the time after the Bulgars. We will have to rethink the period of the Golden Horde, which a number of scholars connect (not without grounds) to the consolidation and deconsolidation of Golden Horde peoples, formed primarily of Kypchak groupings and peoples assimilated to them. To be sure, there are differing views as to the role of the Kypchak component in the ethnogenesis and culturogenesis of the Turkic peoples of the Eurasian steppe-and-forest zone, from the Oka in the west to the Tobol and Ishim in the east. In our opinion, the question should be studied on an interdisciplinary basis, spanning the eleventh to sixteenth centuries, making use of the recently enlarged corpus of sources. Special attention should be paid to ethnohistorical processes in the region in the second half of the fourteenth to the first half of the fifteenth centuries, when the steppe and a portion of the steppe-and-forest zones of the region were almost devastated in connection with the displacement of the population to the north. Similarly, constant attention should be paid to the political and ethnocultural processes involving the role in this entire vast region of the Khanate of Kazan, the

Nogai Horde, the Khanates of Siberia and Astrakhan, and also the political and ethnic formations with which the peoples of the region came into contact at a later time—the Kazakh Zhuzy with the Kazakhs, the Kalmyk Horde with the Kalmyks, etc.

In order to illustrate the significance of the fourteenth to sixteenth centuries in ethnogenetic and ethnocultural respects, we present the following example: among three Turkic (Bashkir, Tatar, Chuvash) and three Finno-Ugrian (Mordva, Mari, Udmurt) peoples during the eighteenth and nineteenth centuries there have been identified about forty ethnographic groups, twenty-five of which were formed in the fifteenth to seventeenth centuries or existed earlier in other conditions. Of the five types of ethnographic groups identified—ethnotraditional, mixed interethnic, mixed intraethnic, ethnic-class, ethnic-religious—the latter four were formed primarily in the sixteenth to eighteenth centuries and were the outcome of earlier processes.[a]

New large-scale migrations and shifts of population began in the mid-sixteenth century, when the entire region began to be gradually integrated in the Russian State in political and economic respects, and the population of the region was drawn into continually expanding ethnocultural contacts with the Eastern Slavic population. The subject of Turkic/Eastern Slav relations in the sixteenth to early twentieth centuries awaits a thorough investigation, taking into account the all-embracing role in the region of the Russian government, the interplay of various types of political and social-class structures, and the reflection of these diverse contacts on the condition and evolution of the underlying ethnic culture stratum, languages, and the ethnic profile of local peoples in general.

Thus, a task of immense proportions arises—to construct an ethnogenetic overview of regional history, i.e., the history of the group of interrelated ethnoses. In other words, it is necessary to move from a monoethnic approach to a polyethnic one. In this regard, the logic of the investigation suggests the need to shift research emphasis from ethnogenesis to culturogenesis, to the problem of the interaction and the mutual enrichment of the cultures of interrelated peoples in the course of their contacts during the ancient period, the Middle Ages, the Early Modern and the Modern ages. Only by carefully probing these questions and the laws and mechanisms of cultural processes will we be able to produce ethnogenetic generalizations on a new and immeasurably higher level.

Toward this end, it is important to study ethnocultural development in a multiethnic environment, more specifically, the collection or combination of factors occasioning both processes of interethnic integration and ethnic consolidation, or having a dialectical or contradictory effect on these processes.

From the standpoint of cultural integration processes, the physical-geographical, political (especially polyethnic government formations in the region), and religious (Islam, Christianity, etc.) factors are in need of special study. Let us mention in passing the special importance of studying the religious factor—especially since it has long been studied outside of ethnogenetic frameworks, and the process of combination or synthesis of the ethnic and the religious self-awareness has been virtually ignored. From the standpoint of consolidation movements, the factors of the social organization deserve careful study, especially the traditional structures (community, *volost'*, social class), lifestyle and customs, which always have an ethnic complexion, the demographic factor (very little studied, by the way), ethnic factors proper—the underlying ethnic stratum of the material and spiritual culture, language, self-awareness, ethnic psychology. Apart from all this, a crucial factor is the influence of a social force, group, or class that acts as the leader and spokesperson of ethnic consolidation. All of this confirms yet again the fundamental importance of a formational approach, over a large span of time, to ethnic processes, and of a class approach to cultural phenomena. Accordingly, it is extremely important to establish adequately the level of development of capitalism among the various societies of the region, the completeness or incompleteness of a social-class structure, the maturity and ethnocultural activity of the various social strata, to provide a characterization of the elite subculture and the level, scale, and degree of access of the masses to reading and writing, literature, art, and professional forms of culture. While giving proper respect to individual conspicuous achievements of the past, they should not be advanced as the general standard of the age or the cultural level of all the people. We must remember and take responsibility for the idea that inadequate representation of historical reality inevitably results in a distorted view of the present reality and may warp our expectation of the future.

The ethnogenetic approach to history may throw new light on the secular variability of ethnoses as ethnosocial organisms. In this case, history is revealed to us in all its complexity, with the ebbing and flowing of consolidation, or even deconsolidation, as happened with the Volga Bulgars and the peoples of the Golden Horde. And the peoples living today have, in their thousand-year history, gone through several periods of developmental consolidation, which have received the designation of "stages," "surges," or "impulses." In this sense, besides two ethnogenetic phases in the development of Volga/Ural peoples (at the turn of the first and second millennia and in the fifteenth to sixteenth centuries), when they twice experienced processes of ethnogenetic formation, there were also many consolidation surges, followed by calm or even decline (for example, in the ethnic existence of the Kazan Tatar and other peoples immediately after the fall of the

Khanate of Kazan and the War of Kazan, or of the Bashkir and other peoples in the postreform period, due to crises in the economy). A dialectic approach to the question impels one to study these aspects as well, since the consolidation of one people may also be the deconsolidation of another.

In summary, then, one can state the following.

Studies of ethnic issues in the USSR, in our opinion, have gone through a necessary phase, when the individual ethnoses were the primary focus of scholars. At present, the interdisciplinary approach and comparative historical studies of the formation of the ethnocultural attributes of individual ethnoses by the methods of archeology, ethnography, anthropology, linguistics, and other sciences have led to the buildup of huge potential of knowledge, the generalization of which will enable further progress in the working out of an ethnos and ethnic processes theory. At the same time, the prevalence of a monoethnic approach to the questions today also has negative consequences, such as inability to compare the results of investigation of the ethnogenesis, ethnic history, and culture of neighboring peoples, significant discrepancies in the established chronology and in understanding the historical phases of ethnogenetic processes, and ethnocentric views as to the formation of certain ethnoses and their cultures. It is these negative consequences that are the source of such common phenomena in the scholarly and especially the popular-scientific literature as the excessive venerability given to the ethnogenesis of many peoples, especially the Turkic ones, the assignment of an ethnic identity to archeological cultures (sometimes as far back as the Paleolithic and Mesolithic), the rivalry for the exclusive right to a cultural heritage, discrepancies in the chronology of development of writing and literary languages in various territories and among various ethnoses, etc.

Further development of a comprehensive method should involve deeper investigation of the group of historically interrelated ethnoses, long in contact with each other on a common territory, of the corresponding historico-ethnographic provinces (Volga/Ural, North Caucasus, Central Asia and Kazakhstan, etc.). This approach is dictated not just by the logic of the research and our attained level of knowledge. It is becoming vital against the backdrop of current events, which urgently demand more profound knowledge of the laws and mechanisms of interethnic, inter-nationality, cultural relations and interactions [72]. It is important to point out that the difficult, but generally progressive, development in Soviet ethnographic science of ethnos theory concerning ethnic and ethnocultural processes (Iu.V. Bromlei, V.A. Tishkov, etc.) makes further improvement in the methodological techniques of ethnogenetic, culturological, and other research both possible and necessary [73–77].

The territorial aspect of the investigation of ethnic processes will also make it possible to discern main phases of both consolidation and integration processes which, unfolding on the Middle Volga and in the Southern Urals since deep antiquity, led to the formation of the Volga/Ural historico-ethnographic province. The polyethnicity of all states existing here has played a significant role in the development of the integration processes.

A regional approach to the investigation of ethnic and cultural processes brings out more clearly not only the many components of ethnic makeup, the processes of mutual acculturation and assimilation of regional ethnoses, the commonality or resemblance of a considerable stratum of their culture—both folkloric and professional—but also distinguishes more precisely the territories acting as zones of common ethnogenesis and culturogenesis. Historico-cultural studies in multinational regions, oriented exclusively or predominantly to the materials and accomplishments of a single ethnos, are fraught with one-sided judgments and an inadequate, or (at the other extreme) hypertrophied emphasis on the cultural potential of a particular group of people. The ethnic components of a culture always have deep roots in the region, yet being an expression of the ethnic (nationality) self-awareness of the respective ethnoses, they are formed with varying intensity among various peoples—starting with the ethnogenetic stages (or impulses) of consolidation (at the turn of the first and second millennia and in the fifteenth to mid-sixteenth centuries)—and reach a high level of development in the twentieth century, when all peoples of the Volga/Ural historico-ethnographic province obtain their own national, Soviet state in the form of autonomous republics.

In general, during the period of the late Middle Ages and Early Modern time (as revealed by the sources), major changes in the ethnic situation take place in the Volga/Ural historico-ethnographic province. The general trend of these changes resulted in a complex and contradictory interaction of processes of ethnic consolidation and interethnic integration. It may be concluded that the dialectic of the interaction and struggle between these two trends becomes the permanent content (pattern) of the ethnocultural processes. They would have been rather hard to detect in the lifespan of a single generation, yet become clearly evident after two or three centuries. It follows from this observation that the initial ethnic situation can never be an exact or even a close copy of the result that an investigator visually encounters. Therefore, despite the identity of ethnonyms, the ethnoses of antiquity, of the Middle Ages, and of modern time, even though preserving certain inherited standards, are altogether different phenomena (apparently, even with different models of behavior and different value judgments). That is why the sometimes heated debates on questions of ethnic heritage, the quest for direct forebears under ethnonyms of antiquity that are identical to those of the present, and so on, are highly dubious, and generally do not lead to the desired results.

We shall now briefly touch on modern ethnic problems.

In terms of methodology, the main priority today is the search for new approaches to analyze objective conditions influencing contemporary nationality processes. The development of a new, contemporary theory of socialism and its practical implementation makes further study of the entire system of national factors a crucial issue, in the interest of harmonizing inter-nationality relations in the country.

Study of the economic aspects of nationality processes among the country's Turkic population takes on special urgency. Beyond question, ethnic (nationality) features have a direct bearing on the economic specialization of the corresponding republics and regions. It is quite legitimate to raise the issue of ethnic proclivities toward certain types of labor and kinds of activity.

In the period 1959–79, the overall Turkic population of the country rose from 11.1 to 15.2 percent. It grew even more according to the data of the last census of 1989. As Bromlei writes: "so strong a change in the national structure . . . causes certain socioeconomic problems," due to the fact that "many Turkic peoples, as well as the Tajiks, remain chiefly rural: in 1979, less than 30 percent of the Uzbeks were city dwellers, less than 20 percent of the Kyrgyz, and so on" [78, p. 32]. Thus the need to make major changes in the understanding and treatment of the issue of optimal utilization of labor resources under conditions of intensification of economic and social development, the issue of real equality of lifestyle in the city and in the village, and, consequently, the formation of identical conditions of education and cultural development for the so-called "rural" and "urbanized" nations. The issues of more active involvement of the Turkic (as well as Finno-Ugrian and other) ethnoses in industrial labor and the most modern and advanced industries remain just as difficult and uncertain in their solution. Connected with these lines of present-day scholarship is yet another highly debated theme, namely, the ethnos mobility, the degree of their participation in migratory processes both within and outside the corresponding republics. A sufficiently effective utilization of the increasingly more agitated human factor seems altogether impossible without serious consideration of the nationality factor, and a consistent analysis of the relationship between traditional and innovative models of work activity—for each people, including the features peculiar to its national culture [79]. Obviously, there should be not only a gradual enrichment, but also a renewal of traditional work habits and a teaching of complicated professions to the young generation in order to hasten the socioeconomic development of Soviet society [80].

In our view, it is legitimate today to raise the question of the national-administrative organization of separated Turkic (e.g., the Siberian Tatar), Finno-Ugrian, Samoedic, and other national groups in the areas of their compact dwelling. Living outside of their own nation-state formations, or having no territorial autonomy at all, they might in such cases take a more active part in the work of the local councils of people's deputies and thus guarantee a timely satisfaction of the needs and cultural requirements of their groups within the framework of the existing structure of the Union.

The wisdom of consulting the experience of the twenties, which was simply consigned to oblivion in the thirties and forties, is beyond question. The development of the new economic policy in the twenties was accompanied by a certain democratization of the social order, during which implementation of nationality policy in local areas was controlled by the nationality-based village committees, regions and districts, specially created in areas of compact settlement of nationalities (including the Turkic peoples), surrounded by different ethnic populations. Study of this experience and the system of representative institutions concerned with regional-level relations between nationalities at that time is surely valuable and necessary.

A crucial issue today is to organize departments on inter-nationality affairs within the executive committees of people's deputies' councils on various levels. It is necessary to decide the matter of personal representation in the councils of not only more or less major national groups, but also of all minor nationalities and ethnic groups not having their own nation-state or territorial formations. This idea requires a new approach to the structure of the future elected councils of people's deputies of the union and autonomous republics, as well as the local councils.

The organization, by the Institutes of History, Language, and Literature of the All-Union Scientific Conference on the Issue of "Ethnographic and Ethnic Groups in the USSR and Their Role in Contemporary Ethnocultural Processes" in September 1989 was extremely timely and opportune [81]. The conference enabled a new and constructive assessment of contemporary issues of ethnic and cultural development of various kinds of ethnic subdivisions, existing under various conditions. In light of the prospects for the formation and functioning of new situations in the development of languages and ethnic cultures, the issue of "nationalities (including Turkic ones) in the city" is becoming extremely topical for the Volga/Ural region.

Exactly what are national groups in a city? We think it appropriate to approach the city and the urban population as a peculiar multiethnic territory, a zone of active interaction and mutual enrichment of cultures with highly developed bilingualism, with actively ongoing processes of acculturation and, perhaps, assimilation; however it may be, we know little about urban life in terms of ethnonational or even ethnodemographical issues. Whatever theoretical postulates we construct for urban issues, it is clear that we shall have to determine the research priorities and major themes, develop an arsenal of tools, and train staff. As for the Turkic peoples in this respect, we feel that the Committee of Turkic Studies should display interest in the organization of this research.[b]

We should also mention a topic that has been left completely untouched in Soviet historical science. We mean the evaluation of individual stages of development of a number of Turkic peoples outside the years of Soviet power, the determination of the time and sequence of formation of nations and the criteria for their consolidation. A regional approach to the study of ethnonational processes, taking into account the entire historical path of development of the nations, permits more objective conclusions in the determination of the level and characteristics of their consolidation. This research is especially essential for a realistic determination of the current status and the tasks of social development of the nations [82–84]. Yet this research is still being hindered by a dogmatic typology of ethnically based societies, a desire to use various terms and concepts (nation, nationality, etc.) to designate ethnos social status, and a ranking of ethnic societies on an artificially constructed scale of cultural progress. Quite a lot of harm has been done here, on the one hand, by the forced and indiscriminate evaluations of the levels of socioeconomic development achieved by the country as a whole and by various peoples individually (especially in terms of the relatively high level of capitalist development prior to the October Revolution and the simultaneous attainment by all peoples of the level of "developed" socialism and the construction of a "communist" society), which have characterized our theory in the past. On the other hand, the absolutist approach proclaiming elimination of factual inequality, and its simplification into the idea of total equalization of all peoples—has often blurred historically determined characteristics. The overcoming of these stereotypes requires new assessments and scholarly consideration of the paths of both social and ethnonational development.

Summarizing the above, we should like to emphasize the following:

1. Investigation of the problems of ethnogenesis, ethnic history, and cultural history should be based in future, both in the Volga/Ural region and in the entire USSR, on an interdisciplinary level, on a synthesis of the achievements of various sciences—history, archeology, ethnography, anthropology, linguistics, study of folklore, demographics, philology, onomastics, and other disciplines, and also in the context of the general history of the peoples from antiquity to the current day.

2. It is necessary to improve the methodology of ethnogenetic and

culturological research and to study the processes of ethnogenesis and ethnic history, paying attention to the specific features of a region and civilization, against the backdrop of broad ethnogenetic and ethnocultural contacts embracing the whole of the Volga/Ural region and adjacent territories.

3. It is advisable to strengthen the research base of sources and their study, making available new written sources and data from archeology, anthropology, ethnography, and various spheres of culture, and to study the traditional social structures, clan and tribe ethnonyms, *tamgi* [clan and tribal symbols], historical legends, etc.

4. It is advisable to orient the strategy of ethnogenetic research to working out the question of the interaction and mutual enrichment of cultures, and to identify the mechanism and laws of cultural contacts and processes in a multiethnic environment.

5. It is essential to organize the preparation and publication by researchers from various scientific centers of joint regional works, collections of papers, and materials setting forth alternative approaches to ethnogenetic and ethnocultural processes.

Editor's notes

a. This typology is typical of the kind of categorizing of Iulian Bromlei (e.g., *Ocherki teorii etnosa* [Moscow: Academy of Sciences, 1983]) that influenced many Soviet scholars in history and ethnography institutes. The heuristic value of the four-way division is that it recognizes the importance of a religion-ethnos nexus, at least for some groups, and it acknowledges interethnic mixing, even while trying to differentiate types. Potential problems with the model include: various groups easily fit into different categories at once, or in different time periods; and fixing time frames for the categories is nearly impossible.

b. This committee no longer exists in this form, but has a counterpart within Russia. In addition, congresses of Turkic peoples have been meeting in the past several years, for example in Alma Alta (Kazakhstan) and Kazan (Tatarstan). The Congress of All Turkic Peoples in Kazan held in spring of 1992 included scholars, businessmen, and politicians from around the world. Within such congresses, committees have been established to further research in Turkic studies, and to stimulate international academic cooperation. The authors of this article are particularly interested in pursuing such contacts.

References

1. *Proiskhozhdenie kazanskikh tatar.* Kazan, 1948.
2. *O proiskhozhdenii chuvashkogo naroda.* Cheboksary, 1957.
3. *Trudy Kirgizskoi arkheologo-etnograficheskoi ekspeditsii*, vol. 3. Frunze, 1959.
4. *Tatary Srednego Povolzh'ia i Priural'ia.* Moscow, 1967.
5. Potapov, L.P. *Etnicheskii sostav i proiskhozhdenie altaitsev.* Leningrad, 1969.
6. *Voprosy etnogeneza tiurkoiazychnykh narodov Srednego Povolzh'ia.* Kazan, 1971.

7. "Arkheologiia i etnografiia Bashkirii." *Materialy nauchnoi sessii po etnogenezu bashkir,* vol. 4. Ufa, 1971.

8. Abramzon, S.M. *Kirgizy i ikh etnogeneticheskie i istoriko-kul'turnye sviazi.* Leningrad, 1971.

9. Eremeev, D.E. *Etnogenez turok.* Moscow, 1971.

10. Kuzeev, R.G. *Proiskhozhdenie bashkirskogo naroda.* Moscow, 1974.

11. *Problemy etnogeneza turkmenskogo naroda.* Ashkhabad, 1977.

12. Gogolev, A.N. *Istoricheskaia etnografiia iakutov: voprosy proiskhozhdenii iakutov.* Yakutsk, 1985.

13. *Voprosy istorii,* 1987, no. 9.

14. *Istoriia SSSR,* 1988, no. 1, 2.

15. *Problemy etnogeneza i etnicheskoi istorii narodov Srednei Azii i Kazakhstana: Tez. dokl. Vsesoiuz. konf. (20–23 Noiab. 1988 g.).* Moscow, 1988.

16. Karmysheva, B.Kh. *Ocherki etnicheskoi istorii iuzhnykh raionov Tadzhikistana i Uzbekistana (XVI-nach. XX v.).* Moscow, 1976.

17. Tomilov, N.A. *Tiurkoiazychnoe naselenie Zapadno-Sibirskoi ravniny v kontse XVI-pervoi chetverti XIX v.* Tomsk, 1981.

18. *Voprosy etnicheskoi istorii Iuzhnogo Urala.* Ufa, 1982.

19. *Materialy k etnicheskoi istorii naseleniia Srednei Azii.* Tashkent, 1985.

20. See *Sovetskaia etnografiia,* 1989, no. 3.

21. Fedorov-Davydov, G.A. *Kochevniki Vostochnoi Evropy pod vlast'iu zolotoordynskikh khanov: arkheologicheskie pamiatniki.* Moscow, 1966.

22. Gumilev, L.N. *Drevnie tiurki.* Moscow, 1967.

23. Vainshtein, S.I. *Proiskhozhdenie i istoricheskaia etnografiia tuvinskogo naroda.* Moscow, 1969.

24. *Narody i iazyki Sibiri: areal'nye issledovaniia.* Moscow, 1978.

25. Gadlo, A.V. *Etnicheskaia istoriia Severnogo Kavkaza IV-X vv.* Leningrad, 1979.

26. *Narody i iazyki Sibiri.* Novosibirsk, 1980.

27. *Stepi Evrazii v epokhu srednevekov'ia.* Moscow, 1981.

28. Pletneva, S.A. *Kochevniki srednevekov'ia.* Moscow, 1982.

29. Kshibekov, D. *Kochevoe obshchestvo: genezis, razvitie, upadok.* Alma-Ata, 1984.

30. Kyzlasov, L.R. *Istoriia Iuzhnoi Sibiri v srednie veka.* Moscow, 1984.

31. Sivinov, D.G. *Narody Iuzhnoi Sibiri v drevnetiurkskuiu epokhu.* Leningrad, 1984.

32. Egorov, V.L. *Istoricheskaia geografiia Zolotoi Ordy v XIII-XIV vv.* Moscow, 1985.

33. Dzhafarov, Iu.R. *Gunny i Azerbaidzhan.* Baku, 1985.

34. Magomedov, M.G. *Obrazovanie Khazarskogo kaganata.* Moscow, 1983.

35. Pletneva, S.V. *Khazary,* 2nd ed. Moscow, 1986.

36. Agadzhanov, S.G. *Ocherki istorii oguzov i turkmen Srednei Azii: IX-XIII vv.* Ashkhabad, 1969.

37. Kumekov, B.E. *Gosudarstvo kimakov IX-XI vv. po arabskim istochnikam.* Alma-Ata, 1972.

38. Idem. *Arabskie i persidskie istochniki po istorii kypchakov VIII-XIV vv.: Nauchno-analiticheskii obzor.* Alma-Ata, 1987.

39. Shaniiazov, K.Sh. *K etnicheskoi istorii uzbekskogo naroda: istoriko-etnograficheskoi issledovanie na materialakh kypchakskogo komponenta.* Tashkent, 1974.

40. Mukhamed'iarov, Sh.F. *Osnovnye etapy proiskhozhdeniia i etnicheskoi istorii tatarskoi narodnosti.* Moscow, 1968.

41. Mukhamedova, R.G. *Tatary-mishari: istoriko-etnograficheskoe issledovanie.* Moscow, 1972.

42. Mukhametshin, Iu.G. *Tatary-kriashcheny.* Moscow, 1977.

43. Kuzeev, R.G. *Istoricheskaia etnografiia bashkirskogo naroda.* Ufa, 1978.

44. Khalikov, R.G. *Proiskhozhdenie tatar Povolzh'ia i Priural'ia.* Kazan, 1978.

45. Fedotov, M.R. *Chuvashskii iazyk v sem'e altaiskikh iazykov,* ed. N.A. Baikakov, pt. 1. Cheboksary, 1980.

46. Ibid., pt. 2. Cheboksary, 1983.

47. *K voprosu etnicheskoi istorii tatarskogo naroda.* Kazan, 1985.

48. *K formirovaniiu iazyka tatar Povolzh'ia i Priural'ia.* Kazan, 1985.

49. *Bolgary i chuvashi.* Cheboksary, 1985.

50. Zakiev, M.Z. *Problemy iazyka i proiskhozhdenie volzhskikh tatar.* Kazan, 1986.

51. *Antropologiia i populiatsionnaia genetika bashkir,* ed. R.G. Kuzeev. Ufa, 1987.

52. Gening, V.F. *Etnicheskaia istoriia Zapadnogo Priural'ia na rubezhe nashei ery: n'ianobarskaia epokha III v. do n.e.-II v. n.e.* Moscow, 1988.

53. Aitmuratov, D. *Tiurkskie etnonimy: karakalpak, chernye klobuki, cherkes, bashkurt, kyrgyz, uigur, tiurk, pecheneg, sak, massaget, skif.* Nukus, 1986.

54. Zakiev. *Problemy iazyka i proiskhozhdenie volzhskikh tatar.*

55. Miziev, I.M. *Shagi k etnicheskoi istorii Tsentral'nogo Kavkaza,* Nal'chik, 1986; idem, *Istoriia riadom: Besedy kraeveda.*

56. Karimullin, A. *Tatary: etnos i etnonim.* Kazan, 1988.

57. Novosel'tsev, A.P. "Drevneishie gosudarstva na territorii SSSR: nekotorye itogi i zadachi izucheniia." *Istoriia SSSR,* 1985, no. 6.

58. Aliev, I. "Neskol'ko slov o skifo-sakskoi probleme." *Izv. AN AzSSR. Ser. istorii, filosofii i prava,* 1986, no. 1.

59. Kuzeev, R.G. *Problemy etnicheskoi istorii narodov Srednego Povolzh'ia i Iuzhnogo Urala s serediny vtoroi poloviny I tys. n.e. do XVI v.* Ufa, 1987.

60. See *Voprosy istorii,* 1986, no. 9, 12.

61. Khalikov, A.Kh. "Problemy etnogeneza permskikh finnov." *VI Mezhdunar. kongr. finno-ugrovedeniia.* Kazan, 1985.

62. Mukhamed'iarov, Sh.F. "K probleme periodizatsii uralo-altaiskikh kontaktov: na materialakh Volgo-Ural'skogo regiona." *Istoriko-kul'turnye kontakty narodov altaiskoi iazykovoi obshchnosti,* vol. 1. Moscow, 1986.

63. *Istoriia Chuvashskoi ASSR,* vol. 1. Cheboksary, 1986.

64. Ivanov, V.A. "O zapadnykh predelakh rasseleniia drevnikh tiurkov v sviazi s problemoi tiurkizatsii Iuzhnogo Urala." *Etnicheskaia istoriia tiurkoiazychnykh narodov Sibiri i sopredel'nykh territorii.* Omsk, 1984 (see also [65]).

65. Ivanov, V.A., and Kriger, V.A. *Kurgany kypchakskogo vremeni na Iuzhnom Urale (XII-XIV vv.).* Moscow, 1988.

66. Kliashtornyi, S.G. *Drevnetiurkskie runicheskie pamiatniki.* Moscow, 1964.

67. *Narody Povolzh'ia i Priural'ia.* Moscow, 1985.

68. Fakhrutdinov, R.G. *Ocherki po istorii Volzhskoi Bulgarii.* Moscow, 1984.

69. *Gorod Bolgar: ocherki istorii i kul'tury.* Moscow, 1987.

70. *Gorod Bolgar: ocherki remeslennoi deiatel'nosti.* Moscow, 1988.

71. *Voprosy etnicheskoi istorii Volgo-Don'ia v epokhu srednevekov'ia i problema burtasov: Tez. k mezhoblastnoi nauchnoi konferentsii 23–27 ianvaria 1990 goda.* Penza, 1990.

72. *Chto delat'? V poiskakh idei sovershenstvovaniia mezhnatsional'nykh otnoshenii v SSSR.* Moscow, 1989.

73. Bromlei, Iu.V. *Natsional'nye protsessy v SSSR: V poiskakh novykh podkhodov.* Moscow, 1988.

74. Idem. "K razrabotke poniatiino-terminologicheskikh aspektov natsional'noi problematiki." *Sovetskaia etnografiia,* 1989, no. 6.

75. Tiskhov, V.A. "Narody i gosudarstvo." *Kommunist,* 1989, no. 1.

76. Idem. *Da izmenitsia molitva moia!* ... *O novykh podkhodakh v teorii i praktike mezhnatsional'nykh otnoshenii.* Moscow, 1989.

77. Idem. "O novykh podkhodakh k teorii i praktike mezhnatsional'nykh otnoshenii." *Sovetskaia etnografiia,* 1989, no. 5.

78. Bromlei, Iu.V. "Aktual'nye zadachi razrabotki natsional'noi problematiki." *Sovershenstvovanie natsional'nykh otnoshenii v svete reshenii XXVII s"ezda KPSS.* Moscow, 1988.

79. *NTR* [Nauchnaia tekhnicheskaia revoliutsia] *i natsional'nye protsessy,* ed. O.I. Shkaratan. Moscow, 1988.

80. Bromlei, Iu.V., and Shkaratan, O.I. "Natsional'nye trudovye traditsii—vazhnyi faktor intensifikatsii proizvodstva." *Sotsiologicheskie issledovaniia,* 1983, no. 2.

81. *Etnicheskie i etnograficheskie gruppy v SSSR i ikh rol' v sovremennykh etnokul'turnykh protsessakh: Tez. dokladov.* Ufa, 1989.

82. "Oktiabrskaia revoliutsiia i osushchestvlenie leninskoi natsional'noi politiki v Povolzh'e i Priural'e (k 70-letiiu obrazovaniia Bashkirskoi ASSR)." *Tez. dokladov regional'noi nauchnoi konferentsii.* Ufa, 1989.

83. "Narody Urala i Povolzh'ia i osushchestvlenie leninskoi natsional'noi politiki (k 70-letiiu obrazovaniia Bashkirskoi ASSR)." Ibid.

84. *Obshchnost' sudeb narodov SSSR: Istoriia i sovremennost': Sb. nauch. tr.* Moscow, 1989.

Several Features of the
Yakut (Sakha) Ethnoculture

Anatolii I. Gogolev

The Yakuts are a people with a complicated ethnic formation, resulting from the differentiation and integration of various ethnocultures. Among the Turkic-speaking peoples of Siberia and Central Asia, they occupy an extremely peculiar position, as shown by features of their language, traditional culture, and physical appearance. Although the Yakut language belongs to the Turkic family, it reveals a large percentage of words of Mongolian origin (25 percent) and around 4 percent of words of Tungusic-Manchurian origin. At the same time, Yakut is one of the ancient Turkic languages, which is perhaps the reason why around 10 percent of its word stock consists of words of unknown origin.

Even before the Revolution, the theory of a southern origin of the Yakuts received a solid underpinning on the basis of predominantly linguistic material. Various proposals had already been advanced regarding a Central Asiatic, Baikal, or Minusinsk origin of Lena herdsmen. Scholars have agreed that the Yakuts had moved to the middle Lena from the south. But they differed in respect to their original homeland. Many of them overly simplified the problem by reducing the ethnogenesis to a mere northward migration of a long-established people.[1]

An original idea was advanced by W.W. Radloff, who believed that the Yakut language originally belonged to an unknown language of non-Turkic origin, and only afterward took on a Turkic character. The Turkization of the Yakut language's original stock began long ago, somewhere in the south, and occurred in a series of consecutively shifting stages. He identified three periods in the people's ethnogenesis: (1) Urankhai, when the

Russian text © 1991 by A.I. Gogolev. "Nekotorye osobennosti Iakutskoi etnokul'tury." Original manuscript, 9 pp. Translated with the author's permission. Translated by Ronald Radzai.

Yakut language (of unknown origin) existed by itself; (2) Mongolian, when the old Yakut language turned into one of the Mongolian dialects; (3) Turkic (Turkish), when the Urankhai-Mongolian dialect was submerged in the Turkic language wave and became the present-day Turkic language, after the Mongols' heyday under Chingiz Khan. Nevertheless, Radloff acknowledged the importance of the Turkic grammatical structure to the Yakut language. For the Turkic linguistic rules, in his opinion, were so strong that they completely overcame this entire diversified heritage, reworked it, and "completely clothed it in the garments of a Turkic tongue."[2]

Even before Radloff, a diametrically opposite view had been advanced by O.N. Bëtling, according to whom the Yakut language is the oldest of the currently existing Turkic languages. Therefore, the Yakuts were the first of all related peoples to break off from the ancient Turkic stock.[3]

Another proposal was advanced by S.A. Tokarev. He also believed that the Yakut language arose from a non-Turkic substratum, but in the north, not the south, as a result of Turkization of local tribes' language, primarily Tungusic, and partly paleo-Asiatic.[4] This view in somewhat different form has been elaborated by S.I. Nikolaev.[5]

Of all these views, the southern origin of the Yakuts is most espoused at present—specifically the Kurykan version, extensively developed by A.P. Okladnikov.[6]

In the late seventies, I advanced the hesitant conjecture of a possible connection between the foundations of Yakut traditional culture and the Scythian-Siberian epoch, dated by archeology to the third–seventh centuries B.C.[7] This thesis was developed in greater detail in the works that I published in the eighties and in R.I. Bravina's summary of her Kandidat dissertation.[8]

The basic point of this proposal is that many aspects of Scythian-Age culture of southern Siberia can be traced in the culture of the subsequent generations of nomadic herdsmen. Many rudiments of this ancient steppe culture of early herdsmen have survived among the Yakuts, as well as its other contemporary descendants. This "pre-Turkic" southern Siberian substratum in Yakut culture points to its oldest "underground" wellsprings, reflecting its prehistoric condition, when the conditions for the "starting ingredients" of the future ethnoculture were created.

On the other hand, this link between Yakut culture and the Scythian-Siberian ("Indo-Iranian") era was able to survive so noticeably because of the involvement in Yakut ethnogenesis of certain ancient, most likely Turkic or Turkicized, ethnic groups of Indo-Iranian (Saka) origin, who had links to the Altai Mountain Pazyryk.[9]

This proposal received later confirmation in an investigation by the immunogeneticist V.V. Fefelova. She found the HL A-A1 antigen, occurring only in Europoid populations, in the blood of hypothesized "aboriginal, pure Yakuts." This antigen occurs in the Yakuts in combination with another antigen, B17, which are also found among the Hindus of India. "It may be conjectured," she writes, "that the Yakuts and the Hindus had common ancestors. As the HL A-A1, B17 haplotype is confined to Europoids, one should classify them as such. And they must have come into India from northern regions. We presume that these were the Aryans."[10] Thus, an ancient Europoid stratum was involved in Yakut ethnogenesis, "but at present it is overlaid by more recent Mongoloid strata."[11]

In contrast to my version, Fefelova assumes a specific Aryan contribution to Yakut ethnogenesis. How likely is this?

She believes that the ancient Aryans formed a separate group within the Indoeuropean family, with a high frequency of antigens HL A-A1 and B17 and the haplotype HL A-A1, B17, and a complete absence or low frequency of the antigen HL A-B8 and haplotype HL A-A1, B8.[12]

At present, a predominant Europoid component in the anthropology of the Aeneolithic, Bronze Age, and Scythian population in western Central Asia and southern Siberia is an established fact. In the Scythian-Tatar period, the population of the Altai steppes and foothills was comprised of the Europoid type, with a slight Mongoloid admixture. All of these peoples formed the Indo-Iranian tribes.[13] According to V.I. Abaev, the languages that they spoke went through a number of stages of development: first, the period of the Aryan community (second half of the third millennium B.C.); second, its division into the proto-Iranian and proto-Indo-Aryan branches (first half of the second millennium B.C.); third, the separation of the northern Iranian (Scytho-Sarmatian) from the southern Iranian group (first half of the first millennium B.C.).[14] The epoch of the Aryan language community, according to scholars, occurred somewhere in the Urals or in northeastern European territory, including the northern Urals.[15] According to archeological data, Indo-Iranian tribes spread through the territory of southern Siberia and western Mongolia from the second millennium B.C. onward.[16] Consequently, any Aryan substratum in Yakut ethnogenesis must be dated to the second half of the third and the second millennium B.C., a time that is not susceptible to a concrete ethnographic treatment. In these circumstances, a link between Yakut ethnoculture and the Iranian-speaking tribes, especially the northern Iranian tribes, appears more realistic. In this regard, I proposed as the starting point of Pazyryk archeological culture ethnogenesis in the Altai Mountains, which dates back to roughly the third–fifth centuries B.C. The Pazyryk people are identified with the Iranian-speaking Yueji (Saka). Nevertheless, there is some sense in Fefelova's proposal.

Indeed, the Pazyryk are a probable component in Altai Turk ethnogenesis. In such event, the antigen HI A-A1 should be found in the blood of the modern Altai in the same high percentage as that of the Yakuts (28 percent). Besides the Yakuts and the Hindi (Hindu), a high frequency of this antigen has been found among the Sherpa of Nepal, in whose origin the ancient Aryans may also have played an important role. The antigen HL A-A1 is found among the Tuvans (8 percent), Tofalars (7 percent), and Buryats (19 percent).[17] The high percentage of the antigen among the latter is fully explained by the ethnogenetic similarity of the Buryats and the Yakuts, via the Kurykan of Baikal. In order to explain how the ancient Europoid substratum was passed on to the Yakuts (southern Siberia—Altai or Baikal—Kurykan?), it is necessary to clarify the distribution of the antigens HL A-A1 and HI A-B17 among the Altai and the Khakass. But there are no such data as yet.

Do other materials exist that corroborate the presence of a Europoid gene pool among the Lena herdsmen? Let us consider several facts.

In anthropological and somatological terms, the present-day Yakuts are typical Mongoloids. They, along with contemporary Buryats, are a local variant of the Central Asiatic race. In all likelihood, the Yakuts can thank Mongolian-speaking ancestors for their Central Asiatic type. Indeed, by analysis of measurable criteria, the Yakuts have proved to be most similar to the Mongols.[18]

It is interesting to remember the findings of G.F. Debets of two seventeenth-century Yakut skulls. He compared them with a small series of thirteenth- to fourteenth-century skulls of Turanian type from the region around Tunka in Baikal province. The similarity between them proved greater than to nineteenth-century Yakut skulls.[19] It turns out that the Baikal region in the twelfth to fifteenth centuries was inhabited by members of two anthropological types—mixed Turanian (burials from Tunka) and Central Asiatic (Ust'-Tal'kin tomb). The first type probably originated in connection with the Sayan Mountains and the Minusinsk Depression, especially since the Tunka Depression is located on the eastern edge of the Sayan foothills. And the Ust'-Tal'kin people have proven to be very similar to the Buryats beyond Lake Baikal. I.I. Gokhman supplements this similarity with craniological materials from the slab tombs of Transbaikalia, and proposes a direct participation of the ancient aborigines of Transbaikalia in the formation of the Central Asiatic type.[20]

Thus, the formation of the Yakuts' contemporary appearance occurs basically not earlier than the middle of the second millennium A.D., based on a mingling of immigrating and autochthonous ethnic groups. The Diring-Urkh type human, a more ancient substratal link in the anthropology of the

Lena herdsmen, combined specific traits of Arctic, Baikal, and Central Asiatic types in a poorly differentiated form. In Yakutia, the process of formation of the Baikal type was evidently completed at the very beginning or in the first centuries of our era with the settling of Tungusic tribes here. Therefore, beyond a doubt, a part of the Yakuts, known as "paleo-Asiatics in Central Asiatic masks," entered into the people's makeup through the Tungusic substratum, since immigrants from the south found no Koriak or other paleo-Asiatic tribes on the middle Lena.

In the southern anthropological stratum of the Yakuts, two types can be discerned—a fairly abundant Central Asiatic type, represented by the Turkic milieu of the Baikal region, subjected to the influence of Mongolian-speaking tribes; and a southern Siberian "Kypchak" type with ancient Europoid (Indo-Iranian?) gene pool. Thereafter, these two types merged into one, forming the southern backbone of present-day Yakuts. Thanks to the Khorinians, the Central Asiatic became predominant. Yet the Central Asiatic and the southern Siberian (Turanian, i.e., mestizo) races, "linked by a chain of transitional forms, represent in pure expression the extreme variants of the enormous racial community."[21]

These surmises are also supported by the observations of prerevolutionary scholars. R.K. Maak identified three types among the Yakuts of Viliui: hybrid, Mongolian, and Turkic. He called the latter type "Yakuts." This was comprised of predominantly tall people with a long, oval face, aquiline nose, and wide, open eyes, "a type that has survived till the present [i.e., the middle of the nineteenth century—A.G.] among the elderly and the wealthy."[22] A somewhat different picture was given by A.F. Middendorf: "The earliest form of Tatar face of the Yakuts is apparently closely related to the facial forms of certain North American Indian tribes."[23] He noted that, among the younger generation of Yakuts during the time of his stay (i.e., the 1840s), there were often found "a preponderance of Mongolian, especially Tungusic, facial features."

V.L. Seroshevskii also confirmed the observations of these scholars. "The Turkic type," he noted, "embraces primarily the true-born *toyons.*"[24] "One gets the impression"—writes Prof. N.K. Antonov, who worked in the region many years later on a Yakut historical lexicon—"that the ruling class in ancient Yakut society was comprised of Turkic-speaking tribes, while the poor, laboring, subordinate group was primarily Mongolian-speaking."[25]

N.L. Gekker, who concerned himself especially with anthropological studies of people of the central Yakutia regions, confirmed the presence of two anthropological types—brachycephalic and dolichocephalic. He noted that such a division is characteristic not only of the Yakuts, but also of all Turkic peoples.[26] Furthermore, he discovered a complete coincidence of the brachycephalic type and tall height. "The Yakuts are not a homogeneous and anthropologically pure medium," he notes, "but are now the product of a long mingling of two or more related tribes."[27] In his abstract understanding, one of these types was tall, long-faced, and long-nosed, the other short in stature, with large spherical head, and a short and very broad, flat face and nose. Yet afterward, a few transitional stages were formed between them. These data are apparently supported by more recent reports. Ia.I. Lindenau, who spent time among the Yakuts during the first half of the eighteenth century, wrote as follows: "The Yakuts are for the most part large and well-made, and their faces resemble the Buryats and the Barabinsk Tatars,"[28] i.e., a Central Asiatic type, represented by the Mongols and Buryats, and a mixed, southern Siberian type, which comprises the Barabinsk Tatars, southern Altaians, Kazakh, and Kyrgyz.

The foregoing are some of the features in the ethnogenesis and formation of Yakut traditional culture, essential for a complete understanding of their ethnoculture.

Notes

1. See A.I. Gogolev, "Istoricheskaia etnografiia iakutov," *Voprosy proiskhozhdeniia iakutov* (Yakutsk, 1986), pp. 4–5.

2. W.W. Radloff [V.V. Radlov], "Die jakutische in ihrem verhältnisse zu den Türksprächigen," *Zapiski ethnoistoriko-filolog. otdelenie*, 1908, vol. 8, no. 8; A.P. Okladnikov, *Istoriia Iakutskoi ASSR*, vol. 1 (Moscow-Leningrad, 1955), pp. 278–79.

3. O.N. Bütling, "O iazyke iakutov. Opyt issledovaniia otdel'nogo iazyka v sviazi s sovremennym sostoianiem vseobshchego iazykoznaniia," *Uchenye zapiski AN*, 1853, vol. 1, no. 4.

4. S.A. Tokarev, "Proiskhozhdenie iakutskoi narodnosti," *Krat. soob. o dokladakh i polevykh issledovaniiakh instituta istorii material'noi kul'tury AN SSSR*, 1941, no. 9, pp. 58–62.

5. See "Neobychnyi vzgliad no obychnye veshchi," *Molodezh' Iakutii*, 28 August 1989, p. 9.

6. Okladnikov, *Istoriia Iakutskoi ASSR*, pp. 294–325.

7. A.I. Gogolev, *Lektsii po istoricheskoi etnografii iakutov: Uch. posobie* (Yakutsk, 1978).

8. Idem, *Istoricheskaia etnografiia iakutov: Uch. posobie* (Yakutsk, 1980); idem, *Istoricheskaia etnografiia iakutov (Voprosy proiskhozhdeniia iakutov)* (Yakutsk, 1986); R.I. Bravina, *Pogrebal'nyi obriad iakutov kak istoriko-etnograficheskii istochnik XVII-XIX vv.: Abtoref. dis. na soisk. uch. step. kandidata ist. nauk* (Leningrad, 1983), pp. 21–25.

9. A.I. Gogolev, "Istoricheskaia etnografiia iakutov," pp. 22–23; idem, *Formirovanie iakutskoi etnokul'tury* (Yakutsk: Tribuna, 1990), pp. 16–23.

10. V.V. Fefelova and G.S. Vysotskaia, *Izuchenie rasprostraneniia antigenov sistemy HI A u korennykh narrodnostei Sibiri kak osnova dlia analiza etnogeneza populiatsii: Preprint VTs SO AN SSSR*, no. 12 (Krasnoiarsk, 1987), p. 9.

11. Ibid., p. 11.

12. V.V. Fefelova, "Participation of Indo-European Tribes in Ethnogeny of the Mongoloid Population of Siberia: Analysis of Hb1 Antigen Distribution in Mongoloids of Siberia," *American Society of Human Genetics*, 1990, vol. 47, pp. 284–301.

13. E.A. Novgorodova, "Rannii etap etnogeneza narodov Mongolii (konets III-I tys. do n.e.)," *Etnicheskie problemy Tsentral'noi Azii v drevnosti* (Moscow, 1981), p. 211.

14. V.I. Abaev, *Skifo-evropeiskie izoglossy na styke Vostoka i Zapada* (Moscow, 1965), p. 221.

15. See S. Zharnikova, "K voprosu o vozmozhnoi lokalizatsii sviashchennykh gor Meru i Khara indoariiskoi (ariiskoi) mifologii," *Mezhdunarodnaia assotsiatsiia po izucheniiu kul'tur Tsentral'noi Azii. Informatsionnyi biulleten'*, no. 2 (Moscow, 1986).

16. Novgorodova, "Rannii etap etnogeneza narodov Mongolii," p. 210.

17. Fefelova, "Participation of Indo-European Tribes in Ethnogeny of the Mongoloid Population of Siberia," p. 298.

18. V.I. Bogdanova, "Antropologicheskii sostav i voprosy proiskhozhdeniia tuvintsev," *Problemy antropologii drevnego i sovremennogo naseleniia Sovetskoi Azii* (Novosibirsk, 1986), p. 152.

19. G.F. Debets, "O cherepakh Suor-Bugduka i Legliu-Bege," *Uchenye zapiski IaLI*, no. 2 (Yakutsk, 1955), p. 26.

20. I.I. Gokhman, "Paleoantropologicheskii material iz mogil'nika Ust'-Tal'kin v Pribaikal'e," *Sb. MAE*, 1963, vol. 21, pp. 358–59.

21. V.P. Alekseev and O.B. Trubnikova, *Nekotorye problemy taksonomii i genialogii asiatskikh mongoloidov (kraniologiia)* (Novosibirsk, 1984), p. 77.

22. R.K. Maak, *Viliuiskii okrug Iakutskoi oblasti*, pt. 3 (St. Petersburg, 1887), p. 83.

23. A.F. Middendorf, *Puteshestvie na sever i vostok Sibiri*, pt. 2 (St. Petersburg, 1878), p. 765.

24. V.L. Seroshevskii [W.L. Sieroszewski], *Iakuty. Opyt etnograficheskogo issledovaniia* (St. Petersburg, 1896), p. 244.

25. N.K. Antonov, *Istoricheskaia leksika iakutskogo iazyka* (Yakutsk, 1971), p. 121.

26. N.L. Gekker, "K kharakteristike fizicheskogo tipa iakutov (antropologicheskii ocherk)," *Zapiski VSORGO po etnografii*, vol. 3, no. 1 (Irkutsk, 1896), p. 89.

27. Ibid.

28. Ia.I. Lindenau, *Opisanie narodov Sibiri (Pervaia polovina XVIII v.)* (Magadan, 1983 [original 1741–45]), p. 23.

The Question of the Khakas Ethnonym

Viktor Ia. Butanaev

The successive connection between the modern indigenous population of the Minusinsk hollow and the Enisei Kyrgyz and Khakas of the Chinese chronicles was first provided with scientific substantiation by the well-known historian N.N. Koz'min in the book *Khakasy*, which was written for the most part before World War I.[1] This term was introduced into the political lexicon by his student, the first Khakas ethnographer, S.D. Moinagashev, who conducted a number of national congresses in 1917–18, at which he affirmed the decision to create a union of the *inorodtsy*[a] of the Minusinsk and Achinsk uezds under the name "Khakas."[2] In the given situation, the local intelligentsia made reference to those distant times when, according to Chinese chronicles, the *Khiagas* existed in the Middle Enisei valley.[3] For the political renaissance of the oppressed people, it was necessary to restore the glorious name of their ancestors, despite its Chinese form. In 1939, the Chulym Turks, proceeding from the premise that until 1835 they had in practice fallen under the Kyzyl' Steppe Duma, likewise adopted for themselves the official name *Khakas*.[4]

However, to this day scholars, stimulating heated debates over the term "Khakas," for some reason have not paid attention to the attitude of the people itself to its ethnonym. This, however, is quite a significant matter. The crux is that in their conversational speech, modern Khakas use the term *Tadar* as a self-designation.[5] Therefore, only a person who does not know the Khakas language could assert that the indigenous inhabitants of the Khakasian SSR use the ethnonym *Khakas* to designate themselves in their

Russian text © 1992 by the Division of History, Russian Academy of Sciences (RAS), Institute of Ethnology and Anthropology, RAS, "Nauka" Publishers, "Etnograficheskoe obozrenie," and the author. "Vopros o samonazvanii Khakasov," *Etnograficheskoe obozrenie*, 1992, no. 2 (March–April), pp. 63–69. A publication of the N.N. Miklukho-Maklai Institute of Ethnology and Anthropology, Russian Academy of Sciences. Translated by Stephan Lang.

everyday life. Throughout seventy years of Soviet power, the "restored ethnonym" did not become the self-designation of the people, despite censuses, the pressure of the passport regimen, the influence of the literary language, and so forth. Only the Russian-speaking part of the population of Khakasia adopted it to signify the region's indigenous people, and they do not use it when communicating among themselves. Persons of the older generation cannot even properly pronounce this word of foreign origin, inasmuch as it does not correspond to the phonetic structure of the language.[6] These data, unfortunately, contradict the important and significant facts in I.L. Kyzlasov's conception.

On the other hand, the self-designation *Tadar* is by all indications of recent origin. It is indeed an echo of the tsarist administrative system, when the Khakas and other Turkic peoples in Russia were called Tatar.[7] In addition to the Khakas, the ethnonym *Tadar* exists among their Turkic-speaking neighbors—the Shor, Teleut, and Northern Altai (Tubalar, Chelkan, and Kumanda).

The majority of Soviet scholars, taking into consideration the historical sources as well as the phonetic rules of the Chinese language, maintain the opinion that in the chronicles of the T'ang Dynasty, the form *Khiagasy* was meant to convey the sound of the ethnonym *Kyrgyz*.[8] We share such a point of view, especially since it is supported by local materials as well. In so doing, we likewise rely on Khakas historical folklore, noting that on the steppes of the Middle Enisei in ancient times there dwelled the *Kyrgyz* (or *Kyrghys*). They erected irrigation structures (*Khyrghys arghylary*), left monuments of ferrous metallurgy (*Khyrghys uzanghan chirler*), and so forth in the valleys of the Abakan and Iusy rivers. To this day, the Khakas call the medieval burial sites *Khyrghys söökter*—Kyrgyz graves.[9] In contiguous zones of contact between neighboring tribes and the Kyrgyz, the corresponding name *Khyrkhys*—that is, Kyrgyz—arose. Rivers named *Khyrghys chul*—Kyrgyz Creek (in Russian pronunciation—*Kirgizka*, *Kirgiziul'*, *Kirgisul'*, *Kurgusul'*, and *Kurgusiul*) border the Khakas-Minusinsk basin along the periphery of the taiga. One can approximately outline the former boundaries of the Kyrgyz state from the indicated toponyms.[10] Data from the Khakas language, folklore, and toponymics testify to the authenticity of the ethnonym *Kyrgyz* on the steppes of the Middle Enisei and to the absence in these unofficial sources not only of the term *Khakas* but even of *Tadar*. Everything indicates that the word *Kyrgyz* was used not only in the political sense but also in the ethnic sense.

The problem of the correlation between the modern population of the Saiano-Altai region and the inhabitants of the Tian-Shan has been attracting the attention of researchers for over two hundred years. In recent times, historians have been inclined to believe that both resettled tribes from southern Siberia and Central Asia and the autochthonic population participated in the ethnogenesis of the Kyrgyz. Ethnographic materials introduced into the political lexicon by Soviet researchers support with sufficiently well-grounded argumentation the opinion expressed long ago by the leading Turkologist V.V. Radlov concerning the common historical roots of the Khakas and the Kyrgyz. In addition to this, the presence of common ethnonyms in the clan-tribal structure (*Childeg, Pugha, Khyrghys*, and so forth) points to the ethnogenetic connection between the two nationalities.[11]

The name *Khaas* as a local ethnonym plays the most important role in Kyzlasov's argument. According to the scholar's treatment, it is apparently a modern derivative form of the actual historical ethnonym *Khakas* from the pre-Mongol period. Just how serious is this attestation? One of the groups of the Khakas, the Kachin [Kacha], actually do call themselves *Khaas* or *Khaash*. Based on the data of written sources, prior to the beginning of the eighteenth century, the bearers of this name resided on the northern periphery of the valley of the Middle Enisei, in the region of Krasnoiarsk, through which region the Kacha River flows to this day.[12] Therefore, the ethnonym *Khaash* (or *Khaas*) can be associated with the inhabitants of the Minusinsk basin only after 1729–40, when the bulk of the population of this group had migrated upstream along the Iusy and the Enisei.[13] In addition to this, as Kyzlasov pointed out, the appearance of the majority of the names of the Khakas tribal groups is associated with gross interference by the tsarist administrative system. According to the testimony of G.F. Miller, the Russian name *Kachi* or *Kachintsy* appeared in the seventeenth century and is associated with the name of the largest *seok, Khashkha* (or *Khaskha*).[14] The Russian form, *Kachi*, was subsequently taken on by the Khakas population as *Khaash* (or *Khaas*), but now already in the sense of a common designation for the livestock herders of the Kacha Steppe Duma. The Kyzyl' received a common name based on the *Khyzyl seok* in exactly the same way, as did the Sagai based on the *Saghai seok*, the Bel'tirs based on the *Piltyr seok*, and so forth. Khakasia, which prior to its annexation to Russia had consisted of four principalities—the Altysar, Isar, Altyr, and Tuba—in tsarist times was divided into the renamed Kyzyl', Kacha, Sagai, and Koibal Steppe Dumas.[15]

In this manner, the ethnonym *Khaash* (or *Khaas*) is of relatively recent origin in Khakasia and is a distorted representation of the original *Khashkha* (or *Khaskha*), which would probably not sound like *Khiagas* in Chinese pronunciation. And L.R. Kyzlasov's assertion concerning a possible rearrangement of syllables that may have taken place in antiquity with the ethnonym *Khashkha* (or *Khaskha*), [turning it into] *Khakhash* (or *Khakhas*), which subsequently produced the form *Khaash* (or *Khaas*) as the result of the contraction of the consonants,[16] does not stand up to strong criticism. If we were to go along such a path, then we could prove that the term *Kazak* likewise derives from the word *Khakas*, to which a rearrangement of syllables had taken place to produce *Kha-sak*, and so forth.

The term *Khashkha* (or *Khaskha*) is general-Turkic and signifies the color white. Its pronunciation has remained unchanged since Ancient Turkic times.[17]

A comparative analysis of the ethnonym *Khaash* (or *Khaas*) makes clear that this was the name for the ethnic formations of the reindeer herders of the Western Saian range—*Khaash* is one of the principal *seoks* of the Tofalar; *Khaash* is the Tuvan name for the Buryat Soyots; *Khaash* is the Darkhatian designation for the Todzhan Tuvans; *Khara Khaash* is the Tuvan name for the Tofalar; *Khara Khaas* is the Khakas name for the Tofalar (the Karagas), and so forth. Alongside the form *Khaash*, the name *Khaasum* is encountered among their clan subdivisions.[18] In all likelihood the term *Khaash* (or *Khaas*) goes back to the Samoedic *khas*, meaning "man."[19] Clarification of the actual distribution of this ethnonym confirms the correctness of the many scholars who believe that it is associated with the Samoedic peoples, who do not have any ethnogenetic ties with either the Turkic-speaking Kachin or the territory of Khakasia. I.L. Kyzlasov, when speaking about the original Samoedic essence of the word *kas* in the multilingual and multifaceted society of the Ancient Khakasian state, contradicts himself when he states "that with time, this initially political term became an ethnonym and signified the Turkic-speaking population." L.R. Kyzlasov declares even more categorically: "Since deep antiquity, we have always been Turkic-speaking."[20] Proceeding from the above, we consider that the ethnonym *Khakas* could not have been used among the indigenous inhabitants of the steppes of the Minusinsk basin. It simply did not exist.

The Kyrgyz state fell in the thirteenth century under the blows of the Mongol hordes. However, during the era of the Late Middle Ages, the population of the valley of the Middle Enisei under the aegis of the Kyrgyz who had partially survived after the Mongol pogroms formed the ethnosocial union *Khongor*, or *Khongorai*.[21] As the result of the process of vowel contraction, this word started to sound like *Khoorai* in the Khakas language. It was widely used in heroic epics, historical legends, songs, and other genres of folklore. For example, *Khoos polghan maldyng ääzi!, khoorai polghan churtyn ääzi!* ("Master of a multitude of livestock, head of the Khoorai country"); *Khoorai churtaan chir aimaghynda khomzynmin churtaan chon choghyl* ("In the country where the Khoorai people live there are no persons who would live without sorrow"), and so forth.[22]

The role of the Kyrgyz elite group in Khoorai (or Khongorai) was so great that even the Russian indentured service-soldiers [*sluzhilye liudi*] in the seventeenth century named the indicated ethnosocial formation *Kyrgyzskaia zemlia* [the Land of the Kyrgyz]. According to historical legends, the Khoorai (or Khongorai) people originated from the Kyrgyz. In storytellers' language, a convention is well established: *Khyrghystyng toghys mung toly Khoorai chony* ("The Kyrgyz union of nine thousand, the Khoorai").[23] The data of historical folklore can be compared with what is indicated in the *Yüan-shi* chronicle: "With the coming to power of the Yüan Dynasty, this people (*Tszili-Tsisy*)[b] was divided, and nine thousand homesteads were created."[24] Comparing relevant facts, we assert: first of all, the population of Khakasia in the thirteenth century comprised a *tumen* that could put nine thousand warriors in the field; second, the formation of the Khoorai ethnosocial union had already started under the Mongol administrative system. Quantitative descriptions are characteristic for the naming of many Turko-Mongol tribes: *Tokuz Oguz*—"The Nine Oguz," *Toguz Tatar*—"The Nine Tatars," *Ü Kurykan*—"The Three Kurykans, *Därbän Oirat*—"The Four Oirots," and so forth. The name of the last, in the opinion of scholars, is associated with the actual division of the Oirots from the time of Genghis Khan into four *tumen*.[25]

The ethnonym *Khongorai>Khoorai* most likely arose on local soil, for already in the tenth century written sources noted the name of the *Kuri* (or *Khori*) people "likewise from the Khyrkhyz." The city of Kemidzhket, where the headquarters of the Kyrgyz khan was located, was adjacent to their place of residence.[26]

At the basis of many Turko-Mongol ethnonyms we can trace the root *khor* (or *kor*). For example, *Khor* is the Tibetan name for the Turks of Central Asia; *Khor* is a subdivision of the Yuigu people; *Khoro* is a designation for the ancestors of the Yakut [Sakha]; *Khori* is a subdivision of the Buryat, Uigur, Kurykan, Bashkort, Bulgar, and Khongor, and so forth.[27] In all likelihood, even the ethnonym *Khongorai* also goes back to this basis. To this day, the word *khor* (or *kor*), signifying masses of peoples [*narodnye massy*], is found in the modern Altaic, Tuvan, Khakas, and Kyrgyz languages.[28] In these cases, the relevant ethnonyms have a Turkic etymology. The linguist B.I. Tatarintsev came to the same conclusion and notes in his research that the term *Khongorai* "goes back to a sufficiently ancient Turkic word."[29] But even if we were to allow that the ethnonym is of Mongol origin (and there are Oirot elements as well within the makeup of the Khakas people), then even in that case, it has a full right to exist, no less so than the Samoedic *Kas*.

The former name *Khongorai>Khoorai* should not have slipped through unnoticed by the researchers of times past. And indeed, in the first half of the nineteenth century, the famous linguist A. Castren reported that "generally speaking, all of the Tatar [i.e., Khakas—V.B.] who pay tribute to Krasnoiarsk" are designated by the name *Khongorai*.[30] In 1854, the existence of this ethnonym for the designation of the Khakas was noted in *Statisticheskoe obozrenie Sibiri* [Statistical Overview of Siberia].[31]

During the time of P. Chikhachev's travels through Tuva, the word "Khakas" was completely unknown to the Tuvans. They clearly knew that if one were to get across the Saian Mountains and continue toward the north, one would end up in a land called *Khonru* (Khongorai).[32] In the second half of the nineteenth century, the Tuvans used this word, already in the contracted form *"Khoorai,"* to designate Minusinsk Okrug.[33] All the great shamans were of Khoorai origin.

The Teleuts and the southern Altais called the fertile steppes of the Minusinsk basin *Kongrai* or *Kongyrai-Sagai*. Kongrai was revered among them as the ancient homeland of the Telengits and the place of origin of Altaic musical instruments.[34]

At the end of the eighteenth century, the Koibal were called *Kongraichien* by the Kettic-speaking [*Ketoiazychnye*] Kotts.[35] The Samoedic tribe of Kamassans [Kamasa], on the other hand, used the contracted form *Khooroi* for them.[36] In this manner, unofficial sources in many languages bear witness to the former ethnonym *Khongorai>Khoorai* as a designation for the inhabitants of Khakasia, but they do not say a word about the name *Khakas*.[c]

The term *Khongorai* was used in Russian diplomatic language as well. When the Abakan fort [*ostrog*] was built in 1707, it was noted in written documents: "On the Khongoroi *urochishchi* [separate lands], Russian people erected a town." "And that Khongoroia . . . for the Kirgiz, the Uryankhai, the Motor—[it is] their nomadic land [*kocheviia*]."[37] On an eighteenth-century map of Siberia compiled by P.I. Stråhlenberg, the valley of the Abakan River and the mountainous ridge of the Western Saians are designated as the territory of Honkoroi [Latin letters].[38]

The ethnosocial formation Khoorai (or Khongorai) had an independent political organization, which permits us to define it as a state formation with undeveloped forms of social institutions.[39] After the annexation of Khakasia by Russia according to the Peace of Kiakhtinsk in the year 1727, the name "Khongorai" disappears from the political arena of southern Siberia and Central Asia. As a result of ethnopolitical processes, the term *Tadar* (i.e., the Tatar) displaced the preceding historical name in the early nineteenth century, and the latter entered the realm of legend. It is possible that the ethnonym *Khoorai* (or *Khongorai*) ceased to correspond to the general content of the community being formed. However, the fact of the continuity of the Enisei Kyrgyz and the Khoorai (or Khongors) on the one hand and of the Khoorai (or Khongorian) people with the Khakas on the other is beyond doubt. By the middle of the nineteenth century, according to written source evidence, Khakas groups (the Kachin, the Kyzyl', the Sagai, and the Koibal) represented a single formation with common lifestyle features, a common spoken language, an identical culture, and the self-designation *Tadar*. The process of the formation of the Khakas ethnos stretched out over time and combine several stages that follow one after the other and differ in their duration. The initial, or Kyrgyz, stage is associated with the period of the existence of the Kyrgyz state (sixth through thirteenth centuries). The Enisei Kyrgyz, being one of the ancient cultured peoples of Central Asia, became the ancestors not only of the Khakas but also of the Tian-Shan Kyrgyz and settled partially among many of the livestock- breeding peoples of the Saiano-Altai region. The Khoorai stage encompasses the time of the establishment and development of the Khongorai>Khoorai ethnosocial union (fourteenth through eighteenth centuries), becoming the basis of the Khakas ethnos. The Russian stage began after the annexation of the Khakas to Russia and is characterized by the completion of the principal processes of their consolidation (eighteenth through nineteenth centuries). The modern stage applies to the Soviet period of development and their further consolidation under the official name "Khakas" within the boundaries of the uezd, okrug, autonomous oblast, and finally the Khakas ASSR. In our opinion, the conception of L.R. Kyzlasov and I.L. Kyzlasov concerning the local sources of the Chinese form *Khiagas* is not defensible. It is not accepted in the scientific literature.[40] Moreover, we ought to take into consideration that the artificial word *Khakas* has not taken root in the language of the former Khoorai (or Khongorai) to this day, and it may likely suffer the same fate as the unsuccessful experiment with the ethnonym *Oirot* for the Altai. The Khakas ethnos, as it has finally evolved after the Russian annexation, does not correspond to the Khakas of the Chinese chronicles, i.e., to the Kyrgyz of the Kyrgyz state period. It is true that this people is related to the Kyrgyz in its roots, but its ethnic basis originated during the Late Middle Ages and has a specific name—*Khoorai* (or *Khongorai*). The first steps have already been taken in the matter of the restoration of historical justice. In connection with the formation of the republic, by a decision of the association of the Khakas people, "Tun," an all-encompassing festival under the name "Ada-Khoorai" was held on August 3, 1991, and was dedicated to the Day of the Restoration of Statehood and of the Memory of Ancestors (starting with the mythological Khoorai-Khan) Who Had Perished for the Freedom of Khakasia.

Editor's notes

a. Here the Russian colonial word *inorodtsy* for non-Russians (literally "nonkin") of the empire was taken over by indigenous leaders themselves, who organized diverse local peoples of the Altai region and urged them to think of themselves as a more cohesive group than had been typical in the region. The political sinews of ethnic solidarity building are evident here, revealing a pattern seen in other areas of Siberia at the time. It is especially relevant that one of the organizers was the Khakas ethnographer S.D. Moinagashev.

b. The "Tszili-Tsisy" transliteration from Chinese is awkward, but this important passage may refer to the Xi Xsi [Hsi Hsia], who in turn have been correlated with "Kyrgyz" peoples and with "Tangut."

c. The Kott, Koibal, and Kamasa are historically known groups of southern Siberia who were heavily influenced by Turkic and Slavic peoples. While the Koibal and Kamasa are usually identified in historical and linguistic sources as southern Samoedic (Samoyedic), Kott designation is more problematic, as is the whole issue of the Ket language and its interconnections. The linguist Greg Anderson is working on Altai-Ket interconnections, which may give the argument presented here some plausibility (Greg Anderson, personal communication; and Robert Austerlitz, personal communication).

Notes

1. N.N. Koz'min, *Khakasy* (Irkutsk, 1925).
2. Gos. arkhiv Khakasskoi SSR (hereafter "GAKhSSR"), f. 204, d. 1, l. 72, 84.
3. Koz'min, *Khakasy*, p. VI.
4. Arkhiv ZAGS Tegul'detskogo raiispolkoma Tomskoi oblasti.
5. A.M. Sukhotin, "K probleme natsional'no-lingvisticheskogo raionirovaniia v Iuzhnoi Sibiri," in *Kul'tura i pis'mennost' Vostoka* (Moscow, 1931), bk. 78, p. 95; M.I. Borgoiakov, *Istochniki i istoriia izucheniia khakasskogo iazyka* (Abakan, 1981), p. 25.
6. *Grammatika khakasskogo iazyka* (Moscow, 1975), p. 33.
7. G. Peizyn, "Minusinskii okrug Eniseiskoi gubernii v sel'skokhoziaist-vennom otnoshenii," in *Zapadno-Sibirskoe otdelenie Imperatorskogo russkogo geograficheskogo obshchestva* (St. Petersburg, 1858), bk. 5, p. 121.
8. S.E. Iakhontov, "Drevneishie upominaniia nazvaniia 'kirgiz,' " *Sovetskaia etnografiia* (hereafter *SE*), 1970, no. 2, p. 116; D.G. Savinov, *Narody Iuzhnoi Sibiri v drevnetiurkskuiu epokhu* (Leningrad, 1984); Iu.S. Khudiakov, *Kyrgyzy na Enisee* (Novosibirsk, 1986); O.V. Karaev, "K voprosu o terminakh 'kyrgyz' i 'khakas,' " *Narody Azii i Afriki*, 1970, no. 4, pp. 255–59ff.
9. V.Ia. Butanaev, "Ob etnogeneticheskikh sviaziakh khakasov s eniseiskimi kyrgyzami (po materialam khakasskogo istorichskogo fol'klora)," in *Etnogenez i etnicheskaia istoriia tiurkoiazychnykh narodov Sibiri i sopredel'nykh territorii* (Omsk, 1979), p. 149.
10. V. Ia.Butanaev, *Etnicheskaia istoriia khakasov XVIIXIX vv. Materialy k serii Narody Sovetskogo Soiuza* (Moscow, 1990), issue 3, *Khakasy*, p. 15.
11. V.V. Radlov, Foreword to *"Manas"—geroicheskii epos kirgizskogo naroda* (Frunze, 1968), p. 18; V.Ia. Butanaev and I.B. Moldobaev, "Kirgizsko-khakasskie etnokul'turnye sviazi," in *Istoriko-kul'turnye sviazi narodov Iuzhnoi Sibiri* (Abakan, 1988), p. 24.

12. L.P. Potapov, *Proizkhozhdenie i formirovanie khakasskoi narodnosti* (Abakan, 1957), p. 84.

13. Butanaev, "Etnicheskaia istoria khakasov XVII–XIX vv.," p. 42.

14. G.F. Miller, *Istoriia Sibiri* (Moscow-Leningrad, 1941), vol. 2, p. 49.

15. Butanaev, "Etnicheskaia istoria khakasov XVII–XIX vv.," pp. 19–20, 54.

16. L.R. Kyzlasov, "Vzaimootnoshenie terminov 'khakas' i 'kyrgyz' v pis'mennykh istochnikakh VIXII vekov," in *Uchennye zapiski Khakasskogo NIIIaLI* (Abakan, 1969), issue 13, pp. 11–12; idem, "Kak nam sebia nazyvat'?" *Sovetskaia Khakasiia*, 1991, 6 August.

17. *Kirgizsko-russkii slovar'* (Moscow, 1965), p. 363; *Drevnetiurkskii slovar'* (Leningrad, 1969), p. 431.

18. G.D. Sanzhiev, *Darkhaty* (Leningrad, 1930), p. 16; Rukopisnyi fond TuvNIIIaLI, no. 46, l. 17; Butanaev, "Etnicheskaia istoria khakasov XVII–XIX vv.," p. 55.

19. S.I. Vainshtein, "Ocherk etnogeneza tuvintsev," in *Uchennye zapiski TuvNIIIaLI* (Kyzyl, 1957), p. 198.

20. L.R. Kyzlasov, "Kak nam sebia nazyvat'?"

21. V.Ia. Butanaev, "Ob etnicheskom imeni khakasov v epokhu pozdnego srednevekov'ia," in *Arkheologiia i etnografiia Iuzhnoi Sibiri* (Barnaul, 1984), pp. 134–38; idem, "K istoricheskoi etnonimike khakasov (termin 'khoorai')," in *Istoricheskaia etnografiia* (Leningrad, 1985), issue 3, pp. 25–28.

22. GAKhSSR, f. 588, d. 115, l. 118; Rukopisnyi fond KhakNIIIaLI, no. 662, l. 1.

23. *Chirim tamyrlary* (Abakan, 1982).

24. E.I. Kychanov, "Svedeniia v 'Iuan'-shi' o pereseleniiakh kirgizov v XIII veke," in *Izvestiia AN KirgSSR* (Frunze, 1963), vol. 5, issue 1, p. 59.

25. L.P. Lashuk, "Opyt tipologii etnicheskikh obshchnostei srednevekovykh tiurok i mongolov," *SE*, 1968, no. 1, p. 102.

26. *Materialy po istorii kirgizov i Kirgizii* (Moscow, 1973), issue 1, p. 41.

27. Iu.B. Iusifov, "K etnogenezu azerbaidzhantsev," in *Fol'klor, literatura i istoriia Vostoka* (Tashkent, 1984), p. 336; Iu.N. Rerikh [Rörich], *Po tropam Sredinnoi Azii* (Khabarovsk, 1982), p. 207; G.N. Rumiantsev, *Proiskhozhdenie khorinskikh Buryatov* (Ulan-Ude, 1962), pp. 121, 125; E.R. Tenishev, "Etnicheskii i rodoplemennoi sostav narodnosti iuigu," *SE*, 1962, no. 1, p. 64.

28. V.Ia. Butanaev and I.B. Moldobaev, "Kirgizsko-khakasskie etnokul'tur-nye sviazi," p. 23; *Tuvinsko-russikii slovar'* (Moscow, 1968), p. 483.

29. B.I. Tatarintsev, "Ob odnom predpolagaemom russkom saimstvovanii v leksike tuvinskogo iazyka," in *Rossiskii iazyk v Tuve* (Kyzyl, 1985), p. 157.

30. "Puteshestviia Aleksandra Kastrena [Castrèn] po Laplandii, Severnoi Rossii i Sibiri," *Magazin zemlevedeniia i puteshestvii* (Moscow, 1860), vol. 6, issue 2, p. 427.

31. Gagemeister, *Statisticheskoe obozrenie Sibiri*, pt. 2 (St. Petersburg, 1854), p. 35.

32. P. Chikhachev, *Puteshestvie v Vostochnyi Altai* (Moscow, 1974), p. 210.

33. E.K. Iakovlev, *Etnograficheskii obzor inorodcheskogo naseleniia doliny Iuzhnogo Eniseia* (Minusinsk, 1900), pp. 19, 117.

34. G.N. Potanin, *Ocherki Severo-Zapadnoi Mongolii* (St. Petersburg, 1883), issue 4, pp. 10, 72; E.E. Iamaeva, "Mify altaitsev," in *Fol'klornoe nasledie Gornogo Altaia* (Gorno-Altaisk, 1989), p. 177.

35. A.P. Dul'zon, "Slovarnye materialy XVIII v. po ketskim narechaniiam," in *Uchennye zapiski Tomskogo pedagogicheskogo instituta* ([Tomsk], 1961), vol. 19, issue 2, p. 158.

36. Tsentral'nyi gosudarstvennyi arkhiv drevnikh aktov, fond 199, delo 529, pt. 2, p. 278.

37. *Russko-kitaiskie otnosheniia v XVIII veke* (Moscow, 1978), vol. 1, p. 106.

38. *Svenska Sällskapet för Antropologi och geografi geografiska sektionens tidskrift*, 1879, no. 26, B. 1. Philipp Johann von Stråhlenberg with a map of Asia. Drawing by August Strindberg.

39. Butanaev, "Etnicheskaia istoriia khakasov XVIIXIX vv.," p. 30.

40. N.A. Serdobov, *Istoriia formirovaniia tuvinskoi natsii* (Kyzyl, 1971), pp. 99–103; Khudriakov, *Kyrgyzy na Enisee*, and others.

II

Political Anthropology: Interpreting Ethnicity, Ethnic Conflict, and Sociocultural Norms

The Former Checheno-Ingushetia
Interethnic Relations and Ethnic Conflicts

Galina U. Soldatova

One of the most dangerously explosive republics in the North Caucasus without a doubt has to be the former Checheno-Ingushetia—the second most populous (1.27 million) republic in the region. Today, it has become a terribly entangled knot of ethnic and political conflicts, one of which—the Ossetian-Ingush issue—evolved into armed conflict in late October 1992. I will attempt here to analyze the historical, political, sociodemographic, and sociopsychological aspects of the development of interethnic conflict situations both around the former Checheno-Ingushetia and within it, working from the position of research on interethnic relations.

The history of the interethnic conflicts

Three interethnic conflicts in the North Caucasus are localized around former Checheno-Ingushetia. These include the following interrepublic regional conflicts: the Akkin-Chechen (on that part of the territory of Dagestan that is contiguous to Chechnia), the Chechen-Dagestan-Nogai (at the juncture of Dagestan, Chechnia, and Stavropol' Krai), and the most acute one—the Ossetian-Ingush (between Ingushetia and Ossetia). In addition to these, Checheno-Ingushetia is being rocked by internal problems: first, the tension between the indigenous nationalities—the Chechen and the

Russian text © 1993 by G.U. Soldatova. "Byvshaia Checheno-Ingushetiia: Mezhetnicheskie otnosheniia i etnicheskie konflikty." Original manuscript, translated with the author's permission. Translated by Stephan Lang.

The results of the All-Union Census of the Population for the years 1959, 1970, 1979, and 1980, data from the statistical administrations of North Caucasus republics, and data from the Central State Archive of North Ossetia and other sources have been used in this work.

Ingush. Second, severe exacerbation of relations between the Russians residing in the republic and the indigenous population, which is to a significant extent determined by the conflict between Chechnia and Russia at the state level.

I will very briefly trace the history of the development of the major internal and external interethnic conflicts that are stirring up not only the population of the former Checheno-Ingushetia, but that of neighboring republics as well.

A high degree of tension between the major ethnic groups residing on the territory of the former Checheno-Ingush Republic has existed there for a long time.

A. The Chechen and the Ingush

The fates of the Chechen and the Ingush have historically always been closely intertwined. A common ethnic eponym—the Veinakh—has come into existence as the result of their linguistic and cultural similarity. However, these peoples have aspired to independent paths of development. This expressed itself first of all because the Chechen and Ingush have lived compactly on separate territories and have had independent political formations and different directions and forms of contact with neighboring peoples [1–4]. Nevertheless, by the common wish of these peoples, a united Checheno-Ingushetia was formed in 1934 through the merger of the Chechen and Ingush autonomous oblasts. In 1936, this autonomous oblast was transformed into the Checheno-Ingush Autonomous Republic.

The declaration by Chechnia of its independence within the framework of its 1934 boundaries placed the Ingush face to face with the necessity of having to address a whole range of problems: territorial, economic, cultural, social, and others. At present, the equilibrium of power and privilege in the various spheres of vital activity has evolved in a way that is not to the advantage of the Ingush. For example, major industrial enterprises of the former Checheno-Ingushetia, its administrative and cultural centers, and so forth, have remained on the territory of Chechnia. As a result, the tension existing between Chechen and Ingush has increased recently.

Principal causes for the escalation of Chechen-Ingush confrontation have been Ingushetia's attempts to create an independent republic within the structure of Russia, which is in contradiction with the desire of Chechnia to see Ingushetia as a component part of itself. The aspiration of Ingushetia to remain within Russia was dictated first and foremost by the following reasons: first, the Ingush counted on the assistance of Russia in resolving their territorial disputes with Ossetians and Chechen. Second, their choice was determined by a desire to avoid ethnic assimilation, which would be a very real possibility not only due to the Ingush's extremely close cultural and ethnic kinship with Chechen, but also because of the significant numerical superiority of the latter. For example, according to the data of the 1989 census, the size of the Chechen population in the former Checheno-Ingushetia in 1989 was more than four times greater than the number of Ingush (57 percent and 13 percent, respectively, of the overall population of the republic).

The position of the leadership of Chechnia concerning the territorial disputes with Ingushetia is exceedingly simple: "if the Ingush remain within the structure of Chechnia, the question of borders will not be raised: if on the other hand they leave and join Russia, the question of borders will have to be decided with Moscow" (from an interview given by the Minister of Press and Information of Chechnia, Moldavi Udugov) [5]. The President of Chechnia, Dzhokhar Dudaev, has expressed himself even more succinctly on the subject: "How will Russia divide up Checheno-Ingushetia into two republics? Obviously by seizing a piece of the ancient Chechen lands for Ingushetia, and of course the Ingush extremists are prepared to ask for Russian aid in the Sunzha and Malgobek regions. They will come there with bayonets. And that means war" [6].

In accordance with a decree of the Supreme Soviet of Russia in October 1992, the Ingush were to elect their own organs of power and begin creating a sovereign Ingush Republic within the structure of Russia. However, the elections did not take place, and the end of October became the beginning of the armed conflict between Ingush and Ossetians. Chechnia has not involved itself in the course of the conflict and has recognized the right of the Ingush to self-determination. But when the Russian forces that were engaged in peacekeeping operations in the region advanced deep into the territory of the former Checheno-Ingushetia, they were obliged to reckon with the 1934 borders between Chechnia and Ingushetia.

B. The Russians, the Ingush, and the Chechen

The Russians among the population of the whole of the North Caucasus are the largest ethnic group capable of seriously influencing the development of inter-nationality relations and the sociopolitical situation in the region as a whole. The Russians occupied a solid second place in the population of Checheno-Ingushetia until 1990 (23 percent of the overall population according to the data of the 1989 census). However, from 1959 to 1989, the proportion of Russians in the entire population of the republic fell by more than half (see Table 1).

Table 1

The Dynamics of the Proportions of Indigenous and Russian Nationalities in the Total and Urban-Only Populations of Checheno-Ingushetia (in %)

	Total Population			Urban Population		
Year of Census	1959	1979	1989	1959	1979	1989
Chechen and Ingush	41.1	64.5	70.8	9.0	37.8	46.0
Russians	49.0	29.1	23.2	77.5	52.6	44.6

These changes tell us that those processes that have today acquired a dangerous force were already clearly identifiable in the 1970s and 1980s. Today, the situation is becoming more and more acute. Representatives of the Russian population permanently residing on the territory of the former Checheno-Ingushetia are often victims of acts of violence perpetrated by representatives of the indigenous population. Confrontations between the Ingush population and Cossacks are particularly volatile.

The crux of the matter is that the Russian population of the North Caucasus is not a homogeneous unit. It is divided into the Cossacks, which have nearly a five-hundred-year history in the North Caucasus, and the Russians proper, who arrived in the Caucasus mainly during the Soviet period. These two groups are estranged from one another socially and psychologically. Their differences from the ethnic point of view should be emphasized. Specifically, the Terek Cossack community has included Ossetians, Cherkess, Nogai, and Kabardei, but never Ingush and Chechen.

The rebirth of the Terek Cossacks was declared on March 24, 1990, in Vladikavkaz. The Cossacks established the following tasks: to strive for historical truth and the rights of the Cossacks, to revive the Cossack culture and way of life, and to promote the social and legal protection of the Cossacks [12]. One of the demands of the Cossacks is for the restoration of the historical borders of the Sunzha Cossack National Okrug, unlawfully abolished in 1928. The reader is reminded that Sunzha region happens to be one of the territories disputed in the conflict between Chechnia and Ingushetia.

The history of relations between the Cossacks and Ingush was initially contentious. Ingush settlements in the Terek valley continued to exist until the early 1860s, when their residents were resettled and Cossack *stanitsas* [settlements] were founded there after the end of the Caucasus War. This greatly increased the hunger for land among the Ingush and became the reason for the antagonistic relations between Ingush and Cossacks throughout the second half of the 1800s and the early 1900s, as well as the irreconcilability of the positions of the parties and the intensity of the struggle during the Civil War. In the 1920s, by an edict of the Mountain People's Republic, the lands in the flatland regions along the right bank of the Terek were returned to the Ingush, while the Cossacks were resettled in various regions of the North Caucasus [2].

On the territory of Chechnia and Ingushetia, the Cossack population resides in indigenous Cossack *stanitsas* along the left bank of the Terek and in Grebenskaia and Sunzha area *stanitsas*. A planned settling of Cossack lands by residents of North Caucasus republics is taking place in the already overpopulated *stanitsas* of the Terek Cossacks, creating an explosive situation potentially leading to crime and to an increase in the number of Cossacks being forced to leave their native lands. In late April 1991, pogroms and murders took place in the area in the Cossack *stanitsa* of Troitskaia. No practical measures were taken in response. From that point onwards, the Cossack population, following the lead of other Russians and Russian-speakers, also began to leave Checheno-Ingushetia *en masse*. And so, in only one month after the tragic events of Troitskaia, over 140 families had left the republic and thousands of families had registered to leave [11]. By the middle of September 1991, out of a mere six Cossack *stanitsas* in Sunzha region, approximately 3,000 persons had already left and 12,500 had submitted applications for resettlement in the heart of Russia [7].

Anti-Russian sentiments have also become stronger as the result of the development of relations in the direction of conflict at the official level between Russia and Chechnia. It is known that the Chechen leadership is attempting to throw the blame for everything taking place in Chechnia onto the Russian authorities. In such an environment, the development of a sociopolitical movement on the part of the Russian-speaking population becomes impossible. The leaders of the Russian-speaking population, representing primarily its Grozny Cossack section, were forced to cancel a congress because of the high level of tension and the instability of the situation in the republic. As a consequence of these and other causes, the Russian-speaking population is leaving the former Checheno-Ingushetia *en masse*. As early as February 1991, a figure of 60,000 persons was cited [11].

The attitude of the Russian population of the former Checheno-Ingushetia toward the indigenous residents has likewise changed drastically. According to data of an ethnosociological study conducted by the All-Russian Center for Public Opinion Research [VTsIOM] in various regions of the territory of the CIS in August 1991, the characterizations given by the Russians residing Chechnia of representatives of the indigenous nationality include not only positive traits (hospitable, respectful of elders, energetic), but also negative ones—power-hungry (38.0 percent of those surveyed), arrogant (36.8 percent), cruel (27.2 percent), hypocritical, sneaky (23.9 percent), and imposing their customs on others (15.9 percent). The characterizations show a high degree of correlation within the group and comprise a significant portion of the heterostereotype of Ingush and Chechen given by the Russians. I should note that such a large number of negative characterizations of the indigenous nationality was not uncovered in any of the other studies regions of the former USSR, with the exception of Tuva.

The process of the forced migration of Russians continues and is increasing in scope. For example, according to data of the Federal Migration Service of Russia, in June 1992 alone, 1,587 refugees (596 families) from Chechnia were registered in the Russian Federation. The Russians are loathe to risk the prospect of being cut off from the borders of the Russian state in the Chechen and Ingush states.

The external conflicts around the former Checheno-Ingushetia, especially the one between Ossetians and Ingush, have become even more intense.

C. The Ossetians and the Ingush

The demands of the Ingush public that a portion of the territory of the Prigorodnyi region of North Ossetia, which had previously been within the Ingush Autonomous Oblast, be transferred to Ingushetia lie at the root of the conflict with Ingushetia. In 1957, three regions had been transferred to Checheno-Ingushetia from Stavropol' Krai in the form of compensation for lands that had been alienated (specifically for Prigorodnyi region, which was transferred to North Ossetia in 1944). However, these lands have ended up on the territory of what is presently the Chechen Republic.

The Ingush, Ossetians, and Cossacks have been living in close proximity to one another for several centuries. The Mountain People's Republic, which existed from 1921 to 1924, included Ossetian, Ingush, and Sunzha okrugs longer than it did other national-administrative formations. The population residing in Sunzha Okrug was primarily Cossack. The administrative center of the Ossetian and Ingush okrugs was the city of Vladikavkaz, the right-bank portion of which is likewise included in the current territorial demands of the Ingush.

However, Vladikavkaz was founded in 1784 on the site of the Ossetian *aul* of Kapkai-Dzhaudzhikau, as a Russian fortress on the border between the lands settled by Ossetians and those settled by Ingush. According to the data of *Kavkazskii kalendar'* [The Caucasian Calendar] for 1852, the population of the Vladikavkaz fortress consisted of 1,031 Russians, 883 Ossetians, 99 Georgians and Armenians, 23 Jews, and 26 foreigners [1]. Ingush began to settle in Vladikavkaz only in the twentieth century. According to the data of the 1926 census, out of an overall population of Vladikavkaz residents in excess of 75,000 residents, there were already approximately 1,500 Ingush residing in the city. According to the data of the 1989 census, 14,500 Ingush resided in Vladikavkaz, including surrounding villages, which comprised 4.6 percent of the total population [10].

Two tragic dates stand out in the history of the Ossetian-Ingush conflict in the period since 1957. The Ingush rallies in Groznyi in January 1973, at which questions concerning the fate of Ingushetia and of former Ingush villages on the territory of North Ossetia were raised, served as the beginning of the events. The tragic events of October 1981 that took place on the territory of North Ossetia, as the result of which troops were brought into the capital of the republic, began with mass demonstrations by Ossetians who were filled with indignation at the brutal crimes perpetrated by persons of Ingush nationality. In both cases, the most active participants in the events were accused of nationalism and sanctions of varying degrees of severity were applied to them.

For more than ten years after the events in North Ossetia, the Ossetian-Ingush conflict remained in a precarious balance on the verge of a dangerous precipice. For nearly all of the past two years (and prior to the adoption of the Law of the Russian Federation "On the rehabilitation of repressed peoples" and of course afterwards), the capital of the republic, Vladikavkaz, and Prigorodnyi region have remained under a perpetual state of emergency. Prigorodnyi region in North Ossetia was multinational and the most densely populated region in the republic. Ossetians comprised 58.9 percent of the residents, 22.1 percent were Ingush, 15.7 percent Russians, and 3.3 percent representatives of the other nationalities. Naturally, Ossetians who were forcibly resettled in this region and who have lived in it for over half a century are not about to give away their homes. The mood of the Ingush has been equally determined. The statistics of the conflict for a month of man losses: 319 persons killed, 750 wounded, and over 65,000 refugees for both sides combined. Nevertheless, it is frightening to contemplate how great the losses might have been had Russia not brought its troops into the zone of conflict in time.[a]

Also serving to exacerbate the Ossetian-Ingush conflict was the fact that Prigorodnyi region was literally swarming with refugees from South Ossetia and the internal areas of Georgia. The refugees preferred Prigorodnyi region first and foremost because a large portion of the Ossetian population already residing there are originally from South Ossetia, having been forcibly resettled there after the deportation of Ingush. According to official data, approximately one-quarter of all refugees registered as of February 1, 1991 (nearly 20,000) were residing in Prigorodnyi region. During periods when the situation intensified, it was specifically refugees living in this region who showed themselves to be the most active part of the population. It is no accident that according to the data of our sociopsychological study, one-quarter of the refugees surveyed described as their most pressing problem fear that the Ossetian-Ingush conflict would escalate [9].

The Russian population of North Ossetia, specifically the Cossacks, may have substantial influence on how the conflict will unfold. In contrast to Ossetian-Ingush relations, relations between Ossetians and Cossacks have historically been amicable. Some Ossetians were actually members of the Cossack community. Even in the years of Soviet power when every member of the right-bank Cossacks was repressed in 1920, those of the left bank suffered only partially thanks to the joint, active intervention of Ossetians and Cossacks. Therefore, if this conflict further intensifies, the local Cossacks and Cossacks from the south of Russia may come forward as possible allies of the Ossetian nationality.

The intensification of the Ossetian-Ingush conflict could not but affect the mutual relations between Chechnia and Russia. Martial law was declared in Chechnia in response to the deployment of Russian troops on the territory of Ingushetia in the Malgobek and Sunzha regions, which Chechnia regards as its territory according to the 1934 borders. The situation has in a sense repeated itself in the contemporary history of Chechen-Russian relations: martial law was declared in Chechnia in response to Yeltsin's edict declaring a state of emergency on the territory of Checheno-Ingushetia on November 10, 1991.

D. The Akkin-Chechen and the Dagestani

The Akkin inter-nationality problem is one of the most serious in Dagestan. Its history is as follows: when the indigenous population of Checheno-Ingushetia was deported to Central Asia for internal exile in 1944, 14,500 Akkin-Chechen were simultaneously deported from Aukh region of Checheno-Ingushetia. The residents of several dozen *auls* in the Mountain People's Krai, Avar, and Lak families were forcibly resettled in their place. The region was renamed Novolakskii [New Lak] region and remains under administrative subordination to Dagestan to this day. In 1957, Akkins began returning to their native lands and demanding that they be settled in their previous places of residence. The tension between the Dagestani and Akkin-Chechen has been continuously increasing since this time. The problem has become especially acute in recent times in connection with the quest for sovereignty and the militarization of Chechnia.

E. The Chechen and the Nogai

The Nogais live in the Kizliar Okrug of Stavropol' Krai, which could actually be called the Nogai National Okrug. This small Turkic-speaking nationality (approximately 60,000 persons) never was able to acquire any level of sovereignty whatsoever or the right to decide its fate under Soviet power. Kizliar Okrug was transferred back and forth several times between Stavropol' Krai and Dagestan; in so doing, the opinion of the Nogai nationality was not taken into consideration. When the Chechen and Ingush were deported in 1944, the Checheno-Ingush ASSR abolished, and Grozny Oblast formed [in its stead], the entire territory of the Nogai steppe was incorporated into the oblast. As is known, when justice was restored relative to the repressed nationalities of the North Caucasus in 1957, this gave rise in its turn to a slew of serious problems. Specifically, the Nogai nationality was divided into three parts, of which one was transferred to Dagestan, one remained with Stavropol' Krai, while the third part—Shelkovskaia region—was transferred to the former Checheno-Ingushetia in the form of compensation. It is perfectly natural that the principal theme of the Second (1988), Third (1990), and Fourth (1992) *Kurultai* [congresses] of the Nogai nationality was the problem of national reunification and self-determination. A Nogai Republic, within the structure of the Russian Federation, was proclaimed at the Third Congress. However, Chechnia, Stavropol Krai, and Dagestan have categorically refused to grant the Nogai the right to secede and form an independent oblast or republic. Given the situation as it now stands, Chechnia would hardly be likely to agree to the transfer of "its" part of the Nogai steppe to Stavropol' Krai or Dagestan.

The political aspect

The principal factors affecting the increase in the potential for conflict in Checheno-Ingushetia, and in the whole of the North Caucasus, are the activization of the processes of political sovereignization in the region and the fact that workable solutions to the problems of the repressed and forcible resettled nationalities have yet to be found. At the present time, the republics of the North Caucasus to some extent have begun the process of implementing their economic sovereignty, against the background of which the processes of political sovereignization are also being activated. Here we may identify a wide range of tendencies:

(a) a change in the form of government in all of the republics of the North Caucasus;

(b) an intensification of the tendency toward internal sovereignization or federalization within the republics themselves (for example, the creation of the Confederation of Kabarda and Balkaria, the attempts to create an independent Kumukstan and Lezgistan in Dagestan, and others). This leads to the development of intrarepublic conflicts and further decreases social stability in the region;

(c) an aspiration toward the unification of all of the mountain nationalities of the Caucasus. This latter is being actively propagandized within the framework of a Confederation of the Mountain Nationalities of the Caucasus (the KNK), which has served to unite representatives of sixteen Caucasian nationalities since 1989. The Confederation reflects the positions of a number of influential North Caucasus sociopolitical organizations, of the type of the "popular fronts" to be found in Abkhazia, Adygei, Ingushetia, Kabarda, Cherkessia, and others. The idea that a Mountain People's Federated Republic be created in the Caucasus, under the banner of Islam, is one of the fundamental principles of the proposed union.[b]

The first two of these tendencies lead to disunification on an ethnic basis, when territorial disputes acquire great significance, becoming the principal grounds for the development of not only interrepublic but also intrarepublic disputes.

In the former Checheno-Ingushetia, all of these tendencies have received the greatest possible development. First of all, it is specifically there that we can observe the most extreme version of political sovereignization—the declaration of the independent Chechen Republic. Laws in the ethnic sphere, specifically certain provisions of the Law "On citizenship in the Chechen Republic" (for example, the section stating that residents of Chechnia who do not possess Chechen citizenship are to be removed from administrative posts), directly affect the interests of representatives of all ethnic groups, including the Ingush and Russian-speaking population. In this case, it is no longer just linguistic and confessional attributes but specifically ethnic affiliation that becomes the first and foremost social criterion. This introduces an additional level of tension both to existing interrepublic conflicts and to relations between the republics and Russia.

Second, Chechnia occupies a leading position in the Confederation, and President Dudaev is clearly striving to consolidate his position as a regional political and religious leader in the North Caucasus. In the Muslim republics of the North Caucasus, the intensification of social, ethnic, and economic problems is now often accompanied by public demonstrations under Islamic slogans. This is characteristic first and foremost in the former Checheno-Ingushetia, where discrimination based on religious affiliation existed for a long time and where the first mosques were officially opened only toward the end of the 1970s, functioning underground until that time.

It is no accident that it is specifically Chechnia that has manifested a desire to lead a "national-liberation" movement of the mountain nationalities of the Caucasus, giving it the shadings of an Islamic revolution. Representatives of those republics in which supporters of Islam are especially gaining in strength likewise dominate in the Confederation of the Mountain Nationalities of the Caucasus. All of these processes testify that the development of antagonism based on religious affiliation is possible in the North Caucasus, and this might substantially exacerbate the growth of interethnic tensions between the indigenous Muslim nationalities, on the one hand, and the Russian-speaking population of the Caucasus and the Eastern Orthodox population of North Ossetia, on the other.

The problems that arose after the return of the deported nationalities at the end of the 1950s intensified after the adoption of the [1991] Russian Law "On the rehabilitation of repressed peoples." Specifically, the matter of forcible resettlements—such as those that took place for the Cossacks in 1918–20, for the Ingush in 1944, and for the Ossetians in 1920, 1944, and 1957—an issue that is closely related to that of the repressions, but that was not taken into account in the Law, began to acquire great significance.

Intensive militarization of the former Checheno-Ingushetia—the steps taken by the Chechen Republic toward the creation of its own army, the creation of paramilitary organizations (of the "Mansur" type), and the formation of national guards both in Chechnia and in Ingushetia—has had a direct influence on the exacerbation of tensions and the deterioration of the status of all of the national groups and social strata of the population in the republic.

Military formations were placed on alert status by a decree of the Council of Defense of the Chechen Republic, "On measures to ensure law and order in the city of Grozny and in the regions of the republic," while people possessing firearms were required to register them within three days. In effect, the right of every citizen of the republic to bear firearms was thereby indirectly confirmed. By some accounts, the Chechen army already numbered over 10,000 as early as September 1992, making it a powerful regional military organization. At the present time, against the background of the Ossetian-Ingush conflict, which has naturally exacerbated Russian-Chechen relations, the entire male population of the republic, from the ages of fifteen to fifty-five irrespective of nationality, creed, or citizenship, has been included in a unified system of defense.

The exceptionally strong intensification of the crime situation in the region has also stimulated the exacerbation of interethnic tensions. To a certain extent, this phenomenon is also a consequence of Dudaev's edict "On the fulfillment of the decisions of foreign courts and arbitrages in the

Chechen Republic," according to which no criminal who is on the territory of the republic is to be turned over to a state that has not recognized the independence of Chechnia.

If in Ingushetia, structures of state power were practically nonexistent prior to the exacerbation of the conflict with Ossetia, which naturally did nothing to help normalize social life in the republic, then in Chechnia it was specifically the internal contradictions within existing structures of power and the interclan and opposition struggle that have directly affected the destabilization of the situation to a significant degree. First of all, these are contradictions in the leadership of the republic: an opposition within the government itself, and an antagonistic relationship between the executive and legislative branches of power. For example, the leadership of Chechnia, in the form of its legislative branch, has taken consistent steps to reinforce the withdrawal of the republic from the Russian Federation (specifically, by declaring that the institution of representatives of the President of Russia has no authority on the territory of the republic). However, some of the parlementarians have spoken out for the preservation of the system of prefectures, albeit with a change in their functions.

Extraparliamentary oppositions, such as the "Daimokhk" [Renaissance] movement, the "Marsho" [Freedom] Union of Democratic Forces, and others, likewise have influence on domestic policy. Specifically, the "Marsho" Union, which is headed by Abdullah Bugaev, a former member of the Presidium of the Supreme Soviet of Checheno-Ingushetia, and by Lechi Saligov, the leader of the Chechen Party of Justice, has been speaking out for the nonviolent overthrow of the government of General Dudaev and for the formation of a people's government.

In pursuing a policy of "active neutrality" relative to neighboring republics, Chechnia actively attempts to obtain international recognition while demonstrating a lack of desire to cooperate with the Russian authorities. Such a position cannot fail to affect the relations between the republic's indigenous nationality and Russian-speaking population. For example, the well-known conflict on the territory of Chechnia with military formations *de facto* representing Russia was regarded in the republic at the level of popular consciousness as a conflict with Russians in general, and was projected onto the Russian-speaking population of the republic. Russian military units deployed on the territory of the former Checheno-Ingushetia became hostages to political disagreements between Russia and Chechnia. As a result of the single-minded policy of the leadership of Chechnia, including the shameful February pogroms on military settlements, Russia was forced to withdraw its armed formations from its *de jure* territory.

Attempts on the part of Russia to normalize relations were expressed by a great number of delegations, toward whom the leadership of Chechnia has made unacceptable demands, and whose activity has yet to meet with success. Chechnia demands that Russia recognize its independence and that the Russian leadership acknowledge Dzhokhar Dudaev as the president of a sovereign state. The President of the Republic and his entourage are inclined to explain all of the multitude of crimes taking place in Chechnia and the poor economic condition of the republic (which has become even worse after Russia's cessation of financial operations with Chechnia) as "the underhanded schemes of Moscow" and of "agents of the secret services of foreign states." Dudaev announced at a Congress of the Chechen Nationality in the middle of May 1992 that virtually the only enemy of Chechen statehood is Russia.[c]

The sociodemographic aspect

The most populous indigenous nationality, not only of the former Checheno-Ingushetia but of the entire North Caucasus, is the Chechen (approximately 750,000 persons). Second place was occupied by Russians, followed by Ingush. In connection with the fact that representatives of the remaining ethnic groups residing on the republic's territory made up a total of about 7 percent according to the data of the latest census, let us pause to compare some of the sociodemographic characteristics of the indigenous and Russian populations of former Checheno-Ingushetia.

If we speak of Russians in the North Caucasus as a whole, the increase in their numbers slowed in the 1960s, virtually coming to a standstill by 1970, and from that point onwards the number of Russians on the territory of the region in question has been steadily declining. A comparison of the data for all North Caucasus republics indicates that these processes took place with particular intensity in former Checheno-Ingushetia.

In recent decades, the proportion of the nonindigenous nationalities of the republic, and first and foremost of the Russian population, has fallen dramatically in former Checheno-Ingushetia. The ratio of the Russian-speaking population to the indigenous population (Chechen and Ingush) over thirty years (1959–89) has changed from 1.2 : 1.0 to 1.0 : 3.0, respectively. Specifically, the number of Russians in Checheno-Ingushetia decreased by 42,000 from 1979 to 1989 alone.

These changes were affected primarily by the following factors: the nature of the ethnodemographic processes in the region, the level of inter-republic and interregional migration processes, and the specifics of the contemporary socioeconomic development of the region's indigenous nationalities.

Demographic shifts have served as an important reason for the decline in the proportion of the nonindigenous nationalities of the North Caucasus. To a significant degree, these dislocations have been determined by higher rates of natural increase among North Caucasus indigenous nationalities. As concerns Checheno-Ingushetia, it has the highest birth rate in the region. The population of Checheno-Ingushetia increased most significantly during the last decade (1979–89), as compared with previous periods of time (the number of Ingush increased by 30 percent and that of Chechen by 26 percent), while at the same time, the natural increase among Russians in Checheno-Ingushetia decreased more than fifteen-fold during the same period.

The large interrepublic migration associated with the beginning of the return of the deported nationalities to the territories of their national formations in 1957 should be recognized as a second important cause affecting the decline in the proportion of the Russian population in the North Caucasus. Besides settling in Checheno-Ingushetia, a significant part of the returning Ingush settled on the territory of North Ossetia, while many Chechen and Ingush settled on the territory of Dagestan. The return of the Chechen and Ingush had a direct influence on the correlation of ethnic groups in the republics neighboring Checheno-Ingushetia, and exacerbated interrepublic and inter-nationality relations in the region.

The rapid transformation of Russians from the majority group in the cities to a minority (see Table 1) has been a vivid example of a nonreversing tendency toward the increase of the proportion of representatives of the indigenous nationality in Checheno-Ingushetia. This tendency, characteristic of the entire North Caucasus, is most explicitly apparent in Checheno-Ingushetia. Internal migrational mobility in the village-to-city direction, which is larger on the whole than among the other nationalities of the region, is an important factor directly influencing the increase of the indigenous population residing in urban areas. The village-to-city migrational processes are affected to a large extent by a widespread trend on the part of the indigenous nationality to work in the nonproduction sphere. As a result, not only has the proportion of the indigenous nationalities among urbanites significantly increased, but their representation among the overall number of office employees in the region has also grown. At the same time, the proportion of Russians within any given social group has fallen significantly. From 1959 to 1985, the representation of Russians among office employees in the region fell to half as many (from 36 percent to 15 percent, respectively). The administrative apparatus and the service sector in Chechnia and Ingushetia are practically exclusively represented by representatives of the indigenous nationality. In this manner, the estrangement of nationalities is being reinforced by social distinctions as well, which significantly enhances the position of the indigenous nationality, diminishes the rights of national minorities, and increases the potential for conflict in this republic.

The decrease in the Russian-speaking population in the North Caucasus region is also affected by Russians' active exodus from the republics in recent years. At the same time, any increase in Russians due to migration has been minimal in this region during the past few years. The intensity of the migrational flow is to a large extent determined by the sociopolitical situation in the republic and the degree of interethnic tension. Not one of the North Caucasus republics could be said to be doing well in this sense. At the present time, the migration of the Russian-speaking population has become oriented toward a "return" [to Mother Russia] and is generally of a forced nature. As has already been noted, there is a strong migrational flow of Russians from Chechnia and Ingushetia.

We have seen a leveling of the social and ethnic structure of Checheno-Ingushetia in recent decades. However, crucial processual tendencies toward the rebirth of the republic's indigenous nationalities, who have had an opportunity to develop openly during the years of *perestroika*, have turned out to be so strong that during a brief period of time, the leadership status of the Russian-speaking population has clearly shifted in many areas in favor of indigenous nationalities. The Russian-speaking population was pressured out of the socioeconomic infrastructure to a substantial extent. In addition to this, it has "aged" in comparison with the indigenous nationalities, which means that it has become less active. The low reproduction level of the Russian-speaking population in the North Caucasus, its loss of leadership positions in social and economic spheres of life, and the increase in the exodus of the Russian population from the North Caucasus republics may lead to a nearly twofold decrease in its numbers in the region as a whole in the next ten years. In former Checheno-Ingushetia, given the same intensity of internal processes and political course, the size of the Russian-speaking population may be reduced to a minimum, despite "measures" being taken by the leadership of Chechnia to stave off this process.[d]

The sociopsychological aspect

Any schema related to perceptions and behavioral models defining specific characteristics of human interaction both in everyday life and in conflict situations are rooted in the specifics of an ethnic community's culture. The Chechen and Ingush cultures should categorically not be regarded as one and the same. We will not speak of cultural differences but will concentrate instead on broad psychological commonalities specific to both these nationalities. In our opinion, the following could be named among the principal features affecting the nature of relations and communication between Veinakhs and representatives of other ethnic groups.

Traditionalism

The everyday life of all of the North Caucasus nationalities is pervaded with a high culture of their own faith and stable traditions and customs passed from generation to generation. The basis of kinship of all North Caucasus indigenous nationalities is the simplicity of their moral teachings, which lie in the foundations of their religion, the predominance of patriarchy, and the cult of elders, reflecting a traditional way-of-life model. A high level of interrelation between traditional culture and religion is particularly characteristic of the Chechen and Ingush. This has directly and specifically affected the strict gender-role differentiation in Veinakh society, its historically established tradition of marriage unions within the same nationality, a negative attitude toward mixed-nationality marriages, and so forth [3].

Acceptable behaviors fit within those models that are closest to highly moral ethnocultural norms, traditions, and religious values. This results in a high level of egalitarianism among North Caucasus nationalities and consequently broad opportunities for a person of any nationality to adapt in the Caucasus. In other words, in an ideal situation, there should be no religious or ethnocultural impediments to outside nationalities implanting themselves in the Caucasus. However, in view of the necessity to resolve acute conflict situations, strong mechanisms lie at the root of broader behavioral models, a necessary component of which is violence: from traditional culture, the tradition of the blood feud, which was inherent in many North Caucasus nationalities in the past and which in some cases has not lost its significance; from Muslim religion, the *hazawat* (or *jihad*), a holy war against infidels. Chechen battled with Russian forces under the banner of Islam during the Caucasus War, and the Ingush declared *hazawat* on Ossetians after the armed clashes of November 1992.[e]

Regimentation

A high degree of religious behavior in society and a strict system of social conventions and prohibitions has given rise to low social mobility and a homogeneous and closed society. The direct result of these factors is a stable system of values, the stability of perpetual schema, the regimentation and firmness of everyday and conventional stereotypes, and a strict adherence to accepted rules and chosen goals.

This is a culture in which hierarchy, seniority, and authority have high significance, a strict leadership is supported, and such qualities as obedience, conformity, and submissiveness have significance. The results of a study of ethnic self-perception among North Caucasus youth have reflected precisely this feature: Russian respondents, in describing Chechen and Ingush, specifically identified such qualities as "siege mentality," "submissive," "introverted," and "isolated from those around them," at the same time that Veinakhs, in describing Russians, emphasized just the opposite: "a great deal of freedom of action," "lacking inhibitions," "no sense of constraint in social interaction," and "outgoing" [8]. Regimentation as a feature of society results in a strong need to avoid uncertainty and gives rise to aggressiveness in the face of defiant behavior.

Collectivism

An active community life, a great deal of importance placed on kinship ties, and a strict hierarchy in clan and extended-family relations are inherent in Chechen and Ingush society. In addition to the high degree of solidarity within a group despite some interclan conflicts, intergroup ties are also strong in these cultures. Among representatives of these cultures, a vividly expressed ethnic "we"-identification is observed, ethnocentric orientations are often possible, and one's own ethnic group occupies one of the most important positions in the system of values. Equally characteristic is an expressed behavioral orientation toward one's own ethnic group and toward intragroup cooperation, a one-for-all, all-for-one attitude, and mutual support.

Speaking of perceptions and behaviors in a context of inter-nationality relations, we must not overlook another feature inherent in the nationalities residing in conflict zones—a reduced level of ethnic tolerance. Residence in a region with a high degree of interethnic tension invariably leaves its trace on persons who have breathed the air of national enmity. Such near-pathological mental states as mass neurosis and frustration are characteristic. These states of heightened emotional arousal produce a variety of negative experiences: anxiety, mass emotional tension and uneasiness, irritability, confusion, and despair. All of this results in an overall reduction in tolerance, including ethnic tolerance, which consequently leads to an increase in the level of animosity and aggressiveness and complicates inter-nationality communication. In addition to this, such processes, as is known, promote broad expansion of negative emotions—social, economic, and other problems are projected into the sphere of inter-nationality relations.

A sharp reduction in the level of ethnic tolerance was identified [by G. Soldatova and Kh. Dzutsev] during our study of attitudes and stereotypes among refugees from South Ossetia [9]. To a certain extent, reduction in the level of ethnic tolerance is characteristic of both Ingush and Chechen, who have been living in a situation of interethnic tension for a long time. Of course, in no way should this characteristic be attributed to features of Veinakh culture. If we were to speak of specific inter-nationality relations—the relations between Veinakhs (the Chechen and Ingush) and Russians—then we must regard the relatively low level of ethnic tolerance relative to Russians as the lamentable result of external influence and historical experience.

As is known, in the process of association with Russia, these nationalities received a series of powerful "vaccinations" against any potential Russification. The start of their close mutual relations with Russia coincided with the beginning of the Caucasus War, which lasted nearly half a century and was fought under the banner of *hazawat* on the part of the indigenous Muslim nationalities of the Caucasus. This was followed by another half-century of colonization of the Caucasus by tsarist Russia, and then by the troubled times of revolution and the establishment of Soviet power, during which a relentless struggle against local beliefs and traditions took place, this last period being associated with Russian rule.

The deportation of Veinakhs to Central Asia is testimony to the fact that they never blended harmoniously into the "close-knit family of Soviet nationalities." The subsequent half-century of the history of the Veinakhs, already within the framework of the USSR (from 1917 to 1957, when the deported nationalities of the Caucasus were returned to their lands) was likewise not able to serve as a foundation upon which relations could be improved, with the Russian nationality as well as some other nationalities of the Caucasus.

In concluding this review of various aspects of the interethnic conflict situations associated with Chechnia and Ingushetia, I would like to point out that the above in no way exhausts the rich palate of distinctive features, interdependences, and nuances in relations between nationalities populating this and neighboring republics of the North Caucasus. The problem of interethnic relations is even more complicated, multifaceted, and dramatic. It has only been sketched out here. In striving toward a full understanding, it is necessary to present as broadly as possible all the aspects of the vital activity of an ethnic community and to attempt to integrate analysis into a unified whole.

Editor's notes

a. It is important to note that this was written before the 1994–95 conflagration in Chechia, and to remind readers that the author of this article comes from North Ossetia. Russians fought more on the side of the Ossetians than the Ingush when they tried to clear a "buffer zone" in the fall of 1992.

b. By 1992, an official Confederation incorporated some Cossacks and was not radically Islamic. Its predecessor Assembly was created in 1989. See *Anthropology & Archeology of Eurasia*, vol. 31, no. 4 (1993), pp. 4–11.

c. Despite these tensions, some progress was made by spring of 1993 in Russian-Chechen legal-political relations, including an agreement to have representation in each other's capitals. This was destroyed with the 1994 Russian invasion of Chechnia.

d. By 1994, the Russian population that remained, in many cases elderly pensioners opposed to the Russian invasion, were as much victims of Russian bombing as the Chechen.

e. It should be noted that only some Ingush used this language. On changing Islamic politics, see *Anthropology & Archeology of Eurasia*, vol. 31, no. 4 (1993), pp. 12–62.

References

1. Volkova, N.G. *Etnicheskii sostav naseleniia Severnogo Kavkaza v XVIII–nachale XIX veka*. Moscow, 1974.

2. Zasedateleva, P.B. *Terskie kazaki (seredina XVI–nachalo XX v.)*. Moscow, 1974.

3. Zaurbekova, G.B. *Mezhlichnostnye otnosheniia v mnogonatsional'nykh kollektivakh i etnokul'turnye vzaimodeistviia (po materialam Checheno-Ingushskoi ASSR)*. Candidate's dissertation. Moscow, 1987.

4. Karpov, Iu.Iu. "K probleme Ingushskoi avtonomii." *Sovetskaia etnografiia*, 1990, no. 5, pp. 29–33.

5. *Kommersant*, 1992, no. 31.

6. *Moskovskie novosti*, 19 March 1992.

7. Ibid., 1992, no. 42.

8. Soldatova, G.U. "Interethnic Communication: the Cognitive Structure of Ethnic Self-Awareness." *Soviet Psychology: Studies in Communication*, 1991, vol. 29, no. 3, pp. 48–66 (originally published in Russian as: Soldatova, G.U. "Mezhetnicheskoe obshchenie: kognitivnaia struktura etnicheskogo samosoznaniia." In *Poznanie i obshchenie*. Moscow: Nauka, 1988, pp. 111–26).

9. Soldatova, G., and Dzutsev, Kh. "Refugees from Georgia in North Ossetia." *Soviet Refugee Monitor*, 1992, vol. 1, no. 2, pp. 14–17.

10. *Statisticheskie materialy ob ekonomicheskom, sotsial'nom razvitii soiuznykh i avtonomnykh respublik, avtonomnykh oblastei i okrugov*. Moscow: Goskomstat SSSR, 1989.

11. *Terskii kazak*, 1991, no. 8.

12. Ibid., 1991, nos. 3–4.

Ethnic Relations in Tuva

Zoia V. Anaibin

In order to analyze the state of ethnic relations in a given region, in this case Tuva, it is necessary to systematize a full range of factors and causes that influence the conditions and level of well-being in one of the most complicated spheres of civic society. Based on the results of the study of such processes, a particular analytic scheme can be proposed. To some degree, this can in turn become a practical instrument for assessing and predicting future developments. The role and place of linkages among state authorities, nongovernmental organizations, and the broad public can also be assessed.

Political factors

Political factors primarily concern issues of the distribution of rights, powers, jurisdictional authority, and assets between federal and republic organs. A whole wave of contradictions has emerged in the process of creating principles of federal statehood, both those based on its classical interpretation and those related to the search for a new formula for Russian statehood. The regions, primarily those based on national-governmental structures, have persistently and insistently pursued policies that can maximize their rights and powers. This is manifest especially in the sphere of the budget, and in the ownership, usage, and management of the natural resources within a given territory.

This paper, "Situatsiia mezhetnicheskikh otnoshenii v Tuve," was written in October 1993 for the project "Postcommunist Nationalism, Ethnic Identity, and Conflict Resolution in the Russian Federation," directed by ethnosociologist Leokadiia M. Drobizheva of the Institute of Ethnology and Anthropology, Russian Academy of Sciences, Moscow, and funded by the John D. and Catherine T. MacArthur Foundation. I am grateful to both Zoia V. Anaibin and Leokadiia M. Drobizheva for permission to publish the manuscript. The paper was first presented at a workshop for the project at Stanford University, November 12, 1993. Translated by Marjorie Mandelstam Balzer.

In connection with this undertaking, the higher echelons of republic authorities have met with full approval and support on the part of local populations. At the same time, federal bodies are no less persistent in their unwillingness to part with control and administration in these spheres, since their very survival is at stake.

In the search for new, increasingly persuasive arguments in this struggle, regional authorities, as a rule, have been actively playing the national card. They introduce slogans concerning the indisputable rights to their natural riches for their indigenous peoples (or the term now accepted, the titular nations, those whose names have long been identified with a given republic or autonomous region). Thus the nonindigenous part of the population finds itself in a kind of opposition to the indigenous residents. This situation creates a volatile breeding ground for interethnic tension, mutual offense, and mutual claims.[a]

Even positing the most beneficial outcome of this dispute in favor of the republic, increased ethnic animosity has been accumulated and may last a considerable time.

It is indisputable that central authorities have initiated action in this interethnic conflict. Thus it is logical that they should take responsibility for searching for a way out of these problems and creating a climate of social accord.

Another political factor influencing interethnic relations is the way in which public propaganda formulates understanding of the notion of "a people" [*narod*]. Established practices do not provide uniform approaches to the interpretation of this word. From a purely legal view, *narod* should refer to a particular civic society unified by territory, history, language, and legislation. However, lately the understanding of *narod* has come to have a more strictly ethnic character. Indeed, frequently it implies emphasis on the priority of ethnic rights even over common citizenship rights and interests.

For this reason, it is important to emphasize, in legislation and in other official documents, the multinational [ethnic] component of the notion *narod*, supporting the rights of the individual regardless of ethnic background.

Another active political factor has concerned the process of formulating and passing the constitution of the republic. Given the degree of public concern with this issue, it can be viewed as one of the most influential factors. Irritating ramifications related to this can be seen in many spheres of ethnic relations.[b]

The most critical issue is the status of the republic. A full sovereign status for Tuva is viewed with alarm by the nonindigenous population, which is afraid of extreme manifestations of nationalism. The examples of the republics of the former Soviet Union serve as grounds for direct analogies.

In constitutional debate, insistence on the right of Tuva to self-determination, including the right of full withdrawal from the Russian Federation, did not receive the necessary number of votes in the parliament (the Supreme Soviet) of Tuva for some time (over two years). It was only after a general easing of interethnic tensions that mutual understanding was reached over the need to have this amendment in the republic constitution. At the same time, as understood by many of the parliamentarians of Tuva, the adoption of this constitutional norm under the current conditions of Russian Republic reform processes had quite a declarative and even prophylactic character. It was passed to enable political pressure to be placed on the federal organs of government so that they would not exclude the possibility that Tuva could break with Russia if groundless centralization of the state system were instituted, infringing too much on Tuva's state sovereignty.[c]

Simultaneously, the passage of the republic's right in principle to secession has had a pacifying effect on those more radical national-patriotic social movements that were active agitators and were thus creating a significant destabilization in the society precisely over the issue of constitutional norms. In practice, this movement lost one of its most critical platforms, having argued that the nation had less than full rights without the right to self-determination. Concern centered on an earlier draft constitution of Tuva, which had no concrete right to secession.

Here it is necessary to mention the mechanism for the realization of the right to secede from the Russian Federation, given that its absence created such a wave of blame over the restriction of the rights of the Tuvan people as a nation. The realization of the right to secede can be accomplished through a referendum on the issue. To have legal weight in Tuva, at least two-thirds of those citizens of the republic who are eligible to participate must pass this referendum.

Added to the list of interethnic disagreements should be some other articles of the Tuva Constitution. These disagreements have taken quite a sharp form in the newspapers of the republic during consultations on the draft Basic Law. Among the subjects of dispute have been the question of the status of the Russian language in Tuva, and the question of citizenship, its definition, its loss, the need for residency, and supplemental rights of individuals stemming from citizenship.[d]

The problem of the knowledge of the Tuvan language by non-Tuvans [or lack thereof] is another constant irritant in interethnic tensions.

The current growth of national self-identity among Tuvans has meant that a considerable expansion of the sphere of Tuvan-language use is presumed, encompassing both everyday communication and governmental language use. This direction is understandable and fully defensible. However, there is a serious conflict with reality, given how few non-Tuvans know the Tuvan language. The whole system of mass education was never oriented toward this expertise, at least in its spoken form. And now, given the serious insufficiencies in technical and material resources, in financing, and in trained personnel, this problem may be regarded as a long-term one.

In discussing the ethnopolitical situation in Tuva, it is impossible not to mention that the past few years have seen a remarkable increase in the activization of public life. Currently, the republic's Ministry of Justice has registered forty-eight social movements, parties, and organizations, including five sociopolitical ones and twelve religious ones—eight Buddhist and four Russian Orthodox.[e]

The five sociopolitical groups are: the People's Party of Sovereign Tuva [*Narodnaia Partiia Suverenoi Tuvy*], the Tuvan Republic branch of the Socialist Workers' Party [*Sotsialisticheskaia Partiia Trudiashchikh*], the Tuvan branch of the Democratic Party of Russia [*Dem(okraticheskaia) Rossiia*], the Tuvan Youth Union [*Soiuz Molodezhi Tuvy*], and the People's Front called "Khostug Tyva" [Free Tyva—*Svobodnaia Tuva*]. These, as a rule, have small memberships and none of them has a broad following among the population. More than 90 percent of their memberships consists of representatives of the titular nation. Nonetheless, not one party or movement has made any effort to be exclusive. This is written into their charters. The proportion of women included in these groups is not more than 10 percent. There are no basic contradictions or serious collisions among these parties and movements, although they do represent differing positions on certain political issues.[f]

The relationship of these movements and parties to the governmental authorities of the republic can be characterized for the most part as favorable, based on mutual understanding and cooperation, with recognition of the need for reaching compromise resolutions of issues. The main exception to this is the movement "Khostug Tyva."

The main goal of "Khostug Tyva," as written in its charter, is the "creation and consolidation of the basis for a civil society, the protection of the rights and freedoms of its citizens, the achievement of economic self-sufficiency, and on this basis the independent statehood of the Republic of Tyva."[1] In the movement platform, this goal is outlined in more detail. The charter ensures the participatory right of any Tuvan citizen who reaches 16 years of age. However, the twelve leading organizations that are listed as collective members are all fully Tuvan in nationality. The organization as a whole is quite small, although collective members include "the Union of Tuvan Buddhists," "the Society of the Homeless," "the Association of

Tuvan Entrepreneurs," and "the Society of Former Convicts."

The People's Front began its activities with an unsanctioned rally. The basic political question raised at the rally was the demand for a referendum on statehood independence for the Republic of Tuva. Tuva does theoretically represent one of only a few, if not the only, republic(s) of the Russian Federation that meets all three conditions for possible secession: in the past (before 1944), Tuva had its own nationhood; two-thirds of its population consists of the titular nationality; and the republic has a "geographical exit point," a southern border with Mongolia.[g]

Despite all this, the majority of the population regardless of ethnic background, not to speak of the republic's leadership, does not support the secessionist slogans and is not part of the activities of the People's Front. The government's position is that Tuva, having been a raw-materials appendage of Russia for many decades, is not capable of self-sufficiency today. Connected with this, in our view, is the point that an economic reason for secession cannot provide a logical explanation, given that the relevant reasoning is first and foremost driven by political concerns.

It is necessary to say that from the first publication of the documents of "Khostug Tyva," the Russian-speaking population has been ambivalent.[h] A resolution was issued by republic authorities (on June 26, 1992) stipulating that "the government ... recognizes pluralism of opinions, freedom of speech, and openness." At the same time, it "rejects ultimatum-style demands and the dictates of any political force, condemns their unlawful actions, and will suppress unsanctioned organized activities."[2]

The local branch of Democratic Russia (whose president is G. Epp) evaluated the demands and program of "Khostug Tyva" as a set of unreasonable and not well-grounded economic and political phrases.[3] Two other political parties have also not given any support to the People's Front "Khostug Tyva": the People's Party of Sovereign Tuva, and the Tuvan Republic branch of the Socialist Workers' Party.

Within the last several months [of 1993], the People's Front published in a main republic newspaper an appeal to the prosecutor of the republic. It demanded "a stop to the persecution and collection of compromising materials on the part of the power structures against the members and followers of the democratic movement of Tuva."[4]

In the beginning of August 1993, a yurt decorated with posters was set up on the central square of the capital. Together with urgent demands to adopt the Republic Constitution, the People's Front called for the overthrow of the "mafia" in the person of the republic's vice-president, A.A. Melnikov, and the economics minister, V.B. Salchak.

In our view, the extreme, impulsive accusations and actions of "Khostug

Tyva" are not conducive to the support of the bulk of the Tuvan population, much less its Russian-speakers. The supporters of this movement, those actively approving of all of its initiatives, are generally Tuvan young people, especially the uneducated or unemployed, who see little future for themselves.[i]

Closely tied to "Khostug Tyva" is the group "Society of the Homeless," and these organizations often act in concert. According to its charter, the "Society" is not a political organization, but its actions indicate otherwise. For this reason, the Ministry of Justice has cited the "Society" for violation of its charter. Members of the organization are mostly young families, recently moved from rural areas, who are actively seeking apartments, even breaking into some and taking them over in the absence of their legal owners. In August 1993, ten families with children, demanding legitimacy for these occupations, announced a hunger strike.[5]

It should be noted that all members of the society are representatives of the titular nationality and that, whenever a demand comes up, it is often couched in terms of the contrast between levels of living standards, especially with regard to housing, between the better-off Russians and the worse-off Tuvans.

Social factors

Social factors [contributing to ethnic tension] are mainly nourished as a result of legacies left from the typical Soviet system of distribution of social and lifestyle benefits, exemptions, and privileges. The weaknesses and failures of the government of Tuva in executing social and economic policy have resulted in a lack of provision for those in need of such basic resources as municipal housing, places in kindergartens, consumer durable goods, and cars. A distribution approach that was in principle calculated to create at least relative social equality has instead resulted in inequities in ownership among different ethnic groups. It is natural that this has stimulated demands, announcements, and denouncements of repression among ethnic groups who consider themselves in the "unfortunate" category.

In this connection, it is impossible not to admit that one of the reasons for interethnic discord in Tuva has been the dissatisfaction of the titular nation with its inferior social and living conditions in comparison with other groups. Tuvans still noticeably lag in numbers of workers in skilled labor, in numbers of specialists with higher and mid-level education, and so forth.[j]

In addition, to some degree the obvious differences between Tuvans and Russians have historical roots. This is related to the "programming" of a good portion of Tuvans in rural areas, so that most Tuvans still work in traditional occupations, especially animal breeding. Statistics have shown that Tuvans as a whole have had the lowest median monthly wage over the past ten years. As regards housing conditions, they are below Russian Federation norms in all aspects.

A source of interethnic tension also remains in the sphere of interpersonal communication, although this is far from characteristic of all population groups. Minor incidents provoked on ethnonational grounds can be witnessed everywhere today, having become common occurrences in the life of the republic's population. These kinds of collisions between people of various ethnic groups at first seem insignificant and innocuous, especially against the background of the spectrum of existing national problems. But the reality behind this, in our opinion, is that they mask deeper causes of ethnic discontent.

It is important to emphasize again, however, that the majority of the republic's residents are oriented toward friendly interethnic communication and contact.

Some research results

Analysis of the results of [1991] ethnosociological research show that more than half of the respondents, regardless of nationality identification, place of residence, or age, acknowledge that they have observed exacerbated interethnic relations in the republic lately.[6] To the question of why the situation had worsened, differences in responses were measured not only by nationality, but also by age and whether respondents were rural or urban. Out of a great range of possible answers, both rural and urban Tuvans indicated that the main reason for tensions is the irresponsibility of leaders, lowered work discipline (31.7 percent), lessening of the power of authorities (29.8 percent), and not enough understanding of the needs and interests of nationality growth (28.5 percent).

Among Russians, the main reasons given for the observed increase in tension among peoples of various nationalities were, first, national egotism, arrogance, a sense of dependency and localism (55.5 percent); second, irresponsibility of leaders (32.7 percent); and third, lessening of the power of authorities (30.7 percent).

It is important to note that, while more than half the Russian respondents cited national egotism as the reason for the unpleasant situation, only a quarter of the Tuvans did.

If we take into consideration the age structure, then we can see a correspondence emerging within respondents of one nationality without regard to whether they were young, middle-aged, or elderly. For example, national egotism as a reason for worsening nationality relations was named by a majority of Russians across all age groups. Among Tuvans regardless of age, "irresponsibility of leaders" dominated, in addition to lowered work discipline and growth of national consciousness.

Analysis of the answers in terms of place of residence revealed that the Russian-speaking population, both rural and urban, consistently named egotism as the basic factor in the worsening of nationality relations. This was cited by 56.6 percent of Kyzyl residents and 52.7 percent in Pii-Khemsk Oblast. Among Tuvans in all the research areas, irresponsibility of leaders was the most frequently cited reason. In Kyzyl, 30.0 percent gave this answer [in Kaa-Khemsk, Pii-Khemsk, and Bai-Taiginsk oblasts, the figure was comparable.[k]]

Conclusion

The study of the interethnic situation in Tuva gives us a basis for saying that recently there has been a tendency toward stabilization. The leadership of the republic has taken energetic measures directed toward reconciling interethnic tension. At the same time, one is forced to admit that these measures have not been sufficient thus far. In addition, the leadership of the republic has not always made itself clear in positions taken on conflicts. For example, decisions were taken concerning unsanctioned meetings of the organizations "Khostug Tyva" and "Society of the Homeless." But, as is typical in such cases, after these or other nationalist actions, there was no response or orientation in the local press on the part of the government, or indeed, from the public.

At this stage, it is clear that it is objectively necessary to establish a legitimate basis for resolutions concerning the peaceful coexistence of various ethnic groups in one territory. In our view, a staged program for improving interethnic relations must be adopted for Tuva, in which the interests and aspirations of all nations residing in Tuva must be considered.

Regardless of the lack of harmony in interethnic relations in Tuva, our research nonetheless allows us to conclude that there is still a fairly high degree of ethnic tolerance among the majority of the population. This is grounds for optimism, and makes it possible to state that the republic does have potential conditions for peaceful resolution of its ethnonational problems.

Editor's notes

a. The unstated but well-known context of this is the interethnic (Tuvan-Russian) violence that broke out in Tuva in the summer of 1990, concentrated in mixed-ethnic areas of high unemployment and relatively recent Russian settlement (for example, the industrial town Khovu-Aksy). Young Tuvans rioted and threatened Russians, contributing to an exodus of Russians from the republic that was estimated at over ten thousand by 1992. Soviet troops were brought in to quell the disturbances, angering Tuvans further and creating increased polarization. See Aleksandra Lugovskaia, "V plenu konflikta," *Soiuz*, 1990, no. 35 (August), pp. 9, 16; M.Ia. Zhornitskaia, "Natsional'naia situatsiia v Tuvinskoi ASSR i Khakasskoi AO," manuscript, Institute of Ethnology and Anthropology (Moscow, 1990); N.P. Moskalenko, "Etnopoliticheskaia situatsiia v respublike Tyva," Document 37, Institute of Ethnology and Anthropology, 1992. For a sampling of Russian press coverage, see *Izvestiia*, 3 July 1990, p. 6; ibid., 3 August 1990, p. 29; *Sovetskaia Rossiia*, 29 September 1990, p. 3. See also Ann Sheehy, "Russians the Target of Interethnic Violence in Tuva," *RFE/RL Report on the USSR*, 14 September 1990, pp. 13–17.

b. Tuva adopted its new constitution on October 22, 1993, declaring the more accurate name of "Tyva" for the republic and creating a working parliament called the Supreme Khural. See "Konstitutsiia," *Tuvinskaia pravda*, 23 October 1993, p. 1; Ann Sheehy, "Tuva Adopts New Constitution," *RFE/RL Daily Report*, 26 October 1993, no. 206, p. 2. The older spelling of the republic's name is retained here because that is the spelling Zoia V. Anaiban used in her manuscript. Despite an official constitutional provision for possible secession, the president of Tuva, Sherig-Ool Oorzhak, made clear the republic's near-term plan to remain inside the Russian Federation by participation in December 1993 elections and by hosting President Yeltsin in June 1994.

c. Zoia V. Anaiban's discussion of the secession debate in parliament is informed not only by her role as an ethnosociologist covering current events; she is also the wife of one of the few Russian leaders of the Tuvan parliament.

d. Both Russian and Tuvan are official state languages. For more on the historical and political context of Tuvan debates, see Toomas Alatalu, "Tuva—A State Reawakens," *Soviet Studies*, vol. 44, no. 5 (1991), pp. 881–95; Mergen Mongush, "Remote and Forlorn," *Far Eastern Economic Review*, 30 January 1992, pp. 25–26; idem, "The Annexation of Tannu-Tuva and the Formation of the Tuvinskaya ASSR," *Nationalities Papers*, vol. 21, no. 2 (1993), pp. 47–53; Robert A. Rupen, "The Absorption of Tuva," *The Anatomy of Communist Takeovers*, ed. Thomas T. Hammond (New Haven: Yale University Press, 1975), pp. 148–50; Marjorie Mandelstam Balzer, "From Ethnicity to Nationalism: Turmoil in the Russian Mini-Empire," in *The Social Legacy of Communism*, eds. James Millar and Sharon Wolchik (Cambridge: Cambridge University Press, 1994), pp. 56–88.

e. The cultural, especially Buddhist and shamanist, religious revival currently under way in Tuva is not emphasized here but is nonetheless significant, according to several other Tuvan colleagues. I am grateful to Gennadii Chash of Chagonar (June 1991) and V.Iu. Suzukei of Kyzyl (August 1992) for their consultations. For background, see Boris Chichlo, "Histoire de la formation des territoires autonomes chez les peuples Turco-Mongols de Sibérie," *Cahiers du monde russe et soviétique*, vol. 27, nos. 3–4 (1987), pp. 380–81; Gail Fondahl, "Siberia: Native Peoples and Newcomers," in *Nations and Politics in the Soviet Successor States*, eds. Ian Bremmer and Ray Taras (Cambridge: Cambridge University Press, 1993), pp. 499–503; Sevyan Vainshtein, *Nomads of South Siberia* (Cambridge: Cambridge University Press, 1980); and Caroline Humphrey's introduction in the same volume.

f. The author is exaggerating the degree of harmony among these diverse groups, but her perspective derives from reading their official charters as well as from a desire to soften the Tuvan republic's reputation for ethnic conflict. The author, as is clear from note 5, below, and from conversations with her in September 1992 and November 1993, has had access to the Ministry of Justice archives.

g. The three criteria referred to here derive originally from Yeltsin's former advisor

ETHNIC RELATIONS IN TUVA 111

for nationalities affairs, Galina Starovoitova, who in many speeches (e.g., at Stirin Castle, Prague, in September 1992, at which Zoia Anaiban and I were present) has suggested the following for minimal secession legitimacy: a history of national group consciousness; a demographic majority of the secessionist "titular" group, coupled with a referendum endorsing exit by at least a solid majority; and a geographical outside border. However, no minister of nationalities affairs (whether Nikolai Egorov, Sergei Shakrai, or Valerii Tishkov) has officially endorsed such criteria. More recently, Starovoitova has expanded them to include a fourth, namely that repression of the group should have reached levels of "unbearability," and has made more stringent the requirements for referenda (personal communication, July 1994).

h. The division "Russian-speaking population" and "non-Russian-speaking" is telling, for in the context of Kyzyl politics, some of the Tuvan elite speak among themselves in Russian and have intermarried with people of Slavic background. In many rural Tuvan areas, however, Russian-language knowledge is quite poor. For more on language and demographic background, see *Pasport Tuvinskoi ASSR* (Kyzyl, 1990); Moskalenko, "Etnopoliticheskaia situatsiia v respublike Tyva."

i. While this generalization may be true of some of the instigators of the more radical actions of "Khostug Tyva," it is not valid for the more moderate wing of the Tuvan nationalist and ecology movement. The Tuvan People's Front leader Kaadyr-ool Bicheldei, for example, is an Orientalist who subsequently became head of the Tuvan Supreme Soviet. ("Khostug Tyva" grew out of the People's Front, with some splits between its more radical and moderate wings.) Complaints concerning opposition persecution, ecological despoliation due to official resource abuses, and corruption among the elite are aspects of Tuvan life that Tuvans themselves concede in personal conversations.

j. For more specific statistics, see *Pasport Tuvinskoi ASSR* (Kyzyl, 1990); Moskalenko, "Etnopoliticheskaia situatsiia v respublike Tyva"; Zoia Anaiban, "K probleme mezhnatsional'nykh konfliktov" (paper delivered at a September 1992 conference held in Prague on "Ethnic Conflict Resolution in Eastern Europe and the Former Soviet Union," to be published as "The Problem of Interethnic Conflict" in *Winds of Change: Ethnic Conflict and Resolution in Eastern Europe and the Former Soviet Union*, ed. Catherine Kelleher [Washington, DC: Brookings Institution Press, forthcoming]).

k. While the methodology of this 1991 survey is not made fully explicit, the regions were selected as representative of mixed-ethnic or monoethnic populations. Although some of the suggested answers seem to be lumped in the analysis, results are nonetheless striking. To questions about the desirability of an ethnically mixed workplace, a majority of Tuvans (89.1 percent) and of Russians (91.9 percent) answered they would like to work in a multiethnic collective, or that the nationality composition of the workplace "is irrelevant." Zoia Anaiban is updating this research as part of the new ethnosociological survey project "Postcommunist Nationalism, Ethnic Identity, and Conflict Resolution in the Russian Federation," led by Leokadiia Drobizheva, using rigorous techniques for 1994 fieldwork. The project is funded by the MacArthur Foundation.

Notes

1. *Ustav narodnogo fronta khostug Tyva*, 1990.
2. *Postanovleniia o khostuge Tyve*, 26 June 1992.
3. *Sibirskaia gazeta*, 1992, no. 31 (July).
4. *Tuvinskaia pravda*, 31 August 1993.
5. Tekushchii arkhiv Ministerstva Iustitsii Respubliki Tuva.

6. Results are from a public opinion survey conducted in 1991 as part of the program "Sotsio-kul'turnye faktory ekonomicheskogo razvitiia respubliki," sponsored jointly by the ethnosociological division of the Tuva Institute of Language, Literature, and History and the economic laboratory of the Tuva branch of the Siberian Academy of Sciences. The survey sample included 1,500 people, including residents of the capital and three rural regions. [This section is an excerpt from "K probleme mezhnatsional'nykh konfliktov," written for the September 1992 conference held in Prague, "Ethnic Conflict Resolution in Eastern Europe and the Former Soviet Union," sponsored by Women in International Security, organized by Catherine Kelleher.—MMB]

The Problems of Sovereignty and Interethnic Relations in the Republic of Tatarstan

Roza N. Musina

Since the disintegration of the USSR, Tatarstan has become a zone of some of the most basic attempts to solve the problem of state building and to change the relationship between the Republic of Tatarstan and the federal center. Many specialists believe that the situation in Tatarstan is not only a specific case, but in many ways may be indicative of the Russian Federation's future development.

As is well known, in the last few years a series of significant events has occurred in the republic's political life. These include: unanimous (with only one abstention) adoption by the republic Supreme Soviet of the Declaration of Sovereignty of the Republic of Tatarstan (August 1990); creation of the post of president and election of the first president of Tatarstan (June 1991); a referendum on the state status of Tatarstan (March 1992); and adoption of the new constitution (November 1992).[a]

Of the various opinions concerning the situation in the republic, two are particularly typical. One opinion is that when Tatarstan passed the declaration on its sovereignty and passed its own constitution, it initiated the inevitable future disintegration of the Russian Federation. Thus the current political leadership of Tatarstan strengthened the process of ethnic polarization and could provoke escalation of nationalist conflict between the two

This paper, "Problemy suvereniteta i mezhnatsional'nye otnosheniia v respublike Tatarstana," was written in October 1993 for the project "Postcommunist Nationalism, Ethnic Identity, and Conflict Resolution in the Russian Federation," directed by ethnosociologist Leokadiia M. Drobizheva of the Institute of Ethnology and Anthropology, Russian Academy of Sciences, Moscow, and funded by the John D. and Catherine T. MacArthur Foundation. I am grateful to both Roza N. Musina and Leokadiia M. Drobizheva for permission to publish the manuscript. The paper was first presented at a workshop for the project at Stanford University, November 12, 1993. Translated by Marjorie Mandelstam Balzer.

principal ethnic groups in the republic—the Tatars and the Russians. Others consider that Tatarstan's method of resolving the issue of the Russian Federation's governmental organization and the mutual interrelationship of the republic with the center is the way out of the impasse in which Russia finds itself. Further, they consider that the current internal policies of specific gradual social changes that Tatarstan is following have created an essentially positive climate that will enable Tatarstan to escape social conflict, including ethnonational conflicts.

Analysts advocating both opinions converge in thinking that Tatarstan lags behind Russia in the development of a societywide democratic movement.

What is the real situation? How are present and future interethnic relations developing in Tatarstan? What is the meaning and understanding of the conception of "sovereignty" in government circles, among leaders of ethnonational and other political parties and movements, and among the mass population? How do the different aspects of Tatarstan's sovereignty—ethnonational, connected with the Tatar national-cultural renaissance, and economic, directed toward economic independence from the center—influence interethnic relations in the republic? How are the political decisions made by the main governmental circles understood and received by the republic population? What are the connections between democratic and national values in the contemporary ethnopolitical situation in the republic? What is necessary to preserve peace and stability here?

All these problems are of the highest relevance. For their better understanding, it is necessary to provide a brief outline of the contemporary demographic, socioeconomic, and cultural-linguistic situation in Tatarstan, with a few historical notations.

Ethnodemographic issues

The Republic of Tatarstan, on the Volga River, almost in the center of the European part of Russia, is a multinational region with a population of more than 3.5 million (3.6417 in the 1989 census), and with representatives of more than 100 nationalities. The main ethnic groups, almost equally represented, are the Tatars (48.5 percent) and the Russians (43.3 percent), together constituting nearly 92 percent of the population. Other Volga-region peoples—Chuvash, Mordva, Mari, and Udmurt—comprise just over 6 percent, and approximately 2 percent constitute the rest.[1] The Russian population began settlement here from the middle of the sixteenth century, after the conquest of Kazan by Ivan the Terrible's troops, when the Kazan Khanate was annexed to the Russian state.

Tatarstan is a considerably urbanized republic: almost three-quarters of its population (72.3 percent) live in urban centers. The Russians characteristically have a higher level of urbanization (85.7 percent) than the Tatars (63.4 percent).[2]

This situation has a historical explanation. Tatars were forbidden to live in towns after Ivan the Terrible's conquest of the Kazan Khanate, in itself a highly developed urban civilization. By the beginning of the twentieth century, less than 5 percent of Tatars in the region lived in towns.[3] By 1926, 10.8 percent of the republic population was urban, but a disproportion continued: Tatars were 3.5 times less urban than Russians (Tatars—5.2 percent; Russians—18.3 percent). In general, the urbanization process from the 1930s to the 1980s proceeded in such a way that the Tatar population lagged about twenty years behind Russians. By the end of the 1980s, there were 42.1 percent Tatar urbanites and 50.8 percent Russian urbanites. The proportion of rural Tatars reached nearly two-thirds (65.5 percent) with Russians just over one-fifth (22.9 percent).[4] This condition, as well as the rushed character of industrialization and urbanization in the republic as a whole (resulting in a disproportionate number of first- or second-generation urbanites), has played an important role in the current situation.

Ethnodemographic differences are closely linked with a disproportion in levels of education between Russians and Tatars: in the 1989 census, for every 1,000 people, 312 Russians had higher, unfinished higher, or mid-level specialized education, while only 243 Tatars had a comparable level. This has had an influence on the population's socio-occupational structure. In 1989, Russian professionals constituted 36.3 percent and Tatars 29.7 percent, with more Russians represented among engineering-technical specialists (13.0 percent and 7.3 percent respectively). The same was true of directors of enterprises and organizations (2.9 percent and 2.1 percent respectively).[5] There was also a disproportion among scientific personnel, with 34.9 percent Tatars and 56.2 percent Russians by the end of the 1980s.[6]

The proportion of Tatars involved in menial physical labor was 70.3 percent, whereas the Russian proportion was 63.7 percent. Tatars tend to be well represented in agriculture, in construction, in transport, in the leather and fur industry, in trade, and in food services. More Russians than Tatars work in machine processing and in metallurgy.[7] The backwardness of the Tatars as compared to the Russians is especially evident in skill levels, particularly in more recently built cities.[8]

It is important here to emphasize certain points related to the republic's ethnodemographic and ethnosocial structure. First, these disproportions are tied to economic and to cultural, lifestyle differences in the conditions of life of various nationalities. Second, in recent conditions of growth in educational and social status for Tatars, competition is created among representatives of various ethnic groups. Third, only with a fully well-rounded ethnosocial structure can the growth of a nation be optimally realized.

Sociocultural issues

Thus far, the unfulfilled growth of the nation is also reflected in the ethnic-language and ethnocultural spheres of Tatar life. In the Soviet period, the spheres in which the Tatar language could be active were drastically curtailed. By the end of the 1980s, grade-school students studying in the Tatar language comprised only 12 percent of students in the republic, and in urban centers this figure was not more than 1.5 percent. The level of Tatar-language knowledge declined. In the town of Naberezhnye Chelny in 1990, up to 40 percent of the children either did not know their native Tatar language or knew it poorly.[9] Tatar had become a household language, and even at home the language spoken tended to be a mix of Tatar and Russian.

In all other spheres, the Russian language predominated. In the 1989 census, 77.2 percent of the republic's Tatar population (and 85.3 percent of urban Tatars) spoke fluent Russian. The bilingualism proclaimed for many years in the Soviet period turned out to be one-sided. Only 1.1 percent of Russians in Tatarstan know the Tatar language. Among other peoples in the republic, the proportion of those knowing the Tatar language is somewhat higher: 13.1 percent of the Udmurt people, 9.9 percent of the Mordva, 6.3 percent of the Bashkir, and 3.5 percent of the Chuvash.[10]

The lowering of language competence among Tatars is one of the factors impinging on their national-cultural interests. There has been a general weakening of Tatar culture, especially in the artistic sphere and in urban environments. To a great extent, this penetrates to the level of professional artistic culture and influences its direction.

A definitive advance in national cultural growth was achieved after the Declaration of Sovereignty was passed in August 1990 and after concrete measures were taken toward the declaration's implementation.

In Tatarstan, conceptions have been developed for the growth of national culture, education, and language learning in schools and preschools. In higher and special education establishments, Tatar-language programs have been developed. In the last few years in the republic, Tatar kindergartens and Tatar-language groups for Russian kindergartens (in which 28 percent of the children were Tatar) have begun.[11] Groups for the study of Tatar by non-Tatar children have also been established. Tatar schools, lyceums, and gymnasiums have opened, as well as Tatar classes in schools with mixed ethnic composition. Now 33.5 percent of children of Tatar background study their native language. At pedagogical institutes in Naberezhnye

Chelny and Kazan, teachers are being trained to teach the Tatar language. And experience is now being gained in higher education classes in the teaching of the Tatar language.

However, Tatar-language schools are still predominantly rural and do not have enough teachers, textbooks, or methodological literature.[b] In Naberezhnye Chelny alone, 700 more teachers of Tatar language and literature are needed.[12]

Tatarstan is the spiritual center of all Tatars, although three-quarters of the Tatars live outside their own republic. In recent years, a consciousness has developed among Tatars that only sovereign statehood can guarantee the nation's preservation and protect its interests. Among the national sociopolitical organizations, a few have demanded a full independent national state—the Ittifak [Alliance] Party, the Tatar youth union Azatlyk [Freedom], the self-named cabinet Milli Mejlis, and representatives of other relatively radical branches of the national movement.[c] They also call for a single state language—Tatar. But these organizations have quite a small membership and are not popular with the majority of the Tatar masses. At the end of 1992, sociological survey research commissioned by the Supreme Soviet indicated that their support was not more than 2 percent (1.4–1.8 percent).[13]

Tatarstan constitutes the homeland for not only Tatars but other peoples of the republic as well. In the Constitution of Tatarstan, as passed in November 1992, there are guarantees for the interests of all residents of the republic, regardless of nationality, language, political position, religious conviction, or any other criteria (article 20).[14] Two languages, Tatar and Russian, have the status of state language (article 4).[15] Residents have the right to dual citizenship, republic and federal (article 19).[16]

Republic of Tatarstan policies are directed toward the growth of all its peoples. In addition to Russian and Tatar schools, 109 Chuvash, 35 Udmurt, and 19 Mari schools are also functioning.[17] Newspapers in the Chuvash, Udmurt, and Mari languages have begun publication. Since 1991, in the republic areas where Chuvash, Udmurt, Mari, and Mordva are living compactly, special governmental programs have enabled the opening of national-cultural centers, financed within the republic budget. These national-cultural centers have entered into direct cultural and practical exchanges with other republics of the greater Volga region. In 1992, an Association of National-Cultural Societies was founded. Various existing societies have become members of this association; for instance, the Jewish national-cultural center "Menorah" (in existence since the end of the 1980s), a German cultural society, a Slavic cultural society, Mari and Chuvash cultural centers, the Bashkir society "Bashkort Iorto," the "Kazakhstan" society, the worker's association "Magrifat," and the cultural workers' group "Madaniat." The goal of this umbrella association was construed to be the coordination of the activities of members, their mutual enrichment, and the propagandizing of national cultures as a way toward mutual national trust and civil harmony in the republic.

To encourage interethnic agreement, trust, and mutual respect, a Congress of the Peoples of Tatarstan was held in May 1992. For many centuries, relations among the region's nationalities have been peaceful and neighborly. In current conditions, with a growth in national self-identity and the politicization of ethnic consciousness, the soundness of those relations is being tested.

As a whole, relations among the peoples of Tatarstan are considered relatively stable, and the Tatars are relatively optimistic. In June 1992, three-quarters of the Tatars and more than half of the Russians considered that interethnic relations would improve or stay the same.[d] It should be noted that despite this general stable interethnic context, there was nonetheless sensitivity to the fluctuations of the political situation in the country as a whole and within the republic.

Sociopolitical issues

In Tatarstan it is possible to differentiate conditionally three main sociopolitical blocks, according to their basic ideological orientations: the *national*, including the Milli Mejlis, the Tatar Public Center, Ittifak, the Republican Party, the youth group Azatlyk, and the Sovereignty movement; the *democratic*, including the local branch of the Democratic Party of Russia [*Dem(okraticheskaia) Rossiia*], the Republican Party of the Peoples of Tatarstan [*Narody Tatarstana*], Citizens of the Russian Federation [*Grazhdany Rossiiskoi Federatsii*], the movement "Accord" [*Soglasie*], the People's Front [*Narodny Front Tatarstana*], and others; the *socialist*, including organizations of Tatarstan's communists, the group "Worker's Union," and others.

The main idea of the ethnonational-oriented organizations is the concept of renewal for the Tatar nation, the development of its culture. While the most radical wing (Ittifak, Azatlyk, Milli Mejlis) is not very popular among the masses, the program of the Tatar Public Center (VTOTs) is more so. Their founding documents advocate a sovereign state for all of the peoples of Tatarstan with two state languages recognized, Tatar and Russian. They also call for creating special conditions for Tatar national development, since Tatarstan is the only place in the world where this can be accomplished. The Tatar Public Center's second [revised] program has come to be used by Tatarstan's government as part of its guidelines for policy.[e]

Democratically oriented parties and programs mostly incorporate demands for democratic reforms in political life and for Western-style changes in the economy. When they began their activities, they paid little attention to national interests *per se*. Later they began to defend the interests of the Russians, and of the Russian Federation in relevant [treaty] discussions. But their rating is not very high. It was less than 4 percent (3.5 percent) by the end of 1992.[18]

Socialist parties, whose main demands are civil equality and social justice, have maintained some degree of popularity. By the end of 1992, their rating was 7.6 percent.[19]

Having been born on the wave of society's democratization in 1989–90, and reaching a peak of popularity in 1990–91, by 1992 many of these groups were losing the sympathy of the masses. By the end of 1992, more than two-thirds (66.8 percent) of the population did not sympathize with any sociopolitical organization, whereas in August 1991 this figure was 46.9 percent.[20]

Parallel with the growth of social apathy in the population, there has nonetheless been a strengthening of trust in the government of Tatarstan and its policies. An indication of this was the republic referendum of March 21, 1992, in which over 60 percent voted for Tatarstan as a sovereign state, a subject of international law, with the ability to build its own relations with the Russian Federation and other republics and governments on the basis of equal agreements.[21]

The Republic of Tatarstan has every basis for changing its state status: the historical experience of having its own governance, as well as economic, scientific, and cultural potential. It should be noted that the question of changing the republic's status arose during preparation of the constitution in 1937 and 1977, and was also discussed at the time of the [Soviet] Union agreement in 1990–91. Only the disintegration of the USSR prevented Tatarstan from achieving the status of a union republic.[f]

After the breakup of the Soviet Union, with the creation of cross-republic economic ties, industrial decline, and an increasingly widespread socioeconomic crisis in Tatarstan and a number of other republics, it became necessary to search for a more self-sufficient route out of the complex situation. This was all the more clear when the Declaration of the Sovereign Russian Federation itself indicated the right of all peoples to self-governance. The federal center's policy was to drag out questions of national-governmental structures within the country, and there was considerable delay in the preparation of the new constitution. Further complicating the political situation was the fact that the Federal Treaty was prepared without a well-planned mechanism for its realization.

The Republic of Tatarstan insisted on a two-sided agreement [rather than signing the Federal Treaty] on the principle that the relations of the republics with the Russian Federation should be based on a mutual delegation of rights and powers through equal and voluntary negotiation. Delegation, as seen by Tatarstan, should be initiated fully from below (from the subjects) to the top, to the federal organs. With this formula, political, economic, cultural, and legal ties can be preserved within the Russian Federation, thus ensuring its wholeness. Indeed, only in this way can a truly democratic federal state evolve.

The center nonetheless has attempted to limit the powers of the republics, dividing power between the republics and the federal organs in order to maintain ultimate dependence on the center. The conception and actions of Russian power have continued to be in the direction of ruling a unitary state.

The process of negotiating an agreement between fully authorized delegations from Tatarstan and Russia has dragged on for over two years. In that time, there have been a number of changes in the Russian leadership, creating change in the composition of the Russian delegation. After each round of negotiations, the Russian members achieve an understanding of Tatarstan's position, and arrive at specific agreements. However, then they are replaced and negotiations must begin again. By the summer of 1993, seven agreements were signed out of twelve that had been prepared by Tatarstan. How this will continue in the current chaos is hard to predict.[g]

The Russian center accuses Tatarstan of separatism, and thus the center is violating its own declaration of human rights. But the point is not separation from Russia or continuation within it—the stereotyped view—but the formulation of new, responsible, and responsive norms of mutual cooperation and relations. In current conditions the sovereignty being sought has a functional rather than territorial character. What is being contested are legal rights with specific goals rather than geographic distances.[22]

Editor's notes

a. "Konstitutsiia," *Izvestiia Tatarstana*, 10 November 1992; cf. Dmitrii Mikhailin, "Voina Konstitutsii?" *Rossiiskaia gazeta*, 11 November 1992, p. 2. A major additional event that has occurred since this chapter was written is the February 1994 bilateral treaty between Russia (signed by President Yeltsin) and Tatarstan (signed by President Shamiev), finally regularizing Tatarstan's relationship within the Russian Federation. The treaty, composed of parts worked out since 1992, is titled "O razgranichenii predmetov vedeniia i vzaimnom delegirovanii polomochii mezhdu organami gosudarstvennoi vlasti Respubliki Tatarstan" (manuscript circulated through the Ministry of

Nationalities, and the Committee for Federal Affairs and Regional Politics under the Russian duma). Mechanisms for its implementation were further discussed during President Yeltsin's trip to Tatarstan in May 1994. Indicative of its role as a potential model, similar agreements were subsequently signed by Bashkortostan (Anatolii Kopsov) and Russia (Viktor Chernomyrdin) in May 1994. For more on the Tatarstan agreement, see, for example, Boris Vorob'ev, "Shag k soglasiiu i progressu," *Vecherniaia Kazan, 15 March 1994, p. 1. See also Mukhammat Sabirov, "My vnosim nalogi v federal'nyiu kaznu,"* *Nezavisimaia gazeta*, 10 October 1993, p. 3; Marat Galeev, "Tatarstan i problemy reforma," *Nezavisimaia gazeta*, 28 December 1993, p. 4.

b. The Soviet system supported some "national-language schools" in which children were taught in their native languages, but in practice these schools were being phased out at the autonomous republic level in the 1970s and 1980s or were converted to mixed-language programs. For background, see Karen A. Collias, "Making Soviet Citizens: Patriotic and Internationalist Education in the Formation of a Soviet State Identity," in *Soviet Nationality Policies*, ed. Henry Huttenbach (London: Mansell, 1990), pp. 73–93. Cf. M.N. Guboglo, *Sovremennye etnoiazykovye protsessy v SSSR* (Moscow: Nauka, 1984). On Tatar culture and diaspora, see the chapter by R.G. Kuzeev and Sh.F. Mukhamed'iarov in this book, and see A. Karimullin, *Tatary: Etnos i etnonim* (Kazan: Academy of Sciences, 1989).

c. The politics of the more radical groups, particularly with regard to their Islamic identity, is not stressed here, mainly because they have been more noisy than mainstream. There is also an Islamic Democratic Party of Tatarstan, founded in 1991. Nonetheless, it is worth mentioning that in the early 1990s, activists of the Ittifak, Vatan [Homeland], and Azatlyk groups staged demonstrations for months in the main square of Kazan demanding secession from Russia and, unrealistically, return of lands that had been Tatar before Ivan the Terrible conquered the Golden Horde in 1552. See, for example, "Tatarstan—Ploshad' Svoboda Kipet," *Pravda*, 17 October 1991, p. 1. For background, see D.M. Iskhakov and R.N. Musina, eds., *Sovremenny national'nye protsessy v respublike Tatarstan* (Kazan: Academy of Sciences, 1992); Azade-Ayse Rorlich, *The Volga Tatars: A Profile in National Resilience* (Stanford: Hoover Institution Press, 1987).

d. The author is using her own ethnosociological research here. See also *Tatarstan naperekrestke mnenii. Problemy, tendentsii, perspektivy* (Kazan: Academy of Sciences, 1993). This work is being updated in 1994 by Roza Musina, as part of the project "Postcommunist Nationalism, Ethnic Identity, and Conflict Resolution in the Russian Federation," directed by Leokadiia Drobizheva, funded by the MacArthur Foundation.

e. While a "rating" is not given here for the all-Tatar Public Center (VTOTs), founded in 1988 as TOTs, its popularity in the republic has been considerable, judging by its successful agitation for the March 1992 referendum, in which a majority of republic citizens (not only Tatars) voted for "sovereignty." One of its leaders is Damir Iskhakov, who has worked with Roza Musina on ethnosociological projects. Its revised program, including ecological and tax policies, was established at a congress in February 1991, and has in part been used as the basis for negotiations with Moscow over delegations of federal rights and obligations. See also Roza Musina, "Sovremennye etnosotsial'nye protsessy i etnopoliticheskaia situatsiia v respublike Tatarstan" (September 1992 conference in Prague on Women in International Security, or as "Modern Ethnosociological Processes and the Ethnopolitical Situation in the Republic of Tatarstan," in *Winds of Change: Ethnic Conflict Resolution in Eastern Europe and the Former Soviet Union* [Washington, DC: Brookings Institution Press, forthcoming]).

f. One theory regarding Tatarstan's original lack of union-republic status is that it involved Stalin's political revenge for the national communism of later-jailed Tatar leader Mir-said Sultan-Galiev, who first sought union status in 1922. Union republics were given mainly to those national groups with over a million in population, and on this basis the Tatars qualified. See Z. Ziubchenko, et al., "O tak nazyvaemoi Sultan-Galievskoi kontrrevoliutsionnoi organizatsii," *Izvestiia TsK KPSS*, 1990, no. 10, pp. 75–88; Alexandre A. Bennigsen and S. Enders Wimbush, *Muslim National Communism in the Soviet Union* (Chicago: University of Chicago Press, 1979).

g. As mentioned above, a treaty was signed in February 1994. The treaty gives Tatarstan some important tax relief and permits considerable economic independence, while placing Tatarstan legally within the framework of the Russian Federation. Before the agreement, Tatar President Mintimir Shamiev refused to encourage Tatarstan citizens to vote in the Russian Federation December elections, but afterward, in March 1994, elections to the Russian duma were held. See "Est' itogi, pochti shto okonchatel'nye," *Izvestiia Tatarstana*, 16 March 1994, p. 1.

Notes

1. *Itogi Vsesoiuznoi perepisi naseleniia 1989 g.* Vol. 2. *Natsional'nyi sostav naseleniia Tatarskoi ASSR* (Kazan, 1990).

2. *Itogi.*

3. D.M. Iskhakov, "Etnicheskaia istoriia," in *Tatary i Tatarstan* (Kazan, 1993), p. 18.

4. *Itogi.*

5. *Mnogonatsional'nyi Tatarstan (informatsionno-spravochnyi material)* (Kazan, 1993), p. 22.

6. M.I. Ganiev, "Sotsial'no-etnicheskaia struktura nauchnykh kadrov respubliki Tatarstan i nekotorye problemy ee optimizatsiia," *Sovremennye national'nye protsessy v Republike Tatarstan.* issue 1. (Kazan, 1992), p. 93.

7. *Mnogonatsional'nyi Tatarstan*, pp. 23–24.

8. Ia.Z. Garipov, "Etnicheskie i sotsial'no-kul'turnye aspekty rosta molodykh gorodov v Tatarstane XX v.," in *Tatarstan—strana gorodov* (Naberezhnye Chelny, 1993), p. 9.

9. F.G. Ziiatdinova, S.P. Dyrina, and F.I. Urmancheev, "Narodnoe obrazovanie v molodykh gorodakh respubliki," in *Tatarstan—strana gorodov* (Naberezhnye Chelny, 1993), p. 33.

10. *Itogi.*

11. *Mnogonatsional'nyi Tatarstan*, p. 48.

12. Ziiatdinova, et al., p. 32.

13. *Tatarstan naperekrestke mnenii. Problemy, tendentsii, perspektivy* (Kazan, 1993), pp. 47–51.

14. *Konstitutsiia Respubliki Tatarstan* (Kazan, 1993), pp. 54–55.

15. *Konstitutsiia*, p. 51.

16. Ibid., p. 54.

17. Ziiatdinova et al., p. 30.

18. *Tatarstan naperekrestke*, pp. 47–51.

19. Ibid., pp. 47–51.

20. Ibid., p. 47.

21. *Konstitutsiia.*

22. G. Islamov and A. Miller, "Natsionalizm v SSSR i Vostochnoi Evrope," *Obshchestvenny nauki i sovremennost'*, 1992, no. 1.

Cultural Norms in the Baikal Region

Zoia P. Morokhoeva

The entire structure of social life usually becomes problematic in a situation of social crisis. In intensely critical moments, a feeling arises among the members of a society that "we can't go on living like this." It is then and only then that there appears the need to change the norms regulating the existing social order. It should be emphasized that only in such circumstances does a true opportunity arise—a unique chance to create new norms in the culture. Being conscious that society in Russia today finds itself in just such a situation, the author of this article justifies the need to rethink the cast-in-stone stereotypes in the ways people interact with their world, nature, and society that have developed in the culture of the region around Lake Baikal.

The author realizes that in using the concept of "the Baikal region," she is provoking the reader to raise objections concerning the validity of such a concept. Given the modern-day cultural crisis situation of the nationalities residing around Baikal, when a breakdown—both of the traditional and the modern in social phenomena, and of society and nature—is clearly evident, one can hardly insist on a holistic approach to such a cultural phenomenon as the Baikal region.

In this text, what the author has in mind by the concept of the Baikal region is the culture characterized by a balance between the natural-climatic and sociocultural traditions of the ethnic groups populating the territory around Lake Baikal. Such a culture existed here until the twentieth century. In characterizing it, we can note the existence of certain stable standards of human behavior in this region that are distinct from those found in other cultural areas of the planet. Influencing the formation of the culture of the Baikal region were such factors as: (a) a combination of various traditions

Russian text © 1993 by the author. "O kul'turnykh normakh v baikal'skom regione." Original manuscript, 10 pp. Translated by Stephan Lang and published with the author's permission.

of human relations with nature, formed in conditions of various natural zones—steppe, forest-steppe, taiga; (b) a coexistence of various ethnic groups, with cultural traditions occasionally mutually excluding one another, but in the conditions of living as neighbors, exchanging elements of their ethnocultural traditions, leading eventually to the creation of a more general syncretic culture (an example of this is the proximity of the Semeiki and Buryats); (c) the nature of the region around Lake Baikal as a border between the cultures of the Christian West and the Buddhist East. These world religions likewise influenced the formation of the cultures in the Baikal region. Indeed, starting in the seventeenth century, these different religious traditions adapted, both to one another and with the existing cultural traditions, thus constituting a unique feature of the region.

In order to observe change in those ideas that define the way in which humans interact with nature and society, and which in the past were inherent to the culture of the Baikal region, the author will make use of the concept of a world model, or, what is the same thing, a picture of the world.

A.Ia. Gurevich, in revealing the content of the world model, writes that "such concepts and form of perception of reality as time, space, change, cause, fate, number, the relation between the sensory and the extrasensory, the relation between the parts and the whole," these universal concepts are associated with one another in each culture, forming something akin to a "world model"—that "grid of coordinates through which people perceive reality and build an image of the world existing in their consciousness" (Gurevich, 1984, p. 30). He defines this concept in the following manner: all of a person's behavior is guided by the "world model" that has evolved in a given society; with the help of its categories, a person selects impulses and notions coming in from the outside world and transforms them into the data of internal experience.

These principal categories in a sense precede the ideas and worldview formed by a society's members or groups, and therefore, no matter how different from one another the ideology and convictions of these individuals and groups might be, one can find at their root those obligatory concepts and notions that are basic for the whole society, without which it would be impossible to build any ideas, theories, or philosophical, esthetic, political, or religious concepts and systems whatsoever. The named categories form the principal semantic "tool-kit" of a culture. The obligatory nature of these categories for all of members of the society needs to be understood, needless to say, not in the sense that the society consciously imposes them on people. What we are referring to here is an unconscious imposition by society and [its] equally unconscious perception, an "absorption" of these categories and notions by the society's members. . . . These categories have been imprinted on the language, as well as in other sign systems (in the languages of art, science, and religion), and to think about the world without making use of these categories is just as impossible as thinking outside the categories of language. . . . It must be assumed that within the framework of one civilization, all of these categories do not represent a chance selection, do not form a closed system, and the change of one set of forms is associated with a change in others (Gurevich, pp. 30–32).

Following Gurevich, the author accepts the concept of culture as a world model. This definition of culture seems to me to be imperative for the revelation of those goals set forth in the article, specifically because the concept "world model" expands one's notions of cultural norms. In the Soviet scientific literature, falling within the meaning of the concept "cultural norm" are notions concerning "a certain rule, standard, or principle of activity recognized by the social organization (system, group) and in one form or another designated for fulfillment by its members" (see *Filosofskii entsiklopedicheskii slovar'*, p. 128). The concept of a world model, on the other hand, includes the idea that the system of values of a given culture is exercised by the society not only by means of those norms, rules, standards, and principles of activity that are perceived and exist as obligatory in society's consiousness, but also in an indirect manner—unconsciously. The latter signifies that a culture's system of values is included in the world model by the organization of this world model itself and by the content of the categories characteristic of it. It is as if the world model suggests and imposes those values that are immanently inherent to it. These values fall into the notion of the world as of a certain whole. They are not perceived by the people living in a specific culture, but are nonetheless present in their consciousness on the basis of deep convictions concerning the way in which the world (nature, society) is made up and how they ought to behave in relation with this world. One believes that the world is the way it appears before one, and that there exist no other possible [courses of] action for oneself as a subject. To put it another way, the system of norms in a specific culture, understood as a world model, consciously and at the same time unconsciously gives form to the relations between a person and nature. But even for those norms that exist as norms of behavior in the social consciousness, the world model is their ultimate justification.

Now we already have the necessary technical conceptual tools in order to determine the question that the author has raised in this article. Underscoring that research into the problem of cultural norms in the Baikal region requires a notion of the culture of the Baikal region itself as a world model, it becomes possible to raise the question of the causes of its crisis today and of the possible avenues for overcoming this crisis.

It ought to be obvious, even to those readers who are not believers in economic determinism, that there exists a cause-and-effect relationship between the culture and the natural conditions of the Baikal region. The huge potential formed in connection with a rift in the physical fields in this region has conditioned the presence of intensive exchange processes in all of the strata of the earth's crust, both in the air and on the land. There is no doubt that all of this cannot fail to have an effect on the processes of species formation of the flora, fauna, and other forms of life. It is not by accident that up to 90 percent of the endemic species of the animal and plant kingdom, which are not found anywhere else on Earth, dwell here.[a] And all of this has to a certain extent influenced the formation of the specific features of the way of life of humans and their ways of adapting to the natural environment.

The harshly continental climate, with its severe winters and hot summers, and, correspondingly, with its sharp swings between the nighttime and daytime temperatures of the atmosphere and the consequences of such influences on nature, has unavoidably flung humans into an extreme situation, in which they had to adapt the conditions of their existence to the swings in the natural cycles. In consequence, a culture developed in the clan-tribal society of hunters and livestock-breeders living in the Lake Baikal region, which aided in the adaptation of the population to the natural climatic conditions.

In the traditional preindustrial culture, preserved here until the early twentieth century, humans lived in nature and perceived their connection with and complete dependence on nature. Ancient humans adapted their actions to natural rhythms, and in consequence, the cultural norms regulating all of their behavior restricted the limits of their activity. For example, a hunter could not kill a female animal because by violating this prohibition he could negatively influence the size of the population, thereby infringing on the balance of nature, with harm to himself. Examples can likewise be given of how, in their economic activities, people observed the norms of such behavior in relation to nature, so that the results of their actions did not provoke irreversible processes in nature.

The mutual interaction between humans and nature in traditional society was based on a belief in the existence of a certain spiritual force that gave life to all that surrounded people and to people themselves. Traces of these animistic outlooks continue to exist today. Beliefs in the presence of local spirits have been preserved in the Lake Baikal region. A multitude of religious sites on the lands surrounding Lake Baikal, as well as along the lake itself, continue to retain their significance as before. It should be emphasized that not only the Buryats, but also members of other ethnoses living here, likewise revere these places.

Until very recently, these worldviews were regarded as religious vestiges, and therefore state policy attempted to displace them as a phenomenon impeding social progress. This attitude was retained even when it already had become apparent that the industrialization of the region had led to a whole series of various types of catastrophes: the erosion of soils, afforestation and shoaling of the rivers whose waters flow into Lake Baikal, and the destruction of the balance of the lake's ecological system brought about by the construction of industrial enterprises that polluted the atmosphere, soil, and waters of Baikal, poisoning its fauna and flora.

Today it would be a truism to point out that the solutions to all these crises must be sought not only in improved industrial technologies, but also in a profound rethinking of the position of humans in relation to the world. However, it is hardly possible to create a new attitude toward the world without taking into account the cultural foundations of the former traditional unity between humans and nature.

This is all the more true in light of the point that all of us who live along Lake Baikal must remember that a unique culture exists here, albeit one that has been significantly destroyed, but thanks to which Baikal and the surrounding region retained their primordial nature and unviolated ecological environment to the middle of the twentieth century. Turning to this culture would not only improve understanding, but could create better norms for an improved attitude of humans toward nature. It was noted above that this culture arose as a meeting place of the cultures of the West and East. In consequence of its geographic situation, starting in the seventeenth century, the region began to acquire significance as a bridge between the West and the East. With the change in the role and significance of the countries of the Asian-Pacific region in the modern world community, Russia has found itself faced with the need to develop a policy in relation to the East that takes these new conditions into account. In connection with this, the Baikal region has been given a unique opportunity in which, participating in the development of the regional aspects of such a policy, it could make use of the experience of its past traditions for future generations. It is possible that as a result of the study of the traditions of the culture that arose here as some kind of integrated whole consisting of various elements, the prerequisites would be created for dialogue between the cultures of the West and the East, and through this, the foundation of interaction between Russia and the countries of the Asian-Pacific region.

The author is concerned about the fate of Lake Baikal and the ecological environment in this region. There is no reason to repeat all the arguments that have been expressed in support of maintaining the lake's purity. It is enough to recall that approximately one-fifth of the world's fresh water reserves are in Lake Baikal. Intensive use of fresh water in modern industry leads to the gradual exhausting of its reserves throughout the world. Science has confirmed that the so-called "greenhouse effect" really does influence the reduction of water reserves on the land surface. To this should be added the consequences of pollution and the dropping of the level of underground waters. Already a shortage of underground waters is being felt in many of the world's industrial regions, for example, in Belgium, Germany, and Switzerland.

Lake Baikal's crisis situation is being brought about by the same factors as the breakdown of traditional culture in the region.

The author considers that the processes of industrialization that began in the late nineteenth and early twentieth centuries in Siberia, and in particular the Lake Baikal region, stimulated a fundamental change in attitudes of autochthonic nationalities toward the world. The process of transforming nature along the Western model, which followed because technologies developed along principles of Western science seeped into the region, required a fundamental restructuring of the consciousness of the people living in the Lake Baikal region.

Characteristic of the autochthonic nationalities—the Buryats and Evenks—was an attitude toward the world whose primary principle is that all actions are to be performed in agreement with nature and the cosmos. The new position in relation to the world, developed through industrialization, ruled out in its very foundation this unity between humans and nature. The underlying principles of such a position, as has already been noted above, were rooted in the content of the Eastern Orthodox religion. Let us examine this matter in greater detail.

The mentality of the West in relation to nature arose under the influence of Christian teachings, according to which humans were created in the image and likeness of God, as a being equipped with an immaterial soul. In consequence of this, humans ended up above nature. According to medieval beliefs, humans were the crown of all of God's creation. They could thus subordinate all of nature to their will without restrictions. In particular, there appeared the conviction in Western Christianity that humans are capable of imitating God only when, just like their Creator, they have a creative and constructive approach toward the surrounding world. These convictions became so firmly entrenched in the world model of Western culture that they served as the foundation for all ideologies, including Marxism, which justified the necessity of industrialization as a condition for society's progressive development in the nineteenth century.

Soviet ideologists, not even being conscious of the origins of these ideas in Christianity, adopted them practically without change. One criterion for social progress was success in the struggle with nature, the subjugation of nature. In the final analysis, these ideological roots resulted in implementation of industrialization as sanctioned human interference in the normal course of natural phenomena.

Modern-day sociological materials, testifying to the changes in the lives of the native population of these parts—the Buryats and Evenks—graphically demonstrate that a partial adaptation of these nationalities to changing conditions took place during the twentieth century. People learned how to adapt their lives to the demands of industrial society. Normative attitudes toward nature characteristic of Western culture appeared in their consciousness. However, the price they had to pay for this consisted of not only the destruction of the harmony of the relations between humans and the natural environment, but also the loss of many traditional forms of accustomed life embracing the unity of humans and nature. In its stead, the culture of industrial society in this region left a spiritual emptiness. The family was destroyed. Alcoholism became a common phenomenon. Cases of psychosomatic disorders became more frequent. But most important was the loss of forms of spirituality that had given a sense of the meaning of one's existence to the people living here. After all, a consciousness of the meaning of life had been built in this region first and foremost on the sense of human connection with the cosmos, with nature, and with the clan or neighboring community in which an individual lived. The cultural norms of industrial society destroy not only the opportunity to exercise the unity of humans and nature, but even, as critics of industrial society have been pointing out since the 1960s, the exercise of a connection between the individual and society.

Specifically because industrialization, irrespective of whether it was socialist or capitalist, had at its foundation the same prerequisites that defined the relations between humans and nature, we assert that today, as we are faced with the urgent problem of the survival of the human race and of the preservation of the Baikal environment, we must study what ideas in a culture define the relations between humans and nature, and explore the possibilities of changing them.

One of the possible ways to achieve this goal is through reexamination in a modern context of past traditional norms. After all, they proceeded from a preservation of the unity between humans and their ecological environment. Consequently, first and foremost, the question must be raised of what was the world model that implemented such a unity.

As noted above, in the Western mentality that served as a fountainhead of industrial civilization, the world appears as a place for the free creativity of humanity. At the same time, the human being appears in the role of the criterion by which all things are measured. What evolves is a special relation between humans and the world created by them. As is noted by the [Belgian] scholar I. Prigogine, who studied the role of the modern scientific worldview in the formation of the relations between humans and nature: "As the leitmotiv of the world, reverential worship fades, the echo of another leitmotiv, that of dominion over the surrounding world, resonates. It is much easier to manage a world before which one does not experience reverence. Any science that proceeds from the notion of a world functioning according to a single theoretical plan and that reduces the inexhaustible wealth and variety of natural phenomena down to the cheerless monotony of the application of general laws thereby becomes an instrument, while one alien to the surrounding world appears as the master of all of this world" (Prigogine and Stengers, p. 74).

Another attitude toward the world, preserving a sense of reverence toward it, can still be observed in Eastern religions—in Buddhism, Taoism, Hinduism, and others. In all of these religions one can find a common principle, formalizing the Eastern style of thought, which the author defines as the principle of connection. It consists of the following. First, all phenomena are interconnected with one another. Second, the relations in which objects appear to the cognitive mind are not external to these objects. Such relations might be called internal, inasmuch as they define the properties of the things that appear in these relations. In such a worldview, the world appears as the aggregate of all possible connections and relations.

In contrast with this, the relations between the properties of things are external to these properties in Western thought. They do not define them. In order to understand both the properties of things and the relations between them, the philosophy of the West assumes the existence of a substantial substratum common to all phenomena and accessible to human experience. In the convictions of the majority of Western philosophers, the essence of the latter is evident both in the properties of things and in the relations between them.

In Eastern thought, it is unthinkable to view relations that evolve between things as being external to the properties evident in these relations. In this is the essence of the conviction, characteristic to Eastern thought, that the relations between properties are not external to these properties. It is impossible in this case to imagine properties capable of existing externally to any relations. And conversely, it is impossible for one to imagine relations that would in some way be external to these properties. In such a world model, there is no need to introduce the category of a substantial substratum as a means for defining the ontological basis of both the relations and the properties of things that are evident in these relations. The aggregate of all the phenomena in the world comprise the relations between things, but not the substratum that is external in relation to them.

If this is so, then we ought to notice that the principle of connection provides the basis for a different understanding of the interrelations between phenomena. The connection between cause and effect is represented here not only in the form of a vertical connection between events or phenomena, but also in their interaction along the horizontal axis. All phenomena simultaneously condition themselves.

In Western thought, the occurrence of events is most often represented in linear form as a function of time. Thus, if *A* is the cause of *B,* then *A* precedes *B* in time. If the manifestation of this sequence is encountered sufficiently often, then it is established by science on a statistical basis as a law of nature.

On the other hand, in Eastern thought, for which the principle of connection is characteristic, the essence of the order of the universe is not exhausted just by the one orderly alternation of cause and effect. The point is not that cause and effect appear simultaneously as moments of all-encompassing connection, but the very distinction between cause and effect appears here in general as something relative. On the basis of the principle of connection, an interpretation of events becomes possible in which phenomena that are being perceived as an effect from a certain viewpoint will later, from another viewpoint and by another observer, be perceived in reverse order, where the effect turns out to have been the cause.

From what has been said above concerning the conception of cause it is possible to guess at the complexity of the notion of time in Eastern thought.[b]

The notion of time in the West evolved by the modern era under the influence of classical mechanics and as the result of the introduction of mechanical clocks as a means of measuring time. The most widespread image of time in Western culture is the line on which are placed the events of the past, present, and future, appearing in strict consecutive order. The future, present, and past are monosemantically localized on a time line and cannot substitute for each other.

The image of time in a school of thought for which the principle of connection is characteristic can be imagined, with a significant measure of simplification, as being cyclical. Without getting into detailed explanation, we will simply note that in this conception, the definition of an event as being past, present, or future depends on the observer's viewpoint. Proceeding from the place occupied by the observer on the circle of time, the past can appear as the future, and the future can be perceived as the past. In such a concept of time, phenomena that comprise the past from the cultural tradition appear in consciousness to be at the same temporal level as phenomena in the present or those imagined in the future. One of the manifestations of such an approach is the recognition of the presence of mythical heroes in contemporary life, and the consciousness of the dependence of the future on the presence of the heroes in it. Such a concept of time makes possible the simultaneous coexistence of different "times" (clan time, tribe time, ethnic-group time), connected by a common notion of time in the annual cycle of nature's development.

The merging of various temporal cycles into a single time is conditioned by the principle of connection, so that it is impossible to think of time as something external to a specific space. Their essential unity is manifest since space defines the quality of time, and, conversely, it is impossible to imagine space without qualitative characteristics that are determined by time.

Everything discussed above allows understanding of why the adoption of a system of thought that places its crux on the principle of connection carries within itself a notion of the place of humans in nature and their connections with it that radically differs from Western notions. Eastern thought lacks that type of anthropocentrism that characterizes the Western approach to nature. In the East, the value of humanity is substantiated by the premise that humans, as the creators of culture, are at once higher than nature, yet never stop perceiving themselves as a part of nature. This in turn is associated with the point that in the school of thought defined by the principle of connection, the part is inseparable from the whole. Consequently, living in such a world model, humans cannot think of themselves as external to the whole, external to nature, external to the cosmos.

In contrast to the Western attitude toward the world, people in Eastern culture do not detach themselves from nature because there are none of the notions of human freedom created in Western culture. The juxtaposition of the world of humans as one of freedom and the world of nature as one of inevitability runs like a red thread through the tradition of European philosophy. All nineteenth- and twentieth-century thinkers who raised the problem of freedom in philosophy proceeded from this dichotomy. In so doing, the difficulties they encountered in the resolution of the problem of human freedom arose for the reason that the philosophers, proceeding from a scientific view of the world, often could not fully substantiate determinism evident in natural mutual interrelations, or relate it to the fatalistic concept of inevitability. We can take the works of I. Prigogine as an attempt to get away from such an identification of determinism with fatalism. In order to interpret order in nature, he makes use of the category of chance. His theory of unbalanced, unstable thermodynamic systems allowed him to see other possibilities for describing the world of nature.[c] Such an approach permits one to judge the mutual relations between natural phenomena from the position not of what already is, but of what is in the process of becoming and what is possible, and consequently, of chance in the formation of the world. Prigogine notes that "stability and simplicity are more likely the exception than the rule" (Prigozhin and Stengers, p. 278).

But nonetheless, Prigogine's elaborations concern the determinism–chance dichotomy only in the interpretation of phenomena in nature. However, the introduction of chance for explaining human will does not eliminate the problem of human freedom. Chance as a foundation of human will makes this will subject to the influence of a factor that it cannot control. This introduces an element of fatalism into the explanation of the actions of the will, because it succumbs to capriciousness, as it were, which for any person acts as something independent of the self, beyond the confines of those actions perceived as decisions of personal reason.

The philosophers who attempted to elaborate the problem of human freedom did not as a rule make use of the category of chance. The concept of freedom in Western philosophy is associated with the concept of the autonomy of the will and a notion of creative abilities to be found in human nature. Humans, as beings possessed of reason, can step out beyond the confines of the deterministic order of nature on the strength of their ability to create goals for themselves that do not have models in nature. In exactly the same way, humans can create the means for accomplishing goals and can adjust these means if they are inadequate for the attainment of these goals. Such a concept of the autonomy of the will does not contradict determinism in the interpretation of the scientific worldview. It finds its justification in the concept of culture as an artificial environment, in which humans live, and which was created by humans themselves. And if, in the philosophy of the Modern Era, freedom is defined as a consciousness of inevitability and the overcoming of this inevitability, the existence of a culture is exactly what proves the ability of humans to step beyond the confines of inevitability in the "natural kingdom." However, in Western philosophy yet another interpretation of freedom exists, one that negates both the scientific worldview and determinism in its explanation of human behavior. As an example, we can submit the philosophy of existentialism. The freedom of a person in this philosophy can be boiled down to the autonomy of the self, interpreted as the manifestation of the absolute independence of human consciousness from the order of the world of nature. Such an understanding of human autonomy permitted Jean-Paul Sartre to say that every person strives to become God.

In Eastern philosophy, it is unlikely that one will encounter the discussion of human freedom outside of the context of politics. The problem of freedom did not arise in Eastern thought because in Eastern culture humans were conscious of themselves as a part of a whole, closely interconnected with the entire surrounding world. In Eastern philosophical texts it is possible to find evidence that human creative nature was recognized in the East as well. But nevertheless, the philosophy of the East did not strive to place the person external to nature and society. On the contrary, the harmony between humans and the world of nature, and the need for the self to follow the traditions of society, was underscored in every possible way.

The acceptance of the Eastern world model would for us signify not only changing the relation of humans as a species with nature, but even a change in the very concept of human personality in comparison with the notions of it in the West. This Eastern concept does not contradict the notion of a personality as something capable of creativity. The harmony between humans and nature manifests itself in how deeply a person fits and dissolves, as it were, into relations with nature, how much of an organic part of the Whole of the universe one becomes. But one can express oneself fully, according to such an understanding, only taking into consideration all of the subtle connections between personal individualism and the world of nature. One's creative capabilities and the wealth of one's nature will manifest themselves when a person, resonating with the surrounding world, becomes capable not only of reflecting all of the complexity of the connections with this world, but also, joining oneself to them, of being able to transfer in creative movement that which is their essence. For example, in creating a picture, a Japanese artist prepares for years for the creative act, imagining an object until ready to transfer the essence of the object to the surface of the canvas or paper with several strokes or even a single precise movement of the brush.

The author became interested in reflecting on the peculiarities of the Eastern world model, which comprises the basis of the traditional culture of the Baikal region, after perceiving some shortcomings in the project of George D. Davis.[d] In the joint American–Russian project on Baikal land use called the Davis project, it is noted that "the basin of Lake Baikal has become the foundation for the elaboration of a new project to preserve and use land and water. The time has come for social, economic, and political changes. With the transition in Russia to a market economy and privatization arises a new attitude toward the land. Both the fate of Lake Baikal and the fate of the people living here will be determined depending on whether this new attitude will be based on a desire to live in harmony with the land and to take into account the mistakes made in the West and in other places" (*Baikal'skii region*, pp. 21–22).

But the question naturally arises of the essence of the change in the approach to the land-use policy in the region. Does not the proposed land-use project appear to be merely another in a long line of variations (although this time a comprehensive one, and in this respect, without doubt, a positive one, eliciting certain sympathies toward the developers of the project) on solutions already in existence that were supposed to have saved the ecology of a unique lake?

The authors of this project have divided all of the lands around Lake Baikal into land-use zones, taking into account not only their significance for the economy of the country today, but also their ecological vulnerability and their role in the preservation of the ecological balance in the entire Baikal region. As the primary instrument for the introduction and implementation of the solutions of the project, its authors propose legal regulation, to be used by government institutions at various levels: the federal, republic, raion, and so forth. In the project is likewise noted the need to observe the traditions of relations with nature of the native population—the Buryats and the Evenks. But these references to traditions did not find reflection in the form of any concrete measures whatsoever in the recommendations of the project.

In my opinion, the authors of the project rely too much on the force of the law. However, as can be seen from the existing experience of different countries, a law works only if it has the support of the moral consciousness of society. There has never been any actual, real rule of law in Russia. But during Soviet times, the instrumental use of the law as a supporting pillar of totalitarian power, juxtaposing law against the moral consciousness of the citizenry, fully discredited society's legal foundation. These negative tendencies have redoubled after the breakup of the USSR and the weakening of central power in consequence of the lengthy opposition between the legislative and the executive branches of power, as well as after the appearance of separatist tendencies in Russia. All of this could not but be reflected in phenomena of legal nihilism, characteristic of the state of Russia's legislation in the past two years.

Assessment of the Davis project here takes into account the fact that the project is being introduced simultaneously with a reform of the economy aimed at the creation of market conditions. As is well known, a market economy promotes the development of individualism. The individualism that will grow on the foundation of Western anthropocentrism characteristic of the worldview of the industrialization era may easily turn into an egoism aimed against nature. Proceeding from the premises of such a worldview, individuals appearing as economic agents will attempt to do everything they can to get around existing laws concerning the protection of nature. If other views of the connection between humans and nature are not introduced in society, it is entirely possible that public opinion will begin to exhibit moral apathy toward violations of the law. It is known from capitalist countries that at the beginning of the development of capitalism, as a rule, economic interests are placed higher than legal norms. For this reason it can be assumed that, in the event of the introduction of a market economy in Russia, a tendency to coordinate legal laws and economic interests will manifest itself here. On the strength of notions concerning the place of humans in nature discussed above, we may expect that doubts will be raised about the laws protecting nature. It is possible that they will be perceived as simply a lack of awareness of reality on the part of legislators.

The author of this article considers that the existing laws regulating land use in Buryatia could remain in force (and thereby avoid the danger that they might be repealed in the future under the pretext of preferring economic interests) only under the condition that reinterpretation begins to enable the holistic approach of humans to nature, and of their relations with it.

In Russia a strong tradition has evolved of seeking solutions to all social problems only at the governmental level. In so doing, appeals to people's internal, spiritual world is left by the wayside. Beyond the borders of Russia in democratic countries, this world is manifest in all the diverse forms of civil society. But this cannot serve as a reliable support in a society promoting instant action as the solution of crisis situations. From the experience of the democracies, it is known that the foundation of any civil society is the moral consciousness of the members of that society. The influence of civil society is decisive for the solution first and foremost of crises of power or natural spontaneous cataclysms.

On this basis, concerning the relation between one's behavioral norms and worldview, it follows that it is impossible to create a moral position with a cautious attitude toward nature without entirely changing the cultural norms that define the relations of humans with the world and nature. The prerequisite of such a change in the Baikal region is the existence of an already evolved Eastern tradition, associated with the culture of the region's autochthonic ethnoses.

Under the conditions of modern-day Russia, a turn to folk traditions appears to be a necessity, inasmuch as it is specifically here that we can find the foundation for a renewal of the moral foundations of society. The crisis of culture in Russia is manifested as a crisis of the principles regulating an individual's normative behavior. Ethnic traditions of family, clan, and community might, under today's conditions, create the necessary conditions for the renewal of those principles that could condition the harmonious coexistence of the individual with society as a whole.

In placing before society the task of rethinking cultural norms in the Baikal region, it is necessary to design prerequisites for the development of society in the twenty-first century. Therefore, one of the main challenges becomes the change in the status of the human personality in a given cultural space.

Public opinion should be used to help develop a system for educating citizens that would promote the training of people capable of actively participating in the process of the formation of a civil society. On the one hand, we need to develop a system of values for reforming the educational system and to create conditions for an autonomous person capable of independently setting goals and finding solutions to problems in the sphere of morals. On the other hand, it is imperative that those traditional institutions whose norms preserve an appeal to the people's internal spiritual world and that aid in the development of their moral capabilities not be permitted to disintegrate.

Before borrowing elements from that tradition, it is necessary to study that tradition as it was in the past, its present state, what has been preserved in it, and how to coordinate it with the consciousness of modern humans, because a return to the tradition in its pure form is impossible. How does one reinterpret traditional norms in modern conditions? It is necessary to organize research to find the answer to the questions raised; the results of this research could then be used in the educational system of the region.

Such research can be conducted within the framework of cultural anthropology. Such a field of scholarship did not exist in Soviet social sciences. In the American literature, it is possible to find definitions of the concept of cultural anthropology as the study of a people's "way of life" [obraz zhizni].[e] In its most general form, the topic of cultural anthropology is the study of standards and models of human behavior in a specific culture. Anthropologists usually use field research as tools for studying the culture. However, in the search for knowledge on the state of cultures in the past, the anthropologist reconstructs these cultures by making use of written sources: the descriptions of travelers, documents from the archives of the territorial administration, folkloric sources, and so forth.

Having in mind the situation as it has evolved in the Baikal region, the author of this article considers that the following problems, among others, must be the topic of cultural anthropology study here:

1. Characterization of the existing institutions that have retained a connection with the traditional past of the society, such as clan-tribal structures and communal-collective ownership of the land, concerning both the native nationalities of the region and the Semeiki Old Believers, Cossacks, and others who have come here.

2. Identification of whether the structures of traditional society have adapted in the conditions of the Soviet system.

3. Determination of the level of their breakdown.

4. Determination of the strength of the influence of the institutions of the Soviet system (the political-administrative system, the official ideology, the Soviet economy) on the region as a whole and on its individual territories depending on natural and geographic conditions. To determine the level of such influence, one could assess how strongly the ideology of industrial society has become anchored in human consciousness.

5. With the same goal, it is necessary to carry out an assessment of the results of the inter-nationality policy carried out by means of the Russification of the native population, as well as by means of control over migrational processes.

6. It is likewise necessary to study the consequences of *perestroika*, in particular the consequences for the social structures as the result of the appearance of elements of private property in the economy.

This research should in the final analysis lead to a familiarity with Baikal region individual types and the characterization of their relations with the surrounding world, identifying their cultural norms of behavior, worldview, and moral positions. Such research must be carried out concurrently with the reconstruction of the traditional worldview. Only by knowing which norms regulate behavior in modern society can we determine which elements of traditions can be used in the future development of society. We must not forget that we must educate a person who will be capable of living in the conditions of the twenty-first century and at the same time will be a true heir to traditions that have been created here for centuries and that have promoted harmony in the relations between society and nature.

Editor's notes

a. On Baikal's unique resources, see Boris Komarov [Ze'ev Wolfson], *The Destruction of Nature in the Soviet Union* (Armonk, NY: M. E. Sharpe, 1980); Ze'ev Wolfson, "Anarchy Mirrored in Lake Baikal," *Report on the USSR* May 1989, Radio Liberty Report No. 231, pp. 4–7; idem, *The Geography of Survival: Ecology in the Post-Soviet Era* (Armonk, NY: M. E. Sharpe, 1994); "Spotlight on Lake Baikal," *Surviving Together*, 1993, no. 33 (Winter), pp. 35–43; John Noble Wilford, "Soviet Lake Offers Look at Evolution," *The New York Times*, 10 August 1990, p. A6.

b. Compare this discussion of Eastern and Western concepts of time to David Landes, *Revolution in Time* (Cambridge, MA: Harvard University Press, 1983); Johannes Fabian, *Time and the Other* (New York: Columbia University Press, 1983); Stephen Toulmin and June Goodfield, *The Discovery of Time* (New York: Harper, 1965).

c. Compare Prigogine's theory to the rise in the last decade of popular Western chaos theories with a recently founded journal, *The Chaos Network*. See also Brian Kaye, *Chaos and Complexity: Discovering the Surprising Patterns of Science and Technology* (New York: Weinheim, 1993); Alexandre Favre et al., *Chaos and Determinism: Turbulence As a Paradigm for Complex Systems Converging Toward Final States* (Baltimore:

Johns Hopkins, 1995); Joanne Wieland-Burston, *Chaos and Order in the World of the Psyche* (London: Routledge & Kegan Paul, 1992).

d. The "Davis Project" is headed by the American ecologist George D. Davis, working closely with the Buryat ecology leader Sergei Shapkhaev and the American land-use attorney G. Gordon Davis. The project began in 1991; by 1993 a proposal for the Baikal region entitled "The Lake Baikal Region in the Twenty-First Century: A Model of Sustainable Development or Continued Degradation? (A Comprehensive Program of Land-Use Policies for the Russian Portion of the Lake Baikal Region)" was printed bilingually. Their views were also spread in Buryatia in part through Davis's "Ob"edini nas, Baikal," *Mezhdunarodnaia zhizn'*, 1993, no. 5–6, pp. 64–69. See also G. Gordon Davis, "Long-Term Solutions for Baikal," *Surviving Together*, 1993, vol. 11, issue 4 (Winter), pp. 35–38. Initial efforts were sponsored by the Center for Citizen Initiatives of San Francisco, the Center for Socioecological Issues of the Baikal Region, and the Russian Academy of Sciences, "at the request of the Buryat Republic, Chita Oblast, and Irkutsk Oblast." Their new "nongovernmental organization," Ecologically Sustainable Development, Inc., received an AID grant in 1993 for continued work in the Baikal region, with one subproject (directed by forester Dan Plumley) to create an "anthropological reserve" in the Okinsk region with local Buryat leaders (personal communication, G. Gordon Davis, June 1994).

e. The author used both Russian and English in the original. Classic American anthropological expressions of this point include Alfred Kroeber, *Anthropology* (New York: Harcourt, Brace, 1948), pp. 1–13. However, more complex and reflexive concepts of cultural anthropology are represented in theoretical literature such as Clifford Geertz, *The Interpretation of Cultures* (New York: Basic Books, 1973); Marshall Sahlins, *Culture and Practical Reason* (Chicago: University of Chicago Press, 1976); Sally Falk Moore, *Law As Process* (London: Routledge & Kegan Paul, 1978; and George Marcus and Michael Fischer, *Anthropology As Cultural Critique* (Chicago: University of Chicago Press, 1986).

References

Baikal'skii region v dvadtsat' pervom veke: model' ustoichivogo razvitiia ili nepreryvnaia degradatsiia? Kompleksnaia programma politiki zemlepol'zovaniia dlia rossiiskoi territorii basseina ozera Baikal. Place of publication not given, March 1993, 179 pp.

Filosofskii entsiklopedicheskii slovar'. Moscow, 1989, 815 pp.

Gurevich, A.Ia. *Kategorii srednevekovoi kul'tury.* Moscow, 1984, 2nd ed., 350 pp.

Prigozhin [Prigogine], I., and Stengers, I. *Poriadok iz khaosa. Novyi dialog cheloveka s prirodoi.* Moscow, 1986, 428 pp.

III

Symbolic Anthropology:
Seeking Riches of Folk Wisdom and
Values in Ritual and Tradition

Nina Pavlovna Geiker, Nanai craftswoman, Achin Village, Khabarovsk Krai, Amur River District. Photo gift of N.P. Geiker to M.M. Balzer, June 1991.

Birth Rituals of the Nanai

Evdokiya A. Gaer

The birth of a child among the Nanai was always a joyous event, and one that was carefully prepared. There were complicated rules for the behavior of a pregnant woman, worked out down to the last detail. In Nanai understanding, these were designed to protect the health and life of the mother and the fetus. As soon as the woman felt herself to be pregnant, her life came to be ruled by special prohibitions:

> *Dan beiun minavambani depuvesi, ekte khoraidoni miavani mangalai.*
> *Mo suembeni diulesi ivambovasi, pikte baldimi, kitapchi nieri.*
> *Diakpon bia sivucheni ilgalavasi, khokochon khadiomba angopovasi, khaivada ulpivesi, khoraori manga osi.*
> *Ele bari diulieleni, dalpochivasi, pikte beunchii dalpopchi.*
> *Ekte ele khoraidoni, khochokon diaka sivesi. Tukuru sicheni, khaida khem sicheni khem a choktaori. Tui tavasi osini, pikte baldimi mutesi osi.*

One must not eat the heart of large slain beasts, or the woman's heart will not withstand childbirth.

Wood must not be placed branches-first in the oven: the child will come out legs-first during birth.

After eight months' pregnancy, it is forbidden to do housework or sew anything "closed": the fetus might be "sewn" to the womb, and the birth will be difficult.

It is forbidden to use glue before giving birth, or else the fetus will be "glued" to the womb.

No vessels should be plugged in a pregnant woman's house before giving birth. All plugged bottles and the like must be unplugged, or the woman will not give birth.[1]

Russian text © 1991 by E.A. Gaer and "Mysl' " Publishers. *Traditsionnaia bytovaia obriadnost' nanaitsev v kontse XIX–nachale XX v.* (Moscow: Mysl', 1991), pp. 37–63. A publication of the Miklukho-Maklai Institute of Ethnography and Anthropology, and the Institute of History, Archeology, and Ethnography of the Peoples of the Far East in the Far-Eastern Division, USSR Academy of Sciences. Translated by Stephan Lang.

There were prohibitions for a pregnant woman which, if violated, could cause harm to the child in the womb or the newborn infant. A.A. Samar also told the author about these prohibitions:

> *Mo garani chapchivasi khuse pikte baldigilakhani ekte ochoi.*
> *Pava sangardolani gurpuchivesi, pikte kesu baldi.*
> *Puiuvukhe sogdata nasalbani depuvesi, pikte nasalni chaki osini.*
> *Nai godiava undiveni, khuldiveni ichedevesi, pikte nasalni kesu baldi.*
> *Dava telgechimi diliani kaltalivasi, pikte pemuni sulde baldi.*
> *Gasana, begdieni dalgachivasi, pikte begdini tatai.*
> *Edii uselte telgechiveni belechimi uselte begdiveni diapachavasi, pikte baldimi begdini diulesi nieri, nanta ana-mat baldi.*
> *But'kin nae nai eseliveni belechivesi. Belechi osini adoliksadida, kholgokta kildechiukhendi omolapi-mat aia. Tui tasi osini boiagavori.*

The birth mother must not chop tree branches: this can harm the fetus or cause an unwanted change in sex, i.e., a girl will be born instead of a boy.

She must not peer through a window opening with one eye: the child will be born cross-eyed.

She must not eat the eyes of roast fish: the child will be born with an eye sore.

She must not watch lead being melted or poured into molds: the child will have squinty eyes.

When carving red fish (salmon), the head must not be cut lengthwise: the child will have a harelip.

She must not singe a duck or its feet: the child will have cramps in its legs.

In helping her husband to skin animals, she must not hold them by the paws: the child will be born legs first and its skin will appear as though flayed.

She must not take part in a funeral ceremony. If absolutely necessary, she must girdle herself with a piece of netting or a reed rope, or else she will have a miscarriage.

N.A. Lipskaia has recorded the following prohibitions on pregnant women: they must not eat the brain of a squirrel, or the child will be excessively playful; several days before the birth, when preparing food they must not chop off the feet of animals or stun a fish with a hammer blow to the head before roasting, or the child will be born with crooked legs or a defective head; the woman must not step over a beam (*diamdia*): a large stomach may remain after the birth; she must not mend bags with handicraft articles (*khukuen*) or sacks (*potachan*) several days before the birth, or else the birth will be difficult.[2]

A number of bans extended to the husband of a pregnant woman and all members of the family. Thus, among the Nanai, the husband during the time of his wife's pregnancy should not go hunting for a long time in the forest. This ban was explained primarily by the fact that, during the last months of the pregnancy, the wife's household chores would be placed on the shoulders of the husband, and hunting (especially for sable) would take him away from the house for many months. Furthermore, in Nanai religious views, a husband's actions while hunting might adversely affect the birth and the condition of the mother and child. Supporting this belief with examples, Nanai mentioned everyday occurrences where, supposedly, the man inadvertently harmed the mother and infant.

An analogous story was told the author by E.M. Digor. A husband went hunting on the eve of a birth, heedless of the mother and mother-in-law pleading with him not to do so. Not far from the Kondon camp, he met a fellow villager, and then a flock of ducks flew overhead. They fired at the same time, and the barrel of the future father's gun burst. He returned home unscathed, but the child was born with a "split" lip.[3]

During the last month of a wife's pregnancy, a husband was forbidden to do work involving the driving of stakes, making of fences, and the like, since it was believed that these operations could be transferred to the wife and injure the fetus in the mother's womb. Nanai elders told tales in justification of these bans. One of them was told to the author by E.M. Digor. In our village of Kondon lived a family. The head of the household, father Naiakana, was planning a fishing expedition. In this process, he had occasion to drive in some poles, whereupon the top part of them became split. The wife was expecting a birth. A child was born, with everted lips and eyes closed over. The birthing mother asks her mother:

> *"Enie! Takto pilanchini iraro!" Enini undini: "Khoni efgenku nae iraori!"*

> "Mother! Take it away to the barn!" Her mother replies: "How can I take away a living child!"[4]

It was held that the harmful effects of violating a ban could be avoided by performing certain operations, for example, by smoothing out the upper split ends of two or three poles in a fence built despite the ban. Again, we cite a tale of E.M. Digor: "Night fell. A mother-in-law whispers to her son-in-law: *'Tyi mengenguchi eneru! Khodova mova eusi-taosi pilkiro!'* ('Go to the fence that was built, straighten out at least some of the flattened top ends of the poles!') The son-in-law went and did as he was told, and in the morning he was awakened by the joyous cry of the mother-in-law: *'Ge! Guchkuli angaka! Ge! Tyi tui ulendi tagokha ulen ochogokha!'* ('Look! What a handsome child! Look! You have fixed the mistake, everything is in its place!')"[5]

Two or three months before the birth, a woman would avoid intercourse with a man for hygienic reasons. At the first sign of labor, the husband or, in his absence, the father-in-law would start to build a temporary shelter, with a bedstead and a hearth.[6] This shelter was cone-shaped. Children were sternly forbidden to come near it.[7] If men or boys were present in the house at the time of the first pangs, they would hastily abandon the room, even climbing out the windows. They did this because they feared losing their hunter's luck.[8]

The Nanai explained the need for isolation of a woman during birth by the desire to avoid possible touching of hunting weapons by an "impure" woman.[a] In the opinion of V.K. Arsen'ev, this custom came about from the desire of early peoples to protect a pregnant woman from dirt and the possibility of contamination by putrefaction and other microbes abundant in the winter and summer dwellings of the scattered peoples living in the south of the Far East province.[9] One should probably agree with both views. The practical experience of many generations in dealing with a pregnant woman was shrouded in the mysticism of religious customs and rituals.

A menstruating woman was strictly forbidden to touch a husband's hunting articles and implements. "In setting out to hunt sable, the husband himself always fit out the sledge."[10] During birth, he made absolutely sure that no hunting articles were in the room. If for some reason they had been left in the house, people would say of them "they touched the blood"— "*sevue bakhani.*" It was felt that these things (gloves, stockings, shoes, hunting clothes) had to be changed, or else no animals would be found.[11]

At the first sign of labor, a woman moved to a temporary shelter. She was usually tended by an elderly woman, the midwife, who presided over the birth. The child was usually delivered in the squatting position, the mother's arms resting on a low stool.

If the birth was delayed (*silgeini*), one of the women present in the temporary shelter made an imperceptible motion of pushing with the heel (*anosi*) in the area of the mother's loins, reciting mentally "*Khonida muteunu!*" ("Help her give birth!") In a difficult birth, the woman was given to drink the slime scraped from the sheat-fish and diluted with water.[12] This generally caused vomiting; the actions induced by this may have helped induce delivery.

As medication, previously prepared shavings would be kept in birch boxes. The shavings would be made from meadow-sweet (*bolokto*), silver willow (*busukte*), and hazel (*achankora*). Usually willow shavings were preferred—they are white. The shavings were a substitute for cotton and bandages, being a common medicinal agent with bactericidal properties. Relatives and friends of a new mother brought her gifts after the delivery, including shavings in birch boxes. The infant was also covered with shavings. In the first days, the newborn was placed on the cover of the birch box, laid with shavings and a piece of cloth. After this, a light cradle (*duri*) was made of birch, and the infant placed in it. Immediately after delivery, the infant was moved to the house through an open window or hole in the wall (*kuren*), while saying allegorically, "Here, take this bone for the dog." In this way, they obfuscated the child's tracks from the evil spirit—*amban*.

The umbilical cord was cut with scissors or the woman's knife (*girso*), tied in a knot, and sprinkled with powder scraped from the inner bark of goat's willow (*varankola*). In two or three days the umbilical cord decomposed. It was then wrapped in a piece of cloth and kept, usually in the woman's needlework pouch (*khukuen*), sewed next to the place where the sewing needles were stuck. The needles also evidently provided protection. Sometimes a mother-in-law, worried that a bride would not give her son an heir, would obtain the dried umbilical cord of a woman with many children, crumble it, and pour it into the bride's food. It was believed that a childless woman could then become pregnant.

During pregnancy, if a woman felt sick, there was a ritual of passing her through a hooplike object (*solbon*). This was made from nine withes. At the bases of five of the withes were carved images of the *burkhanchiki-kirgian*, and at four tips the images of the *burkhanchiki-buchuen*.[13] The *solbon* was laced with threads in places, through which a pregnant woman was supposed to crawl. It was important not to break the threads. How she moved through this hoop was used to foretell the destiny of the future child and the woman herself. The *solbon* ritual was performed by a shamaness or shaman, who pronounced the following spell: "Let all sickness leave the woman! Let her be healthy! Let the child in her grow as fast as the river willow!"[14]

The Nanai also performed the *epileuri* ritual. This was as follows. Willow shavings were obtained and tied around the places thought to be sick. Several sprigs of bog rosemary (*senkure*) were burned. A birchbark vessel containing an infusion of bog rosemary was placed next to the sick woman. Next they took willow shavings, dipped them into this water, and performed flicking motions with them, starting at the head, and chanting: *"Enuveni chopal daliono! Khaolia terenkiguru! Khaolonkova khamniara! Tagdak-hamba tanera!"* ("Remove all sicknesses from her! Let her be well again! Let all sicknesses pass into the shavings, into the willow hoop!") The purificatory motions were performed several times, after which the shavings were plunged into the water, taken out, and splashed in the direction of the sunset. This was usually done by an elderly woman.

The woman assisting at birth would wrap the afterbirth in shavings, place it in a birch box (*khordakhin*), and hang the box from a low limb of a tree, so that dogs could not get it, nor the wind sway the branch. If the afterbirth was chewed by a dog, the woman could no longer become pregnant, and if the wind shook the box with the afterbirth the child would cry and be uneasy.

The afterbirth (*khamoroan*) and the umbilical cord (*chunguru*) were guarded against evil spirits. If the umbilical cord was lost, it was believed that the location of the newborn child's soul would "shine through" and become visible to an evil spirit (*amban*). *"Armoldo gadaigan osi paniani!"*[15]

A woman giving birth stayed in the temporary shelter until she felt herself able to walk home. Usually this took place on the same day as the birth. At home, a special place was set aside for her, near the entrance, close to the hearth—the warmest spot. She was kept away from drafts. It was feared that she might die if her blood was curdled by the cold and turned into a jelly-like mass—*sekseni buldigui.*

A strict diet was observed. Immediately after delivery, the woman drank warm water, into which was placed the powdered root of the Amur and Daur mushroom (*aukhekhin*). This medicinal root was added to all meals. Nanai considered that a woman could have wounds on her internal organs (*doni pueku*), and these had to be healed. Infusions of the roots of the dog-rose and the mushroom *aukhekhin* [*fistularia*] were drunk constantly in place of tea. As a result of prolonged observation, the Nanai were convinced that these roots are good at stopping bleeding and promote uterus contraction. If the tongue was coated, they tied bird cherry and willow shavings about the elbows, knees, ankles, and wrists, and also the neck. After fifteen to twenty minutes, they removed all the shavings. It was thought that the shavings, especially those of the bird cherry, should not be left too long on the body, as the heart could not stand it (*miavan mangalai*).

After returning home, the new mother would strictly follow additional prohibitions. She did not have the right to move freely about the home and was supposed to keep to her place until fully "purified." She ate out of special dishes. In the past, she cooked her own food, separate from the rest; starting in the 1920s and 1930s, several women began to eat from the common pot, but using their own dish.

From the moment an infant was born, the mother and her mother-in-law carefully made sure that she did not did not develop mastitis, and that her milk was good. Her breasts were massaged, and she was given a hot decoction of cereal (*boda*) to drink, into which mushroom root was crumbled. According to Nanai observations, mushroom promotes lactation in a nursing mother. If mastitis did develop, however, folk medicinal remedies were employed. It was determined at what time of the day the woman felt pain—

morning, daytime, evening, or not at all. Accordingly, they employed an abandoned wasp's nest, an ant hill, or the bladder of a sturgeon. If pains came in the daytime, a wasp's nest was applied to the sore spot, since wasps fly in and out of their nest in the daytime. If the pain intensified in the morning and evening, the contents of an ant hill were used, since ants crawl out in the morning and crawl back in the evening, and these are the times when the woman is troubled. But if the woman felt no pain during her mastitis, they used the bladder of the sturgeon or *kaluga*. They explained this healing technique thus: when a boil becomes abscessed, many openings appear at the inflamed spot, and if you cut the fish bladder in two it has the same appearance.

The first "cleansing" of the new mother occurred three days after the birth. She changed her underclothes. She would bathe in warm water, with an infusion of bog rosemary. Bird cherry shavings would be used. After the bath, she carefully poured the water into a shallow pit, without splashing any. For the time being, the dirty linen were not washed, but rolled up and stored in a certain place.[16]

Ten days after the birth, the birth mother had a second "cleansing." As the first time, she washed herself with warm water infused with rosemary. She washed her underclothes. She changed her underclothes and outer garments. Commonly, articles used during delivery were washed in standing water—a pond or a shallow pit. It was forbidden to use river water for laundry, as the current might take the dirty water throughout the river, and somewhere an evil spirit might be able to harm her and the baby. The laundered linen was kept in the proper place until the next birth. Vessels that had been used were washed and cleaned. In certain settlements of the Nanai region, the kettle, bowl, cup, and spoons were held over the fire after washing.[17]

The newborn became an object of special care for the mother and grandmother. The infant was placed in a cradle on the fifth to seventh day. There were two kinds of cradle, wooden and birchbark, among the Nanai. The birch *dura* was used right after birth and at night. The lower part of the cradle was covered with shavings or finely ground, rotting poplar (*polo khutedini*). After a bowel movement, this dressing was changed. Intertrigo was treated with a powder scraped from the brown cambium between the bark and the bast of goat's willow, or with the powderlike substance (*khululuken*) left behind by the bark beetle under the bark of the poplar. For colic, a baby was treated with a meadow herb (*dioldamikta*). The stomach and lower torso was wrapped with this, and the wrappings left on overnight. The illness usually went away after this. For flaking skin, the infant was smeared with fish oil: a sheat-fish would be caught and the layer of fat cut from its back, dried, and used as needed.

If the newborn cried for no reason, the mother watched to determine when he cried most. Protective amulets were made accordingly—images of the moon, the sun, and slippers, carved from fish skin. If the baby cried at night, the moon was hung from the cradle's handle; if in the day, the sun; if in the evening, the slippers (their shuffling sound did not let him sleep).

Sometimes a baby would scream suddenly and start crying. On these occasions, several twigs of rosemary would be lit and the cradle fumigated. The child would stop crying. This was explained as follows: the child is crying for a visitor, and with the arrival of the visitor the child becomes quiet.

The crying of an infant was also thought to be a "need" for an unborn twin.[18] In this case, the likeness of a person was carved from a piece of wood, swaddled in a piece of cloth, and placed in the cradle at the head-piece. When nursing the infant, the mother also sprinkled milk onto the "twin," believing that this would quiet the child.

There were similar birth customs and rituals among the neighboring peoples—the Ul'chi and the Nivkh. As with the Nanai, pregnant Ul'chi women strictly observed precautionary bans. They were forbidden to take part in funeral rites, to sew burial clothing, or to cook food for the wake. If a pregnant woman were forced to take part in these activities for specific reasons, she had to girdle herself with a piece of netting to avoid miscarriage.[19] She was forbidden to look at ice floes, to avoid premature delivery. In the event of a difficult birth, a husband or father-in-law made a sacrifice to the spirit-owner of the land, chanting: "Please do not make trouble!" The seams of recently sewn articles were unstitched, and the poles holding down the dry grass on the roof of the barn were moved apart.[20]

During pregnancy, a husband and other relatives were forbidden to go fishing, put corks in bottles, or sew sacks and pouches. During the last months of pregnancy, a husband was not supposed to go hunting or do anything that might harm the fetus or the mother. According to Ul'chi notions, on the eve of a delivery it was forbidden to melt lead for making spoon baits or shot pellets, and to skin fowl in the presence of the future mother: she was forbidden to look on the carcasses of skinned animals.[21]

An Ul'chi woman delivered in a specially constructed shelter. A.V. Smoliak observed that in the early years of the twentieth century, the Ul'chi had begun to construct heated dugouts or small log cabins for the use of women giving birth.[22] At the first sign of labor, a woman went to this structure. Usually the most experienced woman of the clan presided over the delivery.

Nivkh birth rituals also had much in common with those of the Nanai and the Ul'chi. According to L.Ia. Shternberg, a Nivkh woman, "knowing that she was pregnant, immediately took a number of steps to protect the fetus and ease the delivery."[23] Custom forbade her from tying things tight one month before the delivery, for according to the Nivkh anything connected with tying knots or weaving threads might adversely affect the outcome of the birth. For this same reason, it was forbidden to drive in stakes, cut wood in the path of a pregnant woman, strike her in the face, even in jest, or do anything to a stranger. If the birth was difficult, boxes were opened, patches unstitched, and rifle barrels unscrewed.[24]

A pregnant Nivkh strictly observed bans in her diet. She did not eat certain kinds of fish: trout, red fish or fish with red fins, even spawning fish, or salted or smoked fish.[25]

The husband of a pregnant woman also observed a number of prohibitions, for according to Nivkh notions he in this way encouraged a favorable outcome. "The husband never goes hunting during this time" testifies Shternberg. According to E.A. Kreinovich, "a month or two before his wife gives birth the husband should refrain from tying the sledge, driving in objects tightly, and forging iron. It is especially undesirable and dangerous to tie knots during this time.... When delivery was near, according to certain Nivkh, even the hitching of dogs to the sledge might have bad influence on the outcome. If a voyage is necessary, the future father should ask an outsider to place the collar on the dogs."[26]

The following bans were recorded by the author from informants. As of the seventh month of pregnancy, a husband was forbidden to go hunting or go any great distance to lay snares, and in the last month he was forbidden to tie nets or place nets on frames, i.e., anything involving the tying of tight knots. If a wife's delivery was difficult, the husband tried to remember which containers he had closed recently, and opened them immediately. It was believed that these operations influenced the mother's condition. According to Vladimir Renchik, one resident of the village of Makarovka during the delivery of his wife untied his braid, so that the hair fell freely onto the shoulders, loosened his belt, untied cords, undid clasps, and so forth. It was believed to be harmful to the outcome of the delivery to leave sharp objects (hatchet, awl, knife) driven into wood or boards.[27]

Structures built for delivery among the Nivkh were similar to those of the Nanai and Ul'chi.[28] But unlike the latter, the birth shelter (*lan'raf*) of the Nivkh had a gable roof (Sakhalin island) or the shape of a windbreak.[29] This was described in 1910 by B.O. Pilsudskii: "Knocked together from poles, covered in gable fashion with bark and grass, low, strewn with hay, the booth more resembles our dog kennel than a hospitable chamber for the arrival of a new inhabitant of the world, joyously awaited by its parents."[30] Among the Nanai, Ul'chi, and Nivkh, the woman was considered "unclean" during pregnancy. Therefore, the customs of these peoples prescribed a number of measures to prevent possible "defilement" of a hunter's clothing by a pregnant woman.

Thus, in the birth rituals of the peoples of the Amur it is impossible not to observe, on the one hand, a practical concern for household and sexual hygiene and, on the other, magical tabus, observance of which were to facilitate the delivery.

Rituals concerned with preservation of an infant's life played a significant role in Nanai life, for all Nanai families desired to protect the infant from sickness and death and to nourish it. The birth of a boy meant one more breadwinner—a hunter and fisherman. The birth of a girl involved a future betrothal, bride-money, and wedding. Thus, when a girl was born they would shout *"Arakia! Arakia!"* (Vodka! Vodka!)

One could only use allegory in reporting the birth of a child to friends and family. No ceremony whatsoever was held, to prevent the evil spirits learning of it. Although I.A. Lopatin writes that, on the occasion of a birth, the parents held a feast ten days later, with gifts given and much carousal,[31] our field materials do not confirm this statement. The customs of the Nanai and other peoples of the Lower Amur forbade announcing the newborn child, and this ban was unwaveringly observed, as they took pains to hide this news from the devil. Even the mother was told of the upcoming birth in allegory. Evidently, the author of the monograph "The Goldy ... " happened to record an isolated case in Nanai life.

A pregnant Nanai woman did not make clothing in advance for the future child. It was strictly forbidden to sew garments for an unborn child (*sorombori*). This was one of the major tabus: its violation was said to entail serious consequences—miscarriage, death of the woman, or difficult birth. Therefore, Lopatin's statement that "a fifteen- or sixteen-year-old Goldy girl, recently married, sews a shirt for her future first-born with great happiness and joy,"[32] is unfounded. The actions of the young woman as described by Lopatin contradict the Nanai religious views, according to which she had no right to prepare children's articles. On the same topic, A.N. Lipskii writes: "a number of religious-psychological notions and the tabus formed from them, which are strictly observed, especially before the first child, absolutely prohibit such actions."[33]

The Nanai considered only large families to be happy and prosperous. In many families, however, although ten to twelve children would be born, only one or two would survive. A woman of Dzhuen village, T.A. Khodzher, related:

Mi khun biadoni baldikham bi khomoran dolani khatan nongdido. Sagdi enimbi gusurei bichi: mimbie diokchi ivukhechi—beei diukenekheni. Khoni khoraori? Mi khai kesikui, tue bi.

I was born in the frosts of January, outside, in a shelter. My grandmother
said that, when they brought me into the house, my body was covered with a thin
sheet of ice. How could one survive? I was lucky, to this day I still live.[34]

In each Nanai family the parents performed rituals directed at preserving
the newborn's life. From the instant of his appearance in the world, the
parents and close relatives would take every precaution to divert the attention of an evil spirit from the baby. Even people of a different clan performed the *iliochiori* ritual, "placing on the feet." In the family of Deiade
Kile, all the children had died soon after birth. Their house was on the edge
of the village. On the day a new child appeared, they prepared to welcome it
in the home of a woman of a different clan at the other end of the village: a
pipe (*kuren*) was opened in two places, on the street side and inside the
house. As soon as the child was born, the woman of the other clan (*angdai
ekte*) took it and ran quickly to her house, where people were waiting for
them. The child was squeezed through the hole in a pipe into the house,
placed on the floor in the middle of the house, and everyone in the house
stepped over him, reciting: *"Ilioro! Ilioro!"* ("Get to your feet! Get to your
feet!")[35] According to Nanai beliefs, the devil lost the newborn's track in
the house of a different clan. Stepping over the child was also supposed to
confuse a pursuing evil spirit. After the ritual was performed, the woman
quietly brought the child back to its mother.[b]

In order to confuse an evil spirit, the parents of a future child sought out
in advance people willing to take the infant immediately after its birth and
become its father and mother. M.A. Tumali relates: "My mother had seven
children before me. Another two were born after me. Of these, only my
brother and I remain alive. They found another father and mother for me
before I was born. A Korean agreed to become my father. My real parents
thought it would be safer for a child among foreign people, those of a different nationality." It was believed that Nanai evil spirits are powerless over
people of different nationality. Tumali was raised in the Korean family for two
years. The parents then gave her to an uncle to raise, and this man's wife
announced that she was the betrothed of the woman's adult brother, so that the
devil was at a loss as to who this child, born two years ago, actually was.[36]

This same ritual is mentioned by V. Naimuka, from Lower Khalby village: *"Iliochimi goi naidi-da amilagoandi, enileguendi"* ("Foreigners were
asked to become the mother and father, in order that the child would stand
firmly on its feet and survive").[37]

To ensure that a devil (*amban*) lost track of the newborn, immediately
after birth the child was wrapped up and placed in a woman's sewing
pouch. This was placed in the middle of the floor, rubbish was swept in

from all four corners, and it was all covered with the ritual iron kettle. If the child cried out from beneath the kettle, those present would say they heard a sound like the knocking of something against an iron kettle, and they thought that an evil spirit had knocked against the obstacle in pursuit of the newborn's soul.[38] Nanai customs demanded that various obstacles against the evil spirit be created.

When a physically weak child was born, the ritual of passing the infant through a hooplike object (*solbon*) was performed.

The cradle played an important part in the life of the newborn. If the child was the first born, the Nanai did not prepare a cradle in advance. The first days after birth, the infant would be placed in the lid of a birch box or in a container made from withes (*soro*), laid with shavings on top of which was a piece of fabric.[39] Seven days after the birth, the mother or grandmother placed the child in the cradle and, at night, in a light birch cradle, or *duri*.[40]

The Nanai believed that the cradle used by a family that had raised many healthy children was lucky. They especially valued a cradle that was handed down from a great-grandfather or great-grandmother. In expectation of a child, the future mother would allegorically ask the owners to loan her such a cradle: *"Tyi aliova ingsokhari khaikal, khai-kal-ba etekhiguive"* ("Loan me this container so I can keep some things in it").

A.P. Khodzher, from Upper Nergen village, as she donated to the museum of ethnography a cradle that had been in her attic, said wistfully that such a thing is no longer used in our time, and added: *"Ei emue mi purilbive khem ilionkini"* ("This cradle placed all of my children on their feet").[41]

An empty cradle must not be rocked: people feared that an evil spirit could take the place of the child and injure a newborn's health. The Nanai tried to protect the cradle from the stratagems of *amban* with amulets. On either side of the handle they hung claws of the owl, lynx, wolf, and bear, hedgehog quills, dried pike jaws, animal fangs, a piece of snakeskin (found after the snake had molted). The fangs of the bear and wild boar were thought to be good amulets.[42] Boar fangs were traded outside one's clan in return for a ritual vessel (*oni*).[43] In Nanai beliefs, an amulet having no connection with the birth of a child was fearless and merciless in fighting evil spirits. A.S. Soigor from Upper Ekon' village told how of her mother's fifteen children, only she and her brother survived. In order to "set her brother on his feet," the parents obtained a boar fang from a member of a different clan in return for a black dog (blood payment—*seiukhe*) and a ritual vessel (*oni*). As to how this amulet "did its duty," Soigor reported the following. Once, in the summer, she and her grandmother were sitting at home, when suddenly they heard:

"Tassa! Tassa!" Sagdi enie ichekheni: sochan kalta enekhe. Ambandi sorimi dabdakhani.

"Tassa! Tassa!" Grandmother saw the fang split, making this noise. It had fallen in battle with an evil spirit.[44]

An infant was also guarded by a "double" ("twin"); it was given milk by the mother, and garments were sewn for it from the same fabric as those of the newborn. As the child grew, he carried it on his neck as an amulet of good luck. The "double," like the *seven*, was fumigated with smoke from the bog rosemary, and a fowl was sacrificed to it. The Nanai believed that a child having such a *burkhan* would become a successful hunter.[45] This amulet could defend the child from an evil spirit, entertain him, and afterwards help him in hunting.

Another amulet with the same significance as the "double" was the bear's tooth, which was also worn around the neck as the child grew up.[46]

L.Ia. Shternberg, in 1910, collected ethnographic museum pieces, including cradle amulets, along the Amur.[47] Among the amulets against evil spirits, P.P. Shimkevich mentions the eel head, which the Nanai hung above a child's cradle. According to him, at the end of the nineteenth century many Nanai families raised unfledged owls and eagle-owls, taken from the nest. It was thought that they also would defend a child from the stratagems of *amban*.[48]

The Nanai attributed great importance to a child's clothing: in addition to its direct functions, it also played a protective role. The child's things (bedding, blanket, garments, footwear, headwear, etc.), after being washed or dried, were not left in the street past sundown. It was feared that evil spirits could take up an abode (*diukpi*) in them.

In families where children had died soon after birth, the mother would make a special garment for a newborn. Visiting seven or nine lucky houses, she begged scraps of material from fortunate mothers who had raised many children, and from these scraps sewed a robe, or asked seven or nine fortunate mothers to sew a robe from the pieces, believing that the health of their children and their maternal good fortune would pass to her and her child through these pieces during the sewing.[49]

Sometimes an amulet garment might consist not of seven or nine pieces, but more than two dozen. Each part of the robe—the front, back, and lower part—was sewn from seven or nine pieces. M.A. Tumali had such a robe. She said that her mother even traveled to various villages, asking lucky women to sew at least a few stitches in the robe for her, "so that the devil would not know me" (*"Tui mindu tetuegue enimbi angosikhani. Goigoi ekte ulpiumi. Amban takoasi opogoani"*).[50]

When the children began to walk, again for purposes of fooling *amban* a girl would be dressed in boy's clothing, and a boy in those of a girl. One of a pair of fur boots (or any other footwear) would be placed on the left foot, one of another pair on the right foot.[51]

Objects that, according to Nanai notions, were supposed to scare off an evil spirit, were sewn on the children's clothing:

> *Guchi pikte tetueni daramadoni punchilken kitambani ulpi*
> *Tui ambamba ngeleuchi.*
> *Tetue diugdunduni mut 'ki gorimsani ulpi.*
> *Sagdi ekte dilbani pasiani diapara-da pikte tetuegueni angosi.*

> Hedgehog quills were sewn on the back of a child's robe. This was to scare the devil.[52]
> A piece of snakeskin, after molting, was sewn to the back of the child's clothes, near the neck.[53]
> Pieces from an old woman's undergarments were sewn to make a robe.[54]

Parents whose children could not "stand on their legs" asked the oldest women in the village for discarded hair from their heads. This was braided and put on the child's wrist as a bracelet, or wrapped in a piece of cloth and sewn to the child's clothing, in the hope that the long life of these women would be magically transferred to the newborn.[55] During an elderly person's funeral, their clothing was borrowed for the child.[56] Metallic shamanic mirrors (*toli*) were sewn to the child's robe for their protective properties. Commonly, when using old people's articles or hair, one recited:

> *Mene mepikhechie goidam binuenu! Mene kesilee kesiku baldivanu!*

Give of your long life! Share your good fortune!

The Nanai always treated elderly people with respect. It was believed that they played an important role in the "making" of children. The mother of a child would perform the following ritual, with the consent of an elderly woman: the corners of the robe of the child and the robe of this woman were placed one on the other, sewn together, and then cut apart, so that a piece of the child's clothing remained on the woman's clothing and a piece of her clothing on that of the child. According to Nanai beliefs, the old person's long life, wisdom, and experience passed to the child.

In addition to amulets worn on the body, a dried ruff [the fish *ersha*— Ed.], the head or jaws of a pike with bared teeth, or an eel would be nailed above the door. The head of the snakehead (*khoro diliani*) would be hung behind the window or under the eaves. A spear (*gida*) would be placed at the threshold, behind the door.[57]

When a child reached the age of three, parents performed a ritual thanking the spirits who had helped growth. They killed a pig specially fattened for this occasion. Other villagers were invited to partake.[58] However, not everyone performed this ritual.

In the village of Dada, we recorded a rare *iliochiori* ritual. (It is possible that this ritual was performed by many in olden times.) M. Bel´dy told how, in the "big houses," where there were necessarily good hunters, a revered bear's skull was always found. This was thought to protect the health and well-being of all family members. When young families left the "big house," they asked for the sacred skull to protect the newborn against the attacks of evil spirits. In the old house, the skull was fumigated with the smoke of bog rosemary and addressed with the following words: *"Ge! Nai simbie gelengdekhe! Piktei etuguesi! Ge!"* ("So! They have come for you! Protect the child! So!") After this, the sacred skull was wrapped in a garment, taken to the new home, and placed in the corner (*malo*). An offering of a fowl was placed before it. It was "kept" in this way for three years, until the child had grown. After three years it was felt that the skull had performed its task. The child was no longer threatened by the plots of evil spirits. The amulet skull was "thanked" and treated with an offering of a fowl, then returned to the "big house."[59]

Sometimes the Nanai would even try to cajole and placate an evil spirit. The most dangerous *amban* to the newborn were considered to be the spirits *sat´ka*, *sekke*, and *saika*. These were believed to pursue, torment, and kill children's souls. In Nanai beliefs, only a shaman could render them harmless by conjuring. The shaman, in "dealing" with these spirits, would force them to do good by threats and persuasions. "Placing" them in a birch box, the shaman would say the following:

> *Simbie esi de edengueni nekuri. Khaedi-da didi ambamba si etudechie! Dio edeni, ulen seven ochasia!*

> "We now make you the owner and protector of the house. You will watch out for devils, from wherever they may come! You have become the owner of the house, a good *seven*!"[60]

If the child died, in Nanai belief this meant that the shaman had not succeeded in taming these evil spirits; with impunity they "blighted" the child's soul.

The Nanai even used the death of their children for the *iliochiori* ritual. The funerals of children who died before the age of one year, particularly those who had lived only a few days, were special. According to Nanai notions, the souls of children had the appearance of birds. In order that they might "fly away" to the clan tree, they were not buried in the ground. They were wrapped in cloth and sewn up like a cocoon. Duck feathers were sewn in the area of the back, the arms, and especially the joints. A great many feathers were sewn on the head. After attaching the feathers, the whole was wrapped in a special birch article (the *toiksa*). A tree growing not far from the house was chosen and a lean-to built at its trunk. The dead child was placed on this. It was not permitted to bury it in the ground until the mother again became pregnant, or else the soul of the child would not find its path, fly away, and return to the womb of the future mother. It was especially feared that the soul of a first-born child might "get lost" and the mother would remain childless.[61] In observance of these customs, the Nanai would inter their dead children on tree limbs and in hollow trees. It was thought that these transfered the power of growth and viability to the next child.[62]

The Nanai believed that the soul of all dead children would again return to their mothers after a certain time.[c] S.G. Kile related:

> *Nantai piktei khumuidui, begdieni, ngalani siderilemi, sialbidi, ulendi bekhedi saiori. Ulendi icheuridi baldigoi. Emutu gurundule-de baldigoi.*

> Whenever you bury a child, you make a mark or bracelet on the arm or leg with a piece of coal or soot. When a new child is born, the mark can be seen. He might be born of a different woman, but in the same clan.[63]

Burials of deceased children in a way other than described above are extremely rare among the Nanai. We recorded two instances when desperate parents acted out of custom with the dead child. A.S. Soigor tells how her parents, who had only two surviving children out of fifteen, did the following with one dead infant:

> *Neku ochindoni bosodi pokonda, diolosokha takanchi olbinda, diuer takan aldandoni nere, digdakhachi. Diule talodi khuvukhechi. Tui tavokhamba kaltalaokha, umburi.*

> When the *lial'ka* stopped, they wrapped it in fabric and placed it in rock-hard clay. They put it between two hard pieces and placed a third on top. This burial is known as *kaltalaokha*.[64]

A second instance also occurred with Soigor's relatives. Agaf'ia Semenovna related:

> *Ikhon khangialani, sirgedu Geiker Tegdeuken, Pakari amini, guchi goi gurun, piktei but'kimbeni degdikhechi. Telungudu-de echie doldiva! Degdiurie-ke bue echie sarapoa! Tui takhachi, echie emunde ilira!*

On the edge of the village, at the *relka*, Geiker Tegdeuken, father Pakari, and others burned the dead child. We never even heard of this in the legends! We never saw anyone burn a corpse! They did so, but still none of their children "stood on their feet."[65]

When a grandmother or grandfather died in a family, the young parents feared that they would snatch (literally, "take away") the *namandi*, or souls of their favorite grandchildren. In order to protect the children, a special ritual was performed during the funeral. The essence of this was to break the thread tying the dead to the living—*sirekte khetuliuri*. For this, at the moment of interment (before the lowering into the grave), one end of a thread was tied to the finger of the deceased, and the other end was put into the hand of the child. As soon as this was done, the child was supposed to run home, not looking back, while someone from another clan, *angdai nai*, hit the thread with a whisk or broom, breaking it. The Nanai believed that these magical operations broke the tie of the deceased's soul to the soul of its favorite child while alive, and the tracks of this child would be covered.

Naturally, being born in difficult conditions, without medical assistance, children seldom survived, and if they did, they often became ill. Not being able to give a rational explanation to the causes of childhood diseases or death, the Nanai would try various rituals and amulets to protect a child against the action and influence of mystical forces.

Much that is common in the birth rituals and customs aimed at preserving the life of the newborn is observed among the neighboring peoples of the Nanai—the Ul'chi and Nivkh.

The Ul'chi, like the Nanai, were not wont to announce the birth of a child, or even to hold the slightest ceremony on this occasion, fearing evil spirits would learn of the coming of the newborn.[66] According to Ul'chi notions, the souls of the fetus and the child before the age of one year have the form of nestling birds, very weak and helpless. They are very vulnerable and liable to the attacks of *amban*—an evil spirit. A.M. Zolotarev and A.V. Smoliak, in their day, wrote of the Ul'chi notions about the souls of children.[67]

In the families of both Ul'chi and Nanai, relatives employed every means at their disposal to confuse the trail of a newborn. They frequently resorted to a number of particular actions. A.M. Anga tells how all her six children died, some eight months after birth, some at the age of five, six, or four years. When a seventh child, the girl Ul'iana, was born, relatives sought to protect the newborn against evil spirits by taking her from the hospital and going on unused trails through the hills and bogs to the village of Ferma. Arriving home, they removed the glass from the window frame and passed the child in through this opening. The mother came home the usual way, without the child. At home, the child was placed in the *khure*, the woman's needlework pouch, and dragging this by its bindings, nine circles were made on the floor. Next, all the rubbish on the floor was swept onto it. The pouch was then shaken off, the child removed and placed in the cradle.[68]

As complex a ritual was performed by the parents of E.K. Angina. Her mother gave birth to eleven children, of which only two survived. Ekaterina was born in the village of Auri, opposite the island of Dialdako. To cause an evil spirit to lose her trail, her parents drove the infant to Bulavo village. They rode around the island so as to approach the village from the direction of the sunrise. Upstream from the island (on the Amur), there is a narrow place. Here, a boat was dragged to the other side. They traveled down the tributary to the Amur and again rode in the direction of the sunrise. They lived in Bulavo two days and returned to Auri. In this way, they obfuscated the trail of the newborn when she was about two months old.[69]

The Ul'chi, like the Nanai, attached great importance to the cradle. An infant was placed in the cradle around one week after birth. The birth mother or her mother usually did this. Various amulets—for example, a dried-out perch or an eagle owl's talons—were hung at either side of the bow of the cradle. They were supposed to scare away evil spirits. While bear's claws could also be used as an amulet among the Nanai, the Ul'chi considered it tabu (*eneu*) to touch the bear, even for such an important purpose as the preservation of a child's life.[d] They feared he would attack the person.[70]

Hedgehog quills and dried ruff protected not only the cradle, but also the child's dwelling. They were hung behind the window or above the door.[71]

According to Ul'chi beliefs, an infant's clothing could also protect it. Hedgehog quills and metallic shamanic mirrors were sewn to the clothing for this purpose. A special robe was often sewn from scraps, which the mother collected from nine garbage heaps early in the morning, at sunrise.[72] In order to foil *amban*, boys would wear girl's clothing, and girls that of boys.[73]

In order to "put on its feet" one of the last-born children, E.K. Angina, whom we have already mentioned, performed the following ritual. In the evening, she sought out the trousers of a dead person and prepared them for the ritual. The next morning, while all were still asleep, she ripped apart the trouser legs and passed the infant nine times from one leg to the other. After this, she was sure that the *amban* had lost the child's trail.[74]

The Ul'chi trusted in the magical powers of men's and women's trousers, believing that they would confer protective properties of "getting to one's feet" on the newborn. This was reported by P.L. Dechuli: "In families where the children were dying, the parents would take the trousers from two elderly people (a man and a woman) and sew breeches for the child, one leg from the woman's trousers and the other from the man's. It was believed that devils were much afraid of these."[75]

Like the Nanai, the Ul'chi had clothing sewn for the newborn from scraps of trousers by nine women from different villages. Ordinarily, a mother requested this service of women who were fortunate in having children, hoping that their maternal luck would pass to her.

T.G. Kuisali told how only two of her sister's fifteen children survived. She performed various rituals aimed at safeguarding the child. For example, she drove the newborn to Lake Udel', where there is a rock resembling a gate. They pulled the infant through this "arch" from the sunset side to the sunrise side.[76]

Like the Nanai in the *iliochiori* ritual, the Ul'chi used purple willow withes in an *iluchuvu* ritual. They would perform the *dalapon* ritual (*solbon* among the Nanai) over a pregnant woman and the newborn. In passing the person through the *dalapon*, starting from the head and moving toward the feet, the Ul'chi shaman halted at the nine most important parts of the body to chant incantations (*iaian*). The first halting place was the forehead. "All illnesses, pass to the withes! Grow like the willow grows!" the shaman would charm the infant.[77]

The Ul'chi also had a bracelet amulet woven from the hair of the grandmother or an elderly woman. In their beliefs, this not only protected the infant, but also transfered longevity, wisdom, and the strength of adults to him.[78]

In Bulavo village, in the Kuisali family, all six children had died before the age of one. When the seventh child was born, a son, Pavel, the parents agreed with outsiders for him to be raised in their family. These became his "father" and "mother." Not relying only on this ritual, his real parents performed many others for the purpose of confusing a pursuing evil spirit. They used a ritual vessel, *odi* (*oni* in Nanai) and other articles. One of the rituals, very interesting in our opinion, was performed with a shaman. It was called *ningmako* and consisted of two parts: *ningmako* proper, and *puelepun*, though it combined many elements from the ritual of preserving the life of a child.[79] The articles from this ritual—*ningmako* and *puelepun* (to which twenty willow withes were tied)—have been preserved by Pavel's mother, T.G. Kuisali, to this day, even though her son is grown and has his own family and children. She declared that she was saving them just in case.

The Ul'chi also had a special burial for children dying before the age of one. They were wrapped in white cloth, on top of which was wound specially worked birch bark, and then tied to a tree or placed in the hollow of a growing tree. Zolotarev writes that the Ul'chi "did not consign a child dying before the age of one to the earth. The body would be wrapped in a white cloth, to which a bird's wing would be sewn. A long end would be left on the thread used to sew the wing. After this, the body was placed in a dugout coffin, through an opening in which the long end of the thread was passed, and the coffin would be hung from a tree, not far from camp. The mother would take the end of the thread, tie it to her hand, and stand at the tree. Next, the thread was broken with a stick. This would sever the connection between the mother and the child's soul, which would become a bird and fly away to the clan tree."[80]

The Ul'chi, like the Nanai, made soot marks around the wrists or ankles of a dead child, hoping that the soul would again return to their clan.[81]

A.V. Smoliak was able to record interesting rituals aimed at preserving the life of a child.[82] The Ul'chi, like the Nanai, never ill-treated the corpses of fellow clansmen, much less the body of an infant. Therefore, Smoliak views as an "exceptional case" the ritual that she recorded in the village of Dudi, "when Ul'chi parents cut up the body of their ninth dead infant and threw the pieces among the bushes, with the infant's head to the west, saying: 'Return to me no more.' "[83]

Nivkh birth rituals are similar to those of the Nanai and Ul'chi. The Nivkh strove to conceal the fact of a birth from any evil spirit. For this reason, no feast was held in the newborn's family.[84] Ch.M. Taksami writes of this: "Concerning rituals, the birth of a child was commemorated neither by the clan nor by the family. This was evidently connected with the concern to safeguard a newborn's life since, in Nivkh beliefs, there were many evil spirits, ready at any time to steal an infant's soul."[85]

The Nivkh also used various amulets to ensure their children's growth.[86] They likewise believed in the magical powers of growing trees. When children died before the age of one, the families buried them on trees. It was hoped that the children's souls in the form of small birds would fly off to the clan tree and, after a certain time, again return to their mother's womb.[87] Children that died right after birth were not cremated, but buried on trees.[88]

The Nanai had a particular system for bestowing a proper name on a child. It was important to mark his clan and family affiliation, and to individualize him among those of his clan and other clans.

The birth of a child was accompanied by his induction into the clan. The individualization of the newborn among the members of his clan began at the moment he was given a proper name. I.A. Lopatin thought that a child was given a name immediately after birth.[89] According to our field research, the infant was given a name not at once, but after two weeks to two months, or sometimes even a year.[90] Prior to this, he would be called in allegorical fashion, or various nicknames would be used.[91] During the first days after the birth, the Nanai called the child *angaka*, a sound imitation of the child's cry: *"Angak! Angak!"* with a meaning of "little one."

Personal names were given to children on the basis of certain personality attributes or features. The most characteristic names among the Nanai were the following: *Moranga* (loud one), *Sichin* (nimble), *Korokto* (earlobe), *Khoto* (balding), *Sildu* (bald), *Tente* (righteous), *Sigakta* (gadfly), *Eusi* (white salmon), *Toraki* (rook), *Daicha* (noisy), *Saila* (knowledgeable), *Aodia* (ruff fish), *Singekte* (bird cherry), *Gengie* (light, transparent), *Ara* (bran), *Khaporaki* (nimble, anxious), *Kombo* (pitcher), *Maila* (difficult), *Diuersu* (twin).

Usually names were given by the parents, but they preferred to have their child named by a grandparent or by venerable elderly members of the village. Most often, these were names that incorporated best wishes.

A personal name, distinguishing a newborn from his clanspeople, according to Nanai notions, made him vulnerable to evil spirits. The desire of the parents to protect the life of the newborn against the wiles of *amban* led to the appearance of amulet names. The Nanai, in "placing their children on their legs" (*pikteri iliochimari*), gave them names which, according to their notions, frightened or caused disgust in a devil. These were often the names: *Kachakta* (the Amur swallow), *Kuedie* (dog), *Diakta* (turf), *Logda*, *Lebe* (vomiting, trash), *Polokto* (moldiness), *Adaka* (slovenly), *Inoksa* (snot). Certain names were supposed to arouse fear in a devil: *Aodia* (prickly ruff), *Kachakta* (prickly salmon), *Nekte* (wild boar), *Kekse* (cat, scratching animal), *Keechen* (whelp, young dog, but one able to defend itself), and others.

O.F. Samar tells how his parents first gave him the amulet name *Giokhaton* (vagrant, beggar), hoping that the devil would pay no attention to such a lowly type. And when he grew up, he was named Oktiabr', in honor of the October Revolution. Only two of his mother's eight children lived. Oktiabr' Fedorovich said that his father also was given the amulet name *Suederi*.[92]

The amulet name *Suederi* is the garbled Russian name Fedor. It was thought an evil spirit would not know Russian and would pass by when the infant was called by the unknown name.

Vera Naimuka told how she had several amulet names:

> *Mi baldikhandoe tikin khuekheni. Mimbie iliochimi Tikindi gerbiekhechi. Nuchidueteni Kukuridide gerbiesikhel.*

> When I was born, the sludge ice was very thin, and so I was called *Tikin*, which means the same. I also had the amulet name *Kukuri*.[93]

In families where the children were all dying soon after birth, the new-born might have his name changed several times to confuse the *amban*. Thus, according to U.O. Kile, "they named my little brother *Garada* (twig). Then he became Grigorii" (*"Tui mi nevus Garada gerbiesikhechi. Esi-teni Grigorii ochini"*).[94]

Sometimes the Nanai gave their children names connected with the apellations of the *sevens*, of whom the *ambans* were afraid. In the village of Dzhari, D.S. Bel'dy recalled an instance when a child was given the magi-cal name *Teudu*. A devil, hearing this name, would avoid its owner.[95]

In exceptional cases, parents would name a child after a notoriously bad person. The inhabitants of Dzhari remembered the name of an evil man with a bad character—Bamba. Parents would give their newborn such a name, just to allow him to survive. Once grown, he could be given a decent name.

The Nanai did not have the custom of calling an infant after the grandfa-ther or grandmother. Until adulthood, children and grandchildren did not know the true names of their parents and grandparents. It was forbidden to say aloud the names of adults, so as not to "betray" these people to an evil spirit. If such an event occurred, it was believed that the children had pushed (*anosichi*) their parents out of the world of the living.[96] In Nanai beliefs, a person whose true name was called aloud became so defenseless and vulnerable that the safety of his life could not be guaranteed. M.A. Tumali related:

> *Iliochimari, goiva gerbugueni buri. Bue dai gurun gerbueni sarasi bichi. Esie doldipo, bue et'kepu pikteni Kuediedi gerpuku bichi. Kuedie—vechen. Iliochikhachi.*

> In order to place a child on his feet, his original name was changed to another. Nor did we know how the adults were called. We just now learned that our elder sister was called Kuedie—dog. Our parents gave her an amulet name to protect her.[97]

It often happened that, despite the protective rituals and amulet name, a child would grow up sickly. The parents would then think that an evil spirit had guessed all of their tricks, and the amulet name would be changed to another. Tumali told how she was called Sede; when she grew older, Kat'ia; and when she went to school, Mariia.[98]

Nanai neighbors, the Ul'chi, also placed great importance on the name of a child. They too refrained from giving a child a name immediately after birth. Grandparents, more often than parents, named the child. Smoliak reports that, among the Ul'chi, "names were often connected with some event." For example, *Puchandy* (harvest), *Saldanga* (fine fabric). Like the Nanai, the Ul'chi had magical names and nicknames. To safeguard a child against an evil spirit, "for the first year or two (Smoliak reports), he would be called by a nickname, such as *Zamarashka* (Slob)."[99] There were names with an unpleasant meaning: bald patch (*Khotokan*), piss (*Chiechiktu*), kaka (*Adaka*), and others.[100] By custom, it was forbidden to call a child after a deceased clan member. If two persons in the village had the same name, after one of them died the survivor would immediately change his name. It was considered dangerous to call a dead person.[101]

The Nivkh did not name a newborn right away, usually waiting for the umbilicus to fall off. The name was given to the child by the parents of fellow clanspeople. But there were times when a child was given a name right after birth. Taksami explains this as parental desire to forestall a devil in naming the child and thus prevent him from "making the child his own," i.e., killing him.[102]

Every Nivkh, in addition to their individual name, also knew their clan name. The personal name had the function of segregation, and the clan name the function of inclusion.[103] The parents tried to select for their children names that reflected their main activity: *Ovrin* (fix nets), *Byt'kan* (smith).[104] According to Taksami's observations, Nivkh names reflect "their parent's skills, occupation, and character traits." Such names include the following: *Magon* (from *mangd'*, important), *Chida* (from *chid'*, to smoke without haste), *Tiguk* (from *tid'*, to carry a load on the shoulders), *Tyrguk* (from *tyrd'*, to look),[105] *Umlin* (from *umd'*, to be angry), *Churin* (from *chur*, straight), *Motas* (from *motas*, sledge runners), *Kikun* (from *kikun*, eagle owl),[106] and so on.

The Nivkh had the custom of "giving, besides a real name (*uskr kk"a*), a 'jest' name (*lerun kk"a*). The latter was used in everyday affairs, while the real name might remain unknown to many fellow clanspeople."[107]

The Nivkh had the custom of not calling a child after a deceased clansperson, so as not to attract the attention of an evil spirit; and if a child were given such a name, it would only be several generations after the relative's death. Kreinovich notes: "You will not find Nivkh with the same name, as among the Russians. It is very bad for two people to have the same name."[108]

As we see, the name of a child among the Nanai, and their nearest neighbors the Ul'chi and the Nivkh, became an amulet against any evil spirit, reflecting main character traits and parental occupational skills, but there were no commonly used names. Even Lipskii wrote that "it is absolutely inconceivable, given their religious and psychological notions," for the Nanai to use their personal names in a common way.[109]

The world, in Nanai views, was inhabited by many evil spirits, eating or stealing the souls of children. Therefore, most of the birth rituals were directed at protecting a children from the wiles of a devil and confusing it. At the same time, many of the techniques aimed at ensuring a successful birth and the continued existence of the newborn stemmed from the experience of preceding generations and had a practical, progressive significance.

Not only the parents, but all clan members played an important role in a person's socialization. It was necessary to raise surviving children (*iliokha, iluchukhe*) as the next generation. Everything was directed at this: the strengthening of the will, children's games, the system of teaching boys and girls, the transmission of folk tradition through oral narratives, tales, legends, graphic depictions of activities, contests, and so on.

Birth rituals clearly reveal, on the one hand, a form of what is termed stimulus magic:[110] to hasten birth it is enough to untie knots in clothing, open vessels, pour out water. On the other hand, they reflect sympathetic magic: the driving of stakes, sewing of clothes, tying of nets, gluing of fabric when this could adversely affect the birth.[e]

Many magical notions are stamped on the dietary prohibitions for pregnant women.

Nanai notions about a child's soul deserve special attention. The Nanai thought that the souls of clan members are grown on a special clan tree and then enter women. Therefore, the coming of a child into the world was seen not as a consequence of impregnation, but as a result of a child's soul finding a haven in a woman's body.[f] Accordingly, children were not buried in the ground, but on trees, in their hollows and on their branches, in the form of a cocoon with bird feathers sewn on it. It was thought that the child's soul would "fly off" and again reach the clan tree.

It is important to note the similarity of the rituals of the Nanai, Ul'chi, and Nivkh. Apparently, because of their long cultural relations in the regions of the Lower Amur and Sakhalin, there were similar archaic forms of ritual connected with birth and child raising. Several features of these rituals—the confusing of the newborn's trail, the use of cradle amulets and amulets on the clothing, the special type of infant burial, and others—were characteristic not only of the Lower Amur region, but also of all Siberia.[111] Thus, many of the magical and animistic rituals of Turkic peoples are extremely similar to those of the Nanai.

It should be observed that, although magical operations were clearly predominant in the cycle of birth rituals, the Nanai, the Ul'chi, and the Nivkh did not have a conception of a single goddess, the patroness of childbirth.

All of this indicates that birth rituals of the Nanai and their neighbors go back to deep antiquity.

Editor's notes

a. For a summary and analysis of beliefs about women as "impure," see Marjorie Mandelstam Balzer, "Rituals of Gender Identity: Markers of Siberian Khanty Ethnicity, Status and Belief," *American Anthropologist*, 1981, vol. 83, pp. 850–67; and the subsequent debate in *American Anthropologist*, 1985, vol. 87, pp. 126–30. See also Thomas Buckley and Alma Gottlieb, eds., *Blood Magic: The Anthropology of Menstruation* (Berkeley: University of California Press, 1988).

b. Evdokiya Gaer told me a similar story in Washington, D.C., in November 1991. A shaman's own family had been experiencing tragedy after tragedy, as newborns died. Members of his family, trying to determine what was wrong, went to another shaman, who told them that their own family shaman was the cause, despite his best intentions. It was recommended that a subsequent newborn be brought up in another household temporarily.

c. Reincarnation beliefs are very strong and widespread across Siberia, particularly among the so-called Paleo-Asiatic groups, but also among Turkic peoples and among the Ob-Ugrians. See M.M. Balzer, "The Route to Eternity: Cultural Persistence and Change in Khanty Burial Ritual," *Arctic Anthropology*, 1980, vol. 17, pp. 77–90. Most of these beliefs, however, involve the returning of dead ancestral souls to newborns of a clan or a people. This variation is more specific, and comforting, enabling a particular mother to believe she will regain a lost child.

d. The word "tabu" has been widely used and abused in the anthropological literature, beginning at least in the nineteenth century with Sir James G. Frazer's *The Golden Bough* (e.g., New York: Macmillan, 1922). Here Evdokiya Gaer gives the specific local term *eneu*, which means something closer to a prohibition than a sin. The bear was sacred in many areas of Siberia and North America. See the classic A. Irving Hallowell, "Bear Ceremonialism in the Northern Hemisphere," *American Anthropologist*, 1926, vol. 28, pp. 1–175. But in the Amur region, rituals and prohibitions regarding the bear were particularly elaborate. See especially Alexander Zolotarev, "The Bear Festival of the Olcha," *American Anthropologist*, 1937, vol. 39, pp. 113–30.

e. These terms, as the author uses them, come from S.A. Tokarev, and are a variation on distinctions in Western anthropology. See Ari Kiev, ed., *Magic, Faith, and Healing* (New York: Free Press, 1964), pp. 12–13.

f. Anthropologists have been mocked for years for taking native stories about pregnancy literally and not believing that those they study know the "facts of life." Such discrepancies can perhaps be partially reconciled by understanding native explanations as describing what gives spiritual life to biological substance (two dimensions more often split in European than other ideologies). This Nanai explanation certainly does not preclude that adult Nanai know babies come from sex. And Amur River folklore is famous for being rife with tales, poems, and love songs of considerable explicitness. See Chester S. Chard, "Sternberg's Materials on the Sexual Life of the Gilyak," *Anthropological Papers of the University of Alaska*, 1961, vol. 10, pp. 13–23; Robert Austerlitz, "Ten Nivkh (Gilyak) Erotic Poems," *Acta Etnographica Academiae Scientiarum Hungaricae*, 1984–85, vol. 33, pp. 33–44. The latter daring poems were chanted by women during the Bear Festival, rather than in everyday life.

Notes

1. Samar, A.A., notes taken by the author in 1975, 1979, 1984 at Komsomol'sk.
2. See Lipskaia-Val'rond, N.A. "Materialy k etnografii gol'dov." *Sibirskaia zhivaia starina*, no. 3–4. Irkutsk, 1925, pp. 145–60.

3. Digor, E.M. 1981.
4. Ibid.
5. Ibid.
6. Ibid.
7. Ibid.
8. Samar, A.A. 1982.
9. Arsen'ev, V.K. "Dnevnik ekspeditsii 1914 g." Arkhiv Primorskogo filiala Geograficheskogo obshchestva SSSR, f. 1, op. 1.
10. Lipskaia-Val'rond. "Materialy k etnografii gol'dov," p. 147.
11. Digor, E.M. 1981.
12. Bel'dy, D.S. 1971.
13. The *solbon* ritual was conducted in the village of Dzhari by D.S. Bel'dy.
14. Tumali, M.I. 1975.
15. Samar, A.A. 1977.
16. Bel'dy, D.S., 1971; Tumali, M.I., 1975.
17. Dziapi, N.D., Tumali, M.I., 1975.
18. Dechuli, A.L., 1973. If a mother, after giving birth to a child, again felt birth pangs, as though a second child were being born, it was thought that the twin, although it had taken shape, was not born (*gelkini*), i.e., literally, it "dissolved, vanished."
19. See Smoliak, A.V. *Ul'chii. Khoziastvo, kul'tura i byt v proshlom i nastoiashchem.* Moscow, 1966, p. 120.
20. Dechuli, P.L. 1973.
21. See Smoliak. *Ul'chii,* p. 118.
22. See Kreinovich, E.A. *Nivkhgu. Zagadochnye obitateli Sakhalina i Amura.* Moscow, 1973, p. 339.
23. Shternberg, L.Ia. *Giliaki, orochi, gol'dy, negidal'tsy, ainy: Statistika i materialy.* Khabarovsk, 1933, p. 308.
24. Ibid., p. 336; Kreinovich, *Nivkhgu,* p. 309; Pundik, N.N., 1973.
25. See Shternberg. *Giliaki,* p. 205.
26. Ibid., p. 336; Kreinovich, *Nivkhgu,* p. 339.
27. Pundik, N.N., 1973; Renchik, V.S., 1973.
28. See Smoliak, *Ul'chii,* p. 118; Taksami, Ch.M., *Osnovnye problemy etnografii i istorii nivkhov (seredina XIX—nachalo XX v.),* Leningrad, 1975, pp. 138–39.
29. See Kreinovich, *Nivkhgu,* p. 341.
30. Pilsudskii, B.O. "Rody, beremennost', vykidysh, bliznetsy, urody, besplodie i plodovitost' u tuzemtsev o. Sakhalina." *Zhivaia starina,* nos. 1–2. St. Petersburg, 1910, p. 23.
31. See Lopatin, I.A. "Gol'dy amurskie, ussuriiskie i sungariiskie." *Zapiski Obshchestva izucheniia Amurskogo kraia,* vol. 17. Vladivostok, 1922, pp. 176–77.
32. Ibid., p. 172.
33. Lipskii, A.N., *Gol'dy*; Lopatina, I.A., *Kriticheskii obzor chasti knigi,* Vladivostok, 1925, p. 47.
34. Khodzher, T.A. 1971.
35. Ibid.
36. Tumali, M.A. 1971.
37. Naimuka, V. 1971.
38. Samar, A.A. 1978.
39. Idem. 1983.
40. Ibid. A.V. Smoliak recorded a different variant: "For nine days the infant was kept not in the cradle (*duri*), but in a simple *chumashka*" (Smoliak, A.A., "Magicheskie

obriady sokhraneniia zhizni detei u narodov Nizhnego Amura," *Sibirskii etnograficheskii sbornik*, vol. 4, Moscow, 1962, p. 275).

41. Khodzher, A.P. 1977.

42. Kile, S.G., 1971; Kile, U.O., 1974.

43. Soigor, A.S. 1973. The ritual vessel (*oni*) was also given by the parents of the groom to the parents of the bride, who suffered the loss of their daughter to the clan. But the bride brought an identical vessel with her as an amulet to protect her life in the husband's clan. The ritual vessel was used to pay a shaman for services: "finding" the souls of the sick and the dead and "dispatching" the souls of the dead to the next life (*buni*). A person saved from drowning would give an *oni* to his rescuer, and so forth.

44. Soigor, A.S. 1974.

45. Kile, Polokto. 1971.

46. Kile, U.O. 1974.

47. See Shternberg, L.Ia. "Predmety byta i glavnym obrazom kul'ta i shamanstva." *Opis' etnograficheskikh sborov v seleniiakh po Amuru. Gol'dy, udykhy*, 1910, no. 1765. The items are on display at the Institute of Ethnography, USSR Academy of Sciences (Leningrad).

48. See Shimkevich, P.P. "Obychai, pover'ia i predaniia gol'dov," *Etnograficheskoe obozrenie*, 1897, no. 3, p. 136; ibid., "Nekotorye momenty iz zhizni gol'dov i sviazannye s zhizn'iu sueveriia," *Etnograficheskoe obozrenie*, 1897, no. 3, pp. 8–9.

49. Tumali, M.A., 1971; Soigor, A.S., 1973. See also Smoliak. "Magicheskie obriady," pp. 269–70.

50. Tumali, M.A. 1971.

51. Soigor, A.S. 1973.

52. Kile, U.O. 1974.

53. Kile, S.G. (Polokto). 1971.

54. Soigor, A.S. 1973.

55. See Smoliak. "Magicheskie obriady," pp. 269–70.

56. Naimuka, V., 1971. It should be noted that, in 1971 in the Nanai region, we took down material as related by Makto Bel'dy. He thought that the clothing of a dead person was not fit for the *iliochiori* ritual ("placing on the feet"), but that the articles of living people from a different clan could be used.

57. Gaer, Tairaka, 1975; Kile, U.O., 1974.

58. Naimuka, V. 1971.

59. Bel'dy, Makto. 1971.

60. Soigor, A.S. 1973.

61. Idem. 1974. See also Ivanov, S.V. "Predstavleniia nanaitsev o cheloveke i ego zhiznennom tsikle." *Priroda i chelovek v religioznykh predstavleniiakh narodov Sibiri i Severa*. Leningrad, 1976, p. 180.

62. Soigor, N.S.; Soigor, A.S.; Soigor, A.Z. 1971, 1973, 1975.

63. Kile, S.G. (Polokto). 1971.

64. Soigor, A.S. 1974. In the burial, known as *kaltalaokha*, a thick tree was selected and a piece 1.5–2 m long, depending on the height of the dead person, was sawn off. This piece was split lengthwise with a wedge into two identical pieces. Depressions were made in both halves. In one of them, the deceased was placed. The other half was placed over this, and the corpse was thus enclosed in a block of wood.

65. Soigor, A.S. 1975.

66. Dechuli, P.L. 1973.

67. Zolotarev, A.M., *Rodovoi stroi i religiia Ul'chiei*, Khabarovsk, 1939, p. 40; Smoliak, *Ul'chii*, pp. 120–21.

68. Anga, A.M. 1972.

69. Angina, E.K. 1973.
70. Dechuli, K. 1971.
71. Dechuli, P.L. 1973.
72. Angina, E.K. 1973.
73. Anga, A. 1973.
74. Angina, E.K. 1973.
75. Dechuli, P.L., 1971; Kuisali (maiden name Duvan), T.G., 1971.
76. Angina, E.K., 1971; Kuisali, T.G., 1971.
77. Kuisali, T.G. 1971.
78. Ibid.
79. Ibid.
80. Zolotarev. *Rodovoi stroi i religiia Ul'chiei.*
81. Dechuli, P.L. 1973.
82. See Smoliak. "Magicheskie obriady," pp. 267–75.
83. Ibid., p. 272.
84. Chida, Iauk Padlina. 1975.
85. Taksami. *Osnovnye problemy etnografii i istorii nivkhov*, pp. 138–39.
86. See Kreinovich. *Nivghgu*, pp. 354–57.
87. Chida, Iauk Padlina. 1975.
88. Renchik, V.S. 1973.
89. See Lopatin. *Kriticheskii obzor*, p. 174.
90. Samar, A.A., 1979; Bel'dy, Dapsianka S., 1971. According to material of A.N. Lipskii, taken from the family by family census of the Nanai at the start of the twentieth century, 57 of 160 children under the age of one year had no name; 3 children had no name at one year of age (see Lipskii, *Gol'dy*, p. 48).
91. Samar, A.A.; Bel'dy, D.S.; Tumali, M.A., 1971, 1973, 1980, 1984.
92. Samar, O.F. 1980.
93. Naimuka, V. 1971.
94. Kile, U.O. 1974.
95. Bel'dy, D.S. 1971.
96. Soigor, A.S. 1973.
97. Tumali, M.A. 1971.
98. Ibid.
99. Smoliak. *Ul'chii*, p. 118.
100. Dechuli, P.L. 1973.
101. Idem. 1971.
102. See Taksami. *Osnovnye problemy etnografii i istorii nivkhov*, p. 142.
103. See Otaina, G.A., and Gontmakher, P.Ia. "Lichnye imena nivkhov." *Filologiia narodov Dal'nego Vostoka (onomastika).* Vladivostok, 1977, pp. 86–87.
104. Chida, Iauk. 1975.
105. Taksami. *Osnovnye problemy etnografii i istorii nivkhov*, pp. 142, 224.
106. See Otaina and Gontmakher. "Lichnye imena nivkhov," pp. 86–93.
107. Ibid., p. 89.
108. Kreinovich. *Nivkhgu*, p. 350.
109. Lipskii. *Gol'dy*, p. 48.
110. See Tokarev, S.A. "Sushchnost' i proiskhozhdenie magii." *Issledovaniia i materialy po voprosam pervobytnykh religioznykh verovanii. Trudy Instituta etnografii AN SSSR*, vol. 51. Moscow, 1959, pp. 7–75.
111. See Vitashevskii, N., "Iakutskie materialy," *Zhivaia starina*, 1915, no. 1–2; Karunovskaia, L.E., "Iz altaiskikh verovanii i obriadov, sviazannykh s rebenkom,"

MAE, vol. 6, Leningrad, 1927, pp. 25–26; Zelenin, D.K., "Tabu slov u narodov Vostochnoi Evropy i Severnoi Azii. Zaprety v domashnei zhizni," *MAE*, vol. 9, Leningrad, 1930, pp. 128–36; Vainshtein, S.I., *Tuvintsy-todzhintsy: Istoriko-etnograficheskie ocherki*, Moscow, 1961, pp. 139–41; Vasilevich, G.M., *Evenki: Istoriko-etnograficheskie ocherki (XVIII-nachalo XX v.)*, Leningrad, 1969, pp. 165–79; Gurvich, I.S., *Kul'tura severnykh iakutov-olenevodov*, Moscow, 1977, pp. 134–39; Toshchakova, E.M., *Traditsionnye cherty narodnoi kul'tury altaitsev (XIX—nachalo XX v.)*, Novosibirsk, 1978, p. 159.

A bride's father clinching a tragic deal with a matchmaker, from the play "Lookut and Niurguhun," performed on the stage of the Yakut National Theater in the 1950s. The actors are G.G. Ignat´ev and A.P. Petrov. The photo was a gift of ethnomusicologist Aisa P. Reshetnikova to M.M. Balzer.

Marriage Customs of the Yakuts (Sakha)

Platon A. Sleptsov

The Yakut wedding

Yakut marriage customs involved arranged marriages with payment of bride money and were characterized by complicated and diversified customs and rituals. In attempting to reconstruct the traditional Yakut wedding of the nineteenth and early twentieth centuries, our main sources were published works and archive materials collected by prerevolutionary and Soviet scholars on the territory of Yakutsk, Verkhoiansk, and especially Viliuisk districts of Yakutsk province. Where possible, material pertaining to Northern Yakuts was also used.

It should be noted that, apart from minor local variations, the traditional Yakut wedding of this time was characteristic of all main Yakut territorial groups—southern, central, Viliuisk, and northern.

The traditional Yakut wedding, in our opinion, consisted of four phases: (1) matchmaking or bargaining; (2) the first wedding ceremony held after payment of part of the bride-wealth [*kalym*][a] at the bride's home, and the visiting of the bride by the groom in her home; (3) the second wedding ceremony, including the bride's journey to the groom's house and a banquet there, held after full payment of the bride-wealth; (4) temporary return of the woman to her parents' home a short time after the second ceremony.

The matchmaking usually occurred in the winter months, when there was comparatively more free time. It was not customary to send matchmakers in the latter half of summer, when everyone was occupied with hay-mowing.

Russian text © 1989 by the Yakut Science Center, Siberian Division, USSR Academy of Sciences. Excerpts from P.A. Sleptsov, *Traditsionnaia sem'ia i obriadnost' u iakutov (XIX-nachalo XX v.)* (Yakutsk: "Yakutsk" Book Publishers, 1989), pp. 29–58, 119–24, 131–36, and 145–48. A publication of the Yakut Science Center, Institute of Language, Literature, and History, Siberian Division, USSR Academy of Sciences. Translated by Ronald Radzai.

According to certain testimony, the Yakuts also did not arrange marriages during the ninth lunar month (January), since a famous man was said to have arranged the wedding of his son with the daughter of the forbidding deity, D´ylga toion, during this month.[1] The matchmaker was usually the groom's father or a well-respected relative. Sometimes there were several matchmakers, in which case the main matchmaker was supposed to be thoughtful and eloquent. The bargaining as to the time of payment and the size of the bride-wealth and dowry depended on him. Matchmakers were usually men, but sometimes women also took part in this ceremony.

Having arrived at the bride's home, the matchmakers did not bring up the purpose of their visit immediately. Only after partaking of tea did they begin to talk in circumlocutions: *"Kisi keurdioio kelen olorobun"* ("I have come to ask about a person"). After this, the bride's father was given a gift of money or livestock, *uos asar* ("opening the lips") or *syngaakh khongnoror* ("opening the jaws"). This gift was to guarantee the consent of the bride's father to the wedding.[2] Among the Northern Yakuts, the matchmakers pro-ffered a similar *tumustaakh* ("sharp-nosed") gift.[3] If both parties agreed to the wedding, the bargaining (*keisetii*) began on the size of the bride-wealth, *kyys suluuta*, and dowry, *enn'e*; the time for their payment; and the holding of the wedding ceremony. The bride-wealth was established by mutual agreement. There were obligatory rituals to clinch the bargain. N.S. Berg described the ritual of *ilii okhsusar* ("hand-slapping"), which ended in a handshake, whereupon money or pelts were placed in the hand.[4] N.A. Vitashevskii mentions a similar ritual known as *iutiuliuk atastasar* (ex-change of gloves), inside which money was placed. This ritual was ob-served more often when a marriage of children was being arranged.[5] Among the Northern Yakuts, the "hand-slapping" ritual existed until the end of the nineteenth century.[6] If the matchmaking was successful, the matchmakers received a *tyl baaiyyta* (literally, "binding the word") for their efforts—a reward from the groom's parents in the form of livestock or money.[7] This concluded the bargaining.

At the end of the nineteenth and beginning of the twentieth centuries, the matchmaking ceremony among most of the Yakut population, especially the poor, was simpler. Often, the groom's father arranged the wedding, going with his son to the bride's parents. It was essential to ask the bride's permission about the marriage. If she agreed, the young people, standing in front of an icon, exchanged rings, drank vodka, and kissed. After this, the size of the bride-wealth and dowry was arranged.[8] Christian notions played the main part in this matchmaking ceremony.

After obtaining consent to the marriage, both parties began to prepare for the wedding. The interval between the bargain and the first wedding feast at the bride's house depended on the time of payment of the bride-wealth and the age of those entering into wedlock, varying from several months to several years. After paying a portion of the bride-wealth on the allotted day, the groom and his relatives set out for the bride's house. Usually this trip took place during the time of the new moon or full moon. This is explained by the belief that it was lucky to begin married life at this time.[9] The groom was attended by matchmakers—men, women, invited, and uninvited. In later times, at the end of the nineteenth century, the groom often went alone or accompanied by his father or one of the matchmakers.[10] He took with him the entire *kurum* [bride-wealth], the *kiutiueut keusiiteu* (groom's gift) and the *khoonn'osor kesii* (gift for sharing the bride's bed). It was mandatory to bring an entire boiled horse head, around which was wrapped the roasted entrails, filled with blood and fat.[11] There was a definite order in the groom's procession: in front rode the main matchmaker (often the groom's father), followed by the groom himself and all other relatives and guests bringing up the rear. There might be as many as twenty matchmakers and up to two hundred guests at weddings of the wealthy.[12] Five or six *versts* from the bride's *yurt*,[b] they killed a mare and brought the carcass with them. Arriving at the bride's house, the groom's procession rode three times in the direction of the sun around the tethering post in front of the house or around the house itself (and among the Northern Yakuts, around the tent).[13]

The bride's relatives welcomed the guests. The bride's father took the reins of the horse of his future kinsman and held the stirrup as he alighted. The bride's mother did the same. According to several sources, in the past the groom first entered the *yurt* alone, dropped to his right knee at the right side of the fireplace, and "treated" the fire, dropping pieces of meat and fat into it, while the bride's father and mother stood at the left side of the fireplace. The groom then went into the yard, changed into his festive clothing, and entered the *yurt* along with everyone else.[14] This ritual symbolized the groom's communion with the familial hearth and homage to the ancestors of the bride's house.

In the nineteenth century, the groom was the last to enter the house. He was led by a knout, which he held in his hand, head lowered and eyes closed. On entering the house, he was met by the bride's parents with an icon in their hands. The groom then brought sacks of cooked meat into the house and placed them around the fireplace, took out the horse head, pinched three pieces of fat from the eyes and threw them into the fire, and set up the head directly opposite the fireplace, giving it a "living appearance": special twigs were inserted to open the eyes, the mouth was opened, and the ears straightened.[15] After a certain time, the head was taken to the "sacred" [*krasnyi*][c] corner. Then, without disrobing, the groom was seated in the place where the bride slept and spent the entire evening sitting and facing the wall; the bride, also fully clothed, sat in the other half of the house. The groom ate separately from the guests and sent pieces of his food to the bride.[16] Thus, they actually took no part in the banquet. Among Northern Yakuts, the bride and groom were in a separate part of the tent during the banquet and food was taken to them by a child.[17]

The ritual beginning, connected with the first wedding feast, has been vividly described by I.A. Khudiakov. The main matchmaker and the bride's father entered the *yurt*. They were each given a large cup of *kumys*; standing next to each other, they turned in the direction of the sun's movement, hitting their elbows together during each turn and pouring out some *kumys*, so that there would be happiness and prosperity in the house. After this, they dropped to one knee, facing each other, drank a little *kumys*, knocked their knees together three times, turning in a circle each time, and asked each other a symbolic question three times: *"En tuokh dien sanalaakhkhyn?"* ("What is your thought?"). *"Sylgy, ynakh elbeetin dien sanaalaakhpyn"* ("My thought is that horses and cattle be born"). After asking the question, they tried to drink as much *kumys* as possible. According to Yakut notions, good fortune went to whoever drank the most. This ritual was known as *tiusekhter keuriustekhtere* (literally, "the meeting of the knees").[18]

After this, guests were seated in the order in which they arrived, according to their wealth and standing. The wedding feast began with the ceremony of *kumys* drinking, starting with the groom's father. The "ritual banquet" of the Yakut wedding was comprised of such dishes as *oibon salamaat* (porridge), served in large wooden bowls (*kytakh*), *turang suorat* (simple high-quality kasha), *itin killerer khaasy* ("heat-instilling" porridge), which was always eaten very hot. When this porridge was served, none of the guests began to eat until the hostess sampled it. This custom was known as *iurdiun okhtoror* (literally, "turning up"). Various meat dishes were also served at a lavish wedding: *khaan* (blood sausage), *khatta* (mare's fat), and other things.[19] A characteristic feature of the Yakut wedding feast was the abundant food and expensive dishes with magical symbolism suggesting a rich and happy future life for the young people.

In the evening, various games and amusements began: wrestling, foot races, leaping, weight lifting, horse races, line dancing (*ohuokhai*), and story telling.

On the first night, a wedding gift, *khoonn'osor kesii*, of a cooked liver and heart was placed under the young couple's pillow. Sometimes a cup of melted butter and pancakes were placed as a gift at the head of the bed. The newlyweds were supposed to eat or at least sample the gift prepared for them during the night. This food, according to Yakut notions, had a magical significance and produced a heart-binding attachment between them—*siur-ekhterin-byardaryn kholbuullar*.[20] A similar ritual, but with different significance, is recorded by V.L. Priklonskii. On the first night, a cup with *salamat* [porridge] was placed at the head of the bed; if the bride was chaste, the groom ate all the porridge, if not, he left it untouched. In the morning, the couple's parents examined the cup.[21] The existence of these rituals testifies to the Yakuts' strict attitude toward girls' behavior. Similar in meaning is the unusual custom of placing a horse's skull underneath the newlyweds' bed as an amulet to promote fertility. In the morning, the groom sat on this skull and spoke allegorically about the first wedding night.[22] It should be noted that the obligatory use in wedding rituals of a horse head, symbolizing the entire horse, reflects the elaborate cult of the horse among Yakuts.

During the first wedding feast, the Yakuts observed a complicated ritual of bringing gifts from both parties. The bride's parents distributed some of the cattle received as bride-wealth to their relatives, who were supposed to help afterwards in collecting the dowry. This was known as *kiundiuliuiur*, "bestowal with honor." Such gifts were given only to invited guests, *yngyr-yylaakhtarga*. The matchmakers of the groom were given a "personal gift," *sobolong*, the size of which depended on the recipient's social standing. For example, in the second half of the nineteenth century, male matchmakers of wealthy Yakuts received three horses and female matchmakers received three mares.[23]

The first wedding feast usually lasted three or four days, the last evening being known as *bisirem khonuk* (the "invited evening"). Only the closest relatives and invited guests attended, after which the groom and his kinsmen went home. The groom and all those departing, on horseback, arrayed themselves in front of the doors and were each given a cup of *kumys*; they drank some of this, poured some on the temples of their horses, and returned the rest to those remaining behind. They then rode three times around the tethering post in front of the house and quickly rode off. One of those remaining behind then overtook the groom's procession and rode around it, to prevent them from "carrying away" all the good fortune with them.[24]

There is evidence that white shamans took part in the first wedding feast, *tiuse barar*, in the distant past. This is explained by the possible presence of *kusagan sanaalaakh d'on* (those with bad thoughts) or malicious shamans at the wedding. The presence of a white shaman at the wedding was a guarantee against their wiles.[25] By the end of the nineteenth century, black shamans participated in the wedding ritual only in remote settlements.[26]

In the seventeenth and eighteenth centuries, new elements appeared in the rituals of the first wedding feast, *tiuse barar*, with the adoption of

Christianity. If the couple were adults, they went to the church to be married immediately after the *tiuse barar*. The matchmaker rode in front with the icon, followed by the bride and groom, and then the parents of the couple and the guests. Among the poor, the couple rode a single horse: before the wedding, the bride guided the horse, and after the wedding, the groom.[27] In addition to the *tiuse barar* (the visit of the groom and his kinsmen to the bride's house), among wealthy Yakuts there existed *tiungiur tiuser* (a visit by the groom's father to the bride's house) and *khodogoi tiuser* (a visit by the groom's mother). These occurred prior to the *tiuse barar*: they brought some of the cattle making up the bride-wealth, reveled for two or three days, and returned home.[28] Among Northern Yakuts, the principal rituals and ceremonies of the first wedding ceremony coincided with those described above.[29]

After the *tiuse barar*, the groom was entitled to visit the bride every holiday according to *kiutiueuttiuiur*, the "son-in-law custom," which existed until the bride-wealth was paid in full. He came to spend three or four days. His behavior in the house of the bride's parents was marked by timidity and humbleness. He was bounded by certain restrictions and prohibitions. Thus, he was supposed to walk only along the left side of the *yurt*, without removing his outerwear; sit in the *khappakhchy* (girl's room), and generally show himself as little as possible to the people.[30] Studying this custom, A.N. Maksimov came to the reasonable conclusion that it has great ritual importance, since it is acknowledged to a certain degree by common law as an already fulfilled marriage. "In the visits of the groom to the bride prior to the main wedding feast (the culmination of the marriage ritual), one should see the beginning of the marriage proper; the inception of conjugal relations sanctioned by public opinion and the rules of common law."[31] In the opinion of N.P. Lobacheva, "The secret trysts of the bride and groom are a survival of the dislocal-matrilocal residence of the married couple, governed by matriarchal law."[32] On the other hand, this custom may also have been sustained for economic reasons. The time of the couple's premarital visits usually coincided with the time for full payment of the bride-wealth. Payment of this sum in installments often took a long time, primarily because the groom's family lacked adequate means.

After full payment of the bride-wealth, the ceremony of carrying the bride to the groom's house inaugurated the third stage of the traditional Yakut wedding. The groom came for the bride by himself. In the morning, a little ceremony, *barar malaasyn*, was held at the bride's house. Her close kinsfolk and certain guests were present. A white horse hide with black fringe, *kharalaakh aas tellekh*, was laid in front of the fireplace, on which the bride was placed and dressed in fine clothing.

The wedding clothing of a wealthy Yakut bride in the nineteenth century consisted of a fur or cloth cap, *chopchuurdakh d'abaka bergese*; a finely made winter coat, *buukhtaakh son*, or summer jacket, *kytyylaakh son*; a shirt, *khaladaai*; a sleeveless satin blouse, *kesiechchik*; velveteen trousers; winter boots, *tys eterbes*, or leather shoes, *saary*, in summer; fur or leather gloves, *iutiuliuk*, and a chest piece of squirrel tails, *mooitoruk*. Decorations included a silver or silk belt, *kur*; silver bracelet, *beureukh*; silver or gold earrings, *ytarga*; a necklace, *mooi simege*; braided jewelry, *susuok kiistete*; and a headband, *bastynga*, with silver chains ending in a round silver bangle, *kiun*.[33] A decoration, *kelin kebiser*, was attached to the neck piece; the front [decoration was called] *ilin kebiser*, and the back [decoration] *kyld'yy*. Sometimes the back decoration was attached to the headband. In the opinion of F.M. Zykov, this suggests that the decoration was at one time intended to conceal the bride's hair, and when this custom disappeared it came to be attached to the neck piece.[34] A special feature of the bride's wedding attire was the decoration of her trousers, *kyabaka simege*, consisting of several copper chains and beads with attached rattles hanging to the knees. When first crossing the threshold of the groom's house, the bride was supposed to sound the rattles—a sign of moral purity and virginity.[35] In the late nineteenth and early twentieth centuries, many elements of the Yakut bride's costume were made from imported materials: silk, satin, cloth, printed cotton, etc. Prosperous Yakuts took pains to clothe their daughters in finer wear. In the past, the bride was clothed in furs even in the summer. In the bride's clothing, a hidden seam was left unsewn, so as not to deprive the bride of good fortune in her married life.[36]

When the bride finished dressing, she was given a cup of *kumys* and, after "treating" the fire, she said a blessing, bidding farewell to her father's house and wishing her parents many years of happy life. When leaving the house, she held a thong of the groom's knout in her left hand as he walked in front. On a path strewn with green grass they walked to their horses, in elegant harness. It was essential that the bride's horse be light-colored. The groom tied her horse's reins to his own. The eldest of the remaining party, or sometimes the bride's father, blessed the couple, wishing them happiness and prosperity, and sprinkling *kumys* on the back of the bride's horse. Just before departing, the young couple and everyone attending rode three times around the tethering post, formerly in the direction of the sun, subsequently in the opposite direction, and then quickly rode off. The *tangara keuteugeueuchchiu* ("man with the icon") rode first around the tethering post.[37]

It should be noted that almost all Yakut wedding rituals were accompanied by blessings (*algys*) and song. Scholars distinguish seven types of *algys* accompanying the wedding rituals: the *algys* of the bride's parents, the *algys* of the bride before leaving the father's home, the *algys* when lighting the fire in the groom's house, and others. The import of all these blessings was essentially a desire for good fortune and increased wealth and well-being.[38]

The bride was accompanied by her parents, *tustaakh tiunggiur; tustaakh khodogoi*; close kinsmen, *tustaakhtar*; and invited (*yngyraalaakhtar*) and uninvited (*asasynn'ang*) guests. According to tradition, in the past a wealthy bride was also accompanied by a white shaman, *iuiunn'iut*, literally, "man leading the horse by the bridle"; a *yngyyrd'yt*, "man saddling the horse"; and other people participating in rituals—strongmen, wrestlers, racers, etc. Occasionally the bride's parents remained at home.[39] In taking his bride from the father's house, the groom left in her place a mare, which was known as *ogo onnugar keureur kesii*, "that which is given in place of the child."[40] If, on the day of the bride's journey, it was snowing heavily, the Yakuts said *euliuiutiun suolun saban kelbit kiiiit*, literally "the bride has covered the trail of her death." Rain was also considered a good omen, as it symbolized abundance and prosperity in the couple's future family life.[41]

The first to set out for the groom's house was the *syargalaakh uol* ("boy with the sledge"), who hauled the dowry. The bride's wedding procession was arranged in the following order: in front, the *tangara keuteugeueuchchiu*, the man with the icon; after him the bride's parents; after them the young couple; and finally all the guests, according to their wealth and age. In the winter, if the groom lived far away, the bride traveled most of the way on a sled and mounted her horse only when close to the groom's house. In the summer, the bride traveled the entire road on horseback.[42]

Almost all scholars have mentioned the ritual known as the *siel baaiar* (literally "hanging of the horse hair")—sacrificing to a local spirit-owner, performed on the way to the groom's house. This was done as follows: the bride tied a bunch of horse hairs cut from her horse's mane to a large old tree and beseeched the spirit-owner to look favorably upon the new resident. She knelt on one knee, pronounced an *algys*, and sprinkled the tree with *kumys*.[43] In the past, they made a tethering post, *serge*. Three young men drove three young saplings into the ground, their tops touching each other, saying: "Let these be the three main poles of the *urasa*."[44] This part of the ritual evidently suggests that the *urasa* was once a mandatory part of the bride's dowry.[d]

In addition to this ritual, both parties performed a number of obligatory rituals on the way to the groom's house, characterizing the hostility of the groups entering into a kinship relation. Several *versts* from the groom's house, the wedding train encountered a party of one, three, or nine people dressed in white on white horses. They asked: "How have you traveled, how is your health?" Abruptly turning their steeds, they galloped back again. An agile horseman from the wedding procession raced after them, trying to catch at least one rider. The reins of the captured rider's horse was tied to the horse of the last person in the train. According to Yakut notions, the bride's good fortune "stayed" with her if this was done. This ritual was known as *kiueun keurseur* (single combat).[45] In another ritual, three horsemen from each group in white clothes and on white horses took part. They met one *verst* from the groom's house, their horses collided, and they galloped off with the news of the approaching wedding train, trying to outstrip each other and be the first to report the joyful tidings.[46]

Three young people were the first to ride up to the groom's house. Going inside, they examined all the corners in silence and took up positions near the fireplace. The people there gave them each a large cup of *kumys*, which they tried to drink at one draft. This signified a "draining" of the good fortune of the groom's kinsmen. They then produced their gifts: the *uot yiyyta* ("gift to the spirit of fire"); the skin of a red fox; the *iueur yiyyta* ("gift to the spirit of the groom's clan"); the skin of a Siberian weasel; and the *d'ie n'aad'ytygar belekh* ("gift to the spirit-owner of the house"), the skin of an ermine. This ritual was known as *d'ie keureueuchchiuler* ("examining the house").[47]

The bride dismounted at a special tethering post set up on the east side of the house, not very high, so as not to attract the "attention" of evil spirits, which might result in the bride's death.[48] No one dismounted until a number of rituals connected with fire were performed. It is well known that fire played a very large part in Yakut conceptions and the spirit-owner of fire was often a clan's patron and symbol. The newlyweds' future happiness "hinged" on who struck a fire soonest—a person from the party of the groom or of the bride. This ritual was performed in the courtyard: one man struck a fire, standing on the top of the house at the chimney, another standing at the door. As soon as the tinder caught, the man standing on the roof threw it into the chimney, and the man standing at the door threw it into the house. Occasionally several people climbed up onto the roof, striking fire and vying with each other. This ritual was known variously as *uot uksar*, "the laying of fire," and *uot sardakh*, "the striking of fire."[49]

The next ritual was known as *khari kapsyyta* (literally, "the grabbing of the shank"). Two men stood next to each other at one side of the house. A raw horse shank smeared with fat was thrown to them from the other side, over the house. Each tried to be the first to catch it or grab it from the other.[50] These rituals, characterizing the rivalry of the two groups entering into kinship, attest the strength of survivals of the patriarchal clan system in Yakut daily life at this time.[e]

Only after these rituals were performed did household members take the reins of the newcomers' horses. Two maidens, *tesiin tutaachchylar*, took the reins of the bride's horse, for which they received presents from the bride—rings or coins that were hanging on each side of the bridle. Accompanied by them, the bride rode three times around the tethering post in the direction of the sun.[51] From the tethering post to the door of the *yurt* the path was strewn with green grass—the symbol of good fortune and prosperity among Yakuts.[f]

According to tradition, the bride was brought to the house with her face covered. The wealthiest brides covered their face with sables, the poorer brides with a piece of horse hide.[52] This was a magical technique for protecting the bride against evil spirits and the evil eye.

The bride was ushered into the *yurt* by a venerable, elderly woman, the *iie buolaachchy* ("named mother") or the *sieteechchi* ("woman leading by the reins"), who had traveled with the bride. She led the bride by a handkerchief, which the bride grasped. On the way from the tethering post to the house, the bride was supposed to hang up several bundles of furs and make an obeisance the same number of times (in which direction is not clear—P.S.). A wealthy bride brought *togus yiyylaakh* (nine bundles of nine kinds of pelt), a poorer bride *sete yiyylaakh* (seven bundles), and an even poorer bride *ius yiyylaakh* (three bundles).[53] Just before entering the house, the bride loosened her belt to "release" her good fortune. According to certain testimony, she was supposed to make nine deep prostrations three times as she walked to the door where the groom's parents were standing. Upon entering the house, she broke a willow branch with her chest. The branch was held by two maidens and symbolized the severance from her parents.[54]

Entering the house, the bride performed the *uot ottor* ritual, the "fire tending." According to the description of V.L. Seroshevskii, this was as follows: "In the past, when the bride was taken into the groom's house, while walking past the chimney and before taking her seat behind a curtain, she knelt at the fire, threw three pieces of meat into it, set up three torches and blew several times until they caught fire."[55] While the bride was "treating" the fire's spirit-owner and asking his blessing, the fathers of the young couple stood with their backs to her, facing west and holding cups of *kumys* in their hands. As soon as the bride finished feeding the fire, they drank the *kumys* and shouted "*urui!*" The same was done by the guests assembled in the yard. In the past, a shaman was present to bless the bride. Sometimes a blessing was also pronounced by the "named mother," who asked that the groom's kinsmen treat the bride warmly and fondly. In the nineteenth century, the shaman took part only in wealthy weddings. After the fire's spirit-owner was "treated," the bride bowed nine times to the hearth. If the young couple already had a separate house, they first rode up to it and the bride struck a fire in the hearth of her house.[56] The groom's parents tried to determine what sort of housekeeper the bride was from how she laid the fire, carefully or inattentively.[57] The "fire tending" made the bride part of the groom's clan by placating the domestic hearth's spirit-owner.[g]

After this, the "named mother" took the bride behind a curtain or to the "girl's room," where she sat until the end of the wedding without removing her outer garments. The "named mother" and her friends stayed with her. The bride was not supposed to eat with everyone else or show her face. In the past, the Yakut curtain was of birch bark. At the time of our discussion, it was made of purchased fabric. In the opinion of G.A. Bonch-Osmolovskii, the wedding curtain, having an important role (separation of the girl's corner in her parents' home) among all Turkic peoples, also acquires a different meaning in certain cases. With the vanishing of the movable wedding dwelling from use, the curtain comes to replace it in the bride's wedding train, being her own property and a necessary part of the dowry.[58] This is also confirmed by the findings of our field research. Moreover, the curtain was considered to be a magical item, safeguarding the bride.

In the nineteenth and early twentieth centuries, as mentioned, certain rituals and notions associated with Christianity played no small role in the Yakut wedding. While in the past the central *uruu* (wedding) feature was the ritual of the bride's communing with the hearth and, through it, the husband's clan, the ritual of *tangara keursiusiunnerer* ("meeting of the icons") became important. The young couple was met at the home's entrance by the groom's father holding an icon and by the mother with bread and salt. The man carrying the bride's icon also stood alongside them. The men who were present held lit tapers. The couple, holding hands, came up to them, kissed the icon, and bowed at the feet of the parents, who blessed them three times with the icons and the bread, wishing them good fortune and prosperity. After this, they drank vodka that was brought by the bride. The vodka and bread brought by the bride were known as *kiiiit tangaratyn kesiite* ("the present of the bride's icon"). The bread was placed on the icon case, and the bride's icon alongside the household icons.[59]

Then the wedding feast began. During the banqueting, members of both groups performed various rituals. At first, a pair drank specially prepared *kumys* containing finely chopped horse hair. Each tried to drink as much as possible. This was known as *byiang byld'asyyta* (literally, "taking away abundance"). Another ritual involved contestants vying to eat a piece of mare's fat as quickly as possible without touching it with their hands.[60] Various games and amusements occurred in the evening of this same day.

The young couple's bed was arranged by a venerable old woman, *oron ongoroochchu*, for which she received a cup of butter and cookies, which were brought wrapped up in the bride's blanket. This was known as the *suorgan suuta* ("gift of the blanket"). Throughout this time, the bride sat behind the curtain, showing herself to no one. In the past, the bride slept with the "named mother," who accompanied her everywhere until the parents and relatives went home.[61]

During the first half of the nineteenth century, the ritual of the greeting of the father-in-law occurred on the day after the bride's arrival at the groom's house. For this, the bride was led into the house, where she dropped to her right knee at the left side of the fireplace and "fed" the fire. Her face was covered. A shaman blessed her. Without turning around, she left the house back first, turned around, and returned, again backwards.[62] This ritual was apparently connected with the Yakuts' widespread custom of avoidance. According to tradition, the bride was not supposed to show herself to the father-in-law until his very death.[63] According to our field materials, she could show herself and talk with him and with the elder relatives only three years after performing a ritual "opening of the face." During the time in question, especially at the end of the nineteenth century, the Yakuts did not strictly observe the custom of avoidance, except for the ban on appearing before the father-in-law and other elder relatives of the groom with the head uncovered. Apparently, the ritual of the greeting of the father-in-law was a later transformation of the ritual of the "opening of the face."

The ritual *khaasakh khostoosuna* (literally "taking out of the pouch"), intimately connected with magical notions, also occurred during wedding celebrations. Two women took the articles out of the bride's chest. First, they took handfuls of small beads from the four corners of the chest and scattered them about the house. The women and children present hastened to gather them. After this, each article taken out of the chest was shown to all and carefully set aside. There was supposed to be nine of each article: nine fur coats, nine blouses, etc. After taking out all the articles, the women pierced all four corners of the chest with thin awls, reciting: "Nothing here, nothing here." This ritual was performed only at very wealthy weddings. In addition, the pouch in which the meat was brought was beaten with a switch, so that the evil spirits in it returned home.[64]

At the end of the wedding ceremony, both groups exchanged gifts. The bride's attendants—her parents and close kinsfolk—were given livestock, pelts, money, and meat. This type of gift was known as *atakh sobolongo* (literally "ransom for the legs' efforts") and was not returned in kind.[65] Invited guests also received gifts from the groom's relatives. All members of the groom's party who had received gifts from the bride's relatives repaid them with twice as much. The bride's kinsmen gave gifts (*belekh*) without requital to the groom's relatives. Such a gift was also received by the shaman, strongmen, marksmen, and others participating in the wedding rituals.[66] An interesting custom observed at very wealthy weddings in the past has been described by I.A. Khudiakov. Before departing for home, the bride's relatives were supposed to select mares for themselves, equaling the number of valuable furs that they had brought. For this, the groom's party prepared wild, unbroken horses, which were driven into a special enclosure. A member of the bride's party was supposed to catch them by hand.[67]

The holiday *uruu* usually lasted two or three days. Field materials show that the wedding feast at the groom's house formerly lasted seven days among rich Yakuts, three days among the middle class, and one day among the poor.[68]

On the day of departure of the bride's relatives, in the morning, the ceremony of the drinking of *kumys* again took place, and the young people also participated in it. While doing this, they held green grass against their right side. This meant that they were drinking up their "last" happiness. Evidently, this referred to the end of the premarital period and the commencement of the new, conjugal period. Before leaving, one of the departing blessed the bride, wishing her long years of happy life. As the relatives and guests were leaving the groom's house, the bride sat on her bed, facing the wall, until they left.[69] As soon as the bride's relatives began their journey, a horseman from the remaining party overtook them and crossed their path, so that they did not "carry away" all of the good fortune with them.[70] This concluded the wedding feast at the groom's house.

The last stage of the Yakut wedding, the ritual *teurkiutiuiu*, "returning home," involved the young woman's journey to her relatives and kinfolk for a certain time. She might begin the journey one or three years after coming to the groom's house, usually after the birth of the first child. She brought gifts with her, and every relative with whom she stayed (usually those who had received a gift at the wedding) was supposed to make her a corresponding gift of greater value. The woman went to visit relatives on this occasion only if they had been warned, when receiving their gift at the wedding, that these gifts were *iestebilleekh* ("to be requited"). Relatives who had received gifts *iestebile suokh* ("without requital") were visited without *kesii*, gift exchange. In the same way, she might also visit relatives on the father's side who had not received gifts at the wedding, if they were wealthy.[71] According to some accounts, she performed this journey without the husband; according to others, in his company. She spent two or three days with her parents and one or two with her relatives.[72]

Thus, the traditional Yakut wedding during this time occurred in four stages and consisted of two main ceremonies: first, *tiuse barar*, the journey of the groom with his relatives to the bride after paying part of the bride-wealth and the ceremonial feast at the home of her parents, and second, *uruu*, the voyage of the bride to the groom's house and the ceremonial feast there. Between these ceremonies, the groom "secretly" visited the bride in her father's home. Relatives on either side took an active part in the wedding, which shows the strength of patriarchal survivals in Yakut society.

The traditional wedding with the entire complex ceremonial was performed only for the first marriage. If the woman married a second time, the wedding was limited to performing the rituals of her conjunction with the husband's clan: *uot ottor*, obeisance to the spirit-owner of the husband's hearth, obeisance to members of the husband's clan in the person of his parents and elder relatives (ritual of the greeting of the father-in-law) and *tangara keursiusiunnerer*, the obeisance to the icons of the husband's home. If a man married a second time, the wedding was performed with the minimum of rituals.

The intricate ritual complex of the traditional wedding was fully observed among the wealthy Yakuts; among the poor, the wedding was more simple. The ritualistic ceremonial of the traditional Yakut wedding gradually became simplified. In the early twentieth century, even among the wealthy, a wedding with the full complex of ritualistic ceremonial had become uncommon. At this time, poorer Yakuts performed most of the first and second stages of the wedding: instead of the *tiuse barar* ceremony at the house of the bride's parents, they held a small family gathering, *malaashyn*, and did not observe the customs of the groom visiting the bride or the bride returning home.

In places where contact between the Yakuts and the Russian population was especially strong, the simplification of the ritualistic ceremonial of the traditional wedding occurred more quickly and many innovations appeared.

General characterization of wedding rituals

Religious cultural institutions of each nationality are the most conservative and are marked by considerable stability, especially as regards the various ritual complexes. Therefore, it may be worthwhile attempting a general structural-functional characterization of the traditional Yakut wedding of the period in question and a comparative analysis of this with the wedding rituals of other Turkic-Mongolian peoples of Southern Siberia, Kazakhstan, and Central Asia.

The wedding ritual of each people, especially in the later phases of its development, is a complicated, multicomponent structure, including elements of material culture (the wedding clothing, ritual food, attributes of participants), ritual actions (or ritual behavior of participants), and ritual folklore, i.e., oral behavior in its verbal and musical expression.[73] In a structural-functional analysis of rituals, the primary taxonomic unit is the ritual, consisting of individual elements. The elements are actions of symbolic nature to be performed in a definite sequence. Each action corresponds to a special function in the wedding and to a semantic unit or functional purpose. In turn, a group of rituals forms a ritual cycle (wedding, funeral, etc.).[74] Certain rites constitute the minimum, without which no wedding could occur.[75] The structural complexity of the wedding ritual is due to its many functions, each corresponding to a definite group of rites, appearing as substructures within the ritual. The taxonomic units themselves not only vary objectively (formally and functionally) within a substructure, but also "jump" from one segment (stage) of the ritual to another. The same is true of the ritualistic actions within a rite, substructure, or ritual. In the opinion of Iu.Iu. Surkhasko, the most significant substructures in the wedding ritual of any people are the juridical, economic, religious-magical, demonstrative-symbolic, entertainment-play, and social.[76]

Following the principle of synchronization of functions of certain rituals, we may distinguish the following substructures within the traditional Yakut wedding ritual of the nineteenth to early twentieth centuries, including four stages and, accordingly, four ritual cycles. The first includes diverse rituals of legal and economic significance. The second is comprised of rituals performing a religious-magical function. The third substructure should be assigned to the various rituals of demonstrative-symbolic nature, and it is also necessary to distinguish an entertainment-play substructure. The last substructure is the social, defining the actors' makeup, the degree and nature of their participation in the rituals.

The rituals of juridical and economic function in the wedding complex can be assembled into four main groups. First, there are rituals characterizing the relationship between the parties of the groom and the bride. These include the talks of the matchmakers or clan members on the contracting of marriage, the size of the bride-wealth and dowry, the clinching of the marriage bargain, etc. (the rituals *uos asar, iutiuliuk atastasar, talkychchy okhsusar*, and others). The juridical function may be acknowledged as predominant for this group of rituals. Second, there are the rituals that emphasize the social acknowledgment of the marriage being arranged, as manifested by the active participation in the wedding ritual of the couple's relatives and acquaintances, who provide economic assistance to the future spouses (the basic rituals performed in the second, third, and fourth stages of the wedding). The rituals of this group fulfill both a juridical and an economic function. Third, there are the ritual gifts and redemptions from both groups (gifts to the relatives of the bride and groom; the gift connected with the "treating of the table"; return gifts, etc.). The ritualistic exchange of gifts helped establish good relations between the two families and, consequently, the clans, and strengthen the position of the young woman in her new family.[77] On the other hand, as N.L. Zhukovskaia notes, the communicative action of gift and return gift, including the exchange of gifts during a wedding, is a phenomenon of global order, known not only in class societies, but also in many preclass societies. There are four levels of this communicative action.[78] In the Yakut material, the first level of this communicative action also corresponds to one of the ancient forms of marriage, the "return of the bones of the sister" or "exchange of bones." Fourth, there are rituals accompanying the preparation, handing over, and examination of the bride-wealth and dowry (for example, *khaasakh khostoosuna*, and others). This group of rituals is characterized by economic, juridical, demonstrative-symbolic, and even entertainment-play functions.[h]

Yakut wedding ritual includes a particularly prominent role for the religious-magical substructure. This should be examined simultaneously from various perspectives: specifying synchronous functions, ascertaining the types of action, and identifying a complex of methods. In the religious-magical substructure, a prominent place is occupied by rituals of apotropeic and productive magic. The apotropeic (protective) rituals, aimed at protecting those entering into wedlock against supposed hostile forces, in the opinion of E.G. Kagarov, can be divided into repelling, concealing, deceiving, and avoiding.[79] The main purpose of the "repelling" rituals is to chase or scare away hostile spirits at various times in the wedding (the blessing of the bride's wedding train upon its departure, the "opening of the chest" with some of the dowry, etc.). In addition, the wedding couple were supposed to have a number of individual protective devices, amulets. For example, the Yakut bride carried a knife with sheath, needle, scissors, etc. The concealing rituals were supposed to protect the wedding couple against evil spirits and the evil eye (the custom of covering the bride's face with a skin during the trip to the groom's house, the use of the ritual curtain, the allegorical talk during the matchmaking). "Deceiving" rituals included: the custom whereby a different girl sat on the bride's bed while the bride was traveling to the groom's house and stayed there until the bride's attendants returned; the bride's riding around the tethering post in front of her house when traveling to the groom's house, etc. Among "avoidance" rituals are avoiding an "unlucky" time to hold the wedding ceremony and refraining from inviting childless people to the wedding. The performance of protective rituals, guarding the "happiness and well-being" of the young couple against possible deliberate or accidental machinations of supposed hostile forces, is associated with the universal binary opposition: good fortune/ misfortune.

The productive (stimulating) rituals, directed at ensuring the fertility and material welfare of those entering into wedlock, are divided into rituals involving fertility magic, joining, separating, and dedicatory.[80] The custom of strewing green grass, the ritual drinking of *kumys*, and many other ritual actions are closely connected with fertility magic. The "joining" rituals are the common meal of the young couple on the wedding night, the mutual gifts to clinch the marriage bargain, etc. The "separating" rituals are represented by the bride's "breaking" the willow branch when entering the groom's house, the ritual involving "entering" a new period of life, etc. The main purpose of the "dedicatory" rituals is to acquaint the young couple with the various spirits, such as the spirit-owner of the domestic hearth, the spirit-owner of the locality, and other deities.

An important place in the religious-magical substructure is held by the rituals of propitiatory magic, involving various kinds of treating and feeding—for example, the "treating" of the spirit-owner of the house or hearth. A separate group is formed by rituals associated with the broad system of cults: the cult of the family's spirit-protectors, the ancestors, local spirit-owners, hearth spirit-owners. Special notice should be taken of rituals involving the cult of the horse. All these rituals and customs may be considered extremely old, arising in a setting of dual-clan organization and well-developed animistic beliefs.

Various gifts, obligations, connections, and the like are used in order to determine the kinds of action in the religious-magical rituals. Use is made of verbal-poetic means (blessings, dialogues, songs), implements of work, and various objects of animal and vegetable origin.

Scholars believe that many rituals connected with early forms of magic did not have a religious content: they were based either on the conviction that the matter was "decided" by verbal actions or on various rational techniques to which a magical quality was ascribed.[81] A number of rituals of religious-magic substructure of the Yakut wedding complex also had no religious content (e.g., the common meal of the couple and others). It should be noted that the nonreligious magical actions were especially characterized by polyfunctionality and, in the course of time, many lost their magical significance.[i]

During the time under consideration, many religious-magical rituals can also be found in other substructures, primarily the demonstrative-magical, associated with marriage symbolism, wedding symbolism, commercial symbolism, and demonstration of bridal submissiveness and obedience. Rituals that reflect the joining of the parties (the common meal, the common blessing) are characterized by a distinct marital symbolism. Wedding symbolism is mainly associated with elements of material culture (the ritual costumes of the bride and groom, the ceremonial costumes of the wedding participants, the horse's decoration, saddle, harness). Many rituals symbolize the process of a commercial deal (the "examinations," "hand-slapping," and other rituals). A separate group of rituals is the demonstration of the bride's obedience and submissiveness to the groom, the father- and mother-in-law, and her own parents (the custom of tying the reins of the bride's horse to the tail of the groom's horse, the ritual of "opening the face").

The entertainment-play substructure includes various competitions, games, and dances, symbolizing a contest between the two groups.

The makeup of Yakut wedding participants might vary according to specific circumstances: the makeup of the families entering into wedlock, their wealth and numbers, the season of the year, and so on. The main participants in the wedding ritual are the boy (future groom, husband), the girl (future bride, wife), their parents, matchmakers on the groom's side, relatives on both sides, and guests. A special group was comprised of the participants in the ritual competitions: fighters, strongmen, foot racers, horse racers, and others. There is some evidence that white shamans took part in the wedding celebrations in the remote past.[82] The level of activity of wedding participants varied greatly in each stage. For example, the fathers of the families arranging the wedding were the most active in the first stage, and a significant part was assigned to the bride and groom; in the second stage, their role was comparatively slight, and so on. It should be noted that one or another function came into the forefront during each stage of the wedding ritual, i.e., the rituals of one or another substructure become dominant.

The material components of the wedding ritual are also polyfunctional. This pertains mostly to the wedding costume.[83] For example, the costumes of the bride and groom in the Yakut wedding fulfill (in order of importance) a ritual, celebratory, esthetic, ethnic, social ranking, and practical function; the costumes of the other participants fulfill a celebratory, esthetic, ritual, ethnic, social ranking, and practical function. Other material components of the wedding ritual also have a functional dimension.

Verbal communication has great importance in the traditional Yakut wedding. According to R. Jakobson, any act of speech consists of six elements, performing the following functions: emotive, poetic, conative [directive], phatic [contact], referent, and metalinguistic.[84] Many of these functions of verbal communication play a definite part in the wedding rituals of all peoples.[j] In the Yakut wedding, the phatic function is especially important, reflecting the contact between the wedding participants, since the generalized wedding ritual may be conceived as an interaction between the parties of the bride and groom. The metalinguistic function, expressing the code of the speech act (the allegorical conversation during the matchmaking), is distinctly evident. One should also note the poetic function. Verbal communication among all people is complemented by nonverbal signs—various gestures or symbols.[85] These symbolic gestures also play an important part in the traditional Yakut wedding.

In completing a general structural-functional analysis of the traditional Yakut wedding of the nineteenth and early twentieth centuries, we must emphasize that it includes four invariant phases, joined together by a minimum of ritual. Such a four-part structure, in our view, represents the Yakut wedding ritual in its most general form.

With the spread of Christianity from the seventeenth to the early nineteenth centuries, Christian rituals begin to play a sizable part in the Yakut wedding: the nuptials, the custom of "meeting the icon," kisses. "Imitation of the Russians living nearby and partial similarity to their own ritual resulted in substantial Christian overlayering on the Yakut wedding ritual and on the constituent elements of the Yakut ceremonial cycle."[86]

As determined by E.S. Novik, the traditional Yakut wedding of this time is a modification of a special ritual genre—transition rituals—and has a distinct nature as an exchange of communication.[87] The classical scheme of transition rituals is represented by three main groups: isolation of an object, its resolution ("temporary death") and transformation ("rebirth"), and return of the object to the collectivity in a new status.[88] Rituals of passage or, as Turner calls them, life-crisis rituals, are rituals through which a subject moves from "a place in the mother's womb fixed by the placenta to his death and final place fixed by the tombstone and last refuge, the grave, where the now-dead organism resides—a path marked out by a number of turning points or transitions, which all societies ritualize and publicly mark by corresponding rituals, to impart to the living community members an understanding of personal and group meaning. These are the crucial milestones of birth, maturity, marriage and death."[89] Noting that Novik successfully conducted a detailed analysis of traditional Yakut wedding rituals as secondary modeling systems on the basis of semiotic method and communication theory, it is important to examine more closely the role of space, as among other people. Space plays a modeling role in the Yakut traditional wedding. Not only the physical movement of the wedding participants, primarily the bride and groom, but also the social movement, i.e., change of status, has great importance. The contrasting of the parties of the bride and groom in the spatial code was realized by a contrasting of "our" and "their" sides (locus). The structure of "our" side, i.e., the space that has been assimilated to the utmost economic degree, includes the dwelling, the space immediately adjacent to the dwelling, bounded by the tethering post, the stockyard, other utilitarian structures, and the pastures and hunting grounds, i.e., the territory assimilated by a clan (family).[90] "Our" side was designated by special reference points: a sacred place, a tree, the tethering post, etc. All of the main rituals of the second and third phase of the Yakut wedding (such as the riding around the tethering post, the bride's "breaking" the willow branch when entering the groom's house) are connected with the notions of "our" and "their" side. In this scheme, the most characteristic ritual is *siel baaiar*, performed by the bride while traveling to the groom's house, when the wedding procession crosses the boundary to the groom's "side." In our opinion, this ritual simultaneously indicates the bride's crossing into the ranks of married women. The change in social status occurred beyond "her own" locus, on "neutral" territory. These rituals are symmetrically arranged in the spatial structure of the wedding complex. Of considerable importance in the wedding complex is the distribution of the participants in space, reflecting the social organization, the contextual hierarchy, and kinship relations. The arrangement of Yakut wedding participants in the processions, *tiuse barar* and *kyys siukter*, at the table in the bride's house and in the groom's house, was strictly ordered.

The spatial notions of "our/their," "good/evil" indicate that the house is seen, first, as an enclosed space, protected against the penetration of evil hostile forces, and second, as the maximum assimilated and domesticated world. Thus, egress from this space has great importance: the windows, door, threshold, and smoke opening are signs or symbols whereby the space of the house is fenced off from the rest of the "evil," unassimilated world. The crossing of the boundary of the house in either direction through these boundary markers is coupled with the observance of a number of rituals.[91] When the Yakut bride, crossing the threshold of the groom's house, jangled the ritual rattles, *kyabaka simege*, on her trousers, this was an indication not only of her chastity, but also and mainly of her becoming one of "our" household inhabitants.

Many rituals of the traditional Yakut wedding of the nineteenth and early twentieth centuries have analogies in the wedding rituals of other Turkic-Mongolian peoples of Southern Siberia and Central Asia: the Kazakhs, Kyrgyz, Karakalpaks, Siberian Tatar, Altai, and Khakass.[92] For example, the Kazakhs said: "You have the falcon, we the gyrfalcon," the Kyrgyz: "If God joins, the matchmakers will make it happen."[93] The gift to the bride's father, *uos asar* (the "opening of the lips") was known as *aas palek*, the "gift for the mouth," among the Tuvans. The Altai called the sixth arrival of the matchmakers *aas palek*, the "opening of the mouth."[94] To clinch the bargain, they performed *ilii okhsusar*, a handclasp ritual. A similar ritual was performed by the Kazakhs, Kyrgyz, Karakalpaks, and Buryats. Among the Tuvans, the confirmation of the consent of the parents of both sides is known as *kaldan* ("the striking of hands").[95]

Among the Yakut, the matrimonial night occurred during the visit, *tiuse barar*, after which the groom was allowed to see his bride by the custom *kiutiueutiuiur*, until the full bride-wealth was paid. Similar premarital meetings of the bride and groom were observed among the Kazakhs (*kalandyk oinau*), Kyrgyz (*kiuielee baruu*), Karakalpaks (*kuieleu*) (the "period of secret meetings"), and Nogai. Among the Bashkir, the bride could receive the groom after *izhai kabul*, the "little wedding."[96]

The groom, taking the bride away from her father's home, left the parents a mare in her place, *ogo onnugar keureur kesii* ("cattle given instead of the child"), symbolizing payment for the mother's milk. A similar gift existed among the Kazakhs (*sut aki*), Kyrgyz (*siut akky*), Turkmen (*syit khaky*), Altai (*karysh iichek*), Khakass (*imdzhek afy*), Tuvans (*emik kargyzhy*), and Buryats (*ekhkin su*).[97]

Among the Yakuts, the bride arrived with covered face. Among the Kyrgyz, the bride's face was covered with a shawl (*biurkenchek*, from the Kyrgyz *biurken* and the Yakut *biuriun*, meaning "to cover"[98]—P.S.), and among the Karakalpaks with a white handkerchief (*charsi*).[99] The same custom existed among the Kazakhs.[100] Among the Altai, when the bride was on her way to the groom's house, two young men traveled at her side, holding a curtain of white fabric in front of her until they arrived at the house.[101] As noted by Frazer, "the skin of a sacrificed animal, worn on the body, should be understood as a desire to protect oneself against real evil or a threat. Consequently, the skin plays the role of an amulet. Such an interpretation probably also applies to cases when a ritual is a means of confirming an agreement, since the parties are protecting against the possible danger of a breached agreement."[102]

Arriving at the groom's house, the bride rode three times around the tethering post in the direction of the sun (among the Northern Yakuts, around the tent in the opposite direction). A Karakalpak bride was able to enter the house only after walking around a bonfire near the groom's house. Among the Tuvans, the bride's wedding procession rode three times around the groom's *yurt*. The same was observed among the Khakass. The wedding train of the Buryat bride rode clockwise one to three times around the household of the groom's parents.[103]

Upon entering the groom's house, the bride performed the ritual of "treating the fire"—making an offering to the spirit-owner of the hearth with an entreaty to look favorably upon the new member of the family, also symbolizing homage to the ancestors of the groom's house. The ritual of the bride becoming a member of the groom's clan was observed among the Kazakhs, Kyrgyz, Tuvans, Altai, Khakass, and Buryats.[104]

On the day following the *uruu*, the bride performed the ritual of the greeting of the father-in-law, during which she "fed" the fire of his home hearth. Among Kazakhs, a new wife was taken on the third or fourth day to the father-in-law's *yurt* for the ceremony of *bet ashar*, "face opening." An analogous ritual occurred among the Kyrgyz of Chui (*otko kirgiziu*), the Karakalpaks (*bet ashar*), the Kumyks (*betochyv*, "face opening"), the Tuvans (*algysh*), the Buryats (*berii murgel*, "reverence at the clan hearth").[105]

The last phase of the Yakut wedding, *teurkiuttiuiu*, the "return home," occurred a certain time after the bride's coming to the groom's house, usually after the birth of the first child. A similar ritual is found among the Kazakhs—*torkindeu*, the Kyrgyz—*terkin*, the Turkmen—*kaitarma*, the West Siberian Tatars—*turken*, as well as the Tuvans, Altai, and Khakass.[106]

The symbolism of color and number, having sacred meaning, played a large part in the wedding rituals of the Yakut, as in those of other Turkic-speaking peoples.

The material examined in the first part of this chapter reveals that the traditional Yakut wedding of the nineteenth and early twentieth centuries consisted of two main ceremonies: *tiuse barar* and *uruu*. The first ceremony, performed after partial payment of the bride-wealth, may be seen as a survival of late matriarchal relationships.[107] The second is genetically a creation of a different historical epoch—a time of dissolution of earlier relationships,[108] when the marriage occurs only after full payment of the bride-wealth, and the ceremony itself is devoted to bringing the bride to the husband's house, since the marriage becomes virilocal. With the advent of the second ceremony, an uxorilocal habitation of the wedded couple was preserved in the custom of the "secret" visitation, *kiutiueuttiuiur*, of the bride by the groom in her father's house. According to N.P. Lobachevskaia, the first ceremony of the Yakut wedding was devoted to the wedlock and considered the main and proper wedding, while the second was devoted to transferring the wife to the husband's house. Such a wedding corresponded to an early stage of the bride-wealth marriage, when bride-wealth existed but was not yet given much importance, and wedlock occurred before it was paid in full.[109] However, in our opinion, during the period in question the Yakuts gave primary importance to the second ceremony, including the bride's arrival at the groom's house and the banquet there, although the religious wedding most often occurred after the first ceremony. The Yakuts incurred more expenses and invited more guests during the second ceremony than during the first; even the rituals of the second ceremony were much more complex and substantial. On the other hand, as E.S. Novik believes, from the standpoint of communications theory the existence of two wedding ceremonies is not connected with the residency of the new family. Rather, movements within the ritual complex are symmetrically connected through relationships constituting a larger scheme of exchanges between the parties arranging the marriage:

> . . . the wedding ritual is based on a deeper structure, characteristic of ritual behavior, unconsciously issuing from the fact that the "acquisition" of any new valuable occurs by "receiving" it from "another," and this only by exchanging it for one's "own" valuable. This deeper structure is developed, syntagmatically, by the reduplication of dialogue and exchange actions, first between the groom's clan and the bride's clan in general (exchange of the bride-wealth for the dowry), then between the husband's and wife's parts of these two groups (mutual treats, gifts and services, contests), and finally, between the bride and groom.[110]

Comparative analysis of the basic rituals of the Yakut traditional wedding complex of the nineteenth and early twentieth centuries with the analogous rituals of the wedding complexes of Turkic-speaking peoples of Southern Siberia and Central Asia allows a tentative identification of two phases of chronological importance in the genesis of the wedding complex of these peoples.

The first stage is the period of transition from late matriarchal to patriarchal conditions and from uxorilocal to virilocal marriage by payment of bride-wealth. Most scholars assign the origin of the elaborate wedding ceremonial to this period. Traditional nineteenth- and early twentieth-century weddings of Turkic-speaking peoples (Kazakhs, Kyrgyz, Karakalpaks, the seminomadic Uzbeks, Bashkir, Nogai, Tuvans, Altai, Khakass, Yakuts, plus somewhat the Buryats) have preserved many features pertaining to this epoch: the two-stage nature of the wedding complex, the custom of "secret meetings" in the home of the bride's parents, the custom of the "temporary return," and so forth. It should be noted that, among the Kazakhs, Kyrgyz, some of the Karakalpaks, Bashkir, and Tatar of Western Siberia, the first wedding ceremony (Yakut *tiuse barar*) has simply become a betrothal, while the ritual of matrimony and the first night have come to be performed during the second wedding ceremony (Yakut *uruu*). The main wedding feast among the Kazakhs, Kyrgyz, Karakalpaks, Kumyks, Nogai, seminomadic Uzbeks, and Altai was held in the home of the bride's parents after payment of the full bride-wealth, while among the Tuvans, Turkmen, Buryats, and Yakuts it was held in the groom's house after the bride's crossing over.

The second stage is the period of well-developed patriarchal conditions and supremacy of the virilocal marriage—a time of further evolution of the wedding ceremonial. In the traditional Yakut wedding complex, many relict features belonging to this time have survived: the main wedding ceremony, *uruu*, is concerned with carrying away the bride, although the actual marriage was celebrated (as formerly) during the first wedding ceremony, *tiuse barar*, in the home of the bride's parents; the existence of numerous rituals involving bride-wealth and dowry; the decisive role of the fathers of the two families in conducting the first marital stage, and many others. These two stages may be viewed as a reflection of the subsequent development of the wedding ritual of the peoples in various steps of their ethnic history.[111]

Correlations of many rituals of the traditional Yakut wedding complex of the nineteenth and early twentieth centuries with wedding rituals of other Turkic-speaking peoples of Southern Siberia (Tuvans, Altai, Khakass, Shor), Central Asia (Kazakh, Kyrgyz, some Khorezm Uzbeks), and Western Siberian Tatars may be explained by common ethnic components taking an active part in the formation of the ancestors of these peoples in ancient Turkic times (second half of the first millennium A.D.). In this scheme, scholars assign a major role especially to the Kypchak tribes, the Uigurs, and the Enisei Kyrgyz.[112] Of considerable importance were the close ethnogenetic and ethnocultural contacts between ancestors of these future peoples during the previous epoch, that of pre-Turkic time (first half of the first millennium A.D.), when the basis of the future proto-Turkic community was formed. It seems clear that the ritual minimum of the wedding complex of these peoples had come to be formed in the pre-Turkic epoch and assumed its definitive shape in the proto-Turkic time, which was a time of "maximum exertion of force" for their ancestors, according to D.G. Savinov.[113]

As revealed by the materials that we have examined, a many-component, complex, and colorful wedding ceremonial existed among Yakuts at this time, being one of the major aspects of the people's spiritual culture. From the second half of the nineteenth century onward, the ritual ceremonial of the Yakut wedding was gradually simplified, especially among the less affluent segment of the population.

A general structural-functional approach to the traditional Yakut wedding ceremony of the nineteenth and early twentieth centuries reveals five substructures, performing the following functions: economic, religious-magical, demonstrative-symbolic, entertainment-play, and social. The coincidence between basic rituals of the traditional Yakut wedding and analogous rituals of other Turkic-speaking and some Mongolian-speaking peoples of Southern Siberia, Kazakhstan, and Central Asia is yet another testimony to their ancestors' close ethnogenetic and ethnocultural ties.

Thus, the traditional Yakut wedding ceremony may serve as a historical-ethnographic source to clarify main phases of the ethnogenesis and ethnic history of the Yakut people.

Summary

Study of the history of the development of Yakut marital and familial relations in the nineteenth and early twentieth centuries indicates that the primary form of contracting of marriage was through matchmaking, by payment of bride-wealth, which was governed by exogamous bans in both the paternal and maternal line. Other forms of marriage—forcible abduction of a bride, exchange of brides, marriage through working for a wife, the levirate and sororate—corresponding to earlier stages in the development of marriage—had lost all significance at this time. In addition to arranged marriages, marriages of "runaways" (*kiuretii*) enjoyed a certain popularity, especially among the poorer segment of the population.

The average age of marriage for girls was between sixteen and twenty-one, that for boys twenty and twenty-five. Further development of social relations and progressive changes in the patriarchal system, especially at the end of the nineteenth century, led to restricted parental authority in the marriage of their children and complete disappearance of betrothal of the underaged.

In the nineteenth and early twentieth centuries, the institutions of bride-wealth and the dowry went through a definite evolution in their development: their content, size, worth, and degree of enforcement of payment changed. From the second half of the nineteenth century onward, the importance of bride-wealth declined, owing to a breakdown of the barter economy and further development of commercial and monetary relations—elements of early capitalistic relations—which led to a weakening of the patriarchal clan connection. In this setting, the small individual family, especially that of the poor, was not able to pay a large bride-wealth, which might destroy its economic solvency. Each young family needed economic assistance to start its own separate household. This assistance came in the form of the bride's dowry, which often included livestock and money paid as bride-wealth, i.e., both sides actually provided economic assistance to the new family unit. One must also consider that the worth of the dowry equaled or exceeded that of the bride-wealth, which was not very large in value.

In the early twentieth century, with the ultimate decline in importance of bride-wealth, the importance of the dowry also declined. However, this did not mean that marriage had lost all resemblance to an economic transaction, especially among the wealthy. Thus, the development of the paid marriage among the Yakuts, as among other people, followed a general path of marriage norm development and evolution of payment for a wife.

In the nineteenth and early twentieth centuries, the prevailing form of family among Yakuts was the small individual family—the primary socio-economic unit of society, based on private property and individual consumption. The average size of such a two-generation family was three to five people. Less common was the large, undivided family of between eight and twelve people from three generations. A characteristic element of the traditional Yakut family was that, in the context of a barter economy, feudal exploitation, and harsh natural and climatic conditions of the North, it functioned mainly as the economic productive unit of society and only after this carried out its other roles.

A woman occupied an ambivalent position in traditional Yakut society. On the one hand, her economic, legal, and moral rights were greatly diminished. For example, it was virtually impossible for her to initiate divorce, she did not enjoy many property rights, and so forth. On the other hand, her position in the family was marked by relative freedom; her social status was incomparably greater than that of a woman of the East. In the second half of the nineteenth century, with a weakening of the patriarchal foundations of marital and familial relations and the general democratization of social life, there was a gradual broadening of women's property rights, as reflected in the development of traditional inheritance norms. We may distinguish two periods in the development of Yakut traditional right of inheritance: the first includes the period up to the second half of the nineteenth century, when patriarchal survivals continued to play a substantial role; the second includes the period from the second half of the nineteenth to the beginning of the twentieth century, when women's property rights were substantially enlarged. The important role of a woman's work in the animal-breeding economy, especially among the poor, and her freedom in everyday life served as the basis for her swift and complete emancipation during the first years of Soviet power.[k]

The main goal of traditional Yakut upbringing of children and socialization of youth was the gradual indoctrination of all the rules of social behavior in the spirit of the best ethnic traditions and the transmission of all the riches of the people's spiritual culture.

The traditional Yakut wedding ceremony of the nineteenth and early twentieth centuries consisted of four phases: (1) *kergen kepsetii*, the matchmaking and bargain; (2) *tiuse barar*, the first wedding ceremony, held after payment of part of the bride-wealth in the bride's home, and *kiutiueuttiuiur*, the custom of temporary visitation of the son-in-law; (3) *uruu*, the second wedding ceremony, including *kyys siokter*, the coming of the bride to the groom's house and the banquet held there. The ceremony was held after full payment of the bride-wealth; (4) and *teurkiuttiuiu*, the woman's temporary return to the home of her parents a certain time after the second ceremony. The ritual complex brought together five substructures, performing economic, religious-magical, demonstrative-symbolic, entertainment-play, and social functions. From the mid-nineteenth century onward the traditional Yakut wedding was gradually simplified, especially among the poor. At the beginning of the twentieth century, weddings with complicated ritual ceremonial were rare.

Using three simultaneous principles of classification—cult, celebrant personnel, and performance cycle—the traditional Yakut familial rituals of the period in question can be grouped as follows: solitary rituals performed on rare and exceptional occasions (e.g., the building of a new house); calendrical (seasonal) rituals, performed during a certain interval of time year in and year out (e.g., the procession of the goddess Ynakhsyt Khotun and others); and continual rituals performed at any time of the year (e.g., rituals and customs associated with fire reverence). The traditional familial rituals performed productive, protective, contact, and other functions and were individual, group, or collective in nature. During the time in question, they were universally distributed. Their persistent functioning indicates that they continued to play an important normative and regulative role in the everyday life of all segments of the population at this time.

The structure of Yakut traditional birth ritual includes five groups of rituals involving the birth of a child: rituals "stimulating" childbirth; notions and customs associated with female pregnancy; rituals performed immediately during the time of birth; postpartum rituals; and rituals intended to preserve the life of the newborn. The main purpose of these rituals was to ensure fertility and protect the newborn. A special place was given to the rituals involving the cult of the protector of children, the goddess Aiyysyt. The birth rituals fulfilled productive, purificatory, and other functions and were primarily individual or small group, less often collective, rituals.

Traditional Yakut rituals indicate an echoed existence among the Yakuts of many ancient beliefs: animism, fetishism, totemism, and magic. The rituals were associated with an extensive system of cults: of family protector-spirits, local spirit-owner Aan Alakhchyn Khotun, the domestic hearth spirit-owner, the cult of the horse, the ancestor cult, and so on.

Ritualism is one of the most important characteristics in the functioning and development of a traditional worldview. The underlying structure of Yakut traditional ritual is symbolic, with primary rituals in essence a communicative exchange.

The Yakuts' ethnocultural interaction in a new homeland with the Evenks, Evens, and Yukagirs did not have much influence on their ritual ceremonial development. Among the innovations, however, can be mentioned several Christian customs, primarily incorporated in the wedding and family rituals.

The existence among the Yakuts at the time under consideration of a complex, colorful, and multicomponent ritualism with an ancient Turkic foundation indicates that it was organically incorporated in the lifestyle of all segments of Yakut society and constituted an essential part of spiritual culture. It is this that determines the value and special nature of Yakut traditional ritualism.

Comparative analysis of Yakut ritual and that of other Turkic-speaking peoples of Southern Siberia (Tuvans, Altai, Khakass, Shors), Kazakhstan and Central Asia (Kazakh, Kyrgyz, and especially Khorezm Uzbeks), and Western Siberian Tatars in the nineteenth and early twentieth centuries reveals a convergence of many rituals. This can be explained, first, by the argument that common ethnic components were actively involved in the formation of these peoples' ancestors in the proto-Turkic period (second half of the first millennium A.D.): the Kypchak tribes, the Uigurs and Enisei Kyrgyz; second, close ethnogenetic and ethnocultural contacts were of some importance among ancestors of these peoples in the previous epoch—the pre-Turkic period (first half of the first millennium A.D.), when the foundation of the future proto-Turkic community was laid. Certain ethnogenetic links between Yakut and Buryat ancestors (apparently in the first half of the second millennium A.D.) are suggested by the complete correlation between the Yakut ritual of the procession of the goddess Aiyysyt and the Buryat *toomtolkho* ritual.

Retrospective analysis of the traditional ritualism of the Yakuts and other Turkic-speaking peoples of Southern Siberia, Kazakhstan, and Central Asia in the studied period reveals a significant proto-Turkic foundation. The formation of traditional ritualism of these peoples seems to have moved through the following main chronological stages.

The first stage is the period of transition from late matriarchal relations to patriarchal ones, from uxorilocal to virilocal marriage by payment of the bride-wealth (pre-Turkic to proto-Turkic period, first millennium A.D.). Most scholars assign the origin of fully developed ritualism to this period. Special notice should be given to the proto-Turkic epoch. "In the past, each people or group of peoples living within the same historical-geographical region, i.e., connected by the territory of settlement, continual cultural contacts, language, and general historical destiny," notes D.G. Savinov, "has an epoch of maximum exertion of creative forces, when the foundations are laid for a certain cultural model that subsequently unfolds in the course of all succeeding generations. Such an epoch in the history of the peoples of Southern Siberia, the ancestors of the present Altai, Tuvans, Khakass, Shors, and also the ethnogenetically related Turkic-speaking Yakuts along the Lena, the Kyrgyz and Kazakhs in Central Asia, was the proto-Turkic epoch, including more than five centuries for formation of the proto-Turkic historical and cultural complex."[114] Traditional Yakut ritualism has preserved many features pertaining to this epoch: the two-stage wedding ritual, the *kiutiueuttiuiur*, custom of visiting the bride by the son-in-law at the home of the bride's parents, the cult of the child protector Aiyysyt, the existence of well-developed ritual complexes for the spring, summer, and autumn cycles of the calendrical celebration, and so forth.

The second stage is the period of well-developed patriarchal relations and prevalence of virilocal marriage—a time of further ritual development (post-Turkic period, second half of the second millennium A.D.). Traditional Yakut ritualism preserved many relicts: the critical role of the fathers of the two families in the marriage's first phase, the existence of the *uruu* ceremony of carrying away the bride as the primary wedding ceremony, the patriarchal form of the hearth's spirit-owner, and so forth. These two stages can be viewed as a reflection of the consecutive development of Yakut traditional ritual in different periods of their ethnic history.

The foregoing ethnographic material reveals that many aspects of Yakut traditional marital and familial relations and rituals in the nineteenth and early twentieth centuries, correlated to the level of economic, social, ethnic, and ecological development of the ethnos and the functioning of its traditional worldview, were phenomena of a stadial nature.

Editor's notes

a. A gloss of *kalym* as bride-wealth, rather than bride-price, is used here to conform with an anthropological literature that stresses the complex exchange nature of marital transactions (goods and/or money from the groom's family to the bride's, from the bride's family to the groom's, for the couple from both families, for the bride as dowry) rather than depicting brides as chattel to be sold. See Michelle Zimbalist Rosaldo and Louise Lamphere, eds. *Women, Culture and Society* (Stanford: Stanford University Press, 1974), p. 229. See also E.A. Gaer's article on Nanai marriage ritual, *Anthropology and Archeology of Eurasia*, vol. 31, no. 1 (Summer 1992), pp. 67–87.

b. A *verst* is only slightly bigger than a kilometer, about five-eighths of a mile. A *yurt*, as used here, is a gloss of the Sakha winter house, or *balagan*, which was usually a low, long, rounded building made of a wood frame, and earthen or sod-with-mud walls.

c. *Krasnyi ugol* literally means "red corner" but the more appropriate gloss is "beautiful" or "sacred," this being the icon corner (diagonal from the entryway) in homes influenced by Slavic, Russian Orthodox, culture. The term reveals a common root for the words "red" and "beautiful" in Russian.

d. The *urasa*, a tall conical tent of wooden poles covered with elaborately designed birchbark, was the spacious summer home of Sakha cattle breeders. The *serge* was used not only as a tethering post but also as a sacred marker of special occasions, and it is in this context that it would have been placed in a sacred grove near the groom's house. While not revived in exactly the way described here, *serge* have become important again in renewed, revitalized wedding symbolism. Some Sakha young couples have, since the early 1970s, put up memorial *serge* in their family's courtyards, with their names and the date of their wedding carved on its side, and with various traditional symbols (a horse head, *kumys* cup, eagle) carved on top.

e. In 1991, I witnessed good-humored wrestling over a horse shank, revived as a Sakha sport but no longer associated with marriage. The contest was a small part of an outing sponsored by a cultural and political movement called *Sakha Omuk* (The Sakha People), the head of which is the Sakha Minister of Culture. The winner got the meat.

f. At some weddings, since the 1970s, the practice of sprinkling grass on a couple's path has been revived. This was even done for one couple married in Moscow, at the entrance to a restaurant.

g. The small but crucial fire-spirit offering by the bride in her new home is a tradition that has also been revived, and that never died in some areas of Yakutia. Offerings to the fire of token food, *kumys*, or alcohol are also customary when guests arrive, before leaving for important trips, and during travels that include campfires (among other occasions). Reasoning behind the bridal offering was explained to me in 1986 in very similar terms to that given here. Some recent weddings have both bride's home and groom's home ceremonial stages, although more typical is a celebration at the home of the groom, whether the couple is planning to live there or separately.

h. The exchange theory, drawing on N.L. Zhukovskaia, stems from anthropological ideas developed by Marcel Mauss (e.g., *The Gift* [New York: Norton, 1967, French original 1925]) and Claude Lévi-Strauss (e.g., *Les Structures élémentaires de la parente* [Paris, 1949]). For more elaboration of theories of play, see Edward Norbeck, ed., "The Anthropological Study of Human Play," *Rice University Studies*, vol. 60, no. 3 (Summer 1974).

i. Cf. J. Needham, ed., *Science, Religion and Reality* (London, 1925), and Bronislaw Malinowski, *Magic, Science and Religion, and Other Essays* (New York: Anchor, 1954), pp. 93–148.

j. Cf. Roman Jakobson and Morris Halle, *Fundamentals of Language* (The Hague: Mouton, 1956). It was Malinowski, however, who first focused on the "phatic" function of language, to stress reciprocal contact. For a review of various theories of speech functions, see Dell Hymes, "The Ethnography of Speaking," in Ben Blount, ed., *Language, Culture and Society* (Cambridge, MA: Winthrop, 1974), pp. 189–223.

k. The Orientalism (stereotyping the East) revealed in this paragraph is ironic given the author's own roots in an Eastern Siberian culture that some include in generalizations about repressed women. The points made here about relative degrees of status and the strong prerevolutionary role of Sakha women within their domestic contexts are quite appropriate, however. Given that "freedom" is still relative and variable, it is an exaggeration to say the Sakha woman had "swift and complete emancipation during the first years of Soviet power." Cf. Marjorie Mandelstam Balzer, *Siberian Women's Lives* (forthcoming).

Notes

1. LO AAN SSSR, f. 17, op. 2, d. 158, l. 123.

2. I.A. Khudiakov, *Kratkoe opisanie Verkhoianskogo okruga* (Leningrad, 1969), pp. 182–83.

3. G.V. Ksenofontov, *Uraankhai-sakhalar. Ocherki po drevnei istorii iakutov* (Irkutsk, 1937), p. 227.

4. N.S. Berg, "Svadebnye obriady iakutov," *Vestnik IRGO* (St. Petersburg, 1853), p. 33.

5. N.A. Vitashevskii, "Iakutskie materialy dlia razrabotki voprosov embriologii prava," in Pavlinov, et al., *Material dlia obychnomu pravu i obshchestvennomy byta Iakutov* (Leningrad, 1929), p. 183.

6. Arkhiv IaF SO AN SSSR, f. 5, op. 3, d. 736, l. 1.

7. Khudiakov, *Kratkoe opisanie*, p. 160.

8. Arkhiv IaF SO AN SSSR, f. 5, op. 3, d. 759, l. 1–2.

9. TsGA IaASSR, f. 14, op. 2, d. 28, l. 8.

10. V.L. Priklonskii, "Tri goda v Iakutskoi oblasti," *Zhivaia starina*, 1890, issues 1–3, p. 55.

11. Arkhiv IaF SO AN SSSR, f. 5, op. 3, d. 759, l. 3.

12. Berg, "Svadebnye obriady iakutov," p. 35.

13. Vitashevskii, "Iakutskie materialy," p. 185; Arkhiv IaF SO AN SSSR, f. 5, op. 3, d. 736, l. 2.

14. N.S. Shchukin, *Poezdka v Iakutsk* (St. Petersburg, 1844), p. 293.

15. Khudiakov, *Kratkoe opisanie*, p. 162.

16. Iu. Dzhuliani, "O iakutakh," *Syn otechestva*, pt. 178, nos. 23–27, p. 145.

17. I.S. Gurvich, *Kul'tura severnykh iakutov-olenevodov* (Moscow, 1977), p. 126.

18. Khudiakov, *Kratkoe opisanie*, pp. 162–63.

19. LO AAN SSSR, f. 47, op. 2, d. 158, l. 125.

20. Arkhiv IaF SO AN SSSR, f. 1, op. 12, d. 67, l. 8.

21. Priklonskii, "Tri goda v Iakutskoi oblasti," p. 56.

22. D.M. Pavlinov, "Brachnoe pravo y iakutov," in D.M. Pavlinov, et al., *Materialy po obychnomu pravu i obshchestvennomu bytu iakutov*, p. 52.

23. Arkhiv GO SSSR, f. 64, op. 1, d. 65, l. 188.

24. Arkhiv IaF SO AN SSSR, f. 5, op. 3, d. 97, l. 35–38; Khudiakov, *Kratkoe opisanie*, p. 166.

25. Arkhiv LO IV AN SSSR, f. 11, op. 1, d. 67, l. 1–2.

26. M. Sleptsova, *Zhenit'ba Mikhaily* (St. Petersburg, 1903), p. 36.

27. Arkhiv GO SSSR, f. 63, op. 1, d. 21, l. 34.

28. R.K. Maak, *Viliuiskii okrug Iakutskoi oblasti* (St. Petersburg, 1887), p. 94.

29. Gurvich, *Kul'tura severnykh iakutov-olenevodov*, pp. 123–26.

30. Arkhiv LCh IE AN SSSR, f. 14, op. 3, d. 13, l. 8.

31. A.N. Maksimov, "Iz istorii sem'i u russkikh inorodtsev," in *Etnograficheskoe obozrenie* (Moscow, 1902), issue 1, p. 59.

32. N.P. Lobacheva, "Razlichnye obriadovye kompleksy v svadebnom tseremoniale narodov Srednei Azii i Kazakhstana," in *Domusul'manskie verovaniia i obriady v Srednei Azii* (Moscow, 1975), p. 313.

33. M.M. Nosov, "Evoliutsionnoe razvitie iakutskoi odezhdy s kontsa XVII stoletiia do 1920-kh godov," in *Sb. nauchn. trudov IaRKM* (Yakutsk, 1957), no. 2, pp. 125–52; F.M. Zykov, *Iuvelirnye izdeliia iakutov* (Yakutsk, 1976), pp. 45–52.

34. F.M. Zykov, *Poseleniia, zhilishcha i khoziaistvennye postroiki iakutov (XIX–nachalo XX v.)* (Novosibirsk, 1986), pp. 50–51.

35. M.M. Nosov, "Odezhda i ee ukrasheniia u iakutov XVII–XVIII vekov." In *Sb. nauchn. statei IaRKM* (Yakutsk, 1951), no. 1, pp. 92–103.

36. LO AAN SSSR, f. 202, op. 1, d. 13, l. 145.

37. Arkhiv LO IV AN SSSR, f. 11, op. 1, d. 67, l. 6; Khudiakov, *Kratkoe opisanie*, pp. 168, 170.

38. G.M. Vasil'ev, *Zhivoi rodnik (ob ustnoi poezii iakutov)* (Yakutsk, 1973), pp. 63–64.

39. Author's field materials (1982).

40. Arkhiv IaF SO AN SSSR, f. 5, op. 3, d. 97, l. 32.

41. Arkhiv LO IV AN SSSR, f. 22, op. 1, d. 7, l. 79.

42. Arkhiv LCh IE AN SSSR, f. 14, op. 3, d. 13, l. 2.

43. Arkhiv LO IV AN SSSR, f. 22, op. 1, d. 2, l. 50–51.

44. Ibid., f. 11, op. 1, d. 67, l. 6.

45. Arkhiv LCh IE AN SSSR, f. 14, op. 3, d. 13, l. 2.

46. N.I. Tolokonskii, "Iakutskie poslovitsy, zagadki, obriady i dr." (Irkutsk, 1914), p. 39.

47. Arkhiv IaF SO AN SSSR, f. 5, op. 4, d. 97, l. 45.

48. Vitashevskii, "Iakutskie materialy," p. 191.

49. Arkhiv IaF SO AN SSSR, f. 5, op. 3, d. 788, l. 8.

50. Khudiakov, *Kratkoe opisanie*, p. 175.

51. Arkhiv IaF SO AN SSSR, f. 5, op. 4, d. 97, l. 46.

52. Ibid., f. 5, op. 3, d. 379, l. 52.

53. Khudiakov, *Kratkoe opisanie*, p. 171.

54. Arkhiv IaF SO AN SSSR, f. 5, op. 11, d. 97, l. 95.

55. V.L. Seroshevskii, *Iakuty (opyt etnograficheskogo issledovaniia)* (St. Petersburg, 1896), p. 542.

56. D.M. Pavlinov, "Brachnoe pravo u iakutov," p. 55.

57. V.F. Troshchanskii, "Iakuty v ikh domashnei obstanovke," *Zhivaia starina*, 1908, issue 3, p. 16.

58. G.A. Bonch-Osmolovskii, "Svadebnye zhilishcha turetskikh narodnostei," in *Mater. po etnografii Rossii* (Leningrad, 1926), vol. 3, no. 1, pp. 108–9.

59. Arkhiv LO IV AN SSSR, f. 11, op. 1, d. 67, l. 7.

60. Arkhiv IaF SO AN SSSR, f. 5, op. 3, d. 679, l. 24.

61. Arkhiv IaF SO AN SSSR, f. 5, op. 3, d. 759, l. 4.

62. "Opisanie iakutov," *Severnyi arkhiv* (St. Petersburg, 1822), p. 295.

63. Khudiakov, *Kratkoe opisanie*, p. 181.

64. Arkhiv IaF SO AN SSSR, f. 4, op. 12, d. 26, l. 40.

65. *Istoricheskie predaniia i rasskazy iakutov* (Moscow-Leningrad, 1960), vol. 1, p. 296.

66. Arkhiv LCh IE AN SSSR, f. K–5, op. 1, d. 48, l. 42–44.

67. Khudiakov, *Kratkoe opisanie*, pp. 175–76.

68. Author's field materials (1982).

69. S.I. Bolo, "Proshloe iakutov do prikhoda russkikh na Lenu (po predaniiam iakutov byvshego Iakutskogo okruga)," in *Sb. trudov NII iazyka i kul'tury pri SNK IaASSR* (Yakutsk, 1939), issue 4, p. 141.

70. Arkhiv IaF SO AN SSSR, f. 4, op. 12, d. 52, l. 16.

71. TsGIA SSSR, f. 1264, op. 1, d. 300, l. 58; Arkhiv LO IE AN SSSR, f. K–5, op. 1, d. 18, l. 41–42.

72. Maak, *Viliuiskii okrug*, p. 96; Gurvich, *Kul'tura severnykh iakutov-olenevodov*, p. 130.

73. K.V. Chistov, "Problemy kartografirovaniia obriadov i obriadovogo fol'klora."

Svadebnyi obriad," in *Problemy kartografirovaniia v iazykoznanii i etnografii* (Leningrad, 1974), p. 78.

74. L.S. Khristoliubova, *Semeinye obriady udmurtov (opyt kolichestvennoi kharakteristiki)*, Candidate's dissertation (Moscow, 1970), pp. 2–3; A.V. Gura, "Opyt vyiavleniia struktury severorusskogo svadebnogo obriada," in *Russkii narodnyi svadebnyi obriad* (Leningrad, 1978), p. 72.

75. Chistov, "Problemy kartografirovaniia obriadov i obriadovogo fol'klora," pp. 81–82.

76. Idem, "Tipologicheskie problemy izucheniia vostochnoslavianskogo svadebnogo obriada," in *Problemy tipologii v etnografii* (Moscow, 1979), p. 223; Iu.Iu. Surkhasko, "Religiozno-magicheskie elementy karel'skoi svad'by," in *Etnografiia Karelii* (Petrozavodsk, 1976), p. 141.

77. Ia.S. Smirnova, "Svadebnyi daroobmen y narodov Severnogo Kavkaza i ego sovremennaia modifikatsiia," *SE*, 1980, no. 1, p. 99.

78. N.L. Zhukovskaia, *Kategorii i simvolika traditsionnoi kul'tury mongolov* (Moscow, 1988), pp. 101–2; for details on the theory of communicative action: gift/return gift, elaborated by M. Moss, see: A.B. Gofman, "Sotsiologicheskie kontseptsii Marselia Mossa," in *Kontseptsii zarubezhnoi etnologii. Kriticheskie etiudy* (Moscow, 1976), pp. 116–22.

79. E.G. Kagarov, "Sostav i proiskhozhdenie svadebnoi obriadnosti," *Sb. MAE* (Leningrad, 1929), vol. 8, p. 153.

80. Ibid., pp. 170–75, 182–85.

81. Z.I. Iampol'skii, "O bezreligioznosti pervobytnoi magii," *SE*, 1979, no. 1, pp. 72–76; Iu. Iu. Surkhasko, *Karel'skaia svadebnaia obriadnost' (konets XIX–nachalo XX v.* (Leningrad, 1977), p. 207.

82. Arkhiv LO IV AN SSSR, f. 11, op. 1, d. 67, l. 1–2.

83. P.G. Bogatyrev, *Voprosy teorii narodnogo iskusstva* (Moscow, 1971), p. 301.

84. G.A. Levinton, "K voprosu o funktsiakh slovesnykh komponentov obriada," in *Fol'klor i etnografiia. Obriady i obriadovyi fol'klor* (Leningrad, 1974), pp. 162–64.

85. S.S. Tatubaev, *Zhesty kak komponent iskusstva* (Alma-Ata, 1979), p. 16.

86. T.V. Zherebina, *Religioznyi sinkretizm (traditsionnye verovaniia iakutov i khristianstvo)*. Dissertation (Moscow, 1983), p. 15.

87. E.S. Novik, *Obriad i fol'klor v sibirskom shamanizm* (Moscow, 1984) pp. 182–91 [or *Shamanism*, ed. Marjorie Mandelstam Balzer (Armonk, NY, 1990)—M.M.B.]; on the structural theory in ethnography see Lévi-Strauss, *Strukturnaia antropologiia* (Moscow, 1985), pp. 397–421 [or *Structural Anthropology*, New York, 1967—M.M.B.].

88. Novik, *Obriad i fol'klor v sibirskom shamanizm*, pp. 163, 182–91; cf. M.M. Bakhtin, *Problemy poetiki Dostoevskogo* (Moscow, 1979), p. 143.

89. Cited in: V. Turner, *Simvol i obriad* (Moscow, 1983), p. 233 [or *The Ritual Process* (Ithaca, 1977), Symbol, Myth and Ritual series—M.M.B.].

90. N.L. Zhukovskaia, "Prostranstvo i vremia v mirovozzrenii mongolov," in *Mify, kul'ty, obriady narodov zarubezhnoi Azii* (Moscow, 1986), p. 126; E.L. L'vova, N.V. Oktiabr'skaia, A.M. Sagalaev, and M.S. Usmanova, *Traditsionnoe mirovozzrenie tiurkov Iuzhnoi Sibiri. Prostranstvo i vremia. Veshchnyi mir* (Novosibirsk, 1988), p. 11; A.K. Baiburin and G.A. Levinton, "K opisaniiu organizatsii prostranstva v vostochnoslavianskoi svad'be," in *Russkii narodnyi svadebnyi obriad. Issledovaniia i materialy* (Leningrad, 1978), p. 89.

91. N.A. Levonen, "Funktsional'nyi rol' poroga v fol'klore i verovaniiakh karel," in *Fol'klor i etnografiia. U etnograficheskikh istokov fol'klornykh siuzhetov i obriadov* (Leningrad, 1981), pp. 171–72, 178.

92. N.A. Kisliakov, *Ocherki po istorii sem'i i braka u narodov Srednei Azii i*

Kazakhstana (Leningrad, 1969), p. 100; A. Dzhumagulov, *Sem'ia i brak u kirgizov Chuiskoi doliny* (Frunze, 1960), p. 35; Kh. Esbergenov and T. Atamuratov, *Traditsii i ikh preobrazovanie v gorodskom bytu karakalpakov* (Nukus, 1975), p. 50; F.T. Valeev, *Zapadnosibirskie tatary* (Kazan, 1980), p. 159; V.I. Verbitskii, *Altaiskie inorodtsy* (Moscow, 1983), p. 81; E.K. Iakovlev, "Etnograficheskii obzor inorodcheskogo naseleniia doliny Iuzhnogo Eniseia," in *Opisanie Minusinskogo muzeia* (Minusinsk, 1900), no. 4, p. 90.

93. Kisliakov, *Ocherki po istorii sem'i i braka*, p. 100; Dzhumagulov, *Sem'ia i brak u kirgizov Chuiskoi doliny*, p. 35.

94. L.P. Potapov, *Ocherki narodnogo byta tuvintsev* (Moscow, 1969), p. 224; N.I. Shatinova, *Sem'ia u altaitsev*, p. 51.

95. P.E. Makovetskii, *Mater. dlia izucheniia iuridicheskikh voprosov kirgizov* (Omsk, 1886), no. 10, pp. 3–4; Kisliakov, *Ocherki po istorii sem'i i braka*, p. 115; Lobacheva, "Razlichnye obriadovye kompleksy v svadebnom tseremoniale," p. 305; I.I. Inkizhinov, *Buriatskaia svad'ba* (Irkutsk, 1912), p. 4; Potapov, *Ocherki narodnogo byta tuvintsev*, p. 224.

96. Kh.A. Argynbaev, *Sem'ia i brak u kazakhov*. Dissertation (Alma-Ata, 1975), pp. 33–35; S.M. Abramzon, *Kirgizy i ikh etnogeneticheskie i istoriko-kul'turnye sviazi* (Leningrad, 1971), p. 226; A.T. Bekmuratova, *Brak i sem'ia u karakalpakov v proshlom i nastoiashchem* (Nukus, 1970), p. 67; S.Sh. Gadzhieva, *Ocherki po istorii sem'i i braka u nogaitsev (XIX–nachalo XX vv.)* (Moscow, 1979), p. 76; S.I. Rudenko, *Bashkiry (istoriko-etnograficheskie ocherki)* (Moscow-Leningrad, 1955), p. 261.

97. Argynbaev, *Sem'ia i brak u kazakhov*, p. 86; A.A. Divaev, *O svadebnom rituale kirgizov Syr-Dar'inskoi oblasti* (Kazan, 1899), p. 21; A. Dzhikiev, "Svadebnye obriady u turkmen-salyrov v kontse XIX–nachale XX v.," *TIIAE* (Ashkhabad, 1983), vol. 7, p. 161; E.M. Toshchakova, "Altaiskaia zhenshchina v dorevoliutsionnom proshlom," *Uch. zapiski* (Gorno-Altaisk, 1958), no. 2, p. 136; V.Ia. Butanaev, "K istorii sem'i i semeinogo prava khakasov (XIX–nachalo XX v.)," in *Traditsionnye verovaniia i byt narodov Sibiri* (Novosibirsk, 1987), p. 158; K.V. Viatkina, "Kul't ognia u mongol'skikh narodov," *SE*, 1968, no. 6, p. 118.

98. Abramzon, *Kirgizy i ikh etnogeneticheskie i istoriko-kul'turnye sviazi*, p. 235.

99. L.S. Tolstova, *Karakalpaki Ferganskoi doliny* (Nukus, 1959), p. 119.

100. Kisliakov, *Ocherki po istorii sem'i i braka*, p. 113.

101. Verbitskii, *Altaiskie inorodtsy*, p. 81.

102. J.G. Frazer, *Fol'klor v Vetkhom Zavete* (Moscow, 1986), p. 238 [*Folklore in the Old Testament* (London, 1919), 3 vols.—M.M.B.].

103. Tolstova, *Karakalpaki Ferganskoi doliny*, p. 120; Potapov, *Ocherki narodnogo byta tuvin-tsev*, p. 242; Iakovlev, "Etnograficheskii obzor," p. 84; K.D. Basaeva, *Sem'ia i brak u buriat (vtoraia polovina XIX–nachalo XX v.)* (Novosibirsk, 1980), p. 181.

104. Kh.A. Argynbaev, "Svad'ba i svadebnye obriady v proshlom i nastoiashchem," *SE*, 1974, no. 6, p. 73; T.D. Baialieva, *Doislamskie verovaniia i ikh perezhitki u kirgizov* (Frunze, 1972), p. 44; Potapov, *Ocherki narodnogo byta tuvintsev*, p. 261; Verbitskii, *Altaiskie inorodtsy*, p. 81; Iakovlev, "Etnograficheskii obzor," p. 84; K.V. Viatkina, *Ocherki kul'tury i byta buriat* (Leningrad, 1969), p. 52.

105. V.V. Vostrov, "Kazaki Dzhanibekskogo raiona Zapadno-Kazakhstanskoi oblasti," *TIIAE AN Kaz. SSR* (Alma-Ata, 1956), vol. 3, pp. 36–38; Abramzon, *Kirgizy i ikh etnogeneticheskie i istoriko-kul'turnye sviazi*, p. 233; Tolstova, *Karakalpaki Ferganskoi doliny*, p. 121; S.Sh. Gadzhieva, *Kumyki* (Moscow, 1961), p. 277; Potapov, *Ocherki narodnogo byta tuvintsev*, p. 242; Basaeva, *Sem'ia i brak*, p. 184.

106. Argynbaev, *Sem'ia i brak u kazakhov*, p. 39; Abramzon, *Kirgizy i ikh etnogeneticheskie i istoriko-kul'turnye sviazi*, p. 232; G.P. Vasil'eva, "O roli etnicheskikh

komponentov v slozhenii svadebnoi obriadnosti turkmen," in *Istoriia, arkheologiia i etnografiia Srednei Azii* (Moscow, 1968), p. 33; F.T. Valeev, *Zapadnosibirskie tatary* (Kazan, 1980), p. 158; Potapov, *Ocherki narodnogo byta tuvintsev*, p. 262; N.P. Dyrenkova, "Perezhitki materinskogo roda u altaiskikh tiurkov," *SE*, 1937, no. 4, p. 34; Iakovlev, "Etnograficheskii obzor," p. 84.

107. For more on the terms "matriarchate" and "patriarchate" see *Svod etnograficheskikh poniatii i terminov. Sotsial'no-ekonomicheskie otnosheniia i sotsionormativnaia kul'tura* (Moscow, 1986), pp. 82–83, 131–32.

108. A.I. Pershits, A.L. Mongait, and V.P. Alekseev, *Istoriia pervobytnogo obshchestva* (Moscow, 1982), p. 172.

109. N.P. Lobacheva, "K istorii slozheniia instituta svadebnoi obriadnosti," in *Sem'ia i semeinye obriady u narodov Srednei Azii i Kazakhstana* (Moscow, 1978), p. 160.

110. Novik, *Obriad i fol'klor v sibirskom shamanizm*, p. 191.

111. P.A. Sleptsov, "Svadebnye obriady kak istochnik po etnicheskoi istorii iakutov," in *Etnicheskaia istoriia tiurkoiazychnykh narodov Sibiri i sopredel'nykh territorii. Tezisy dokladov* (Omsk, 1984), p. 60.

112. L.P. Potapov, "Istoricheskie sviazy altaesaianskikh narodov s iakutami," *SE*, 1978, no. 6, p. 93; D.G. Savinov, *Narody Iuzhnoi Sibiri v drevnetiurkskuiu epokhu* (Leningrad, 1984), pp. 146–48; A.I. Gogolev, *Istoricheskaia etnografiia iakutov (Voprosy proiskhozhdeniia iakutov)* (Yakutsk, 1986), pp. 33–35 [or *Anthropology & Archeology of Eurasia*, vol. 31, no. 2 (Fall 1992)—M.M.B.]; R.I. Bravina, *Pogrebal'nyi obriad iakutov kak istoriko-etnograficheskii istochnik (XVII–XIX vv.)*, dissertation (Leningrad, 1983), p. 24; V.I. D'iachenko, "Ritual'nye funktsii konia v svadebnoi obriadnosti iakutov," in *Tiurkologiia–88. Tezisy dokl. i soobshch. V Vsesoiuznoi tiurkologicheskoi konferentsii* (Frunze, 1988), p. 548.

113. Savinov, *Narody Iuzhnoi Sibiri*, p. 3.

114. Ibid.

Abbreviations

Arkhiv GO SSSR—Arkhiv Geograficheskogo obshchestva SSSR
Arkhiv LO IV AN SSSR—Arkhiv Leningradskogo otdeleniia Instituta vostokovedeniia Akademiia nauk SSSR
Arkhiv LCh IE AN SSSR—Arkhiv Leningradskoi chasti Instituta etnografii Akademiia nauk SSSR
Arkhiv IaF SO AN SSSR—Arkhiv Iakutskogo filiala Sibirskogo otdeleniia Akademiia nauk SSSR
EO—Zhurn. Etnograficheskoe obozrenie
IaRKM—Iakutskii respublikanskii kraevedcheskii muzei im. Em. Iaroslavskogo
Izvestiia VSOIRGO—Izvestiia Vostochno-Sibirskogo otdela Imperatorskogo Russkogo geograficheskogo obshchestva
Izvestiia OAIE—Izvestiia Obshchestva arkheologii, istorii i etnografii
KSIE—Kratkie soobshcheniia Instituta etnografii
LO AAN SSSR—Leningradskoe otdelenie Arkhiva AN SSSR
Sbornik MAE—Sbornik Muzeia antropologii i etnografii
SE—Zhurn. Sovetskaia etnografiia
TIIAE AN Kaz SSR—Trudy Instituta istorii, arkheologii i etnografii AN Kazakhskoi SSR
TIE—Trudy Instituta etnografii

Trudy TKAEE—Trudy Tuvinskoi kompleksnoi arkheologo-etnograficheskoi ekspeditsii
TsGA Iakutskoi ASSR—Tzentral'nyi Gosudarstvennyi arkhiv Iakutskoi ASSR
TsGIA SSSR—Tzentral'nyi Gosudarstvennyi arkhiv SSSR
Vestnik IRGO—Vestnik Imperatorskogo Russkogo geograficheskogo obshchestva
Zapiski SOIRGO—Zapiski Sibirskogo otdela Imperatorskogo Russkogo geografiche-
skogo obshchestva
Zapiski IRGO—Zapiski Imperatorskogo Russkogo geograficheskogo obshchestva
Zapiski IIaLI IaF SO AN SSSR—Zapiski Instituta iazyka, literatury i istorii IaF SO AN
SSSR

List of informants

Namsk region (1982)

G.P. Vasil'ev, 65 years old, Khomustakh
P.D. Dmitriev, 81 years old, Betiuntsy
A.I. D'iakonova, 67 years old, Khatyryk
I.P. Kutukov, 90 years old, Modut
M.I. Nikitin, 75 years old, Betiuntsy
I.I. Sleptsov, 90 years old, Khatyryk
K.S. Everstov, 72 years old, Appaany
P.S. Everstov, 70 years old, Appaany
A.V. Ushnitskaia, 82 years old, Modut

Megino-Kangalasskii region

A.P. Govorova, 101 years old, Balyktaakh
A.I. Kychkina, 66 years old, Balyktaakh
A.I. Fedorova, 73 years old, Rassoloda
E.N. Uvarovskaia, 76 years old, Rassoloda
I.D. Izbekov, 79 years old, Maandai

Gornyi region

V.S. Alekseeva, 68 years old, Berdigestiakh
V.F. Andreeva, 64 years old, Mytaakh
G.N. Zhirkov, 87 years old, Berdigestiakh
M.M. Kirillina, 80 years old, Mytaakh
K.I. Kononova, 79 years old, Berdigestiakh
A.N. Mikhailova, 100 years old, Berdigestiakh
A.Ia. Pavlova, 73 years old, Mytaakh
M.G. Romanova, 90 years old, Mytaakh
E.Ia. Stepanova, 76 years old, Mytaakh
T.S. Chemezova, 83 years old, Berdigestiakh

Suntarskii region (1983)

M.S. Grigor'ev, 72 years old, Suntar
A.A. Ivanov, 83 years old, Bordon
G.E. Fedorov, 72 years old, Suntar

Traditions, Rituals, and Beliefs
of the Asiatic Eskimos

Tassan S. Tein

*Ancient traditions and rituals are a fascinating research subject for histori-
ans and archeologists. Knowledge of material culture sheds light on the
everyday life of an ancient people and their system of spiritual values.
Tassan Tein, a researcher at SVKNII [Combined Scientific Research Institute of North-Eastern Studies], talks of his research.*[a]

**Do not raid the mice's hoard or they will take offense,
believed the ancient Eskimos**

The Eskimos attached much importance to the *baidara* [large, open skin
boat—M.M.B.], their hope and provider during the warm season. In their
leather vessels they not only hunted in the seas, but also visited the remote
villages and nomad camps of the reindeer breeders. For that reason, in the
spring, ritual celebrations [*qamigaqut*] preceded the release of the *baidara*
into the water. A *baidara* owner approached his vessel from the bow,
lightly striking its sides with his right hand and chanting incantations
[*qanimsut*]. This meant that he was awakening the *baidara* after its long
winter hibernation. The owner's wife brings her husband a round wooden
dish containing herbs and water. The owner wets or "washes" the bow of
the *baidara*. According to the Eskimos, just like a human being, the vessel
had a face—the bow. These types of rituals were conducted by sea mammal
hunters before transporting the *baidara* to the berth prior to leaving for the
hunt.

During the first days of possible hunt in the *baidara*, any hunter whose
relative had recently died was not permitted to take part, nor was a hunter

---

Russian text © 1992 by Tassan Tein. "Traditsii, obriady, pover'ia." Original manuscript, 5 pp. Translated with the author's permission. Translated by Olga Zaslavsky.

who had kept his weapons and implements in his *yaranga* [large winter skin tent, sometimes fortified with turf] while his wife or dog was giving birth, instead of storing the equipment with his relatives.[b] This was done because the sea animals will flee from a *baidara* occupied by sinful hunters.

A woman should not hang her washing above her husband's head in the canopy of a *yaranga*, for this brings bad luck on the hunt. If a seal swimming in open water between ice floes points its snout skyward, a northerly wind is approaching. The hunters know signs: if a whale jumps out of the water or shows his tail above the surface, the weather will change. In addition, a whale will show his tail when preparing for a deep dive. If the hunters caught a small dolphin, they nonetheless performed the same ritual of greeting given to a full-fledged whale. When the dolphin was dragged ashore, the hunters had to pretend that their prey was very heavy and difficult to budge. If this greeting ritual were violated, the dolphin would take offense and some misfortune would befall the hunters. Seeing blood in a dream, however, brought good fortune in the hunt.

The mice that live in the tundra store up edible roots near their burrows. Upon finding such a hoard, women pilfered the supply but left some reindeer fat or other foodstuff in the burrow so as not to offend the mouse by the "robbery."

Losing a tooth in one's sleep is considered a bad omen: a relative will die. Another omen presaging a death in the family was a snow bunting flying in through the air hole in the cold canopy of the *yaranga*. Finding an egg of a large bird in a deserted spot is a sign of future wealth. Seeing a deceased relative in a dream means a change in the weather. If a dog urinates on his master, it indicates misfortune: the master will soon not be of this world.

Chaplino Eskimos have the following belief: a woman serving meat to her husband should place the dish in such a way that it will not rock; otherwise, her husband can be rocked in the waves or the wind can break the ice and her husband may drown. Another belief of the Naukan Eskimos is that if meat is served at the evening meal in a wooden dish, the dish should not rock or the rocking will summon evil spirits who are up to no good. After serving her family a dish of rendered deer fat mixed with snow, a woman should take the dish out into the cold part of the *yaranga* and always remember to cover it with a bundle of grass. Without the grass, evil spirits will come to feast on the leftovers and a relative will fall ill.

The Eskimos believed in life after death. When a human being dies, they believed, the soul lives on. It is said that on the fourth day after the funeral the men and, on the fifth day, the women would check the entire village to be sure dwellings were carefully shut. Otherwise, the deceased could enter at night and steal the soul or shadow of a loved or a hated person. To safeguard a dwelling from the deceased, the living undertook necessary precautions. In order to prevent the deceased from gaining entry to a *yaranga*, the mother of the household sprinkled human urine around the dwelling with a bundle of grass dipped into a wooden chamber pot.[c] Sometimes, for the same purpose, urine was simply poured on the ground and snow by the entrance to the *yaranga*. To cast out a dead person's soul, a shaman's drum beater was tossed in various directions. It was thought that if the deceased's body suddenly became very heavy during a funeral, one of the close relatives would soon follow.

All these traditions, rituals, customs, omens, and beliefs of Asiatic Eskimos are closely connected with their religious beliefs.

Do not eat the heart of a bird or you will be a coward all your life, believed the ancient Eskimos

The birth of a boy in the family was treated as a great stroke of luck. A boy is a future hunter and a provider. The family members paid great attention to his upbringing. The father, uncles, and older brothers devoted themselves to his physical development and the cultivation of his hunting skills. Spiritual upbringing was entrusted to the shaman. This was believed to be of utmost importance in the life of a boy or a youth. The shaman imparted the myths, legends, and tales of the past and revealed the "secrets" of his shamanistic activity.

An interesting ritual was the initiation of an adolescent as a hunter when he caught his first seal or bearded seal [*erignatus barbatus*]. An elderly man would throw the boy on top of his first catch, signifying that the young hunter had already come into contact with the animal and thus would have good hunting fortune in the future. Usually, the youth presented his first catch to an older hunter, a relative. On the second day, there was a complex ritual during which the youth's lower lip was pierced with a labret made from a walrus tooth. This tradition of hunting initiation persisted into the Soviet period, albeit without the elaborate initiation ritual.

Particularly prized among the hunters was the taking of a Greenland whale. A single whale provided the settlement with meat and blubber for the entire year. Joyful about such good fortune, the settlement would hold a month-long celebration. During the whale festival, the whale's soul was welcomed with a thanksgiving reception and then sent off to the sea. The whale was greeted and seen off with all possible honors and ritual ceremony. For the duration of the whale festival all arguments and quarrels between family members and clans were curtailed, for otherwise the whale's soul could take offense and no longer bring his comrades to the familiar shores.

When a wounded whale is in agony, he does not dive but swims in wide circles following the sun's movement. Should a whale circle in the opposite direction, against the movement of the sun, then, according to Eskimo beliefs, a misfortune will befall the family of that *baidara* owner who first harpooned the whale. If the taken whale is missing several whalebones, that is also a bad sign—the whole clan of the *baidara* owner will die out.

The Naukan Eskimos had a custom: when encountering a dead swallow at sea, her soul was cajoled to bring good fortune to all the hunters' families and was "fed" with a pinch of meat. The Provedenia region Eskimos held a different belief: a dead swallow found on the shore brings misfortune—the hunter will not live for long.

According to an ancient custom, a bear belonged to the hunter who spotted him first, even if another hunter made the kill. Before skinning and cutting up the carcass, special rituals were performed to placate the bear's soul. The bear's head was placed in his right paw, facing the direction of the rising sun. A hunter addressed the head, chanting: "Return home now. The road to my house is poor, you should visit us later sometime." After boiling the bear meat, the oldest family member had a youth stand so that an elongated wooden dish containing the boiled meat was between his legs, while another elder whispered incantations to make the youth a successful hunter of sea animals.

A Chaplino hunter who killed a white bear celebrated his dear guest for five days, playing the drum day and night to please the bear's soul. During these days, this hunter did not leave his dwelling nor engage in hunting.[d]

The remains of the white whale were returned to the sea by the family of the hunter who had caught the animal. First, small pieces were cut from the whale's head, front flippers, and rear fin, a piece for each family member living in the *yaranga*. The *yaranga* residents then threw their pieces through the entrance toward the sea, with the family elder throwing first. This ritual was devoted to celebrating the whale's return to her natural element—the sea. On the Kruzenshtern island (Little Diomide) in the Bering Strait, after taking a white whale the hunter does not hunt for a full month and does no other work. The women in his family stop sewing clothes or shoes. The ancients thought that if this prohibition was violated, the hunter would have no luck in the future.

If a seal has bald patches on its skin, that is a bad sign. The hunter who killed this seal will not live long. A seal with white claws was a bad omen for Naukan Eskimos, but a good one for Chaplino Eskimos. If a hunter caught a seal with six phalanges [bones] per flipper instead of five, he would be successful for the rest of his life and his descendants would also hunt well. Fewer than five phalanges, on the other hand, brought bad luck.

If a young hunter caught several seals and an older relative caught none, the younger hunter was obliged to hand over one seal. Before giving the seal away, he cut off the whiskers from the right side of the snout for good luck. Failure to do so made it difficult for him to catch animals in the future.

There was a specific quota for the number of animals to be taken in a single hunt. In one trip to the sea, a hunter should take only four seals. If a fifth one was taken, she belonged to the sea spirit. Taking the fifth seal could endanger the life of his relatives.

Different omens and meteorological observations contributed to successful hunting. If windless weather set in, hunters did not approach the edge of the ice, as strong currents could take them into the open sea, where they would perish. A lasting southerly wind and flocks of ducks sitting in the water or flying with the wind meant not to bother waiting for good weather. If duck flocks are flying against a southerly wind, the wind will blow from the north on the next day. If in wintertime a seal swims out to sea in the open water between ice sheets, a northerly wind is coming.

The sandpipers' arrival signaled the opening of the summer walrus-hunting season, which hunters awaited with great anticipation. The walrus, taken close to the settlement, was skinned on the shore and everyone savored the sea mollusks that came from the walrus's stomach. This was considered a rare delicacy by Eskimos.

Walrus meat was not permitted to be fried over a fire. The ancients were afraid that, during the hunt, an enraged walrus could overturn the *baidara*. A young hunter was not allowed to eat scraps of food remaining on the dish, as this would cause him to take only thin, malnourished animals. If you cook a duck or any other bird outdoors, a strong northerly wind is bound to blow. Eating a bird's heart can make a life-long coward, and a coward always returns from the hunt empty-handed. It was not proper for a young hunter to partake of a seal's muscles, as this was believed to bring physical weakness.

If a dog howls woefully at night, the master of the dwelling will depart from life.

The Eskimos ate uncooked seaweed with blubber. When fresh walrus meat was boiled, it was garnished with seaweed. Seaweed was never burned in a fire, as this can cause the weather to deteriorate and bring on a great storm.

All of these traditions, rituals, omens, and beliefs of the Asiatic Eskimos were closely connected with their religious beliefs.

Editor's notes

a. This prologue was in the original manuscript and has been kept as written by the author.

b. This is one aspect of very widespread, though not universal, tabus associated with concepts of women (especially their pregnancy and menstruation) as both potent and "impure." For a survey, see Marjorie Mandelstam Balzer, "Rituals of Gender Identity: Markers of Siberian Khanty Ethnicity, Status and Belief," *American Anthropologist*, 1981, vol. 83, pp. 850–67. In 1990, when the cultural anthropologist Anna Kertulla was in Sireniki, Chukotka, about to take a trip with Eskimo sea mammal hunters, she mentioned such traditional tabus and was laughed at for thinking they might still pertain today. (I am grateful to her for sharing this story, November 1991.) Elsewhere Tassan Tein describes women as threats to evil spirits, the strongest shamans, and considered "holy beings, since they provided offspring" ("Shamans of the Siberian Eskimo," *Arctic Anthropology*, 1993, vol. 30, no. 1).

c. Tein relates a legend to go with this custom, based on a story of two friends who vowed to visit each other, even after the death of one. The fourth night after one of the friends had died, he returned to his village and escorted his surviving friend through a world of noisy spirits and sleeping humans. Those protected by urine or oil fat glittering around their *yaranga* were unharmed, the friend was taught. Those who only had fetishes and amulets inside their homes could have their souls stolen ("Shamans of the Siberian Eskimo," *Arctic Anthropology*, 1993, vol. 30, no. 1).

d. For a rich survey of beliefs and rituals associated with the sacredness of the bear, see A. Irving Hallowell, "Bear Ceremonialism in the Northern Hemisphere," *American Anthropologist*, 1926, vol. 28, pp. 1–175.

Tuvan Shamanic Folklore

Mongush B. Kenin-Lopsan

Oral folklore has great importance in studying early forms of religious beliefs. The shamanic worldview found expression not only in rituals, but also in folklore. During their seances, Tuvan shamans "voyaged" in the "subterranean" world, the "celestial" world, and the "middle" world, populated by people. The shamans told their listeners of their impressions and actions. It might be said that shamans created worlds through words. Yet shamanic poetry has not yet been investigated as a part of Tuvan folklore.

Folk memory preserves the names of certain authors of shamanic verses, but most of the shamanic texts are anonymous. Indeed, among the shamans were both genuine masters of poetic speech and their imitators. But since shamanic folklore developed in the context of religious tradition, distinct individuality of authorship was not an essential condition for creation. Therefore, the specimens of shamanic folklore that we have recorded at varying times and from different people exhibit mostly typical and similar features. Our task at the present stage is to discover the main themes of shamanic poetry and to analyze their plots and style.

Composition of the curative seance

The seance—a collective ritual event—was a kind of creative laboratory for the shaman. Verses were conceived during the seance. Examining shamanic texts, we see that the seance is a complex and well-structured event, where one can discern a prologue, exposition, plot, author's digression, culmination, dénouement, and epilogue. This scheme would have varying degrees of completeness in different rituals. The duration of the seance could also vary.

Russian text © 1987 by "Nauka" Publishers. *Obriadovaia praktika i fol'klor tuvinskogo shamanstva. Konets XIX–nachalo XX v.* (Novosibirsk: Nauka, 1987), pp. 89–151, 157–63. A publication of the Institute of History, Philology, and Philosophy, Siberian Division, USSR Academy of Sciences. Translated by Ronald Radzai.

Prologue

The curative seance was generally held at the onset of night and before daybreak. After the shaman attired himself in his ritual costume, he took up his drum and rattle, performed the ritual of fumigation with juniper, and began to imitate quietly the voices of birds and beasts—crows, ravens, magpies, eagle-owls, wolves, and bears, so as to select the proper sound for the anaphora or refrain, choose a definite rhythm for the verses, and find the central word or thought that would become the means of healing the patient.[a]

As our informants report, at the start of the seance the shaman spoke of his shamanic duty, of himself. In this way, he introduced himself to the patient and the listeners. For example:

> Aiym, khunym chaazynda
> Aldai tangdym aldyn o"du—
> Aldy kyrlyg artysh-bile
> Aramailap sangym salgash,
> Artyzhanyp-artyzhanyp,
> A"ttanyptym, tonnanyptym.

> Chakpalyg-la charnym chaiyp,
> Sannaashtyp-la bazhym chainyp,
> Keuzuldur-le kheureem chaiyp,
> Keurgen karaam keurup, shiiip,
> Argalyktyg moinum sunup,
> Attyg digesh adap keldim.

(Recorded from Saaia Sambuu)

As my moon, my sun began to rise
I burned the golden herb of my wondrous mountain—
The six-jointed juniper—
Fumigating myself.
And carefully refreshing myself with its aroma,
I then mounted my steed and donned my cloak.

And now I am galloping with my shoulder-blades,
Nodding my head with the bird feathers,
Opening and closing the all-seeing eyes,
And dropping my neck in a bow.
And so I come to that which has a name, and so I come to this
that has become known.

Search for the cause of sickness

After telling the audience of his duty to help the sick and describing his abilities, the shaman tried to explain the cause of the sickness. He "mingled" with his spirits, psychologically preparing the patient for the upcoming emotional strain, encouraging him, and creating a "case history of the disease." All of this served as a kind of exposition for the "cure." The shaman would say something like the following:

> *Ashpas arty, chuge ashkan?*
> *Keshpes khemni chuge keshken?*
> *Ishpes shemni chuge ishken?*
> *Ketpes khepti chuge ketken?*
>
> (Recorded from Kyrgysa Biurbiu)

Why did he cross the pass, to where he durst not go?
Why swim the river, where he durst not swim?
Why eat the food, which he durst not eat?
Why wear the clothes, which he durst not wear?

In these lines we see a reflection of the views of the Tuvinians that each person has his own path, swerving from which meant destruction, as well as a special attitude to rivers, passes, and certain kinds of food and clothing. In the present case, the shaman found that the patient committed four "sins," failing to observe the traditional rules, and therefore fell sick. A number of seances would now have to be held to "cleanse" the patient from his "sins."

The plot of the seance

The shaman "found" the cause of the sickness with the help of his helper-spirits, whom he "dispatched" into various parts of the world. Returning from a lengthy voyage, they were supposed to tell their master everything they had learned.

> *Kaiyyn yndyg bolgulaaryl,*
> *Kaigyyl kylyp choruptaaly,*
> *Changgys chovag kaiaa kalbas,*
> *Chakpalygny chadyptaaly.*
> *Kheurlug-Taiga baary chedir*
> *Khandyr-sundur choruum-na bar,*
> *Kalgyp orungar, chaiaannarym!*
> *Karai tyrtyp keurgesh keliil.*

Kara cherning keugun seukken
Kalchan keuktu munupkai-la.
Deushtug cherning keugun seukken
Keunggur keuktu munupkai-la.
Kandyg-kandyg didir siler?
Kham-na irem chugaalangar.
Kham-na yiash kilengneen-dir.
Khaazhylyg ka"ttar edee
Kara-dagnyng baarynda
Ka"ttar edee belchigeshte
Kham-na yiash kilengneen-dir.
Kara chirik artyndyva
Khaia keurnu bergen-ne-dir.

(Recorded from Kuzhuget Balgan)

It is strange why this has happened,
We shall go with you to look,
We shall share your grief.
And thou, my soul, spread thy wings.
To the valley of Mount Khorlug-Taiga
I must go,
Go forward, my creatures, with soft steps!
There from the heights we shall watch.
We shall ride the bald blue one,
Who digs the roots from the dark earth.
We shall ride the hornless blue one,
Who tears the grass from the slope.

Of what do you speak, of whom do you speak?
Please speak, my shaman-grandfather,
Yes, the shaman-tree is wrathful.
Truly, the shaman-tree is angry and wrathful,
Standing in the meadow before the Dark Mountain,
Beyond the distant hills,
So beautiful.
Yes, the soul of the patient has gone away for good
To the dark ravine of the dark abyss.

Here, the cause of the sickness is announced as being the wrath of the tree-shaman.[b] To find this out, the shaman consulted first the winged *eeren*, or raven, then the "bald" badger, then the "hornless" bear, then the moth:

Kheueurtkuinung keergenchiin,
Kheulegesi argyp kalgan, ooi-ooi.
Sunezini kanchap bargan,
Surdurgenge tutturgan be, ooi-ooi.
Chuuden desken?
Chuuden kortkan? Ooi-ooi.
Duruiaa kushtung ununden be, ooi-ooi.
Erlik oran chetken-dir be, chetpeen-dir be, ooi-ooi.
Choorattyn oranynda doktaagan be, doktaavaan be, ooi-ooi.
Soonaidan surungerem,
Sogun oktan durgen choram, ooi-ooi.
Alys cherge chetkelekte
Atkan o"ktan durgen choram, ooi-ooi.
Algash-tutkash, ekkelinger, ooi-ooi.
Khovui-khovui khovuganym, ooi-ooi, ooi-ooi, ooi-ooi.

(Recorded from Saaia Sambuu)

How pitiful he has become, this sick man,
Hardly his shadow remains, *ooi-ooi.*
What has happened to his soul?
Has it been caught by the hand of the runner, *ooi-ooi?*
Why did it run away?
What has frighted it? *Ooi-ooi.*
Perhaps it was struck by the voice of the lark, *ooi-ooi?*
Perhaps it has gone to the [underworld] land of Erlik?
      or not gone, *ooi-ooi?*
Perhaps it has stayed in the land of Choorat? or not stayed, *ooi-ooi?*
Chase after it.
Fly swifter than an arrow, *ooi-ooi!*
Go swifter than a bullet,
Before it reaches the appointed place, *ooi-ooi,*
Catch and hold the soul and bring it here, *ooi-ooi.*
My little one, my dear little moth, *ooi-ooi, ooi-ooi, ooi-ooi.*

After repeating the exclamation *ooi-ooi* three times, the shaman lifted the drum even higher, gradually ceasing to strike it with the rattle. The mood of the patient was lifted—now he knew that the *eeren* moth had been sent to where his soul was. But the seance would last much longer. The patient was afraid to hear of the possible loss of his soul. An evil spirit now speaks through the mouth of the shaman. He sings a song of the captured soul:

Chylan shokar, kyyt-kyyt
Chyraa shokar, kyyt-kyyt,
Chyraa-saiak, kyyt-kyyt.

Bazyp olur, kyyt-kyyt,
Chychyy tonnug, kyyt-kyyt,
Torgu tonnug, kyyt-kyyt,
Kaidal irgi, kyyt-kyyt.

Khunnug cherning, kyyt-kyyt,
Khureng arnyyn, kyyt-kyyt,
Khulup alyyl, kyyt-kyyt,
Tudup alyyl, kyyt-kyyt.

Ailyg cherning, kyyt-kyyt,
Arny kyzyl, kyyt-kyyt,
Aalynda, kyyt-kyyt,
Organ-na boor, kyyt-kyyt.

Tangdaa chydar, kyyt-kyyt,
Seueugu artsyn, kyyt-kyyt,
Tamaa chydar, kyyt-kyyt,
Sunezinin, kyyt-kyyt,
Surup algash, kyyt-kyyt,
Chorui baar men, kyyt-kyyt.

(Recorded from Saaia Sambuu)[c]

Thou brightly colored one, like a snake, *kyyt-kyyt*, thou ambling
   steed, *kyyt-kyyt*,
Go pacing, *kyyt-kyyt*,
Go ambling, *kyyt-kyyt*.
He wore a serge robe, *kyyt-kyyt*,
He wore a silk robe, *kyyt-kyyt*,
Where is he now, *kyyt-kyyt*.
He was from the land of the sun, *kyyt-kyyt*,
His face was ruddy, *kyyt-kyyt*,
I shall bind him by the hands, *kyyt-kyyt*,
I shall take him alive, *kyyt-kyyt*.
He was from the land of the moon, *kyyt-kyyt*,
His face was red, *kyyt-kyyt*,
He is in his *aal* [settlement], *kyyt-kyyt*,

And there he sits, *kyyt-kyyt.*
Let his bones remain, *kyyt-kyyt,*
In the country where there are mountains, *kyyt-kyyt,*
I must return homeward, *kyyt-kyyt,*
With his captured soul, *kyyt-kyyt,*
I shall drive his soul onward, *kyyt-kyyt,*
It shall lie in the ground, *kyyt-kyyt.*

Thus, the shaman disclosed a page from the case history of the patient's sickness, in keeping with the traditional notions. Having learned of his hopeless situation, the patient asked the shaman to continue the seance.

The interim seance

The Tuvan shamans practiced the *algysh arazunda alganyr algysh*, a seance held during an intermission of the main seance—a kind of lyrical digression.

Having learned of the presence of a great shaman at a particular camp, anyone from the surrounding *aal* (settlement) could go there to meet with him. Entering the *yurt*, the person tied a white ribbon to the door and asked: "Oh great shaman, I beg you to visit my *aal* and to stay in my native places. I also beg you to foresee that which is not permitted me to know. I ask you to prevent that which threatens my well-being. I ask you to tell me the unknown." Saying these words, the visitor handed the shaman a pipe with tobacco and offered him liquor, *arak*, from his leather flask, and offered a white silk cloth, *kadak*, to the spirits. Interrupting the seance, the shaman smoked the offered pipe and received the offerings. An unexpected interruption would occur—an interim seance within the main seance, devoted to healing the patient. But even if no outsider arrived, the shaman himself could hold an author's digression, serving as a kind of link between the opening and the culmination of the main seance. The digression could have almost any given subject or nature, except that it was based on mythological themes.

They are beholden to me, they are in debt.
I have the mandate of my people, *oo-ooi.*
He has come with white *kadak, oo-ooi.*
He offers bitter tobacco, *oo-ooi.*
My stout one,
My black bear, *oo-ooi!*
And all his children, and all his *aal*

I ask you to guard, *oo-ooi!*
Let his dogs not bark, *oo-ooi!*
Do not chase away his herd, *oo-ooi!*
Do not trouble the peaceful sleep of his children, *oo-ooi.*
Is there a fire burning at his house?
Does a hat appear on a head?
What has departed? What has arrived? *oo-ooi.*
Who is creeping on all fours? *oo-ooi*
My stout one,
My black bear [*Mashpak kara, Mazhaalaiym*], go and see!

(Here the shaman paused a bit.)

What did you see? What did you learn?
Why are you frightened? Why run away?
Thou—my fearsome honored one, *oo-ooi.*
You sit on the right side of the *yurt,*
Your high chest mutters.
You chew and crunch beetles.
My fierce black thundering one, *oo-ooi.*[d]
You chew black worms, *oo-ooi.*
Thus far all is normal,
Thus far life is quiet.
But the camp of the *aal* grows dark,
It will be dangerous in future. *Oo-ooi.*
Sickness will break out,
Be vigilant! Be smart!
Someone will fall sick,
Someone will burn up.
His path is open to the *aza* [spirits], *oo-ooi.*
It is a straight path to the graveyard.
Is this because of the anger of the water and the earth? *oo-ooi.*
Be vigilant! Be smart!

(Recorded from Saaia Sambuu)

The new visitor, hearing the dismal conclusion of the shaman, humbly said: "Whatever is possible, great shaman, must be done for the cure. Not everyone has all-seeing eyes, only you, who have double vision, can do something." Thus the shaman ensured himself a clientele in future. This was a customary technique of all powerful shamans.

The culmination of the seance

The culmination was a proclamation (direct or oblique) of the prognosis of the disease. We shall present an example when, in a moment of highest tension, a woman bade farewell to her children, husband, and native land:

> My dear, sweet children,
> Your mother is sad and forlorn.
> And tears flow from my husband's eyes,
> When he sees his wife in sadness.
> She bids farewell to her people,
> She leaves her native *aal* forever.
> Her life cannot be saved,
> She shall soon go away from here.
> To be born and die is the law,
> You grow and then you go away—such is life.
> Pay it no heed, do not be sad,
> For she has sons and daughters.
> She has many children, born late,
> They will live where she lived.
> Yes, she has many children,
> They will take the place of their mother.
>
> (Recorded from Kuzhuget Balgan)

The dénouement of the seance

Apparently, the spirits have at last returned from Kara-Tal, where they have found the true explanation of the patient's condition. The dénouement is at hand.

> His life cannot be saved.
> It seems he chopped wood on the other side—
> A terrible ill has come from there,
> Before the winter month is out,
>
> Before the summer moon appears,
> He shall be lying in that graveyard.
> There, on our northern side,
> There, at the entrance to the narrow hollow.

I searched for his departed soul,
I asked for kindness and humbly prayed,
And went beyond the great range Sumber,
But was not able to catch it

Do not say I helped you not,
I was unable to return his soul,
Do not say I did not drive it here—
It is already in chains and shall not return from there.

When one is summoned from the kingdom of Erlik,
Not even the Khan Ezhen can help one.
He, this sick man, has left his native people,
He, this sick man, shall never again appear.

(Recorded from Kuzhuget Balgan)

Summary

Brevity of information is a characteristic trait of the shamanic seance. The ritual traditionally ended with verses, in which were heard words about fatigue, the difficulties of lengthy travels on the steed (drum), and the victories gained by the shaman with the aid of his helpers over the enemies of the sick person. Here is a characteristic epilogue used by the shaman to end a seance:

My seance, my action, is coming to an end,
I wish to return home from the seance.
Lo, my morning is already beginning,
And my chestnut steed is also tired.

It is time for me to go home,
Leading the seance in a lively dance.
It is time for me to go back to my dark, rundown hut
Leading the seance in a frenzied dance.

(Recorded from Viktor Kok-ool)

The time of the epilogue was in the morning. Night was ending, and the time had come to return home on the chestnut steed or drum—such was the theme of the shaman's epilogue. At the end of the ritual, the shaman reminded the audience not to forget to invite him on another occasion, to another *aal*.

Basic themes and techniques of shamanic poetry

Frequently the shaman began the seance praising his predecessor shaman (or shamaness) or his first teacher in this difficult art. Occasionally, one might hear an entire autobiographical poem. Praising predecessors, the shaman spoke of the shaman's fame, the geography of the travels of specific ancestors—great shamans, and the native places where his relatives lived from earliest times. For example:

> My dear father Delger, *oo-oo!*
> My grandfather, *aa-aa, oo-oo.*
> From a family of shamans, *oo-oo.*
> I was the youngest, *oo-oo.*
> I am the hereditary grandson of a shaman, *oo-oo,*
> The lot of a shaman fell to me, *oo-oo,*
> I come from six shamans, *oo-oo,*
> I became the youngest shaman, *oo-oo,*
> I am the heir of my father's clan, *oo-oo,*
> I have already become a far-famed shaman, *kham-na, oo-oo.*
> (Recorded from Shokshut Salchak)

One of the basic themes of shamanic folklore was that of the native land. As the shaman gained experience and made long voyages to distant *aals* (occasionally to neighboring countries, especially the Altai Mountains and the steppes of Mongolia), the geography of the folklore of Tuvan shamans naturally broadened. Yet the native land, with which the shamans connected their destiny and associated the mighty force of their spirit-helpers, is an object of their pride and an eternal theme of shamanic poetry.

> *O-oo-ooo!* *Eeren*—lords of the very foundation,
> *O-oo-ooo!* Sovereigns of the mountain ranges,
> *O-oo-ooo!* Come hither, one after the other, to me,
> *O-oo-ooo!* My treasure, my dear taiga!
> *O-oo-ooo!* Show mercy to me!
> (Recorded from Kuzhuget Balgan)

"Mingling" with the spirits—the masters of the water, sky, and earth—is evidently one of the oldest customs of the Tuvan shamans. Such rituals are evidently connected with the cult of mountains, water, natural phenomena, etc. The shaman questioned his spirit-helpers:

Let us rise from the ground to the skies,
Let us play there, past the seven-colored rainbow.
Let us set out on a steed from the lower world,
Let us rise to the upper world, where Azar is.
Let us play there,
Past the seven-colored golden rainbow.
Riding on the motley-red dragon,
Striking red sparks with a whip,
Giving out peals of thunder,
Oh you, the hail and the rain,
Calling forth the beautiful downpour!
Come, fellows, let us play, knocking down the beautiful larches
   with arrows.

   (Recorded from Viktor Kok-ool)

Every shaman was supposed to compose songs about his attributes and trusty spirit-helpers. Here is an example of how the shaman treated his headgear:

Ai, my hat with feathers spread wide,
With partridge feathers, resembling the sun and the moon,
My seven-feather *kaskak* hat,
How do you feel?
Let us fly away, fly together!

   (Recorded and translated by S.I. Vainshtein)

Here is an example of how a shaman might praise his headgear:

My yellow hat sways so nicely,
It is made of eagle feathers.
My yellow hat changes colors,
It is made of bird feathers.

or:

My hat of bird skin
Reaches to Kurbustan.

The shamans were convinced that their spirit-helpers had a universal ability to comprehend and mimic the speech of any person, the voices of birds and animals, and the conversations of spirits. The seance necessarily included a poetic dialogue between the shaman and his idols.[e]

It was thought that the shaman was not able to discover the intention of an evil spirit and understand the cause of the sickness and the fate of a patient without verses addressed to the *eereni*. For example, the shaman addressed his main helper— the mirror *kuzungu*:

> My *kuzungu* of golden copper
> Descended from yellow thunderclouds,
> Quickly touched ground,
> Splitting a yellow rock with one blow.
> My *kuzungu* of red copper
> Descended from red thunderclouds.
> It flew as a red light,
> Breaking a red rock with one blow.
>
> (Recorded from Kenden Khomushku)

During the seance, the shaman created an imaginary history of the disease. The content of these verses was exceptionally diversified and multi-leveled. For example:

> Could this be the curse of a shaman,
> Which loudly cries in these *aals*?
> Could this be the curse of the *turpan* bird,
> That cries in the striped willows?

> You say this is from the water and from the earth?
> Was she really so frightened and splashed so much?
> You say she defiled
> The source of the spring?
> Then go there and see,
> What she did, when and where.

> Yes, at the spring
> The woman spilled water,
> And showed her shame there—
> And from this has come her woe.

> A spider also lives there,
> At night he will creep up to the doomed woman—
> And the master of the lake himself, Uspa—
> Not his daughter and not his son—

He sent his scout here,
To prevent this from being done.

Yes, they say the girl is sick because
She defiled the sacred water *arzhaan*.
Clean your shame yourselves,
Bless the water of the spring.

Organize a great festival,
Serve brisket and the fatty tail of the sheep.
Let there be archery, wrestling, and races,
And heated competitions, and merry games,
And they will clean the dirt and shame forever.

Your daughter shines with laughter,
But she is seeing an outsider.
With the smoke of the juniper
Cover the tracks of this cursed tramp.

In her belly, in the inner organ,
Already lies a two-month child.
Time will pass, and the day will come,
And I will make your happiness.

Among your herds
There is an ambling colt.
There also lies a chest,
In which is silk for a robe, that too is possessed by the devil.

And in your box
Is silverware.
In one chest, in your chest—
There lies a golden talisman.

Bring all of this
As an offering to the master Uspa.
To the spring, whence you draw your drinking water,
As an offering, please bring silk.
I shall fumigate with juniper, wash with water—
And then your sick daughter will be well.

(Recorded from Seree Khertek)

According to the scenario, *eereni* came to help the sick one at the shaman's request. The shaman appealed to them for advice:

> Such is the reason for our talk!
> Let us speak, let us smoke,
> You must come here and find a solution—
> What need be done, what must be done.
>
> You have tried the taste of the milk,
> You have tasted the best milk.
> I beg you, do not rush away,
> Shrouding yourselves with a white cloud.
> I beg you to free the sick one,
> From the heavy burden of his illness,
> Which violently squeezes his chest and does not let him
>   breathe freely.
>
> What method, what advice is necessary?
> I beg you to tell me, *eereni*.
> Where, do you say? Which, do you say?
> In what direction is it found?
> Where is it hiding? What does it have with itself?
> What has occurred, and how has this come about?
>   (Recorded from Aldyn-Kherel Ondar)

Here is how a shaman asks his spirit-helpers to save the life of a man dying from tuberculosis:

> *Eereni*, make him spit strongly,
> So that the bloody pus comes out in a stream. Do so!
> Stop his loud coughing,
> Let the bloody foam come out of him. Do so!
> Make his belly swell,
> So that he belches and does not sit down. Do so!
>
> Disturb him so he sneezes,
> So he passes his illness down below,
> So that it comes out with the gases. Do so!
>   (Recorded from Viktor Kok-ool)

The theme of illness in general occupied a major place in shamanic poetry. The motif of forestalling mournful events, the approach of illness, and a person's tragic death was also often sounded.

The shaman constructed his predictions so that listeners became afraid of unknown forces. According to stories of the old people, after a shaman was consulted for a prediction every healthy person felt sick and again appealed to the shaman.[f]

The shamans liked to pose as prophets. The nature of the prediction often depended on the social status of the applicant. To the poor, the shaman made a short prediction, to the rich a more elaborate one. If a patient was rich, the shaman deliberately avoided a clear formulation of the prognosis in order to repeat the seance after a certain time and receive a larger reward.

> Your companion-soul
> Has flown away to the upper world of Kurbustu.
> In the country where it is dwelling,
> There is nothing foul.

> These people have their own *eeren*
> Who makes all the bones of the body shake.
> If you will feed me meat, then I
> Might vanquish such *eeren*.

(Recorded from Viktor Kok-ool)

If the shaman were no longer called upon, he would have no income. In order to enlarge the clientele, a shaman resorted to intimidation:

> A ways from your *aal*
> There is a cave, facing the north.
> There a company of *aza* is gathered—
> They might be dangerous.
> This cave requires a great offering-payment,
> A wicked evil is brewing there.
> A stranger will arrive to visit you,
> He is placing his foot in the stirrup.
> Together with him shall come a spirit from the land of Erlik,
> He is waiting at the roof of your *yurt*.

(Recorded from Seree Khertek)

Shamanistic followers dreaded the shaman's wrath. Even so, the shaman might become angry. For example, a person who inadvertently "offended" a shamanic spirit-helper by walking in front of its image became his personal enemy. The highest pitch of passion was achieved in rivalry between two shamans. A folklore expedition recorded an imprecation of the former shaman Oorzhak Shokar:

Ah, let the *aza* consume the cursed one,
Let it devour his children,
Let it tear open the bosom of his parents,
May you be eaten piece by piece!

Oi, let him have no descendants,
Oi, let him be alone, like a stake,
Oi, let him be like a withered tree.[1]

Followers believed that if a soul abandoned a person they would take sick and die. The soul of the deceased would visit its native places, where its friends and relatives lived, at least twice: after seven days and after forty-nine days. In visiting the familial hearth, the soul of the deceased, according to Tuvan notions, attempted to tell its kin about itself, to express its displeasure with a particular ungrateful living relative or to impart its last wish to a friend.

If no children were born to a family, this meant in Tuvan belief that the soul of a child was not inhabiting their *yurt*. The parents of the newlyweds then invited a well-known shaman to summon this soul. Here is a fragment of text of a seance intended to "summon the soul" of an unborn infant:

Naryyn-naryn! Alaas-alaas!
And you, multitude of idols,
And you, ancient elders,
And you, sovereigns of Burkhan![g]

And my drum, like a mountain,
And my rattle, like a stone,
And my gray mother's grandmother.
You know how things grow,
You know the life of he who shall die.
My gray-headed ancestors!
You are the protectors of he who is in the cradle,
You bestow good fortune on the infant!

I sing your praises, I sing your praises,
Having prepared delicious food for all of you.
I solemnly bless you,
Giving you a white *kadak*—a silken handkerchief,

A soul of the infants—the golden-headed children,
Playing in the *saizanak* of stones,
I call, I summon and invite.
Kurai-kurai! I call the souls of children.

Boys who will carry the flint,
Girls with ribbons—
Call their fortunate souls.
My dark and fearsome *khaiyrakan*,
Who stands at the bedside, near the pillow!

My snakes, my four-sided ones!
My creator, copper-headed old one!
Give us happiness, give us goodness!

(Recorded from Saaia Sambuu)

Or:

Let the souls of tiny children come down
Onto the surface of the milken food.
Kurai-kurai! Kurai-kurai!
Children, whose cradles are made of gray willows,
Children who feed at their mother's breast,
Children whose cheeks are round, let your souls come here!
Kurai-kurai! Kurai-kurai!

Children, whose cradles are made of willow withies,
Children who lie on the goat skin,
Children, let your souls return here!
Kurai-kurai! Kurai-kurai!

(Recorded from Saaia Sambuu)

Fire enjoyed great veneration among shamanic followers. The autumn ritual of fire reverence was supposed to ensure the well-being and good fortune of the family year-round. A "great" shaman was generally invited to the celebration of the hearth.

He has a fast steed—a yellow goat with an apple on its brow,
He has an encirclement—an iron ring,
He has a birch enclosure.

This fire, he is the master of the smoke-darkened idols [*eeleri*].
Be quiet! Be courteous!
Kurai! Kurai! Kurai!

He is the well-being of the livestock,
He is the happiness of growing children.
Kurai! Kurai! Kurai!

You, O smudged creator idols,
Create a protection, a fence around the hearth,
So that no loss is suffered!

And the souls of boys carrying the flint and knife,
And the souls of girls skilled in the needle and ring,
Protect and guard them.
Kurai! Kurai! Kurai!

(Recorded from Aleksei Bair)

In this poem devoted to fire, we notice an intertwining of mythological and real motifs. At first, the shaman describes the general appearance of the domestic hearth. This is a very familiar picture to those who were born and grew up in the *yurt*: a tripod for the iron kettle, a square of birch wood around the hearth—all of this is absolutely essential. Every hearth has a domestic animal devoted to it (the "yellow goat with an apple on its brow"). The hearth has its own protector *eereni*, which are supposed to prevent the entry of evil spirits into the *yurt*. Death, disease, birth, misfortune—all depends on fire. "Fire is my god, fire is my creator," Tuvans say.

The shamanic seances also reflected themes connected with productive activity—the hunt, animal husbandry, and farming. For example, the shaman Oorzhak Mortui-ool once held a seance at the request of a hunter. To ensure a successful hunt, the shaman appealed to the tall mountain range of Khan-Deer. According to a Tuvan legend, once many animals lived here and the hunters killed so many of them that their blood flowed in a river, in which the sky was reflected (hence the name of the locality: Khan-Deer, "Bloody Sky"). Here is the text of the shaman's propitiatory poem:

I light the censer,
I sprinkle the holy water,
I offer a white and blue ribbon in sacrifice,
To you, my Khan-Deer!

What you wish to give me—
Please give.
What it is rightful for me to take—
Please grant.

If one should come insolently to you—
Let him have no place to hunt,
If one should steal from you—
Give him no riches,
O wealthy Khan-Deer!

Do not conceal
Your wealth under yourself.
Do not hide
Under branches.

Where there is level ground,
Where there is a handsome tree,
There bestow, my wealthy Khan-Deer!
My dark taiga,
You have a thousand dark trees,
You have a hundred hearts,
You have nine pitchers.
My taiga, bestow that with the shiny earrings,
My taiga, bestow that with the bushy tail.
Be good, my taiga,
Guard me, my taiga,
Give me strength, my taiga,
Give my horse strength, my taiga!
Kurai! Kurai! Kurai!

(Recorded from Aleksei Bair)

If one of the members of a family took ill, or if the head of the family suffered a misfortune, the shaman was invited to hold a seance in honor of the sacred horse. The shaman conducted the ceremony and composed verses addressed to this animal, so that a horse with its mane decorated by a red ribbon was sanctified.

Whose eyes are like a spyglass?
Whose teeth are like a shell?
Whose breath is like a fog?
Say thy word,

Stretch forth the golden shoe,
Do not be angry,
Do not be distracted,

Be the guardian of your yard,
Never abandon your gates!

I have washed you with holy water—*arzhaan*,
So that your anger disappears.
I have bathed you in the smoke of the juniper—*artysh*,
So your fright disappears.

Do not be angry with your master,
Who fed and raised you.
If you pace in a circle,
My head will be dizzy.

If you get angry,
My throat will choke. And so be good!
I beg of you,
Do not weaken me, be good!

(Recorded from Aleksei Bair)

The poetics of shamanic folklore

Most of the shamans held the seance in the Tuvan language, although there were some exceptions. Shalyk Darbaa told of the "great" shaman Shadyk who held seances in Tuvan, Mongolian, and Chinese. His only son, Don, was mute. The people said that shaman Shalyk, who was fluent in three languages, spent his whole life in battle with hostile shamans, and though they could not "devour" him they nevertheless took vengeance in his son being born without a tongue.[h] And Saaia Sambuu told how the shaman Kaldar, who died in 1930, migrated from the nearby Altai Mountains to the Mongun-Taiga region in the early twenties. He shamanized only in the Altai language. Another shaman, Askak, also held seances in Altai. According to information obtained from Tash-ool Kungaa, the famous shamaness Kurgak Kyrgys lived beside the rivers Kachyk and Saigal, which are on the border with Mongolia. Her entire life she "serviced" the sick of the Tuvans and Mongols, shamanizing in the Mongolian language.

Even in the same seance, the language often changed. Each of the characters had their own style and speech, with a rich symbolism of sound. This intensified the emotional aspect of the seance. The elder Chimba Lopsan said that if a shaman was cursing his enemy he imitated the raven; summoning rain, he imitated the crow; frightening people, he imitated the wolf or the eagle-owl; uncovering a lie, he imitated the magpie; showing off his power, he imitated the bull; and expressing rapture, the bear. In a word, the shaman could imitate the voices of many wild animals, birds, and domestic animals. According to Soruktu Kyrgys, the shamaness Shimit-Kyrgys also imitated various voices in the same seance. If it turned out that the patient was ill from "meddling of the spirits" of water or earth, the shamaness imitated the voices of the raven, crow, wolf, Siberian stag, billy goat, marmot, and bear. Having decided that the patient was the victim of the anger of domestic animals, Shimit-Kyrgys imitated the voices of the nanny goat, sheep, camel, horse, and dog.

Words and sounds had a definite symbolism. In Tuvan beliefs, if a horse bites his bridle, his master could take ill and die. By imitating the neighing of a horse, the shaman predicted a bad outcome. If the cry of the raven was heard at night, this meant the soul of a person was going away. By imitating the voice of the raven, the shaman predicted the imminent passing of a person with his soul.[i]

Before the start of the seance, the shaman turned to the audience and shouted onomatopoeic words, selecting those needed for the anaphora of the verses; in a quiet voice he conversed with the spirits, choosing a rhythm. Salchak Tamba recalls that the shaman Suiziuk never began by singing verses. First he imitated the raven, the magpie, and the bear; then he performed a shamanic dance; and only after this did he begin the seance.

The Tuvans are great masters in making onomatopoeic words; they have a special throat singing (of the *kargyraa, sygyt,* and *khomei* types):[j]

> *Aa-uu-aa-uui! Kelbes cherge chuge kelding?*
> *Choruvas cherge choraan sen.*
> *Aa-uu, aa-uui! Euzheen-kylyyng algan-dyr sen*
> *Alyryngny algan-dir sen.*
>
> (Recorded from Saaia Sambuu)

> *Aa-uu, aa-uu!* Why did you come to the forbidden place?
> It seems you have already been where it is not permitted.
> *Aa-uu, aa-uu!* You have already taken back your anger,
> And you have taken that which need be taken.

The beast about which the shaman is singing is not mentioned here, but it is recognized from the voice, and it is clear to the audience that the shaman is singing about a wolf. The seemingly senseless words, according to our informants, produced an intoxicating effect on the onlookers. The shaman's helpers usually sat at his right and left and echoed the same words.

Azyg aksyng, oo-ooi,
Aazatpa, oo-ooi,
Azyg dizhing, ooi-ooi,
Shaaratpam, Ooi-ooi.

(Recorded from Saaia Sambuu)

Your mouth, *oo-ooi,*
Do not open, *oo-ooi,*
Your fangs, *ooi-ooi,*
Do not show, *Ooi-ooi.*

This is how the shaman addressed the spirit-helper, *eeren moosa,* so that he did not reveal his "fearsome outer form" to the people. The words *ooi-ooi* in this case perform a magical function.[2]

The seance began in standard fashion, occasionally with pairs of onomatopoeic words; this is characteristic of an archaic construction. For example:

Aryyng-aryyn!
Alaas-alaas!
Aryglanyp,
Naryydap aain!

(Recorded from Seree Khertek)

I wish to be cleansed
And I prepare myself for cleansing!

The Tuvans say: *"Khalak deerge—khalas barbas"* ("Say *khalak*—there will be a sacrifice"). When the shaman conjures a thief, he necessarily uses the "magical" word *khalak*:

Aa khalak-khalak!
Algash baardy, kulugurnu!
Aa khalak-khalak!
Azalarnyng, aldyn shalba!
As khalak-khalak!
Ara kirzin, kulugurnu!

(Recorded from Viktor Kok-ool)

Aa khalak-khalak!
He took the cattle, the scoundrel!
Aa khalak-khalak!

A golden lasso should [take him] to the devils!
Aa khalak-khalak!
Let the scoundrel not reach his home!

The word *khalak-khalak* in this incantation, indicating fresh milk and having lost its independent meaning, plays the part of an interjection and expresses the shaman's hatred of the thief.

Word-symbols could also be placed at the end of a text. It is said there was once a "mighty" shaman Keldir Khirligbei, who liked to sing songs of the daughter of the mythical subterranean king Erlik. At the end of each line of verse were interjectory words of purely abstract semantics:

Erlik's daughter, *shalyr-shalyr,*
My friend, *shalyr-shalyr,*
I would like to come to you, *shalyr-shalyr,*
I would like to meet you, *shalyr-shalyr.*

Never, *shalyr-shalyr,*
Shall I die, *shalyr-shalyr,*
Erlik's daughter is mine, *shalyr-shalyr,*
She is my friend, *shalyr-shalyr.*

(Recorded from Saaia Sambuu)

Onomatopoeic words of the *shalyr-shalyr* type are often found in shamanic verse and designate a loud rustling sound.[3]

By its very nature, shamanic verse is musical. We find striking parallels in the use of interjections and onomatopoeic words in ancient folk songs and shamanic texts. Here is a folk song:

Kuu dagnyng baaryndan, konggurgai,
Kuduk kassa ugmein kanchaar, konggurgai,
Kuskun kara uruglarny, konggurgai,
Kudalaza albain kanchaar, konggurgai.[4]

If you dig underneath the mountain Kuu, *konggurgai,*
There will be a well, *konggurgai,*
If you woo girls with tresses like a raven's wing, *konggurgai,*
They will become women, *konggurgai.*

Another song, a recent one, is called *"Dembildei."* The composer, Saaia Biurbee, wrote the music for it to the words of the national poet of the Tuvan ASSR, Sergei Piurbiu.

Orai kezhee syldys karaa chetchip-tip,
Salgyn bolchaang euiu keep-tip, ezhikei,
Oglaa-saryg dynyn tyrtyp, chutkui-dur.
Salgyn-bile charzhyptar-dyr, dembildei.
Dembil, dembil, dembildei.[5]

In the late sky the eyes of the stars appear,
My dear, the hour of the meeting has come.
The restless piebald horse is anxious to go,
Let us fly, speeding with the wind, *dembildei,*
Dembil, dembil, dembildei.

In these two examples, we find a succession of onomatopoeic words of exceptional vivacity. Such words intensified the rhythmical sounds of shamanic incantations, and they also beautify the melody of modern songs. Rasul Gamzatov has written on the rhythmical, poetic, and melodious nature of words of this type. The word *"dolalai"* that he uses and the Tuvan *"dembildei"* or *"agarooi"* are identical in their function:

I, composing verse, sometimes sing:
Dolalai, dolalai, dolalai.[6]

Obviously, word-symbols, word-music, and word-interjections participate in creating the rhythm of song and cannot be replaced by any other words of purely lexical meaning.

We shall present some examples characterizing the riches and diversity of the figurative-expressive means of the language of shamanic poetry. A classic example of the use of epithet is the following text:

Kalchaa dalai keustup deldi,
Kanchalyyly, chalgynnygbai?
Chadgynnarym chadyptain che,
Chalbaraashtyng kiripteeli.

(Recorded from Salchak Tamba)

Lo, the raging sea, has appeared,
What shall we do, wingèd one?
Let us stretch out our wings
And make a prayer.

Such was the song of the popular shaman Siuziuk in the Kaa-Khemsk region during his seance. Addressing his raven idol [helper spirit-image] shaman Siuziuk created an image of a mythological sea, to which only he and his helper could fly. Or an example of simile:

> My aorta, my liver have dried up.
> Like a snake in a hollow,
> I am the shaman Burbu, I am the pock-marked shaman.
> I ask for good things from the benefactor,
> I ask for mercy with my seance,
> So that death will go away forever.
>
> (Recorded from Arkadii Bazyr-Taraa)

The true meaning of what was sung in the shaman's verse could only be understood by knowing the historical and lexical meaning of each word. For example, the shaman could talk at length about his *eereni* without naming them. Whoever knew the shaman's helpers would understand what he was singing about. Allegory was a favorite technique of the Tuvan shamans. We present an example:

> Have you indeed come to take him away?
> Have you indeed come from his *aal*?
> He has gone from the *yurt* and stands beyond the threshold,
> He is looking back, there he stands.
> What must I do for it to be well?
>
> (Recorded from Salchak Tamba)

The poet Salchak Tamba, who provided this text, was present in his youth at a seance of the shamaness Kham-Kadai. She was "curing" a man who could not get up from his bed and she was talking to someone. After the seance the shamaness explained: "A very strong *buk* (evil spirit—M.K.-L.) has appeared in this *aal*. I wrested him away from the sick man and chased him from the *yurt*. But he went out and is standing there, beyond the threshold, he is standing and looking at the sick man. However much I chased the *buk*, he does not want to go any further. He wants to take the one he came for."

The shaman might speak in his verses of a living person as though he were dead. He might sing of a long-deceased person as of one who has come from afar to take someone back with him. The shaman might speak of a tree, a spring of water, a mountain, as of a living being. Many examples of personification can be found in shamanic folklore. Here is a fragment from the seance of a shaman appealing to the high mountains Khattyg-Taiga and Buura-Taiga:

My Khattyg-Taiga!
My shamaness—my Buura!
Look, listen!
When you, the watchful one, when you, the careful one,
With your storm, with your rain
Let the plague pass by,
I humbly beg of you.

(Recorded from Arkadii Bazyr-Taraa)

The shamans liked to exalt their spirit-helpers. For example, a shaman spoke about the meaning of his small wooden raven *eeren*:

He flies swiftly—
The flute sounds piercingly.
On his wings is an inscription,
On his tail is drawn an ornament,
He flies to where the beast with red blood dwells,
He ascends to the zenith,
Such thou art, my slender, my black raven.

You are carried easily through the air,
My black raven, hungry raven!
You are my black scout, you are my white scout.
I beg you to come to me, to come nigh!
[*Arai-la beer, oon-na beer!*]

Descend from the skies,
Drop on my head with a dance.
There, between my shoulder blades, hang little bells,
They are of bronze, amuse yourself with them!
On my shoulders are little bells—
They are black, they are masculine.
Play to the sound of these bells.
[*Konggalarnyng, unu-bile oinazhyngar!*]

In this poem the shaman created an extremely vivid and poetic image of the raven: it flies headlong, it cuts the air with its wings, it soars in the skies, it lightly descends to earth. All that is on the earth and in the sky is subservient to the raven-spirit.

Shamans could conjure with special respect for *albys* [witches; Russian *ved'ma*]:

Under the lowering skies, under the storm clouds,
Above the spreading trees
My golden *albys* fly,
My *albys* fly with a rustle, with a noise,
Each one has a forked tongue.
My amber-golden ones, my all-powerful ones,
With forked tongues.
You are sharper than an awl,
More clever than a spy.

(Recorded from Aleksei Bair)

In the images of the *albys*, we see legendary creatures, but to the shaman the *albys* were real forces.

The shamanic rituals made use of *chazhyg*, a pitcher of holy water, and *san*, or juniper, which was strewn on a flat stone, resembling a small plate. How the shaman exalted these in verse can be seen from the following example:

Eei-ei!
At the beginning of the moon, at the beginning of the sun, *oo-oo-oo!*
At the very dawn of this day, *oo-oo-oo!*
Eei-ei!
I offer holy water, like a large sea, *oo-oo-oo!*
I burn juniper, like a large mountain, *oo-oo-oo!*

(Recorded from Salchak Shokshut)

Here, the pitcher of holy water is called a sea and the handful of juniper is compared to a mountain. There are many such examples of exaggeration of the qualities and dimensions of attributes in shamanic mythology.

In the lexicon of shamanic poetry one can find words that have gone out of the word fund of the modern Tuvan language. Here is an example of the words used by a shaman in creating a portrait of his white *eeren*:

His *baryndak* is of white silk,
His *ovaadai* is of lynx and sable skin,
His food is wormwood,
His *chegedek* is of white *kadak*,
His food is the aspen tree,
His *chegedek* is of yellow *kadak*.

(Recorded from Aleksei Bair)

Here, *baryndak* is a handkerchief, *ovaadai* a hat, *chegedek* a vest. It should be noted that certain words and phraseological combinations employed in shamanic texts are also missing from dictionaries, in particular the *Tuvan-Russian Phraseological Dictionary*.[7]

A primary characteristic of shamanic verse is the repetition of an identical number of vowel sounds in a line. The quatrain is the basic unit of shamanic poetry. In rhythm, the shamanic verse has an equal number of syllables. The strict alternation of interjections at the beginning and end of the line sets the rhythm.

The oldest determinants of the sound organization of the shamanic seance were interjections, which are totally absent from modern Tuvan poetry. Without the musical instrument of the drum, without the music composed by the shaman himself, and without his performance of it, these archaic determinants lose their emotional force. We shall present several examples in which the most characteristic rhythmical determinants of shamanic song are easily seen.

The use of interjections at the start of a line:

Alas. Alas. I have been to Erlik's land.
Alas. Alas. I am very tired, I have suffered much.
Alas. Alas. I have been in Aza's land.
Alas. Alas. I am very hungry, I wish to drink.

(Recorded from Arkadii Bazyr-Taraa)

The use of interjections at the end of the line:

The red mountain range, *doot-doot*,
Where I shall lie, *doot-doot*,
The red blossom, *doot-doot*,
Which I have eaten, *doot-doot*.

(Recorded from Saaia Sambuu)

Example of four-syllable verse:

Dunggurlugnung
Duvu changgys.
Orbalygnyng
Oruu changgys.

(Recorded from Dezhit Tozhu)

He who has the drum,
Only one bottom.

He who has the rattle,
Only one road.

Example of eight-syllable verse:

Kalgan-bargan chuvelerni
Katap ergeesh, kanchaar onu.
Eulgen-bargan chuvelerge
Eurgul kylyp kanchaar onu.

(Recorded from Kuzhuget Balgan)

One need not return to those,
Who have gone away forever.
One need not honor the dead,
Who are long since deceased.

Example of twelve-syllable verse:

Artysh, shaanak chydy dolgan bedik taigam,
Arzhaan sugnung uner deuzu ulug synym,
Azhy-teuldun amy-tynyn alyr deeshting,
Artysh, shaanak, agy-kanggy kypsyp tur men.

(Recorded from Viktor Kok-ool)

My high taiga full of the scent of the juniper and heather,
My high mountain, where the water *arzhaan* takes its source,
In order to save the life of small children,
I burn the juniper, heather, and wormwood.

An identical number of syllables in syntactic parallelism functions as a rhythmical determinant of shamanic verse. The singer (shaman) places primary attention on the first syllable of the line and thereafter on the parallel harmony of vowels in couplets (according to the type of the proverb). Thus, the full vigor of shamanic verse depended on the rhythmical alternation of vowels. As an illustration, we take one stanza of shamanic poetry:

Aalyngarnyng kedeezinde
Aksy dedir ulug kui bar,
Aza-chetker ynda chyylgan—
Alys baryp ondaktyg-dyr.

(Recorded from Seree Khertek)

In the back of your *aal*
There is a cave, facing north.
There a company of devils is gathered—
In future they may be dangerous.

The scheme of harmony of the vowels in the above stanza is as follows:

aa-y/a-y e-ee/i-e
a-y e-i u-u u/a
a-a/e-e y-a yy-a
a-y a-y o-a y-y.

Here, we observe the equal number of syllables in parallel syntactical lines. This is an important feature of shamanic versification. Eight-syllable stanzas are the most common, four- and six-syllable stanzas considerably rarer. Five-, seven-, and ten-syllable stanzas are almost never used. The words and the order of presentation in our example preserve the archaic form of syntactical parallelism: the vowels of the first line harmonize with the vowels of the second, those of the third with the vowels of the fourth. The principle of equality of symbols in paired couplets and quatrains dictates the rhythmicity of shamanic poetry. Tuvan shamanic verse is synharmonic in nature, based on rhythmical syntactical parallelism.

An essential organizer of the sounds of shamanic versification was lexical or phonetic refrain, anaphora. To the characteristic sounds of shamanic verse, anaphora was not merely a repetition of words or syntactical constructs, but also a means of unification of sounds at the beginning of sentences, verses, and stanzas.

A classical example of a shamanic text:

Kady taakpy tyrtyzhaaly,
Kady araga izhizheeli,
Changys a"tka ushkazhyyly,
Changys tonga khoigazhyyly.
Dyngnaan chuve chazhyrbaaly,
Typkan chuve kamnaaly.[8]

Let us smoke tobacco together,
Let us drink *arak* together,
We shall travel on the same steed,
We shall wear the same coat,
We shall not conceal the tidings heard,
We shall guard that which is found![9]

In this example, the verbal parallelism initiated by the words *kady* and *changys* is accompanied by a rhythmical highlighting of these parallel terms. Every composer of shamanic song considered a uniform beginning of his speech to be an essential condition, not paying attention to the random repetition of words or sounds in the middle and at the end of lines. Anaphora is the basic technique of shamanic versification. We shall present several examples characterizing anaphora as the organizing principle of shamanic versification.

An example of sound anaphora:

> *Idiingerning khonchuzunda*
> *Iii dangza taakpy bar-dyr.*
> *Ishtingerde, khyrnyngarda*
> *Iii-le ailyg urug bar-dyr.*

> (Recorded from Viktor Kok-ool)

> There, tucked in behind the shoe,
> Is tobacco enough for two pipes.
> There, in your belly,
> Is a two-month child.

Each line begins with the same vowel, "i," on which the shaman placed special emphasis during the seance. Lexical anaphora, intensifying the role of rhythm in the verse, imparts a sing-song quality:

> *Kyzyl kyrny kyrlai kakkash,*
> *Kyzyl charyk askyn keureel.*
> *Kyzyl khany ynda teuktur,*
> *Kyzyl tyny ynda kalyr.*

> Along the red slope we shall gallop,
> There we shall see the mouth of the red ravine,
> Red blood turns crimson there,
> It bids farewell to the red breath there.[10]

Here, lexical anaphora of the same word is used by the shaman to highlight the beginning of the lines and hold the listeners' attention.

Anaphora of paired words is seldom found in shamanic verse. We have an example of such anaphora from the seance of Kham-ool, the hero of a play by V. Kok-ool:

Oozhum-oozhum boluulungar,
Ooldar, kystar chyglyp kelzin.

Softly-softly sit,
Let the boys and girls gather round.

A peculiar technique of shamanic versification is strophic anaphora. The eminent expert in Tuvan folklore, B.K. Mongush,[k] has provided me with a characteristic specimen of strophic anaphora:

Agarooi!
My *kuzungu* of golden bronze,
It is a gift of the skies.
It is the terror of six men,
It took its breath from six sheep.
Agarooi!
My *kuzungu* of iron bronze.
It is the gift of devils.
It is the terror of seven men,
It took its breath from seven sheep.

When we speak of anaphoric parallelism, we mean syntactical parallelism. Many examples of syntactical anaphora can be found in shamanic folklore. For example:

Chedi kudai shavyzy men,
Chedi khamnyng cheeni men,
Aldy kudai shavyzy men,
Aldy khamnyng anynaa men.

(Recorded from Kenden Kuular)

I am the follower of seven skies,
I am the grandson of seven shamans.
I am the follower of six skies,
I am the youngest of six shamans.

Alliteration is a powerful means of vocal expressiveness of shamanic verse. If the shaman began one line with a consonant, he would start the parallel line with the same consonant.

Beudei kara chadyrymche
Beueuldei khamnap chanain yngai.
Samdar kara chadyrymche
Samnai khamnap chanain yngai!

(Recorded from Viktor Kok-ool)

It is time for me to return home,
Leading the seance in the wild dance.
It is time for me to return to my rundown, my dark hut,
Leading the seance in the wild dance.

In this example, the first and second lines begin with the consonant "b," while the third and fourth begin with the consonant "s." Thus, our analysis shows that shamanic verse, in its composition, is anaphoric verse.

There is no rhythm, in the full meaning of this term, in shamanic poetry. Instead, the principal form of metrical composition is atrophic epiphora. This appears as a repetition of the same vocal combinations, sometimes words or combinations of words. One should emphasize the special role of epiphora at the end of syntactically parallel lines. For example:

Terek bashtap kagaalyngar,
Tereng suglap kezheelinger,
Oorug bashtap kagaalyngar,
Ottuk-dashtap alyynyngar.

(Recorded from Viktor Kok-ool)

Over the tops of the poplars we shall fly,
The deep rivers we shall swim across,
Over the tall mountains we shall roam,
Flintstone we shall gather.

The identical (consonant) endings of the lines and verbs of identical rhythmical meaning are quite characteristic of shamanic verse. A repetition of morphologically identical endings is also found in the form of nouns, singular or plural:

Ailar, sholban karaktyymny,
Aldyn, meunggun syrgalyymny,
Kydyr-kydyr karaktyymny,
Kyzyl khureng shyrailyymny.

(Recorded from Viktor Kok-ool)

Her eyes resemble the moon and the morning star,
She has golden and silver earrings,
Her eyelids have delicate creases,
Her face is of ruddy amber.

The words for eyes, earrings, and face have the same declensions, which intensifies the phonic rhythm, in which the long vowel "y" is most clearly delineated.

Anaphora at the start of lines is a conscious choice of sounds or words. The coincidence of sounds at the end of lines of verse, as I.V. Stebleva correctly writes, is forced, and therefore not creative.[11] The epiphora of shamanic verse is not a rhythmoid, much less a rhythm. It arises by chance, as a result of the coincidence of terminal sounds of identical grammatical forms, as a compulsory euphonic technique.

Alliteration and assonances as constituent elements of root anaphora are an organic part of the general organization of shamanic versification, where the archaic order of words is preserved in its primordial form. The expressive force of the root syllable has not been suppressed here by the influence of other languages. The principal element of the vocal organization of shamanic verse, as shown by our analysis, was the root syllable. The most important for a characterization of shamanic verse are the active role of the beginning of the word, the passive role of the end of the word in each line, the presence of a constant accent, the tendency to balancing of syllables in parallel lines of verse, the archaic construction of the sentences, and the major role of synharmonism as the basic rhythmical law of shamanic verse. Thus, the form of shamanic poetry, according to V.M. Zhirmunskii, was based on rhythmical-syntactical parallelism, characteristic of the ancient epic style of the Turkic peoples;[12] but with strict observance of vowel harmony. Shamanic verse is anaphoric in composition and synharmonic in rhythmics.

Editor's notes

a. The author's use of the masculine for shamans and their dress is preserved here, although ahead it is clear that some Tuvan shamans were women. It should be noted that some still are (personal communication V.Iu. Suzukei, Tuvan ethnomusicologist, August 1992). See also V.Iu. Suzukei, "Shamanizm i muzykal'nyi fol'klor Tuvinstev," in A.I. Gogolev, A.P. Reshetnikova, K.N. Romanova, P.A. Sleptsov, Z.F. Semenova, eds. *Shamanizm kak religiia (Tezisy dokladov mezhdunarodnoi nauchnoi konferentsii)* (Yakutsk: "Iakutsk" Gosudarstvennyi Universitet, 1992), pp. 57–58.

b. Word order is preserved here, so that the meaning of "tree-shaman" is differentiated from the more general concept of a shamanic, or world-tree. See for context: Mircea Eliade, *Shamanism* (Chicago: University of Chicago Press, 1972), pp. 37–42, 70–71,

271–82; Vilmos Dioszegi, "Tuva Shamanism," *Acta Etnografiia*, 1962, vol. 11, pp. 143–90.

c. Subsequent poems translated here were also provided in the original text in the Tuvan modified Cyrillic, with Russian translations. Readers interested in linguistic subtleties of the highly alliterative poetry should consult the original text. Where discussion of word musicality makes transliteration crucial, it is provided. Tuvan used Mongolian and Tibetan scripts into the 1930s. In 1930, a modern Tuvan Latin alphabet script was also devised. This was changed into Cyrillic in 1943, and is now the subject of political debate.

d. Poetic license seems to have been taken in Kenin-Lopsan's Russian translation, for he uses the refrain "*oo-ooi*" more in the Russian poem than the Tuvan original. More significant, he twice glosses as "idol" two phrases that are metaphorical, referring to the bear helper-spirit as "honored one" and "thunderer." Euphemisms for the bear are widespread throughout Siberia and also in Slavic tradition.

e. "Idols" is used in the original, although the terms "spirit images" or "ancestral images" have less pejorative meaning and are more specific. *Eeren*, which also means spirit, appears most frequently in the Tuvan incantations, glossed as *idol* or *idol-bog* by Kenin-Lopsan but kept here as *eeren*.

f. For other, more positive, dimensions to the psychology of consumers of shamanism, see S. Shirokogoroff, *Psychomental Complex of the Tungus* (London: Routledge & Kegan Paul, 1935); M.M. Balzer, "Introduction," in *Shamanism: Soviet Studies of Traditional Religion in Siberia and Central Asia* (Armonk, NY: M.E. Sharpe, 1990), pp. vii–xviii; Lola Romanucci-Ross, Daniel Moerman, and Lawrence Tancredi, eds., *The Anthropology of Medicine* (New York: Bergin and Garvey, 1991).

g. This refers to Burkhan, a Mongolic name for a manifestation of the Buddha worshipped in Burkhanism, called *ak di'an* or the "white faith." It developed among the nearby Altai-Kizhi at the start of the century, and can be interpreted as an ethnic revitalization or "nativistic" religion, syncretizing aspects of shamanism and Dzhungar Lamaism. See Liudmilla I. Sherstova, "Shamanizm i Burkhanism: Dinamika vzaimootnoshenii," in A.I. Gogolev, et al., eds., *Shamanizm kak religiia*, p. 86; Lawrence Krader, "A Nativistic Movement in Western Siberia," *American Anthropologist*, 1956, vol. 58, pp. 282–92.

h. Sadly, this idea of revenge of hostile shamans or their helper-spirits on family members of shamans has not died, and is widespread through much of Siberia, judging from discussions on this with Khanty (Ob-Ugrian Ostiak), Sakha (Turkic Yakut), and Nanai (Amur River Goldy) consultants. Related to a perceived need for protection, the Tuvan words for *kham*, seance, and to guard, *khamna-*, probably have the same root, also widespread.

i. The raven holds a special place in the ranks of shamanic spirit-helpers among many of the Eastern Siberian peoples, and also in Northwest Coast Alaskan traditions. The Sakha also specifically associate the raven with messages of death.

j. A Tuvan throat master is able to sound like more than one person singing at once by creating deep, gutteral resonances through a highly controlled system of song types. The echoing magic of this music (created in and for the mountains of the Altai) can be heard on the Melodiia record (D–030773–74) "Melodii Tuvy," and is forthcoming in the Smithsonian/Folkways series, produced by ethnomusicologist Ted Levin. Throat singing has been part of the Tuvan cultural revival, with groups led by activist-singers such as Genadii Chash, to whom I am grateful for insights into Tuvan culture. See *Soveshchanie po problemam razvitiia khomeiia* (Kyzyl: Ministerstvo kul'tury, 1988).

k. Borakh K. Mongush is the author's father.

Notes

1. "Rukopisnyi fond Tuvinskogo NIIIaLI," t. 57, d. 250, l. 15.

2. A similar technique was used by the author in the poem "End of the Shaman," the main character of which, the shaman Shagar, begins a strophic anaphora with the onomatopoeic interjection *agarooi*:

> *Agarooi!*
> Pour out your rage,
> Sounding like the rain,
> Yet do not hurl at me
> The lightning-snake!
> *Agarooi!*
> Water is needed,
> Celestial chief,
> Send the rain
> Speedily here!
>
> (Translation Iu. Razumovskii)

See M.B. Kenin-Lopsan, *Selected Works* in 2 vol. (in Tuvinian) (Kyzyl, 1975), vol. 1, p. 203; idem, *Kinovar'* (Kyzyl, 1973), p. 115.

3. F.G. Iskhakov and A.A. Pal'mbakh, *Grammatika tuvinskogo iazyka: fonetika i morfologiia* (Moscow, 1961), p. 462.

4. "Tyva ulustung yrlary" (Tuvan folk songs), musical arrangement by Maksim Munzuk, texts gathered by Kara-Kys Munzuk (Kyzyl, 1973), p. 37.

5. Biurbe Saaia, *Kush-azhylga maktal* (Glory to Labor!), in Tuvan (Kyzyl, 1967), p. 37.

6. R. Gamzatov, *Chetki let* (Moscow, 1973), p. 213.

7. Ia. Sh. Khertek, *Tuvinsko-russkii frazeologicheskii slovar'*, ed. D.A. Tatarintsev (Kyzyl, 1975).

8. *Obraztsy narodnoi literatury tiurkskikh plemen, izdannye V.V. Radlovym* (St. Petersburg, 1907), pt. 9. Dialects of the Uriankhai (Soiot), Abakan Tatars, and Kargas. Texts collected and revised by N.F. Katanov, p. 48.

9. Ibid., p. 45.

10. D.P. Potapov, "Materialy po izucheniiu etnografii tuvinskikh raionov Mongun-Taiga i Kara-Kholia," *Tr. TKAE* (Moscow-Leningrad, 1960), no. 1, p. 223.

11. I.V. Stebleva, *Poeziia tiurkov VI–VII vekov* (Moscow, 1965), p. 39.

12. V.M. Zhirmunskii, *Tiurkskii geroicheskii epos* (Leningrad, 1974), p. 580.

Afterword

The time when the Tuvans believed in the "voyaging" of the shamans, their strength and might, is a thing of the past. Professional shamanism, seances with traditional attributes, remain only in the people's memory. To a slight extent, elements of the cult of the shamanic tree, the mineral spring *arzhaan*, and certain beliefs indirectly related to shamanism are preserved. The bearers of the traditional religious consciousness are primarily people of advanced age. And only a few of them are able to perform the ceremony of the shamanic seance, and even these no longer use a drum or staff, but instead a saw harp, *vargan*.*

---

*See, for example, V.N. Basilov, *Izbranniki dukhov* (Moscow, 1984), p. 204.

The disappearance of shamanism from the daily life of the Tuvans, however, does not mean that the atheistic propaganda has accomplished its goals. There is yet much to be done to overcome the religious superstitions in the minds of the people. At the same time, it is difficult to overlook the tremendous problem faced by Siberian ethnographers. Along with the shamans and other beliefs, an entire stratum of cultural effects is gone from the life of the people. This applies, first and foremost, to the wealth of folklore.

Ancient folklore, including the shamanic type, is a unique source telling of the pathways of development of Tuvan culture and the life of the people itself in the recent past, not having their own literature. Classical specimens of shamanic folklore are used by scholars studying the history, ethnography, and language of the Tuvan people, as well as by writers who make creative use of the themes and images of ancient poetry in their own compositions.

List of informants

(The complete list of informants is given in the supplement to the manuscript dissertation: M.B. Kenin-Lopsan, "Siuzhety i praktika tuvinskogo shamanstva: Opyt istoriko-etnograficheskoi rekonstruktsii," GPB im. Lenina, dissertation collection.)

Aldyn-Kherel Ondar (1892–1980?), born in Man-Churek of Siut-Khol′ (Dzun-Khemchik) region, lived his last years in the village of Chyraa-Bazhy, Dzun-Khemchik region, a great expert in Tuvan mythology.

Bazyr-Taraa Arkadii Dambaevich (b. 1917), born in Ezhim, Ulug-Khem region, lives in the village of Khaiyrakan of the same region, took part in the First Republican Gathering of National Poets and Musicians.

Bair Aleksei Shirinmeevich (1904–85), born in Aldyy-Ishkin of Dzun-Khemchik region, very familiar with Mongolian and Russian languages.

Balgan Kuzhuget Lenchaevich (b. 1913), born in Tele-Gol, Bai-Taiga region, a wood carver. Recording taken in the village of Kara-Khol′.

Biurbiu Kyrggys Oidupovich (b. 1936), born in Torgalyg, Oviur region. Now lives in Kyzyl., Baitaiga region.

Dazhy-Bilbin Khovalyg Balchyi-oolovich (1905–80?), resident of the village of Tor-galyg, Ulug-Khem region, storyteller, very familiar with Russian and Mongolian languages, knew many *algyshy.*

Dezhit Tozhu Lopsan uruu (b. 1912, former shamaness), born in Sorug-Chazy, Kaa-Khem region, now lives in the village of Kungurtuk, Kyzyl region. A great expert in shamanic folklore.

Dongak Barykaan Kuralbai uruu (1898–1975), born in Bedik-Khavak, Dzun-Khemchik region. The first poetess of Tuva, writing in Mongolian, an expert in Tuvan folklore. Recording taken in the village of Khon-dergei, Dzun-Khemchik region.

Dulush Chamyian Kalbak oglu (b. 1914), born in Kara-Sug sumona Tarlag, Pii-Khem region, a teller of folk tales.

Dulush Sharap, born in Khaiyrakan, Ulug-Khem region.

Kok-ool Viktor Shogzhapovich (1906–80), born in Torgalyg, Oviur region, a great expert in shamanic folklore, dramatist, actor, writer.

Kungaa Tash-ool Buu oglu (b. 1940), born in Sergek-Khem, formerly Erza, now Kyzyl region. Was raised among reindeer herders and hunters of the Tepe-Khol' state farm, near the Mongolian border.

Kuular Badat Davyndai oglu (1906–74), hunter and expert in Tuvan oral folklore. Born in Teve-Khaia, Dzun-Khemchik region. Recording taken in the village of Khondergei, Dzun-Khemchik region.

Kuular Kendenchik Sembil oglu (1904–75), born in Ak-Aksy, Siut-Khol' region, a remarkable performer of shamanic *algyshy*, an expert in shamanic folklore.

Kuular Sengil Davyndai oglu (1903–73), a hunter and expert in folk songs, proverbs, and legends.

Kuular Chanzan-ool Bolunmai oglu (b. 1901), born in Aiangaty, Barun-Khemchik region, storyteller.

Kyrgys Soruktu Samdanai oglu (1901–?), born in Ol-Aryg sumona, Mezhegei-Tanda region, lived in the village of Erzin, could do guttural singing.

Lopsan Chimba Sendelchikovich (b. 1910), born in Ush-Terek, Barun-Khemchik region.

Mongush Belek Mandylaazhyk oglu (b. 1894), born in Ulaan-Byra, Dzun-Khemchik region.

Mongush Bora-khoo Kendegei oglu (1892–1970), born in Teve-Khaia, Dzun-Khemchik region, hunter, storyteller.

Mongush Opai Angyrban oglu (b. 1900), born in Shemi, Dzun-Khemchik region.

Mongush Sendinmaa Shiizhek uruu (1895–1962), born in Ush-Tei, Khondergei village council, Dzun-Khemchik region, storyteller.

Oiun Seden Khuragandai oglu (b. 1907), born in Khaialyg-Odek, across the Chargy mountains, on the right bank of the river Ulug-Khem, a former lama, very familiar with Tibetan.

Saaia Seren Sotpa oglu (b. 1927), born in Ergi-Barlyk, Barun-Khemchik region. Recording made in the village of Khondergei.

Sambuu Saaia Chuvurekovich (1908–86), born in Migur-Aksy, Mongun-Taiga region, Distinguished Cultural Worker of the Tuvan ASSR, a great expert in Tuvan folklore.

Saryg-ool Stepan Agbanovich (1908–83), born in Torgalyg, Oviur region, National Writer of the Tuvan ASSR, a great expert in oral folklore.

Sat Sotpa Oiduu oglu (1901–76), born in Orten-Tei, Barun-Khemchik region, story-teller, a remarkable expert in the old ways of the Tuvans. Recording made in the village of Khondergei, Dzun-Khemchik region.

Seree Khortek Burulbaaevich (b. 1924), born in Kara-Tal, Bai-Taiga region, an expert in Tuvan folklore, writer.

Solaan Duger Segbe oglu (b. 1902), born in Tere-Khol', former shaman. Recording made in the village of Kungurtuk, Kyzyl region.

Siukterek Tadar Endan uruu (b. 1918), born in Baian-kol, former Pii-Khem, now Kyzyl region.

Tagba Boris Uvazhaevich (b. 1906), born in Erzhei, Kaa-Khem region, an expert in Tuvan ethnography.

Tamba Salchak Odekeevich (1918–83), born in Oshtan, Kaa-Khem region, journalist, poet, and folklorist.

Tarzhaa Khertek Naiyrovich (b. 1905), born in Koop-Sook, Bai-Taiga region, teacher, a great expert in Tuvan ethnography, fluent in Mongolian and Russian.

Toibukhaa Khertek Koshtaiovich (1917–81), artist, a great expert in Tuvan folklore.

Shalyk Darbaa (b. 1912), born in Bai-Tal, Tes-Khem region, an expert in the old ways of the Tuvans and Mongols.

Shokshui Salchak Sunduevich (1906–72), born in Mongun-Taiga region, hunter, story-teller, well versed in Mongolian. Recording made in the village of Mugur-Aksy, Bai-Taiga region.

Choodu Chorbaa Donduula oglu (b. 1912), born in Terektig, Tes-Khem region.

IV

Native Ethnographers Unite:
A Folklore Manifesto

The Study of Northern Languages, Folklore, and Cultures

Aleksandr B. Soktoev

Linguistic research on Siberian and Far Eastern languages and dialects is aimed first and foremost at recording as much as possible of those that are on the verge of disappearing. As many as twenty-six are in danger of extinction to varying degrees. They include practically all of the principal language groups on the territory of Siberia, the North, and the Far East: the *Samoedic* (Nenets, Enets, Selkup, Nganasan, and other languages), the *Paleo-Asiatic* (Ket and others), the *Ob-Ugrian* (Khanty, Mansi, and others), the *Tungus-Manchu* (Evenk, Negidal, Nanai, Ulchi, Udegei, Orok, and others), and the *Turkic* (Dolgan, Tofalar, Yukagir, and others).[a]

As an example of how scholars at the Institute of Philology, Siberian Division, Russian Academy of Sciences are organizing their work in the immediate recording of languages in the danger zone, I will describe the research being conducted on the Udegei, Negidal, and Orok languages.

The *Udegei* are a small Tungus-Manchu people residing in the Ussuri taiga in the southern Far East. Their total population numbers 1.9 thousand persons, according to the 1989 census. The number of persons speaking the Udegei language is decreasing with each year. At present, Udegei is used only in the home environment, primarily by the older generation.

The situation is the same with the *Negidals*. Out of a total of 354 persons, 224 can speak their mother tongue.

Or let us take the *Oroks*, one of the smallest of the nationalities in the

Russian text © 1993 by Aleksandr B. Soktoev. Presentation (Principal Directions of Scholarship of the Institute of Philology of the Siberian Division of the Russian Academy of Sciences) for the International Scholarly Conference "The Languages, Spiritual Culture, and Future of the People's of the Arctic" (Yakutsk, 17–22 June 1993). Translated by Stephan Lang.

Tungus-Manchu group, who reside on Sakhalin Island. There are only 300 of them, and not more than 30 know their mother tongue—primarily persons of the older generation.

Considering the dangerous situation, linguists from the Institute undertook a number of expeditions into regions where these nationalities reside, and, on the basis of the materials obtained, immediately began a description of these languages at all linguistic levels—in particular their vocabulary (the *Udegeisko–russkii* and *Oroksko–russkii* [Udegei–Russian and Orok–Russian] dictionaries compiled by M.D. Simonov and L.V. Ozolini); every lexical unit will be accompanied by illustrative material.

The dictionaries represent an important contribution to the study of these languages and will eliminate the danger of their disappearance without a trace.

B.V. Boldyrev's fundamental work, the *Russko–evenkiiskii slovar'* [Russian–Evenk Dictionary], which will be published in the near future, is unquestionably one of the substantial results of this task.

Scholars at the Institute of Philology are heading a large-scale project, "Experimental-phonetic research on the sound systems of the indigenous nationalities of Siberia and adjacent regions," which will cover approximately thirty languages and territorial dialects, among which the overwhelming majority are northern.

This large and multifaceted project encompasses many languages of the nationalities of Siberia, including a large group of Turkic-language nationalities. Linguistic approaches that evolved in central Siberia are continuing at the Institute of Philology—the schools of Avrorin, Ubriatova, and Nadeliaev. Their legacy is carried on by Doctor of Philological Sciences Professor M.I. Cheremisina, N.N. Shirobokova, and I.Ia. Seliutina, all of whom are participating in this international conference.

Of central concern is the collection, study, and publication of those monuments of folklore that are disappearing before our eyes.

Why is this so important?

The folklore of the northern peoples is little known and little studied, but it is one of the world's most interesting and rich in content.

Why is this folklore so obscure? Because the northern nationalities are the smallest in number of all of the indigenous nationalities of Siberia and the Far East. But what are "small-in-number" nationalities and what do the concepts "large" and "small" peoples mean?

These concepts may be important for statistics, but they have no significance for understanding the role of each of these peoples in the artistic development of the world.

One can always discover world-level and world-class treasures of poetry in the folklore works of even the smallest nationality. All of them represent equally great artistic wealth for the culture of humanity and its history.

Despite the fact that a movement was organized by the Russian Academy of Sciences at the end of the nineteenth century and in the 1920s and 1930s to select, study, and publish folklore heritage and linguistic and cultural material, this movement began to wind down in the mid-1930s due to the political regulations and doctrines then in force.

People gradually became accustomed to the idea that nothing could be done about the small nationalities—they would not have enough strength for internal or external resistance. Although the flame of the movement to collect cultural material never died, it was nonetheless weak and ephemeral, at times blazing forth brightly, at other times flickering.

Be that as it may, a dangerous process was taking place: outstanding masters of oral folk literature, with their incredible wealth of unrecorded material, were leaving this world forever. A drama of gigantic proportions was being played out before our eyes—a priceless body of culture, containing thousands of years of history, was withering away, disappearing into nothingness.

In the North, especially among nationalities of the Far East, when researchers obtain unique living data, they simultaneously experience the fortune of coming into tangible contact with humanity's "dawn of art."[b] They can find here a centuries-old history of oral folk arts, illustrating their sources and archaic forms (for example, the earliest song [*prapesnia*] and story [*praskazka*], and so forth).

But folklore is not only the past; it is a mighty force, one that addresses the present and the future. I would like to emphasize that we must actively try to save the languages of the indigenous nationalities of Russia, especially those of the northern nationalities.

But how should we save them? By reviving and expanding their capability for daily use, in the conducting of business, and for official documentation? This is a weak incentive for those who would like to return to a forgotten mother tongue. Few people have an interest in reviving language for use in the bureaucratic sphere.

Instead there exists a living and deep fountainhead of highly organized national speech, and this is folklore. The language of folklore is an extremely rich and invigorating source; it is only by taking advantage of it that we can start to do something about the problem of language restoration.

In this sense folklore is not only the past but also a constructive force turned to the future of a nationality, its language, and its culture.

I hardly need mention folklore's independent spiritual, artistic-poetic, and cultural significance. Yet it is specifically this rich folk culture of peoples of the North, Siberia, and the Far East that, like their languages, is in danger of collapse and destruction. This is why, starting in the 1970s and continuing to the present, work has been undertaken to save the folkloric heritage of these peoples.

The most ambitious project in this direction has become the organization and scholarly preparation for publication of the sixty-volume academic bilingual series, *Pamiatniki fol'klora narodov Sibiri i Dal'nego Vostoka* [Monuments of Folklore of the Peoples of Siberia and the Far East], undertaken by the Institute of Philology, Siberian Division, Russian Academy of Sciences in conjunction with the Scientific Research Institute of Siberia and the Far East. In this undertaking, priority was given to comprehensive folkloric expeditions.

Taking part in preparation of the volumes of northern nationalities' folklore are experienced folklorists, well known for their work in Russia and abroad. They include N.A. Alekseev, N.V. Emel'ianov, A.N. Myreeva, G.N. Kurilov, G.V. Varlamova, V.A. Robbek, N.Ia. Bulatova, Zh.K. Lebedeva, A.N. Zhukova, Antonina Kymytval', Chuner M. Taksami, N.B. Kile, A.I. Chudoiakov, G.A. Otaina, Anastasiia Sainakhova, V.I. Rassadin, the late V.T. Petrov, and P.E. Efremov. Musicologists, headed by Eduard E. Alekseev, include: Iurii I. Sheikin, Tat'iana Bulgakova, Nadezhda Nikolaeva, Galina Alekseeva, Aiza P. Reshetnikova, R.B. Nazarenko, M.A. Vakhitova, and many others.[c]

The series represents the academic publication of classical oral-poetic works, as recorded by the finest performers of the past and present. The series includes texts in the languages of the original, along with Russian translation and commentary, musical notation for vocal performance and instrumental accompaniment, sound recordings on records (examples of the artistry of contemporary epic singers, songwriters, and storytellers), a researcher's interpretation of the wealth of artistry and ideas in published works, and ethnographic and historicocultural illustrative material.

The novelty of this series lies not only in the strict new guidelines—especially developed for this project—for selecting and presenting the texts. It is also due to the multiple genres of the folklore works being published—epic tales, myths, legends, lyrical songs, and ritual poetry. These genres contain a thousand years of oral folk art history, starting with its sources and archaic forms and going back to the earliest songs and stories. The works were selected from the entire body of available recordings—from the first recordings in the nineteenth century to materials gathered by folklore expeditions under my direction from 1984 to 1991.

In effect, this is a scholarly publishing project unprecedented in its scale and in its new editorial requirements and principles. Participating in preparation of the series are folklorists from fourteen scientific research institutes of the former USSR Academy of Sciences (Siberia, the Far East, Moscow, St. Petersburg, Minsk, and Kiev), as well as from institutes in the now-sovereign constituent republics of the Russian Federation (Mountainous Altai, Khakassia, and Tuva) and from over twenty higher educational establishments in the country. The managing editors' team and authors' collectives for volumes in the series include folklorists who have received broad recognition in Russia and abroad for their experience in publishing oral folk creative works.

The main scholarly institution for the fulfillment of this large program of publication is the Institute of Philology, Siberian Division, Russian Academy of Sciences. General scholarly-methodological leadership over the series' publication is being implemented by the Division of Literature and Language of the Russian Academy of Sciences, the Scientific Council on Folklore of the Russian Academy of Sciences, and the head editorial board of the series.

In conclusion, it must be admitted that in the past few years, the Institute has been conducting its research in preserving and restoring the languages, folklore, and traditional culture of the nationalities of the North, Siberia, and the Far East under extremely difficult and unfavorable circumstances. Remuneration of scientific personnel in the entire Russian Academy of Sciences has fallen sharply, funding for expeditions and scholarly travel has effectively ceased, and the Institute has been deprived of the means to acquire scientific equipment and relevant materials.

What is most tragic in these sad circumstances is that works that are ready for publication by the Institute are not being published due to lack of funds. From 1990 to 1993, manuscripts of upcoming volumes of the *Pamiatniki fol'klora narodov Sibiri i Dal'nego Vostoka* series, the major work of Turcologists at the Institute (*Dialektologicheskii atlas tiurkskikh iazykov (byvshego) SSSR* [Dialectological Atlas of the Turkic Languages of the (Former) USSR]), and monographs on vital problems in linguistics and literary criticism have been sitting on a shelf at Nauka Publishers.

The problem of funding

The situation is more acceptable when it concerns publication of the folklore volumes of large Siberian nationalities with the status of national republics: the Republic of Sakha (Yakutia), the Republic of Buryatia, the Republic of Tuva, the Republic of Mountainous Altai, and the Republic of

Khakassia. The presidents and heads of government, who are doing every-thing possible in deeds as well as in words to save, perpetuate, and develop their people's folklore, are finding the money in their inadequate budget to bring to light the volumes of their national classics in the sixty-volume *Pamiatniki fol'klora narodov Sibiri i Dal'nego Vostoka* series [Folklore of Siberia and the Far East].

The volumes of folklore of the small groups of the North and the Far East remain the most neglected, and, paradoxical as it may seem, so do volumes of the folklore of the largest peoples, our brother Slavs—Russians, Ukrainians, and Belarusians, who long ago also qualified as native residents of Siberia and the Far East.

While Tuva, Yakutia, Buryatia, Mountainous Altai, and Khakassia have already transferred their share of the funding for the publication of their national volumes, the Administration of Khabarovsk Krai responded cyni-cally to the editorial board regarding its possible financial participation in the publication of the Nanai, Udegei, Ulchi, and Nivkhi series volumes, stating that these volumes are intended for a narrow circle of readers and that the administration does not consider it possible to finance their publication.

In sharp contrast to this heartless, colonialist, snobbishly chauvinistic ap-proach is the situation that is evolving in the Republic of Sakha (Yakutia), where, in these difficult conditions of transition to free-market relations, the republic's leadership, its president, Mikhail Efimovich Nikolaev, the govern-ment, and parliamentary deputies are creating a "most-favored" status for the development of the sciences, education, and culture, and not only for their own Yakut [Sakha] nationality, but also for the small northern nationalities—the Evenks, Evens, Yukagirs, and Chukchi, and the Yakuts' relatives, the Dolgans.

I am convinced that in participating in the financing of the publication of the Yakut volumes, the leadership of the Republic of Sakha (Yakutia) will do everything possible to publish the folklore of northern nationalities re-siding in Yakutia. It is here, after all, that an Institute of the Problems of the Northern Minorities was created, thanks to the concern of the republic's leadership for its small northern groups. This Institute, headed by the tal-ented scholar and scientific director, Doctor of Philosophical Sciences V.A. Robbek, has been functioning for three years.

The very fact that the republic's leadership organized and carried out our present International Conference, "The Languages, Spiritual Culture, and Future of the Peoples of the Arctic," is eloquent proof that the problems of saving, restoring, and developing the languages, folklore, and traditional spiritual and material culture of all of the nationalities—even of the small ethnic groups—in this republic are not simply acknowledged but are being handled by a well-planned strategy.

I have brought with me a proof copy of the first Yakut [Sakha] volume, which is called *Iakutskii geroicheskii epos "Kyys Debiliie"* [The Yakut Heroic Epic "Kyys Debiliie"]—that magnificent classical monument of Yakut folklore prepared for publication by your compatriots—the veteran of our all-Siberian folklore studies, Doctor of Philological Sciences N.V. Emel'ianov, leading scientific researcher at the Institute of Language, Literature, and History of the Yakutia Scientific Center, with splendid musicological interpretation by Aiza P. Reshetnikova[d].

In sum, this is a realistic, businesslike report on what is being done to perpetuate the folklore heritage of the native peoples of Siberia. The realization of the long-term, large-scale scholarly program to publish the sixty-volume *Pamiatniki fol'klora narodov Sibiri i Dal'nego Vostoka* series is destined to become an inspiring motivation for all those researchers engaged in efforts toward saving, preserving, and developing the spiritual wealth of the world's native peoples.

Editor's notes

a. Yukagir is not usually included as a Turkic language, but may be here because of the admixtures of Turkic with a more aboriginal language in the original Yukagir homeland of far-northeastern Siberia. For language family background, see Bernard Comrie, *The Languages of the Soviet Union* (Cambridge: Cambridge University Press, 1981). cf. Roman Jakobson, Gerta Huttl-Worth, and John Fred Beebe, *Paleosiberian Peoples and Languages: A Bibliographical Guide* (New Haven: Human Relations Area Files Press, 1957).

b. This assertion of direct, almost mystical links to an archaic human "dawn of art" may be the most controversial and romanticized statement here. However, it is quite representative of the views of Russian Federation folklorists. Searching for archaic links does not prohibit awareness of profound cultural changes, mutual influences of various groups, and syncretism.

c. It is worth stressing again that nearly all of the participants named here are native ethnographers and folklorists. Aleksandr Soktoev is the director of this vast project.

d. This Yakut (Sakha) volume of epic poetry, of the genre called *olonko*, was published in 1993, and includes its own phono record, as do all the volumes in the series. At the time of his address, Aleksandr Soktoev had to add a plea for publication aid, saying "The manuscript has already been typeset, and all that is needed is a modest little push of 2 million rubles in order to print the planned edition, which all true admirers and connoisseurs of the Yakut heroic epic have been awaiting for a long time."

Index

A

Abaev, V.I., 65
Akkin-Chechen, 90
Alekseev, Eduard E., 260
Alekseev, N.A., 260
Alekseeva, Galina Grigor'evna, 260
Altai, marriage customs of, 192–94
Amur River peoples, 11–12
Anaibin, Zoia V., 10
Anderson, Greg, 77*note c*
Angina, E.K., 160
Antigens, Yakut, 65–66
Antonov, N.K., 67
Arsen'ev, V.K., 146
Aryans, and Yakuts, 65
Avtonova, Isabella Vasil'evna Mimykg, 17

B

Baidara, 209–10
Baikal region, 11
  cultural norms in, 123–38
  categories, 124–25
  and changes in Russian cultural
    traditions, 136–37
  and Eastern thought, 130–34
  and industrial society, 129
  and land-use policy, 134–36
  and natural conditions, 126–28
  and Western worldview, 128–30
  and world model, 125
Banzaroz, Dorzhi, 4
Bashkir, 116

Bel'dy, D.S., 164
Bel'dy, M., 157
Berg, N.S., 174
Birth rituals. *See also* Nanai, birth
    rituals of
  of Nivkh, 150–51, 162, 165, 166
  of Ul'chi, 150, 159–62, 164–66
  of Yakuts, 199
Boldyrev, B.V., 258
Bonch-Osmolovskii, G.A., 183
Bravina, R.I., 64
Bromlei, Iu. V., 41, 46–47
Bromlei, Iulian, 7
Bugaev, Abdullah, 94
Bulatova, N.Ia., 260
Bulgakova, Tat'iana, 260
Buryats
  antigens among, 66
  and Baikal, 11
  cultural norms of, 126, 128, 129, 135
  marriage customs of, 193–96
Butanaev, Viktor Iakovlevich, 8
Bütling, O.N., 64

C

Checheno-Ingushetia, 89, 831–00
  interethnic conflicts in, 83–91
    Akkin-Chechen and Dagestanis, 90
    Chechen and Ingush, 84–85
    Chechen and Nogai, 91
    Ossetians and Ingush, 88–90
    and Russians, 85–88
  political factors of conflicts in, 91–95
  sociodemographic changes in, 95–97

Checheno-Ingushetia *(continued)*
  sociopsychological factors in, 97–100
Chechen
  Ingush, conflict with, 84–85
  Nogai, conflict with, 91
  Russians, conflict with, 85–88
Cheremisina, M.I., 258
Chikhachev, P., 75
Chimba Lopsan, 235–36
Chingiz Khan, 64
Christianity, and marriage customs of
  Yakuts, 177–78, 183, 191
Chudoiakov, A.I., 260
Chukchi, 17
Chuvash, 49, 116, 117
Circassians, presentation of self by, 9
Confederation of the Mountain
  Nationalities of the Caucasus
  (KNK), 92
Constantine Porphyrogenetus, 32
Constitutions, 103
  Tatarstan, 117
Cossacks
  in Checheno-Ingushetia, 86–88
  in North Ossetia, 90
Curative seance. *See under* Tuvans

D

Dagestanis, conflict with
  Akkin-Chechen, 90
Davis, George D., 134–35
Debets, G.F., 66
Dechuli, P.L., 160–61
Democratic Party of Russia, 105
Digor, E.M., 145
Dudaev, Dzhokhar, 85, 92, 94, 95
Dzutsev, Kh., 99

E

Eastern thought, and cultural norms in
  Baikal region, 130–34
Efremov, P.E., 260

Emel'ianov, N.V., 260, 263
Epp, G., 106
Erzia, 32–35, 37–43
Eskimos, 14–15, 209–13
Ethnogenesis, 46–48
Ethnohistory, 5
Evenks, 128, 129, 135

F

Fedorov, Afansii, 20
Fefelova, V.V., 65–66
Freedom, 133–34

G

Gaer, Evdokiya Alexandrovna, 11–12,
  12, 17–18
Gamzatov, Rasul, 239
Gasprali, Ismail Bei (Gasprinskii), 4
Geiker, Nina Pavlovna, 142
Gekker, N.L., 67–68
Genetic anthropology, of Yakuts, 65–67
Gogolev, Anatolii Ignatevich, 2, 78, 19
Gokhman, I.I., 66
Guillaume Rubruquis, 33
Gurevich, A. Ia., 124–25

H

Hermanarich, 32
Herodotus, 49
Hunting rituals, of Eskimos, 211–13

I

Ignat'ev, G.G., 172
Industrial society, 129
Ingush
  Chechen, conflict with, 84–85
  Ossetians, conflict with, 88–90
Ingushetia. *See* Checheno-Ingushetia
Iosif (Kagan of Khazaria), 33
Islam, in Checheno-Ingushetia, 92–93
Ittifak (Tatarstan), 117, 118

Ivanov, V.A., 50
Ivan the Terrible, 115

J

Jakobson, R., 190
Jordanus, 32

K

Kachin (Kacha), 72
Kagarov, E.G., 188
Kamasa, 77*note c*
Karakalpaks, 193, 195
Karatai, 42
Kazakhs, 192, 193, 195
Kazan Khanate, 115
Keldir Khirligbei, 238
Kenin-Lopsan, Mongush B., 15–16, 18
Khaash (Khaas), 72–73
Khakas, 8
    ethnonyms for, 70–76
Khatanov, Nikolai F., 4
Khazars, 34
Khodzher, A.P., 154
Khodzher, T.A., 152–53
Khoorai (Khongorai), 74–76
Khorinians, 67
Khostug Tyva, 105–7, 111*note i*
Khudiakov, I.A., 176, 185
Kiev, 34
Kile, N.B., 260
Kile, S.G., 158
Kile, U.O., 164
Kliashtornyi, S.G., 50
Koibal, 77*note c*
Kott, 77*note c*
Koz'min, N.N., 70
Kreinovich, E.A., 151
Ksenofontov, Gavril V., 4
Kuisali, T.G., 161
Kulakovskii, Aleksei E., 4
Kurgak Kyrgys, 235

Kurilov, G.N., 260
Kurilov, Nikolai N., 21, 22
Kurykan, 66
Kuzeev, Raul Gumerovich, 7
Kymytval', Antonina, 260
Kypchak, 51
Kyrgyz, 71–74, 76
    marriage customs of, 192–96
Kyzlasov, I.L., 71, 72, 73, 76
Kyzlasov, L.R., 72–73, 76

L

Lebedeva, Zh.K., 260
Lenin, 36
Lipskaia, N.A., 144
Lipskii, A.N., 152, 165
Lobacheva, N.P., 178
Lobachevskaia, N.P., 194
Lomovatskaia culture, 49
Lopatin, I.A., 152, 162

M

Maak, R.K., 67
Maksimov, A.N., 178
Mari, 117
Marriage customs. *See also* Yakuts
    (Sakha), marriage customs of
    of Altai, 192–94
    of Buryats, 193–96
    of Kyrgyz, 192–96
"Marsho" Union of Democratic Forces,
    94
Matchmaking rituals, of Yakuts, 173–74
Melnikov, A.A., 106
Middendorf, A.F., 67
Mikhailov, Taras, 18
Miller, G.F., 72
Moinagashev, S.D., 70
Moksha, 32–35, 37–43
Mokshin, Nikolai Feodorovich, 67
Mongush, B.K., 247

Mordva, 67, 31–43, 116, 117
  in early Soviet period, 36–38
  ethnic subdivisions among, 39–43
  ethnonyms for, 31–34, 38–39
  Mordva Autonomous Soviet Socialist
    Republic, 37–38
Morokhoeva, Zoia I., 11
Mountain People's Republic, 87, 88
Mukhamediarov, Shamil Fatikhovich, 7
Musina, Roza N., 10
Myreeva, A.N., 260

N

Naimuka, Vera, 153, 163
Nanai, birth rituals of, 143–66
  amulets, 155–57
  childbirth, 146–48
  "cleansing" of new mother, 149
  cradle, 154
  death of infants, 157–59
  elderly, role of, 156
  epileuri ritual, 147
  evil spirits, protection of child from,
    166
  husband of pregnant woman, rules for,
    144–45
  iliochiori ritual, 157–58
  infant's life, preservation of, 152–56
  labor, 145
  mastitis, treatments for, 148–49
  names, bestowing of, 162–64
  newborn, care of, 149–50
  pregnant woman, rules for, 143–44,
    152
  shelter, birth, 145–46, 148
  solban ritual, 147
  umbilical cord, 147–48
  willow shavings, use of, 145–46
Narod, 103
Nationality processes, 56
Native anthropologists, 35, 16–17
Natural conditions, and folk beliefs in
  Baikal region, 126–28

Nazarenko, R.B., 260
Negidals, 258
Nikolaev, S.I., 64
Nikolaeva, Nadezhda, 260
Nivkh, birth rituals of, 150–51, 162,
  165, 166
Nogai, 193, 195
  Chechen, conflict with, 91
Novik, E.S., 191–92, 195
Novolakskii region, 90

O

Oiunskii, Platon A. (Sleptsov), 4
Oka River, 32
Okladnikov, A.P., 64
Oroks, 258
Ossetians, conflict with Ingush, 88–90
Otaina, G.A., 260
Ozolini, L.V., 258

P

Pazyryk, 65–66
Pechenegs, 49
People's Front (Tuva), 105–7
People's Party of Sovereign Tuva,
  105
Petrov, A.P., 172
Petrov, V.T., 260
Pilsudskii, B.O., 151
Piseral'sko-Andreevsk mounds, 49
Piurbiu, Sergei, 238–39
Political anthropology, 6
Polomskaia culture, 49
Prigorodnyi region (North Ossetia),
  89–90
Prigogine, I., 130, 132–33
Priklonskii, V.L., 177
Purgas, 34–35

R

Radlov, V.V., 63–64, 72
Rashad-al-Din, 33

Rassadin, V.I., 260
Relations, Eastern view of, 130–31
Renchik, Vladimir, 151
Reshetnikova, Aiza, 260, 263
Robbek, V.A., 260
Russian cultural traditions, changes in, 136–37
Russians
  in Checheno-Ingushetia, 85–88, 95–97
  in Tatarstan, 114–15
Rybakov, B.A., 47

S

Saaia Sambuu, 235
Sainakhova, Anastasiia, 260
Sakha. *See* Yakuts
Salchak, V.B., 106
Saligov, Lechi, 94
Samar, A.A., 144
Samar, O.F., 163
Sartre, Jean-Paul, 133
Scythians, 64–65
Seals, capturing of, 212–13
Seance. *See under* Tuvans
Seliutina, I.Ia., 258
Semenovna, Agafia, 158–59
Seroshevskii, V.L., 67, 182
Shakhmatov, A.A., 33
Shalyk Darbaa, 235
Shamans, Tuvan, 215–49, 251–52
  and curative seance, 215–24
  poetics of folklore of, 235–49
  poetry of, 225–35
Sheikin, Iurii I., 260
Shimit-Kyrgys, 236
Shimkevich, P.P., 155
Shirobokova, N.N., 258
Shnirel'man, V.A., 34
Shoksha, 41–42

Shternberg, L.Ia., 4, 150–51, 155
Siberian Division of Russian Academy of Sciences, 257–63
Sibikov, Gomozhap, 4
Simonov, M.D., 258
Siuziuk, 239–40
Skulls, Yakut, 66
Sleptsov, Platon A., 12–14, 13
Smoliak, A.V., 150, 159, 162, 164–65
Socialist Workers' Party, 105
Society of the Homeless (Tuva), 107
Soigor, A.S., 154, 158
Soktoev, Aleksandr Badmaevich, 21, 263*note c*
Soldatova, Galina U., 910, 99
Soruktu Kyrgys, 236
Sovereignty, of Tatarstan, 113–14, 116, 119–20
Stalin, 9
Stebleva, I.V., 249
Stepanov, P.D., 38
Sunzha Cossack National Okrug, 86
Surkhasko, Iu.Iu., 187
Symbolic anthropology, 6

T

Tadar, 70, 71
Taksami, Chuner, 260
Tamba, Salchak, 240
Tatar language, 116–17
Tatar Public Center, 118
Tatars, 10
Tatarstan, 113–20
  ethnodemographic issues, 114–16
  sociocultural issues, 116–18
  sociopolitical issues, 118–20
Tein, Tassan S., 14–15
Terek Cossacks, 86–87
Teriushevians, 42–43
Throat singing, Tuvan, 236–37
Time, 131–32
Tiuse barar, 177–78

Tofalars, 66
Tokarev, S.A., 64
Tumali, M.A., 153, 155
Turkic peoples, 7
  in Volga and Ural regions, 46–49
Tuva, ethnic relations in, 10–29
  political factors, 10–27
  social factors, 10–78
Tuvan language, 10–45
Tuvan Youth Union, 105
Tuvans, 10, 66, 75, 193
  curative seance of, 215–24
    cause of sickness, search for, 217
    culmination, 223
    dénouement, 223–24
    interim seance, 221–22
    plot, 217–21
    prologue, 216
  poetics of shamanic folklore of, 235–49
  shamanic poetry of, 225–35

U

Udegei, 257
Udmurt, 116, 117
Ul'chi, birth rituals of, 150, 159–62, 164–66
Uzbeks, 195, 196

V

Veinakh, 84, 991–00
Vakhitova, M.A., 260
Valikhanov, Chikan Ch., 4
Varlamova, G.V., 260
Vitashevskii, N.A., 174
Vladikavkaz, 88–89
Volga Bulgars, 50–51
Volga River, 32

W

Western worldview, 128–30
Whale, capturing of, 211–12

Y

Yakut language, 63–64
Yakuts (Sakha), 78, 12–14, 19, 63–68
  birth rituals of, 199
  marriage customs of, 173–201
    bridewealth and dowry, 197–98
    Christianity, influence of, 177–78, 183, 191
    entertainment-play substructure, 190
    and family structure, 198
    first wedding, 174–78
    legal and economic significance, rituals of, 187–88
    makeup of participants, 190
    matchmaking, 173–74
    material components, 190
    other Turkic-Mongolian peoples, compared with, 192–97
    religious-magical function, rituals with, 188–90
    "returning home" by bride, 185
    second wedding, 178–85
    and status of women, 198
    as transition ritual, 191–92
    verbal communication, role of, 190–91
Yukagir language, 263note a

Z

Zhirmunskii, V.M., 249
Zhukova, A.N., 260
Zhukovskaia, N.L., 188
Zolotarev, A.M., 159, 162

Also from *M.E. Sharpe*

RUSSIAN TRADITIONAL CULTURE
Religion, Gender, and Customary Law
Edited by Marjorie Mandelstam Balzer

SHAMANISM
Soviet Studies of Traditional Religion
in Siberia and Central Asia
Edited by Marjorie Mandelstam Balzer

CENTRAL ASIA READER
The Rediscovery of History
Edited by H.B. Paksoy

MOSCOW'S LOST EMPIRE
Michael Rywkin

THE NEW RUSSIAN DIASPORA
Russian Minorities in the Former Soviet Republics
Edited by Vladimir Shlapentokh, Munir Sendich, and Emil Payin

**NATIONAL IDENTITY AND ETHNICITY
IN RUSSIA AND THE NEW STATES OF EURASIA**
Edited by Roman Szporluk

THE PEOPLES OF THE USSR
An Ethnographic Handbook
Ronald Wixman

HM896
IL-68

DE PAUL UNIVERSITY LIBRARY

3 0511 00559 2928